D1537692

OBJECT-ORIENTED ENVIRONMENT IN C++

A USER-FRIENDLY INTERFACE

DAVID HU

ADVANCED COMPUTER BOOKS

MIS. PRESS

MANAGEMENT INFORMATION SOURCE, INC.

COPYRIGHT

Copyright © 1990 by Baldur Systems Corp.
Published by Management Information Source, Inc.
P.O. Box 5277
Portland, Oregon 97208
(503) 282-5215

Second Printing

Book: ISBN 1-55828-014-6
Book & Disk: ISBN 1-55828-039-1

All rights reserved. Reproduction or use, without express
permission, of editorial or pictorial content, in any manner, is
prohibited. No patent liability is assumed with respect to the use
of the information contained herein. While every precaution has
been taken in the preparation of this book, neither the publisher
nor the author assumes responsibility for errors or omissions.
Neither is any liability assumed for damage resulting from
the use of the information contained herein.

For information about our audio products, write us at:
Newbridge Book Clubs, 3000 Cindel Drive, Delran, NJ 08370

ACKNOWLEDGMENTS

The author is indebted to those whose enthusiasm inspired him to write a series of object-oriented programming/expert system books and to those who contributed their ideas, cases, and reviews. Thanks are expressed to the following companies, (listed below in alphabetical order), who provided their products for use in preparing programs and text in the manuscript:

- Digitalk, Inc. (distributing Smalltalk V)
- Guidelines Software, Inc. (distributing Guidelines C++)
- Lifeboat (distributing Advantage C++)
- The Stepstone Corporation (distributing Objectiv-C)
- Zortech, Inc. (distributing Zortech C++)

Oregon Software and Servio Logic Corp also provided information/assistance for the preparation of the manuscript.

DEDICATION

To: Lise, Eileen, Emily

Special thanks to Michael Song, John Kallen, and Walter Liew, who have contributed greatly to the preparation of this book in software and hardware.

TABLE OF CONTENTS

PREFACE

This book is written for programmers who would like to integrate a new programming technique, object-oriented programming (in C++ for the most part), into their programs.

Object-oriented Programming (OOP) is a new concept that is rapidly entering the mainstream of software development. Combining with artificial intelligence, OOP is heralded as the technology that will lead to computer-integrated manufacturing which in turn could lift U.S. competitiveness.

The book leads the reader, and user, to the idea of incorporating object-oriented environment (in C++) features in daily programming work by providing details about using the main strengths of OOP to build a user-friendly, intelligent software environment.

Key elements of object-oriented programming provided in this book include:

- data encapsulation
- inheritance of attributes
- polymorphism (overloading of operator names)
- basic classes and examples (as well as source code) on windows
- bit-mapped icons
- mouse cursors
- menus

These elements can be used to rapid-prototype a graphical user-interface environment. This capability gives the user's personal computer the look of a Smalltalk- or MacApp window-like (Macintosh) environment. It also allows the creation of a Microsoft window-like interface.

The text compares the differences between programming in C and C++ and examines the strengths and weaknesses of the three main OOP languages (Smalltalk, C++, and Objective-C). It demonstrates building or adopting an object-oriented environment on to existing C programs. Guidence is provided about using the basic classes which include: integrating icons, menus, and mouse operations into a C program for friendly, intelligent user interface. The text further discusses building an object-oriented database or intelligent database interface by integrating OOP/expert system programs presented.

The sequence of chapters presented includes:

- Chapter 1 uses an automobile parts inventory problem to demonstrate OOP's close relationship to the real organization of daily routines and methods to use it as a problem solver.

- Chapters 2, 3, and 4 introduce three most frequently mentioned OOP languages with a description of the evolution of OOP. While the graphics user interface of Smalltalk is analyzed in depth emphasizing the user-friendliness of a good OOP environment, the important features of C++, are clarified in Chapter 2.

- Chapter 5 coaches the reader about using C++ by going through each step of building classes, member functions, and overloading, for a text-mode window.

- Chapter 6 discusses the structure of the kernel classes for designing a graphical interface environment using facilities, such as bit-mapped icons, menus, and panes.

- Chapters 7 and 8 discuss the application of OOP in organizing and deriving knowledge and data to make intelligent programs.

- Chapter 9 integrates a graphical interface environment with an existing C program, and uses an inventory accounting system as an example.

- Chapter 10 synthesizes the classes previously discussed into an intelligent data base interface for communication among various types of data bases, such as dBase, Lotus 1-2-3, and SQL.

The C++ source code of more than 30 classes is presented in the book. Even though the **Zortech Compiler** is used to compile them, no major modification is required for compilation on other compilers.

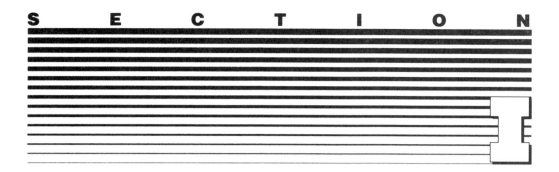

BASIC CONCEPTS AND TERMS OF OBJECT-ORIENTED PROGRAMMING

This book introduces the reader to features of **object-oriented programming** (OOP) to be incorporated in your programming work by providing details about using the main features of OOP to build intelligent, user-friendly software systems. This book also provides fundamentals for creating essential user-friendly components, such as windows, menus, icons, intelligence, and database interfaces.

Section I focuses on basic OOP concepts and terms. To help the user quickly and easily comprehend the new terms, the description of OOP draws heavily on an analogy between new and conventional programming techniques.

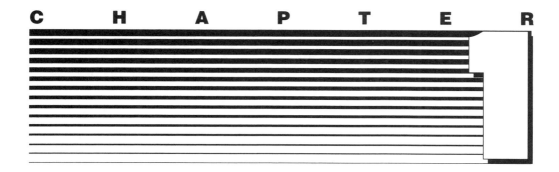

FUNDAMENTALS OF OBJECT-ORIENTED PROGRAMMING

Object-oriented programming (**OOP**) is a new programming concept rapidly entering mainstream software development. The combination of artificial intelligence and OOP is being heralded as the technology that will lead to computer-integrated manufacturing, which could improve U.S. competitiveness. OOP techniques allow programmers to reuse code components previously developed under rigid sets of specifications, much like reusing integrated circuits in hardware systems engineered and tested with given specifications. Reusing available code components reduces the bulkiness of code and the time and effort needed to develop programs.

Object-oriented programs are different from conventional programs that focus on numbers and mathematical formulas. Conventional programs treat data and procedures separately, and programmers (users) must ensure appropriate data types when they attempt to use the procedures. Object-oriented systems are different from database systems which manipulate data under rigid database management methods. Object-oriented programming allows programmers and users to view concepts as a variety of units or objects — a hierarchy of different components or structures of various organizations. By using main OOP techniques, programmers can conveniently and neatly represent (encode) the relationships among components, objects, tasks that must be performed, and conditions that must be met. The code can be reused and easily changed by subsequent users. Generally users do not need to worry about the data type, repeated variable names, or function names; they are able to concentrate on their professional knowledge instead of programming.

This chapter begins with an example of inventory control to explain the object-oriented concept, review the difference between OOP and conventional programming, and focus on the three key features of object-oriented programming languages.

OBJECT-ORIENTED CONCEPT

Assume that you are asked to build an inventory control system prototype in three months. In the prototype, such user-friendly features as icons, windows, pull-down menus, and the mouse cursor are required. Because the code might be expanded in the future (if the prototype is good), the user must ensure that the code will be reusable, tight, and well-documented. To allow future programmers to reuse the code, the code should be transparent to users as in real-world objects and structures.

Assume that the inventory control system (ICS) prototype will be an information system allowing a parts dealer or shop owner to cost-effectively control inventory; maintain an optimal level of stocks; record translations; reorder stocks; and check at any moment the status of a given part, such as the cost, degree of customer satisfaction, and supplier's delivery schedule.

The intended functions of such a system include the following:

1. Organizing parts inventory information in an easy-to-understand manner utilizing windows, icons, menus, and the mouse.

2. Accepting rules about parts being sold, purchased, priced, and other procedures.

3. Communicating with other information systems that contain necessary information, such as dBASE or Lotus 1-2-3.

These icons, menus, rules, or other information systems will be treated as objects and organized in a hierarchy similar to the natural organization of parts and components. In this example, these relationships will be represented with classes by using Mazda automobile parts. Chapters 7 and 8 include a more detailed discussion of the ICS.

Using the Class Structure to Represent the Real-World Problem

Like items in an organizational chart, a **class** is a set of closely related objects sharing similar attributes. The class structure closely resembles the organization of parts in the inventory system. Classes also serve as templates for the creation of objects. The initial class is always the basic class, that is, the origin (**root class**). Subsequently, every class created is a child class (**subclass**) of the root class, as shown in Figure 1.1. The end-class is called a unit. A class can have attributes (**slots**). Some attributes will be passed down (**inherited**) to subclasses or other classes; some will not be inherited to children classes. The value of the slots determines whether they can be passed down to those of the subclass. Slots can be classified as **member slots** or **own slots**:

Member slots	the value of the slot will be inherited by those of the subclass.
Own slots	the value of the slot will not be inherited.

A **slot** is an object that holds information regarding a particular attribute of a class. A class can have as many slots as needed. The primary items of information in a slot include the following:

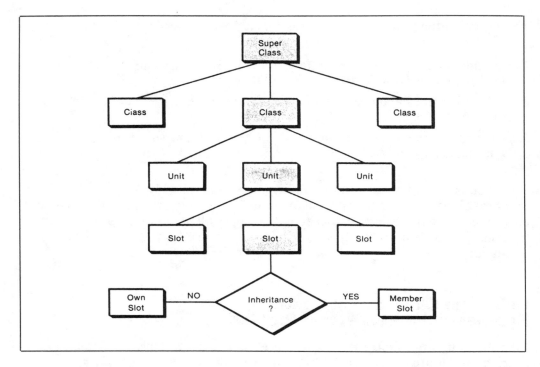

Figure 1.1   Organization of a frame structure.

Slot Name	name of the slot
Slot Value	value provided by the user
Slot Type-Restriction	restriction on the type of value that can be entered for this slot
Slot Source	location from which the attribute is inherited
Slot Destination	location to which the attribute is passed
Slot Inheritance	indication of whether slot inherits value or not
Slot Default value	value used if none is provided
Slot Certainty	certainty the user feels about the information
Slot Prompt	prompt at which the user enters values

Slot Documentation   documents the purpose, function, and other attributes of the slot

Slot name and **slot value** are self-explanatory. **Slot type-restriction** restricts the value of the slot entered by the user. To restrict a slot value, set its type-restriction to the following:

Expression	the value can be any expression
Number	the value can be any number
String	the value can be any string
Boolean	the value must be yes or no
(member (*atom***))**	the value must be one of the atoms in the list
(class *classname*)	the value must be an entity of class *classname*
Name	the value must be a name

Slot source and **slot destination** are used in the inheritance to indicate the source and destination of the slot. **Slot default value** is the value used if the user does not input a value. **Slot certainty** indicates how confident the user is of the entered value. To help in calculating probability, slot certainty is selected to range between zero and one. **Slot prompt** allows the user to input a value. In a more sophisticated tool, a procedure name can be entered to compute the appropriate value. The procedure is called a **method** or a **demon**. **Slot documentation** is provided for the user to enter helpful information regarding the slot for future users.

Create Classes and Display Class Hierarchy

The structure of classes created in the ICS is similar to the hierarchy of a typical organization. The ICS allows the user to create the appropriate number of classes. The sample classes created for MAZDA-PARTS include the following:

- A root class of Madza parts called MAZDA-PARTS

- Two classes of cars — WAGON and SEDAN

- Several classes of part groups, such as ENGINE and FUEL-SYSTEM

- Several end-classes (called **units**) of fuel-system elements, such as carburetor and fuel pump

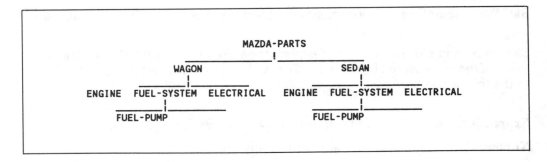

Figure 1.2   The partial structure of the Mazda Parts Inventory .

The partial hierarchy of MAZDA-PARTS classes is exhibited in Figure 1.2. Figures 1.3 to 1.6 provide sample descriptions of the classes discussed. The root class MAZDA-PARTS shown in Figure 1.3 contains the common characteristics and their default values, such as **dealer-name, preference** (preferred supplier) to be passed down to lower classes.

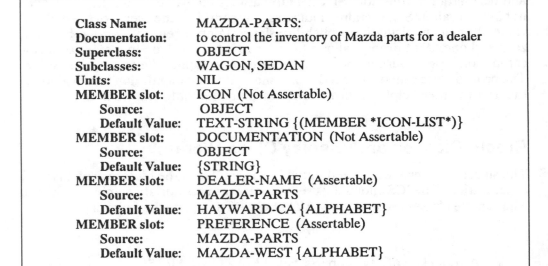

Figure 1.3   Creating a class for the Mazda parts inventory problem .

Figures 1.4 and 1.5 (see following page) indicate the difference between parts needed for the two types of cars. In Figure 1.4, the superclass of the WAGON class is MAZDA-PARTS, and WAGON inherits the two common characteristics of MAZDA-PARTS: PREFERENCE and DEALER-NAME. Because DOCUMENTATION and ICON have not been changed, they are inherited from the OBJECT and used as the origin of any root class, such as MAZDA-PARTS. WAGON has a common characteristic to be passed down to its subclass, COMMON-PARTS, which has default values of BATTERY, TIRE, ENGINE. More common characteristics can be added to the slot of the class. The third layer of classes includes FUEL-SYSTEMS, ENGINE, ELECTRICAL, and BRAKING-SYSTEMS which are not elaborated.

Class Name:	WAGON
Documentation:	parts for Mazda wagons
Superclass:	MAZDA-PARTS
Subclasses:	ENGINE, FUEL-SYSTEMS, ELECTRICAL, BRAKING SYSTEMS
Units:	NIL
MEMBER slot:	PREFERENCE (Assertable)
Source:	MAZDA-PARTS
Default Value:	MAZDA-WEST {ALPHABET}
MEMBER slot:	DEALER-NAME (Assertable)
Source:	MAZDA-PARTS
Default Value:	HAYWARD-CA {ALPHABET}
MEMBER slot:	DOCUMENTATION (Not Assertable)
Source:	OBJECT
Default Value:	{STRING}
MEMBER slot:	ICON (Not Assertable)
Source:	OBJECT
Default Value:	TEXT-STRING {(MEMBER *ICON-LIST*)}
MEMBER slot:	COMMON-PARTS (Assertable)
Source:	WAGON
Default Value:	(BATTERY TIRE ENGINE) {(ALPHABET ICON)}

Figure 1.4   *The wagon class of the Mazda parts (CLASS WAGON)* .

Class Name:	SEDAN
Documentation:	Mazda sedan class of cars
Superclass:	MAZDA-PARTS
Subclasses:	ENGINE, FUEL-SYSTEMS, ELECTRICAL, BRAKING SYSTEMS
Units:	NIL
MEMBER slot:	PREFERENCE (Assertable)
Source:	MAZDA-PARTS
Default Value:	MAZDA-WEST {ALPHABET}
MEMBER slot:	DEALER-NAME (Assertable)
Source:	MAZDA-PARTS
Default Value:	HAYWARD-CA {ALPHABET}
MEMBER slot:	DOCUMENTATION (Not Assertable)
Source:	OBJECT
Default Value:	{STRING}
MEMBER slot:	ICON (Not Assertable)
Source:	OBJECT
Default Value:	TEXT-STRING {(MEMBER *ICON-LIST*)}
MEMBER slot:	COMMON-PARTS (Assertable)
Source:	SEDAN
Default Value:	(BATTERY LIGHTS TANK) {(ALPHABET ICON)}

Figure 1.5   The sedan class of Mazda Parts Inventory (CLASS SEDAN) .

The fourth layer of classes, for example, fuel system elements, can have subclasses if the complexity of the element deserves further subclassification. Otherwise, a unit called an **entity** can be created to compile all information about this element.

A sample unit is created for FUEL-PUMP. The characteristics of FUEL-PUMP will include all features inherited ranging from MAZDA-PARTS, WAGON to FUEL-SYSTEM, plus all characteristics belonging only to FUEL-PUMP. The FUEL-PUMP's own characteristics include the following:

- Current inventory level
- Optimal inventory level
- Minimum order size
- Availability
- Repair frequency

- Customer complaining frequency

- Best source, name, telephone number, terms, and conditions

- Least desired source, name, telephone number, terms, and conditions

- Cost

- Discount

- Storage space required

- Location of the storage

- Substitute

These characteristics can be edited, deleted, and added with ease. A sample
FUEL-PUMP inventory is shown in Figure 1.6.

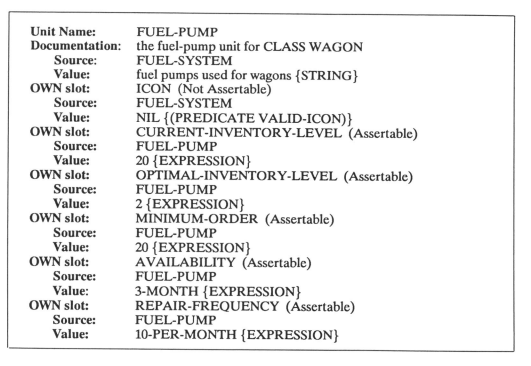

Unit Name:	FUEL-PUMP
Documentation:	the fuel-pump unit for CLASS WAGON
Source:	FUEL-SYSTEM
Value:	fuel pumps used for wagons {STRING}
OWN slot:	ICON (Not Assertable)
Source:	FUEL-SYSTEM
Value:	NIL {(PREDICATE VALID-ICON)}
OWN slot:	CURRENT-INVENTORY-LEVEL (Assertable)
Source:	FUEL-PUMP
Value:	20 {EXPRESSION}
OWN slot:	OPTIMAL-INVENTORY-LEVEL (Assertable)
Source:	FUEL-PUMP
Value:	2 {EXPRESSION}
OWN slot:	MINIMUM-ORDER (Assertable)
Source:	FUEL-PUMP
Value:	20 {EXPRESSION}
OWN slot:	AVAILABILITY (Assertable)
Source:	FUEL-PUMP
Value:	3-MONTH {EXPRESSION}
OWN slot:	REPAIR-FREQUENCY (Assertable)
Source:	FUEL-PUMP
Value:	10-PER-MONTH {EXPRESSION}

Figure 1.6   *A partial unit (end-class) for FUEL-PUMP.*

Observation of the ICS Example

Figures 1.2 to 1.6 illustrate the following key points of the object-oriented concept: data hiding (encapsulated) within the class; information passing between classes; and function names being reused in different classes in the same program.

The hierarchy of MAZDA-PARTS partially displayed in Figure 1.2 mimics the physical organization of the parts inventory classification. Information (including icons) regarding a given object — such as a Mazda wagon — is well documented and encapsulated in the template "The WAGON class of MAZDA-PARTS" as shown in Figure 1.3. Once the template is created, other similar objects, such as "The SEDAN class of MAZDA-PARTS," can use it. Subsequent users or programmers can understand the information, make changes, expand the lists, or modify the structures of the hierarchy and reuse the class of Figure 1.3.

As shown in Figures 1.2 to 1.5, data in a class can be designed to be inherited or not inherited by designating the slots to be member slots for inheritance or own slots for non-inheritance. Subsequent users can change the status of inheritance easily by alternating "member" and "own."

Variable and function names can be reused in classes in the same program, and they can be recalled easily by using the **classname.slotname** convention, as in the following example:

```
Fuel-pump.minimum-order   (as shown in Figure 1.6)
```

The name "minimum order" will be used as many times as required by relevant inventory classes.

For example, the following statements will define a minimum order policy for fuel pumps and engines for the wagon class:

```
WAGON.OPTIMAL-INVENTORY-LEVEL:
   - WAGON.FUEL-PUMP.MINIMUM-ORDER <<= 5
   - WAGON.ENGINE.MINIMUM-ORDER <<= 3
```

Note that MINIMUM ORDER can be used as a variable name or a function name.

COMPARING OOP AND CONVENTIONAL PROGRAMMING

Object-oriented programming requires tools other than conventional programming languages because most conventional programming languages (without extension) cannot accomplish the object-oriented concept discussed in the previous section. Different OOP languages provide different degrees of ability to encode object-oriented concepts. Smalltalk and C++, the two most commonly mentioned languages, are briefly discussed to demonstrate the difference.

Smalltalk

In a conventional programming language, such as C, FORTRAN, or Pascal, procedures and functions are written to manipulate data and obtain solutions. In object-oriented languages, such as Smalltalk, classes such as Boolean, Directory, and Menu, are first defined to represent underlying abstract types. Each class is encompassed with an associated set of operations (called **methods**, which are analogous to procedures and functions) to characterize the behavior of the subject type. Then objects (for example, beta) are declared to be of specific classes (**instances**) for desired operations, such as **sin** (requesting the object name "beta" to compute the sine of itself—beta sin). Such objects inherit the entire field of data defined by their class. Actions may be performed on these objects by invoking one or more of the internal underlying functions (methods) defined in respective classes. The process of invoking a method in the class is called sending a **message** to the object. A message is sent to an object to evaluate the object itself for example., beta sin. Messages perform a task similar to that of function calls in other languages. In this case, the user of the code does need not to be concerned with the type of data in "beta." For example, a Smalltalk expression contains at least an object and a message, as shown in the following:

Example 1.1   `3 factorial => 6`

The user need only be concerned with creating the right order of a message and using the right message; the user does not need to be concerned with data type. If a wrong data type—such as non-integer—is used in Example 1.1, Smalltalk will detect the discrepancy and provide details for debugging.

C++

Bjarne Stroustrup developed C++ at the AT&T Bell Laboratories in 1983. An extension of C, it retains C's efficiency and flexibility. Earlier versions of the language were collectively known as "C with Classes." The key concept in C++ is **class**. A class is a user-defined type. Classes provide object-oriented programming features, such as data hiding, inheritance, and operator name overloading (discussed in the next section). C++ retains the interface facilities corresponding directly to computer hardware and enhances facilities for designing interfaces among program modules. C++ modules are compatible with C modules and can be linked freely so existing C libraries may be used with C++ programs.

C++ provides many facilities available in OOP (but not in C) for programmers to use in reducing code and development time. C++ also makes code more transparent to the subsequent users and makes programs more user-friendly. Classes provide programmers with power tools to make their code secure and efficient. For instance, in OOP, data in a class can be declared **private** and can then be accessed by only a group of designated functions in this class (member functions). This feature can be used to protect data from interference or alteration by unauthorized modification. For example, the inventory files of each individual department must be kept separate and properly labeled. In a corporate inventory system, this requirement can be accomplished by using a class declaration in C++, **class Idxfile**, as follows:

```
class IdxFile : public OurFile {
private:
   char      fidxname[MAXFILENM];// index file
   FILE      *fidxp;            // index file id
   int       ixblksiz;         // the size of a index record
   int       dtblksiz;         // the size of a data record
   unsigned int Inv_Dat_N;     // # of data records
   struct INV_IDX *Inv_Idx;    // points to the index block
   struct INV_HDR Inv_Hdr;     // used for search index block
public:
   IdxFile(char[],int,int):(char[]);// constructor
   ~IdxFile();             // destructor
      int GetStuff(char[],struct INV_DAT*);// Get the inventory data
   int GetStuff(char[],struct CUS_DAT*);// Get the customer data

      int SrchStuff(char[],int*);    // search the index file for item

      int AddStuff(char[],struct INV_DAT*);// add an item
in                                        // index file
   //   .......
};
```

The **FILE** pointer **fidxp** can be accessed by only member functions in this class, such as **GetStuff, AddStuff**; therefore, inventory data cannot be mixed with other inventory data. For a more detailed discussion, see Chapters 3 and 9.

THE THREE KEY ELEMENTS OF OOP

The examples shown in the previous two sections indicate that the three key elements of object-oriented programming are, as follows:

- data encapsulation
- inheritance of attributes
- polymorphism (overloading of operator names)

Most OOP languages implement these three elements differently; as a result, the use of each language varies significantly.

Common characteristics, using C++, are outlined in this section. Detailed implementation in Smalltalk, C++, and Objective-C is discussed in Chapters 2, 3, and 4, respectively.

Data Encapsulation

Data encapsulation is defined as an orderly, structural arrangement of the internal data of an object and the associated action on the manipulation of these data, and the selective access of data through a filter, as shown in Figure 1.7.

Data encapsulation makes representation and organization of knowledge and data relatively easy, and it affects the subsequent uses of the object. Listing 1.1 shows a class written in C++, **specialIcon**, for making an icon of a Chinese character "large." Encapsulating is achieved by appropriately arranging data, such as foreground color (fg_color_t) pattern. Data in the class can be accessed through sending messages with a symbol of "->", as in the following statements:

```
yellow->FillRect(this,0,0,xmax-1,ymax-1);
red->Put(this,0,0,pattern,16,16);
```

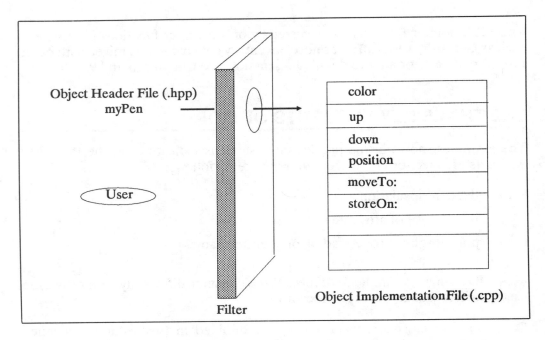

Figure 1.7   Data encapsulation for the user.

Listing 1.1 Special Icon to Write a Chinese Character "Large"

```
#include <stdio.h>
#include "queue.hpp"
#include "manager.hpp"
#include "pen.hpp"

/*
** test.cpp
**
**
**
*/


class specialIcon : public Pane {
    Pen *blue, *white, *red, *yellow;
public:
    specialIcon(fg_color_t,int,int);
    void Draw();
};
```

continued...

```
specialIcon::specialIcon(fg_color_t col,int x, int y) :
(x,y,16,16)
{
    white  = new Pen(FG_WHITE);
    blue   = new Pen(FG_BLUE);
    red    = new Pen(FG_RED);
    yellow = new Pen(col);
}


void specialIcon::Draw()
{
    static char pattern[] = {
    0x0,0x0,
    0x0,0x0,
    0x1,0x0,
    0x1,0x0,
    0x1,0x0,
    0x1,0x0,
    0x3f,0xFE,
    0x1,0x0,
    0x1,0x80,
    0x2,0x40,
    0x2,0x40,
    0x4,0x20,
    0x8,0x20,
    0x70,0x10,
    0x0,0x0c,
    0x0,0x0
     };

    yellow->FillRect(this,0,0,xmax-1,ymax-1);
    red->Put(this,0,0,pattern,16,16);
    Flush();
}
```

The rationale and usage of the program in Listing 1.1 is discussed in Chapter 6.

In addition to these benefits, data encapsulation is also called **data hiding** since access of a given set of data structures is restricted to a list of functions explicitly declared by the designer. Functions not authorized to use these private data will cause an error. For example, the following code is written for a generic "pen" for drawing icons in C++:

```
class Pen /* to declare "Pen" is a class */
private:
   int     mode;// private data (member)
   fg_color_t     color;
   int     x,y;
      public: /* "public" means open to other classes */
```
```
Pen(fg_color_t   c=FG_BLACK);
void SetColor(fg_color_t c) { color = c; } /*  member function
*/
   void SetLinePattern(int lp) { linetype = lp; }
   void SetMode(int m) { mode = FG_MODE_SET; }
   void XorMode(int m) { mode = FG_MODE_XOR: }
   void MoveTo(Pane*, int, int);
   void Plot(Pane*,int,int);
   void Text(Pane*,char*);
   void Line(Pane*,int,int,int,int);
   void Rect(Pane*,int,int,int,int);
   void FillRect(Pane*,int,int,int,int);
   void Put(Pane*,int,int,char*,int,int);
};
```

In the above example, "mode", "color", and "x","y" are defined as private members of the "Pen" class; they can be manipulated only by the functions declared in the program (**member functions**), such as "SetMode". Nonmember functions are barred from using these private data. Consider the following example:

```
    void nonmemberfun()
{
md = Pen.mode;// error
}
```

The above statements will cause an error because the "mode" is private data that can be accessed by a member function as follows:

```
md = Pen.SetMode(m); //getting access through SetMode
```

If an error is found in the private data, you need only examine the member functions rather than the entire functions in the program. This data-hiding feature makes debugging relatively easier than with conventional programming.

Inheritance of Attributes

Inheritance of attributes can mean different things for different OOP languages. Inheritance has at least four meanings:

- **Code Sharing and Reuse:** a subclass can use the member functions of its superclasses as if they were defined in the subclass itself. Even though this definition is opposite to the second definition, C++ and many other OOP programmings are built on this definition.

- **Variable Inheritance:** a subclass contains all the local variables of the superclass (member slots). In addition, the subclass can have more variables of its own (own slots), for example:

  myColor= {red, blue, myName}

  is a subclass of

  color= {red, blue}

  because **myColor** has the two colors of **color** plus one additional variable **myName**.

- **Function Inheritance:** a subclass receives all the member functions of its superclass plus additional functions of its own, for example:

  myPen = {north, east, west, south, center}

  is a subclass of

  pen = {north, east, west, south}

- **Simple Polymorphism:** a concrete operation is a subclass of a generic one, for example, a FORD-SEDAN class is a subclass of the FORD-AUTO class.

OOP languages often combine some or all of these definitions of inheritance; as a result, these combinations appear to cause confusion among users. The inheritance defined in this book is mainly for the purpose of reducing code sharing.

If two sets of data structures (classes) have significant amounts of data in common, the inheritance mechanism can be used to avoid duplication of code. For example, inventory structures, such as "inventory category" and "inventory object" (Category and InvObj) are similar in nature. A class hierarchy can be declared so that InvObj can be a subclass of Category to make code more compact:

```
    class Category {
    int   catcod;
    char catdesc[20];
    int   catsals;
    int   catcost;
    friend class InvObj; /* to declare InvObj is a */
/*  "friend" class that can share the private data */
    public:
    Category();
    ~Category();

    void SetCatcode(int);
    void CalSals();
    void CalCost();
    .....
    }


    class InvObj : public Category { /* to declare InvObj */
/*as a subclass of Category.*/
    char       itemno[20];
    class     *anIcon;
    public:
    InvObj();
    ~InvObj();

    .....
    }
```

Since the class "Category" has been declared as the superclass of class "InvObj", subclass "InvObj" inherits all the properties of the class Category in addition to those declared specifically for itself. Note the following example:

```
void demofun()
    {
        class InvObj aninvety = new class InvObj;
       /*the "aninvety is called to reserve space for */
/* the subclass InvObj                        */

       aninvety.SetCatcode(10);  /* inherited a     */
/* member function from superclass Category  */

       . . . . . .
```

After being declared to reserve a space for subclass InvObj under the name "aninvety", the member function of the superclass "SetCatcode" is inherited as "aninvety.SetCatcode(10)" to avoid rewriting of the similar code as if C were used for coding.

Polymorphism (Overloading of Operator Names)

Polymorphism (overloading of operator names) is used to reduce the bulkiness of code because the same operator names are used for many data types. For example, C++ provides functions in a base (root) class that can be redefined in each subclass. (The compiler guarantees the correct correspondence between objects and functions). This feature is called polymorphism, which allows a message to be sent to an object without worrying about the mechanics of the system implementing the action.

A virtual function must be declared in a parent class (or the class in which it is first declared) by using the keyword **virtual** in front of the function definition. Virtual functions allow you to use the function names repeatedly in the subclasses and to slightly modify the content of the function. The following is an example:

```
class parent_class1
{
protected
  int  version ;
public :
  parent class1 ( ) { version = 1 ;}
  virtualvoid  print  ( )
  {
```
continued...

```
        printf ("\n  the parent class.   version%d," version):
    }
    };

class  subclass1 : public parent_class1
{ private :
    int  layer ;
public :
//...

void print ( )
{
    printf ("\nSubclass1  layer:%d.   version%d",layer,   version);
}
};
```

In this example, the two **print** ( )'s are slightly different, even though they use the same function name.

Your program may have many functions with the same name but different types of arguments. The compiler will choose the correct function. This valuable feature hides data details and makes code more readable. Consider the following example:

```
class Window {
    protected:
      int lastchar;
    int wrapmode;
    .....
     public:
       Window(int,int,int,int);
    ~Window();

    Window &operator<<(const char *);
    Window &operator<<(long a);
    Window &operator<<(int a);
    Window &operator<<(double a);

    ......
};
```

The "<<" is an overloaded operator. Using this same operator, the user can output different types of items to the window without being concerned that the data type may not match. If C is used, you may need to make the function name different for each type of argument; otherwise, the compiler will complain of data-type mismatching. The same example is rewritten in C, as follows:

```
For integer type:    &operatorINT<<(int a);
For character type:  &operatorCH<<(char *a);
For double type:     &operatorDB<<(double a);
For long int type:   &operatorLNG<<(long a);
```

The user must be concerned with the function name that should be called when outputing items in the window, because each function in C is tightly restricted to fixed numbers and types of arguments. It is impossible to achieve this function overloading in C.

Furthermore, even the created class can be initialized with different types of data (called **constructor overloading**). For example the following class, **InvntObj**, after first being created can be initialized with char type stock number (in Case A) or integer type stock number (in Case B):

```
class InvntObj {
  char stokn[16];     /* stock number*/
  class Icon *invicon;    /* icon stands for this invnobj*/
public:
  InvntObj(char*);
  InvntObj(int);
  ~InvntObj();

    void  GetInvDat(struct INV_DAT*); /*find data from
the user.*/
    void     SetIcon(class Icon*); /*set a new icon*/
    class Icon*     GetIcon(); /*get the icon*/
    void  SetStokn(char*);    /*set a stock number*/
    char*   GetStokn();       /*get the stock number*/
    int    StokSrch(int*);         /*search the pos# in the
data file*/
    int      GetFmFile(FILE*,FILE*,struct INV_DAT*);
    int      ItmSav(struct INV_DAT*,FILE*,FILE*);
    int      ChgVal(struct INV_DAT*,FILE*);
    int      Delete(FILE*);
    int      AddVal();
};

  // Define member functions


// Case A: the input stock number is char type
    InvntObj::InvntObj(char* x)
  {
    strcpy(stokn,x);
    invicon = deficon; /*initialize as default icon*/
  }
```

continued...

```
// Case B: the input stock number is int type
   Invntobj::Invntobj(int x)
   {
     char c[20];

     itoa(x,c,10);
     strcpy(stokn,c);
     invicon = deficon;
   }
```

See Chapter 3 for further discussion of C++ features.

SUMMARY

- Object-oriented programming (OOP) is a new programming concept rapidly entering the mainstream of software development. Together with artificial intelligence, OOP is heralded as the technology that will lead to computer-integrated manufacturing which could improve U.S. competitiveness.

- OOP techniques allow programmers to reuse code components previously developed under rigid specifications, much like reusing integrated circuits in hardware systems engineered and tested with given specifications.

- Object-oriented programs are different from conventional programs that focus on numbers and mathematical formulas, in which data and procedures are treated separately, and programmers (users) must ensure appropriate application of data types are applied when they try to use the procedures.

- Object-oriented systems differ from database systems in which data are manipulated under rigid database management methods. By contrast, object-oriented programming allows the programmer and the user to view concepts as a hierarchy of different components or structures of various organizations.

- By using main OOP techniques, programmers can conveniently and neatly represent (encode) these relationships among components, objects, tasks to be performed, and conditions to be met. The code can be reused and easily changed by subsequent users. Generally users do not need to worry about the data type, repeated variable names, or function names. The programmer can concentrate on their professional knowledge instead of programming. A variety of OOP languages provide different degrees of ability to encode object-oriented concepts; C++ and Smalltalk are two the most commonly mentioned languages.

- C++ was developed by Bjarne Stroustrup at the AT&T Bell Laboratories in 1983. Earlier versions of the language were collectively known as "C with Classes." The key concept in C++ is class. A class is considered as a user-defined type.

- Three key elements of object-oriented programming are data encapsulation, inheritance of attributes, and polymorphism (overloading of operator names)

- Most OOP languages implement these three elements differently; as a result, the use of each language varies significantly.

- Data encapsulation is the arrangement of an object's internal data, the associated actions on the manipulation of these data, and the access of data through a filter.

- Data encapsulation is also called data hiding because access to a given set of data structures is restricted to a list of functions explicitly declared by the designer. Functions not authorized to use these private data will cause errors.

- Inheritance of attributes can mean different things for different OOP languages. Inheritance is used to mean at least four things: Code Sharing and Reuse, Variable Inheritance, Function Inheritance, and Simple Polymorphism.

- The inheritance defined in this book is mainly for the purpose of reducing code duplication. If two sets of data structures (classes) have significant amounts of data in common, the inheritance mechanism can be used to avoid code duplication.

- Polymorphism (overloading of operator names) is used to reduce the bulkiness of code because the same operator names are used for many data types.

- A virtual function must be declared in a parent class (or the class in which it is first declared) by using the keyword **virtual** in front of the function definition. Virtual functions allow function names to be used repeatedly in subclasses and modify slightly the content of the function.

- If C is used, programmers may need to provide different function names for each type of argument; otherwise, the compiler will complain of data-type mismatching.

CHAPTER REFERENCES

Special Report. "Smart Factories: America's Turn?," *Business Week*, ", 142-150, May 8, 1989.

Hailpern, B. and Nguyen, V. "A Model for Object-Based Inheritance," *Research Directions in Object-Oriented Programming*, edited by Bruce Shriver and Peter Wegner, MIT Press, 147-164, 1987.

Cox, B. "Object Oriented Programming: An Evolutionary Approach," Addison-Wesley Publishing Company, 1987

Thomas, D., "What's in An Object?," *Byte*, 231- 240, March 1989.

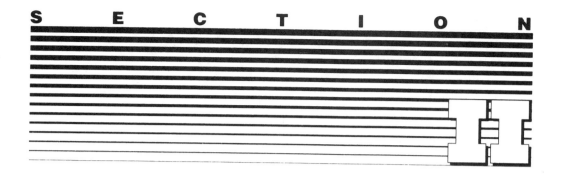

OBJECT-ORIENTED LANGUAGES

Confusion often occurs regarding what constitutes an object-oriented language. Most frequently mentioned terms are object-based languages, class-based languages, and object-oriented languages. Each of these language groups has slightly different characteristics.

A programming language is defined to be **object-based** if it allows direct modeling of objects in the real world, such as parts, machines, cars, ships, people, or bank accounts. An **object** is defined as a set of operations and a state that "remembers" the effect of the operations. Objects may be contrasted to **functions**, which have no memory and are determined by their arguments when invoked. However, objects in an object-based language do not belong to classes or have inheritance. **Ada** is a good example of object-based language in objects. These objects are called "packages" and do not belong to any classes.

Class-based languages are defined as languages that support object classes such as "clusters," which allow objects to be collected and "bundled" in templates. Objects in these classes can be passed as parameters, assigned to variables, and organized into structures; however, these classes do not have hierarchical relation-ships in which data on the higher layers can be controllably passed down to the lower ones. **CLU** is a good example of class-based languages.

A language is defined as **object-oriented** if it is object-based and supports classes that allow inheritance, as in the following summary:

Object-oriented = object-based + classes + inheritance

The derivation of object-oriented programming languages is depicted in Figure II.1. Three examples of object-oriented languages are Smalltalk, C++, and Objective -C.

Smalltalk is more than a language; it is an object-oriented, interactive environ-ment that provides windows, graphics, editors, and debugging facilities. **C++** is the other extreme. C++ supports only mechanisms for classes (data hiding), inheritance, and overloading and nothing else. **Objective-C** supports capabilities somewhere between C++ and Smalltalk. The difficulty with Smalltalk is derived from its strength: everything programmed in Smalltalk must live in the Smalltalk environment. However, since C++ can be used to program all the facilities provided in Smalltalk such as windows and graphics, these features can be integrated in C programs to enhance programs for the end-users.

Smalltalk is presented first and in the greatest detail to familiarize the reader with facilities such as windows, menus, and icons. Methods for building these facilities and sample programs in C++ are discussed in later chapters in other sections.

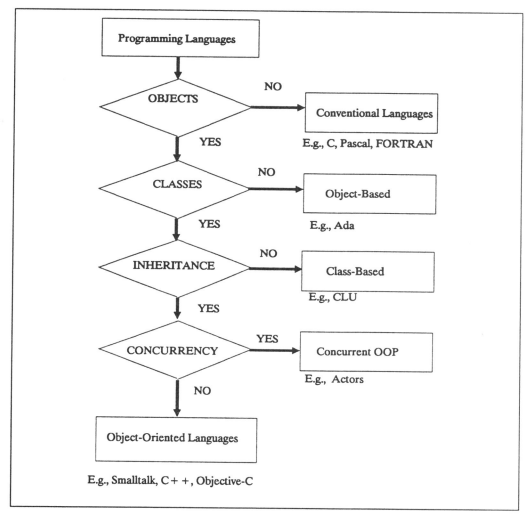

Figure II.1   Object-oriented language classification.

SECTION REFERENCES

U.S. Dept. of Defense. . *Ada Reference Manual,*. July 1980

Liskov, B., Snyder, A., Atkinson, R., & Schaffert, C. "Abstraction Mechanisms in CLU," *CACM*, August 1977

Agha, G. *Actors: A Model of Concurrent Computation in Distributed Systems*, Cambridge, MA, MIT Press 1986.

Wegner, P. "Learning the Language," *Byte*, 245-249 March 1989,

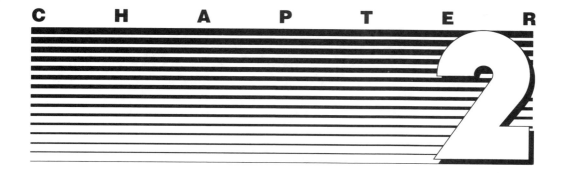

OBJECT-ORIENTED PROGRAMMING IN SMALLTALK

Smalltalk is an object-oriented language environment. As with other relatively new languages, no language standard has emerged yet, so the text in this chapter is based on the implementation of Smalltalk V /286. Structurally, Smalltalk V/286 is similar to other implementations, such as Smalltalk-80. Smalltalk V/286 is an interactive environment where a mouse is more convenient than the keyboard for executing Smalltalk expressions or creating and maintaining Smalltalk programs.

As an object-oriented language, Smalltalk allows the user to classify all information into a hierarchy of related characteristics, such as classes and subclasses. Problems can be broken down into more comprehensible subproblems. These subproblems can be prototyped rapidly without extensive preplanning or flowchart analysis.

Smalltalk is different from conventional programming languages. A programmer must know extensively the class and method library before becoming proficient in using the full power of the language. Good documentation and well-planned development programs are critical in the mastering of Smalltalk. A list of Smalltalk's main classes and methods is included in Appendix A.

This chapter focuses on familiarizing the reader with distinctive Smalltalk expressions, classes and methods in manipulating data, graphics, and windows.

BASIC SMALLTALK EXPRESSIONS

Basic Smalltalk expressions may contain objects, messages, and variables. Simple Smalltalk programs are composed of those three elements.

Objects

Objects are the basic building blocks of Smalltalk, analogous to pieces of data in other languages. The three elementary Smalltalk objects are integers, strings of characters, and arrays:

Object	Example
Integer	1050
String of characters	$ABC
Array	#('array' 'of' 4 'strings' and 6 'integer')

Notice in the examples that a "$" sign is required to indicate the object is a string of characters and a "#" is required to indicate the object is an array. As shown in the example of an array, all objects contained inside of an object do not have to be of the same type or size.

Messages and Methods

In Smalltalk, a **message** is sent to an object to evaluate the object itself. Messages act similar to function calls in other languages. **Methods** are the internal algorithms performed by an object after receiving a message. They represent the internal implementation of an object. A Smalltalk expression contains at least an object and a message, as in the following:

Example 2.1:   `3 factorial => 6`

In Example 2.1, **3** is an object (an integer), and **factorial** is a message that requests 3 to perform a factorial. The internal structure of **factorial** is a method. A message consists of three elements: a receiver object, a message selector, and optional arguments (the message may include no arguments). In Example 2.1, **3** is the receiver object, **factorial** is the message selector, and no argument is used in the expression. As in functions, the message selector is the function name, the receiver object is the function parameter, and the function definition is the method. A message always returns a single object, the result, the following are additional examples:

Example 2.2:   `5+7  =>12`

Example 2.3:   `10*3 =>30`

Example 2.4:   `5+4*3 =>27`

Note that in Example 2.4, the result is 27 — not 17 — because Smalltalk evaluates an arithmetic expression strictly from left to right.

Example 2.5:   `#('what' 'time' 'is' 'it?' ) at: 3   => 'is'`

In Example 2.5, an array is the receiver object, **at:** is the message selector, **3** is the argument, when arguments are present, and a colon is added after the message. The message requests display of the third element in the array.

Example 2.6   `#(7  8  9),  #(10  11  12  13)`
                   `=>  (7  8  9  10  11  12  13)`

In this example, the special character (non digits and non letter), comma, is the selector, which concatenates the argument with the receiver object.

Example 2.7   `3 factorial between: 2+1 and: 'Time" size *5`
                   `=> True`

Example 2-7 is a message inside messages. The expression asks whether (3 factorial) is between (2+1) and: "Time" size*5. It is true that 6 is between 3 and (4*5=20).

Expressions can be grouped together as a series which then can be evaluated as a single unit. Each expression except the last expression is separated from the next with a period. If all of the messages in the series are sent to the same receiver, they can be cascaded. The receiver is written only once, and each message (except the last) is terminated with a semicolon instead of a period. For example, the following two series of expressions are equivalent:

Example 2.8   `Series 1`
                   `    Pen up.`
                   `    Pen go: length.`
                   `    Pen down`

Example 2.9   `Series 2`
                   `    Pen`
                   `    up;`
                   `    go: length;`
                   `    down`

Variables

Smalltalk variables are containers for objects. The two types of variables used in Smalltalk are temporary variables and global variables. Temporary variables are declared after the program is executed. They are declared by enclosing them in pairs of vertical bars at the beginning of an expression series and their names must start with a lower case letter as follows:

Example 2.10   `| tempVariable   index value |`

Temporary Variable can be assigned values as follows:

Example 2.11
```
index:= 1.
tempVariable := value at: index
```

The first line in the example assigns object, 1, to the temporary variable **index**. Note that the symbol for value assignment is `:=`. The second line in the example assigns the result of a message. A caret (^) symbol is used before the value to be returned as the result of the expression series:

Example 2.12 `^value`

Global variables are systemwide objects and are not automatically disposed of after a program has been executed; they are not confined only to use in an expression. Global variable names always begin with an upper case letter. When a global variable does not currently exist, a menu will pop up automatically to allow the user to decide whether or not to create one. Examples of global variables available in Smalltalk are:

- Disk
- Transcript
- True

As with temporary variable, global variables can be assigned value, for example:

Example 2.13 `Family := 'David Lise Eileen Emily`

Control Structures and Iterations

The concept of control structure and iteration in Smalltalk is fairly similar to other programming languages. Generally, a control structure consists of a series of testing expressions and conditional executions. An iteration is composed of an index and looping statements.

Control Structures

Certain messages such as **odd**, **=**, **<**, **isVowel**, **isUpperCase**, **between**: can be used to test whether the expression involved is true for a control structure. Examples are:

- 9 odd   =>true
- $t= $T   =>false
- $C> $D   =>true
- $c isVowel => false
- ('Yellow' at:2) isVowel =>true
- 3/2 between: 0.5 and: 2 => true

The class that contains these methods, **Magnitude**, will be discussed in the next section. These test expressions can be combined by using logical connectors such as **or, and, not.**, for example:

Example 2.14   (x < 3 or: [x > 5])

In the above example, a pair of parentheses is required for the whole expression and a pair of brackets is required for a testing expression after the logical connector message. The test expression can be nested such as:

Example 2.15   (X is Digit and: [X < 3 or: [X > 5])

Example 2.15 is to test whether X is a digit and its value is either smaller than 3 or greater than 5. Two messages are required to express a conditional execution following the testing expressions: **ifTrue:** and **ifFalse:,** for example:

Example 2.16
```
(goalStack isEmpty)
    ifTrue: [ subgoal := nil]
    ifFalse: [subgoal := goalStack].
```

Example 2-16 is a conditional execution expression; therefore, it starts with the testing expression, then the **ifTrue:** and **ifFalse:** expression, and ends with a period. The sequence of **ifTrue:** and **ifFalse:** can be reversed.

Iterations

Four iteration methods can be selected to send a message to an object to request an iteration service:

- do:
- select:
- reject:
- collect:

The format and special features of the four iterators are discussed.

The do: iterator   The **do:** message iterates across its receiver and returns all elements in the range of the arguments. The three variations of the **do:** format are as follows:

Example 2.17
```
i to: j do: [:x|
x timesRepeat: [
.......
.........]]
```

Example 2.18
```
i to j by: k do: [:x|
y := y+x
.......]
```

Example 2.19
```
#(i,j,k,l) do: [:x|
x timesRepeat:[
.......
```

```
. . . . . . . ]]
```

In the first example, the temporary variable **x** increases from **i** to **j** by 1 each time, and the expressions that follow are evaluated. This iteration format includes the compound message **to: do:**, which has two arguments. It takes the receiver object **i** as the lower limit of the iteration and uses the first argument **j** as the upper limit. The second argument is a block of expressions embraced by a pair of brackets. The **to: do:** message allows users to specify their own increment on the receiver. In the second example, the temporary variable **x** increases from **i** to **j** by a **k** increment.

The third variation of the format causes either an array, a string, or a file stream to iterate across itself. In the third example, the elements in the array **i, j, k, l** are substituted into **x** for iteration.

Select: iterator

The **select:** message gives the user an additional feature to select the elements that are evaluated to be true, for example:

Example 2.20

```
(#(1,10,12,16,19) select: [:x| x odd]
x := y+x
```

Example 2.20 indicates that only the elements in the array that are odd will be substituted in the iteration.

Reject: iterator

The **reject:** iterator works just like **select:** except it substitutes all elements of the receiver when the block of expressions returns false, as in the following example:

Example 2.21

```
(#(1,10,12,16,19) reject: [:x| x even]
    x :=y+x)
```

Example 2.21 performs exactly the same task as Example 2.20 even though the message is different.

Collector: iterator The **collector:** message works exactly like the third variation of **do:** because the block of expressions returns always true, for example:

Example 2.22   "Comment: Increase each element in the array by 5"   #(0 5 10 15) collect: [:x| x+5]

Writing a Program

A basic program consists of a comment statement embraced by a pair of double quote marks (") as the title of the program, declaration of the temporary variables, and assignment of values and expressions (including control structures), for example:

Example 2.23

```
"Explain how the reason originates in a reasoning process"
whyFrom: aMessage with: arguments
tempVariable subgoal|
goalStack isEmpty)
ifTrue: [subgoal := nil.
    'Because you have told me' asSymbol printOn: Transcript.
    Transcript cr.]
ifFalse: [subgoal := goalStack removeLast.
    'To prove ' asSymbol printOn: Transcript.
    ((subgoal at: 1) at:3) printOn: Transcript. Transcript
cr].
tempVariable :=self perform: aMessage withArguments: arguments.
subgoal isNil ifFalse:[goalStack addLast: subgoal].
^tempVariable!
```

In Example 2.23, the first line is a comment about the title of the program and the second line is the declaration of local variables. Because no assignment is required for the local variables, the first expression (**goalStack isEmpty**) appears. The local variables are assigned in the condition statements following the first expression.

Evaluating Expressions

Three commands can be chosen to evaluate expressions: **show it**, **do it**, and **save**. To evaluate an expression or a short series of expressions, activate the text pane, select the expression or the series of expressions, and select one of the three commands. For a long series of expressions, the series is better stored in a file, such as **prntst7.st**. The **FileIn** message is used to compose an expression as follows:

Example 2.24   (file pathName: 'prntst7.st') fileIn

The directory browser window is activated, Example 2-24 is selected, and **do it** is then chosen to evaluate the expression.

CLASSES AND THEIR PROGRAMMING

The concept of classes is one of the most distinctive features of Smalltalk. Together with the other three concepts, objects, messages, and methods, it forms the basis of programming to solve problems. Objects, messages, and methods have been discussed in the previous section. This section focuses on major classes available in Smalltalk and how to program classes.

Definition Of Classes

Classes describe data structures (objects), algorithms (methods) and external interface (messages). Each object is an instance of a certain class and all objects in a class are similar because they share the same structure and respond to the same class message and methods. The classes themselves are objects that are contained in global variables. Consequently, all classes begin with a capital letter.

Classes from a hierarchy consist of a root class, **Object**, and many subclasses. Subclasses in turn may contain more layers of subclasses. Each class inherits the functionality of all its superclasses in the organization. A class builds on its superclasses by adding its own methods and "instance variables" to characterize its behavior. Instance variables are their own internal variables accessible only to the objects they belong to; they are similar to fields of a record structure and contain either pointers, words, or bytes. Most object instance variables contain pointers.

Smalltalk makes more than 100 classes available for user selection, modification, and editing to meet the requirements of their applications. The major classes that serve as the basic building blocks for most applications include:

- Magnitude
- Stream (Input/Output)
- File and Directory (DOS System Interface)
- Collection
- Classes for Windows
- Classes for Graphics

Each of these classes contains more subclasses which are discussed in the later sections. However, the discussion focuses on the critical subclasses. The summary of main classes is presented in Appendix A.

Before the details of these critical classes are discussed, we will first concentrate on programing a class, that is, modifying its class methods and instance methods to meet the needs of an application.

Programming Class Features

To program class features, pop up the **Class Hierarchy Browse** window by selecting **browse class** in the system menu. The window allows the user to browse and to modify existing method definitions, and to create new ones. The five types of class features that can be created are global variables, instance methods, class methods, class variables, and new classes. Each requires a different format and is discussed separately.

Adding Global Variables

The procedure for adding global variables is, as follows:

1. Install the relevant file by evaluating (clicking **do it**) the following expression:

    ```
    (file pathname: 'filename') fileIn
    ```

2. Activate the **Class Hierarchy Browser** Window by clicking **browse classes**.

3. Pop up class list pane menu and select **update** .

4. Select the target class.

5. Create global variables by assigning global variables to the class and methods. For example, to create a new dog in class **Dog** of the subclass of class **animal** which has a method of **name**, write the following expressions:

    ```
    "creating a dog, Snoopy"
    Snoopy := Dog new.
    Snoopy name: 'Snoopy"
    ```

    Note the **new** is used to create a new variable, **Snoopy**.

6. Pop up the pane menu and select **save**.

Modifying and Adding an Instance Method

The procedure for modifying or adding an instance method is as follows:

1. Same as steps used for adding global variables.
2. Same as steps used for adding global variables.
3. Same as steps used for adding global variables.
4. Same as steps used for adding global variables.
5. Select **instance** by clicking the right mouse button when the cursor is over **instance**.
6. Select the appropriate method for modification that shows in the top right pane above **instance**
7. Modify the code in the text pane or add a new method by changing its name as well as contents.
8. Evaluate the new code by selecting **save**.
9. The new name if any will appear in the top right pane.

Adding Class Variables

Class variables are global variables accessible to all instances of a class and they begin with a capital letter. The procedure for adding a class variable to a class is, as follows:

1-4. Same as steps used for adding global variables.

5. Edit the class definition to include the string of the new class name following the **classVariableNames:** selector.
6. Pop up the pane menu and select **save**.
7. Add the class variable name to related methods to connect it to the class functions.

Adding a Class Method

The procedure for adding a class method is ,as follows:

1.-4. Same as those used in adding a global variable.

5. Select the pane labeled **class** by clicking the right mouse button.

6. Pop up the method list pane menu and select **new method.**

7. Create the new method by following the template shown in the text pane.

8. Pop up the pane menu and select **save.**

Adding a Class

The procedure for adding a subclass to a class is, as follows:

1-4. Same as those for adding global variables.

5. Pop up pane menu and select **add subclass.**

6. A prompter appears to ask for the name of the subclass.

7. Enter the name, hit return key.

8. Another menu appears, select **variable Subclass..**

9. Specify the new class's instance variables by following the template shown in the text pane.

10 Pop up the pane menu and select **save.**

CRITICAL CLASSES FOR DATA MANIPULATION

Critical classes for data manipulation include the following class groups:

- Magnitude
- Stream (Input/output)
- File and Directory (DOS System Interface)
- Collection

Magnitudes

The magnitude class group defines objects that can be compared, measured, ordered, and counted, such as characters, numbers, dates, and times which are most frequently used. The hierarchy of the magnitude class is shown, as follows:

Superclass (inherits from): Object
Superclass (inherited by): Association
Character
Date
Number
    Float
    Fraction
    Integer
    LargeNegativeInteger
    LargePositiveInteger
    SmallInteger
Time

Magnitude assumes its subclass and implements the ordering relationships and comparison methods, such as =, < =, > =, <, >, and =. Based on these methods, **magnitude** provides its subclasses with interval testing (**between:**) and **max/min** computation. For example:

Example 2.25

```
11 between: 20 and: 10  => True
25 max: 30              => 30
25 min: 30              => 30
```

The definition of these classes can be found in Appendix A. Let us discuss the most frequently used subclasses: **Number, Character, Date** and **Time**.

Number

Class **Number** supports three subclasses: **Float** (for floating point), **Fraction** (for rational), and **Integer** (for integer). Class **Number** implements binary arithmetic operators, such as **+, -, *, /, qus** (integer quotient), **rem**(integer remainder), **raisedTo** (raised to the power of), **log**. Class **Number** also supports other unary arithmetic operators, like **sqrt, exp, Cos, arcSin, tan, ln, floor** (nearest integer less than or equal to), **ceiling, reciprocal, truncated,** and **rounded. Number** also implements testing methods, such as **even, odd, negative, positive** (true if > =0), **strictlyPositive** (true if >0) and **sign** (-1 if negative, 1 if positive, and 0 if zero). The internal testing and max/min methods are inherited from the superclass, **Magnitude**. All iteration methods are implemented in **Number** also.

The difference among **Number's** three subclasses is discussed below. Real numbers in class **Float** are represented in an 8-byte IEEE format and are given an approximate 18 digits of precision in the value range of (+ /-) 4.19 e- 307 to (+ /-) 1.67 e 308. A math co-processor is required to perform arithmetic operations in **Float**. Rational numbers are represented by instances of class **Fraction** and are described by a pair of integers (instance variables numerator and denominator), for example:

Example 2.26   5 / 4

In this example, the slash message is sent to the integer receiver, 5, with an integer argument 4 to form a fraction.

Class **Integer** contains integers as its instances. The class is divided into three subclasses: LargeNegativeInteger, LargePositiveInteger, and SmallInteger for high efficiency in computing speed and memory requirement. For example, small integers are not represented as objects in memory and their values are between -16,384 to 16,383. However, the large integers can be represented in up to 64 k bytes of precision.

Character

Class Character contains the extended ASCII character set from ASCII value 0 to ASCII 255. Characters need not be created and may be referenced by either of the two messages, **asCharacter** or **value:**. For example:

Example 2.27
```
65 asCharacter  => $A
Character value: 65 => $A
```

The interval testing and comparison methods are inherited from class **Magnitude**. For example,

Example 2.28
```
$B <$F     =>True
75 asCharacter max: $F => $K
$d between: $A and $E   => False
$d asUpperCase => $D
```

Date and Time

Instances of class **Date** represent specific dates such as January 3, 1987. Instances of class **Time** indicate specific times of the date, such as 3:00 a.m. A variety of methods for classes Date and Time are listed in Appendix A (in the method section). They can be identified by searching through the names of methods which contain terms, such as day, date, month, or time. The testing and comparison methods are inherited from class **Magnitude**. Examples of simple Date or Time expressions are , as follows:

Example 2.29
```
Date today
Time now
Date newday: 4 month: #January year: 1989
```

New global variables such as Birthday, Lunchtime can be created for comparison of dates. For example, if Birthday is created, as follows:

Example 2-30

Smalltalk at: #Birthday put: '1 January 1989' as Date

Then we can make the following comparison:

Example 2.31   `Birthday > Date newday => false`
                    `Birthday  max: Date newday => 'January 4, 1989'`

Stream (Input/Output)

The **Stream** class is used for accessing file devices, and internal objects as sequences of characters and is used to access messages to get or to put the next object at the current position. Stream is used for scanning input and writing edited output. The hierarchy of class **Stream** is, as follows:

Superclass: Object

Subclasses: ReadStream

                   WriteStream

                   ReadWriteStream

                   FileStream

                   TerminalStream

To create an input stream as an instance of classes **ReadStream** and **WriteStream**, the **on:** message with string as the argument is used. For example, the variable **familyAnimals** is created to accept the stream read from the text pane:

```
familyAnimals: =ReadStream on:
#(Cat Dog Mouse Goldfish).
```

Important messages for screening the input stream are, as follows:

- **fileIn**, Read and execute the Smalltalk source code chunks from the receiver. If a chunk starts with ! send it the message fileInFrom: self (read chunks from a stream until an empty chunk, a single '!' is found).

- **next: anInteger**, answer a collection of the next anInteger elements of the stream and advance the stream position by an integer.

- **skipTo: anObject**, set the stream position beyond the next occurrence of anObject in the stream; and answer true when there is an occurrence.

- **atEnd**, answer true if the receiver is positioned beyond the last object.

Examples are, as follows:

```
(File pathname: 'chapter7.st') fileIn
familyAnimal isEmpty => false
familyAnimal next:2 => (Cat Dog)
familyAnimal skipTo: #Dog => true
```

The first example will be discussed in class **File**. The remaining three examples are self-explanatory. Important messages to writing streams are, as follows:

- **contents**, answer the collection over which the receiver is streaming.

- **nextput: anObject**, write an object to the receiver stream and anInteger times and answer anObject.

- **cr**, write a line-terminating character to the stream.

- **space**, write a space character to the stream.

- **nextPutAll: aCollection**, write the elements of a collection to the stream at once and answer a collection.

The above messages need to be combined with the message **printOn**: whose argument is a stream to produce a character description of the receiver object on the argument stream. For example, to print a rectangle, the message **printOn**: is sent to the origin and corner points and the message **nextPutAll**: is sent to write corner point to the stream:

Example 2.33
```
origin printOn : aStream.
aStream nextPutAll: 'corner:'
corner printOn: aStream
```

Next the user needs to read and write arrays of objects in a program such as

Example 2.34
```
"Read and Write an array of Objects"
|input output anArray|
input := ReadStream on: anArray.
output := WriteStream on: Array new.
[input atEnd]
whileFalse := [output nextPut: input next aMessage].
^output contents
```

In the above example, **aMessage** represents a message sent to **input next**; **anArray** can be an array of objects. If one wishes to produce a printed report, a subclass, **PrintStream** needs to be created under class **WriteStream** and the following sample expressions can be modified:

```
Printer   := PrintStream new

"print the report on the printer"

x   y..........

..........

Printer

NextPutAll:  X,' ';

NextPutAll: y;

cr]
```

File and Directory (DOS System Interface)

Classes **File** and **Directory** together provide the programmer with a facility for obtaining files stored in a DOS directory. Both classes are subclasses of class **Object** and have no subclass of their own. The most useful expression often combines messages from the two classes to read a file that contains a Smalltalk program code. The following is an example:

Example 2.35   `(file pathname: 'c:\Smalltalk\chapter7') fileIn`

In the example **file** is a message from class Directory, **pathname:** is a message from class **File**, and **fileIn** is a message from class **stream**, as also shown in Example 2-32. The disk name and pathname in the example may not be required if the defaulted values are used.

Other useful methods include :

- **copy:** oldFile **to:** newFile, transfer the file named oldFile into the file named newFile.

- **remove: aString**, remove a file named aString.

- **close**, close the file.

- **create: newPathName**, create a DOS directory on disk with complete pathname, newPathName.

Collection

Class **Collection** is the superclass of all the collection classes; and collections are the basic structures used to organize and to store objects in a group manner. Two kinds of collections have already been discussed: **Arrays** and **Strings.** Arrays are fixed-size sequences of objects. Strings are fixed-size sequences of characters. The hierarchy of class **Collection** is shown, as follows:

Superclass: Object

Superclass: Bag
                  IndexedCollection
                      FixedsizeCollection
                      Array
                      ByteArray
                      Interval
                      String
                          Symbol
                  OrderedCollection
                      SortedCollection
                  Set
                      Dictionary
                      IdentityDictionary

The definition of these classes can be found in Appendix A. Among them, the most frequently used classes are **Dictionary**, **Bag**, and **Set**. Features, attributes, and common protocols of class collection and the special characteristics of the three classes will be discussed.

Features, Attributes, and Common Protocols of Class Collection

Generally, any subclass in class **Collection** provides the following capabilities to the user:

- Searching, adding, removing, accessing, and changing elements of a collection
- Iterating over the elements of a collection

The four attributes that characterize a collection class are:

- Order of the elements in a collection
- Flexibility of collection size, fixed or expandable
- Duplicability of collection elements
- Accessibility of a collection by a set of keys

The attributes of the three most frequently used classes are shown, as follows:

Class	Ordered	Fixed Size	Element Dup's	Key	Class
Bag	No	No	Yes	None	Any
Set	No	No	No	None	Any
Dictionary	No	No	No	Lookup	Any

A special message **with:** can be used to create an instance of any collection classes as follows:

```
with: firstObject

with: secondObject

with: thirdObject

with: fourthObject
```

For example, assume we want to create a parts base with two global variables, Engine and Battery. Arbitrary objects and duplicates may be used in the base classes, so Bag is more appropriate. Initialize the variable, as follows:

Example 2.37
```
Engine:= Bag with: #GM
             with: #Toyota
             with: #Ford
             with: #Nissan
Battery:= Bag with: #(Sears JCPenny)
```

Common protocol for manipulating collections includes adding, removing, and testing messages and iteration messages, such as **do:**, **select:** to process all elements of a collection. Examples are, as follows:

Example 2.38
```
Engine add: #Mazda      =>Mazda
Engine remove: #GM      =>GM
Engine size             =>4
Engine addall: Battery  =>(Sears JCPenny)
Engine select: [: aPart| aPart ==#Mazda]
Engine includes: #Mazda   =>true
```

Dictionary

Class **Dictionary** stores and retrieves objects with an external lookup key. A dictionary can be easily created using **Dictionary**. For example, let us create a **ClientDictionary** , as follows:

Example 2.39
```
ClientDictionary := Dictionary new
```

In the example, **ClientDictionary** is a global variable, and **new** is a message indicating a new variable. The following tasks can be performed with **Client-Dictionary**:

- Add telephone numbers to it, use **at: put:**

  ```
  ClientDictionary

          at: 'David' put:  '582-0000'

          at: 'Lise' put:  '583-1111'
  ```

- Retrieve a telephone number, use **at:**

  ```
  ClientDictionary at: 'David' => '582-0000'
  ```

- Check whether a name is in the directory, use **at: ifAbsent**

  ```
  ClientDictionary at: 'Emily' ifAbsent: ['not in the
  Directory']
  ```

- Review all the names in the directory, use **inspect**

  ```
  ClientDictionary inspect
  ```

Be sure to follow the above formats precisely with respect to the keys and arguments of the messages.

Bag and Set

Class **Bag** stores an arbitrary number of objects of any kind including duplicates without implied order or sequence to the elements in the bag. Messages used to create, add, retrieve, and test elements in a bag are shown in Examples 2.37 and 38. These are the common protocols available in class **Collection**.

Class **Set**, like **Bag**, stores arbitrary objects. However, class **Set** does not store the same object more than once. The common messages available for class collection are inherited in Class **Set**. The special message that is unique to this class is **asSet**. The message **asSet** can be used to create a set out of the receiver collection object that eliminates duplicates from the collection. For example, to calculate the odd numbers in a string, evaluate the following expression:

Example 2-40   `'1 2 2 3 3 3 3 4 5 5' asSet select: [:x| x odd]`

CLASSES FOR MAKING GRAPHICS

Smalltalk graphics are generated by bitmapped operation. A bitmap is a linear array of bits; each bit has a value of 1 or 0, with 1 representing white and 0 representing black. Four classes are involved in bitmapped graphics: **Point**, **Rectangle**, **Form**, and **BitBlt**. Points are used to refer to a position of an individual dot within a bitmap. Rectangles are employed to denote areas where a group of dots can be moved from one place to another. Dots are displayed on a monitor screen as colored pixels and stored internally as a bitmap that is contained in a form. Due to the complexity of bitmapped operation, class **Bit-Blt** is needed to handle the moves of blocks of bits.

Point

A point has two instance variables to represent a dot's location: x representing the column (horizontal) coordinate and y representing the row (vertical) coordinate. The @ message is sent to an integer to create a point, as in the following example:

`5 @ 6`

Three important features of point operations are:

- **x:** and **y:** message can be sent to alter the coordinates of a point,

  ```
  (10 @ 120)  x: 60  =>60 @ 120
  (10 @ 120)  y: 100 =>10 @ 100
  ```

- **x** and **y** message can be sent to retrieve the coordinates of a point,

  ```
  ( 10 @ 120) x  =>10
  (10 @ 120) y   =>120
  ```

- points can be compared and performed arithmetically,

  ```
  (-1 @ 50) < (0 @ 60) => true
  (-1 @ 50) max: (-2 @ 60)  =>(-1 @ 60)
  (-1 @ 50) + (-2 @ 60)       => (-3 @ 110)
  (-1 @ 50) dotProduct: (-2 @ 60)  => 3002
  (-1 @ 50) Transpose             => (50 @ -1)
  ```

Rectangle

A rectangle is represented by two points: the **original** (the top left point) and the **corner** (the button right point). Its width and height can be calculated by:

```
width:= corner x - origin x
height:= corner y - origin y
```

The above expression can be used to represent the extension of the rectangle from the original point, as follows:

```
extent:= corner - origin
```

A Rectangle is created by sending the **corner:** or **extent:** message to a point,

```
0 @ 1 corner: 50 @ 50
0 @ 1 extent: 50 @ 49
```

Major Rectangle operations include: **top, button, left, right, center, width, height, origin, corner, containsPoint: expandedBy:, insetBy:, intersect:, merge:, translateBy:, moveBy:, and moveTo:.** Consider the rectangles Box1 and Box2 to illustrate some of these messages:

```
Box1 =10 @ 5 corner: 100 @ 125

Box2   50 @ 60 corner: 180 @ 120
```

The following are examples of rectangle operations:

```
Box1 top            =>5

Box2 bottom         =>120

Box1 left           =>10

Box2 right          =>180

   Box2 containsPoint 100 @ 100 =>true

   Box1 merge Box2     =>10 @ 5 corner: 180 @ 125

   Box2 moveTo: Box1 corner => 100 @ 125: 230 @ 185
```

Form

Class **Form** is a subclass of class **DisplayMedium**, which is a subclass of class **DisplayObject**. Both parent classes are abstract classes and contain no data. A form is used to provide a two-dimensional view for a bitmap. The three major variables in **Form** concerning the user are **bits**, **width**, and **height**. The variable **bits** contains a bitmap, and the content of the form represented by the other two variables, as follows:

```
0 @ 0 extent:(width @ height)
```

Major messages that can be sent to class **Form** to create new forms are:

- **width: w height: h,** answer a white Form whose width is **w** and height is **h**, and allocate its bitmap with the appropriate size.

- **displayAt: clippingBox:,** display the contents of a form on a restricted screen area .

- **outputToPrinter** print the contents of a Form on a printer.

- **copyFrom:** or **copy: from: to: rule:,** copy the contents of one Form onto another Form.

Examples of these messages include:

```
white:= Form width: 60 height: 120   "This example creates a
        white Form of (60 @ 120)"

white displayAt: 50 @ 50 clippingBox: aRectangle "To display
        the white box at 50 @ 50 within aRectangle."

(Form new width: 100 height: 100 initialByte: 16rFo)

outputToPrinter        "To create a new Form and display at the
                        printer."
```

BitBlt

Class **BitBlt** has two subclasses: **CharacterScreen** (for writing text) and **Pen** (for drawing). It is used to move a rectangular area of bits from one portion of a Form or DisplayScreen to another. The source rectangle is defined as:

```
sourceX  @ sourceY extent: width @ height
```

The destination rectangle is defined as:

```
destX @ destY extent: width @ height
```

and the clipping rectangle (as in **ClippingBox:**) is defined as:

```
clipX  @ clipY extent: clipWidth @ clipHeight
```

The sourceForm must be either nil or an instance of Form or its subclasses.

The following messages are used to move one Form to another:

- **destForm: sourceForm:,** specify the destination and source form.
- **copyBits**, move bits from one place to another.
- **drawLoop X: xDelta Y: yDelta**, draw a line from the destination origin to a point of Delta distance to the original.

A sample code employing some of these messages to move the top left quarter area of the screen to the right is shown, as follows:

```
(BitBlt destForm: Display sourceForm: Display) "Display used
    as both the source and destination Form"
sourceRect: (0 @  0 extent: Display rectant / / 2); "The top
            left quarter of Display is the source rectangle"

destOrigin: (Display width / / 2 @ 0); "The top center point
            is the destination origin"

   copyBits  "Move the bits"
```

An effect of gray tone can be created by using messages such as **Form gray, black, darkGray, lightGray**, as shown in the following example:

```
(BitBlt destForm: Display sourceForm: nil)
mask: Form gray;
destRect: (0 @ 0 extent: 100 @ 100);
copyBits
```

Note that the second line in the example, **gray** can be changed to any of the shades mentioned, such as **black or darkGray** in the message.

CharacterScanner is a subclass of BitBlt to be used for writing text. To allow the user to express various styles of writing, the instance methods of class **Font** are used. Useful messages are, as follows:

- **Font: aFont**, specify aFont as the current Font
- **setFont: aFont**, change the font to aFont

The following sample program displays "I love you." at the top left corner of the screen using a Font of 8 lines height initially and then switching to a Font of 14 lines:

```
"Display ' I love you.'"
CharacterScanner new
initialize: Display bounding Box
font: Font eightLine
display:'I love you.' at 0 @ 0;
setplay: Font fourteenLine;
display: 'I love you.' at: 40 @ 0
```

A Pen is used to draw pictures. It has three parameters, **location, direction, and downState:**

- **location,** tell the Pen where to start the next movement.

- **direction,** calculate the ending point when the **go:** message is used.

- **downState,** when **downState** is true, the Pen draws while it moves; otherwise, it moves without drawing.

Useful messages include:

- **black,** change the Pen color to black.

- **gray,** change the Pen color to gray.

- **white,** change the Pen color to white.

- **direction: aNumber,** set the direction to aNumber degree.

- **home,** center the Pen on the destination Form.

- **north,** set the direction to 270 degrees.

- **place: aPoint,** position the receiver Pen at aPoint.

- **go: distance,** move the receiver Pen for length distance.

- **goto: aPoint,** move the receiver Pen to a Point.

- **down,** set down the Pen.

- **up,** lift up the Pen.

These messages are employed to create **aForm** that will be executed by either one of the following two expressions:

```
Pen new aForm

Pen new
```

aForm contains parameters about location and direction. Its **downState** is equal to true. **Pen new** draws on Display rather than on **aForm**.

Examples of the uses of these messages are, as follows:

```
pen

    home;

    north.
 side timesRepeat:[

    pen

       up;

       go:length / / 2;

       down;

       go: length. "length: a local variable"

    side - 1 timesRepeat: [

       pen

          turn: 360 // sides; "sides: a local variable"

          go: length]]
```

Class **Pen** has a subclass called **Animation** which contains several collections of images of the objects in motion and displays Forms continuously to create the illusion of a moving object, as in a cartoon. Useful messages include:

- **tell: name bounce: increment**, tell the object with the **name** to bounce for **increment** distance.

- **tell: name direction: anInteger,** tell the object with the name to change its direction to anInteger.

- **tell: name go: distance,** tell the object with the name to go for distance.

- **tell: name place: aPoint,** tell the object with the name to be placed at aPoint.

- **tell: name turn: anInteger,** tell the object with the name to turn by anInteger degrees.

- **speed: anInteger,** change the distance between the consecutive copies to anInteger. The larger the distance, the faster the object moves.

- **shiftRate: anInteger,** display the current picture anInteger times before going to the next picture.

Examples of sending these messages are:

```
tell: 'David' bound 800;

tell: 'Lise' go: 360;

tell: 'Eileen' direction: -180;

tell: 'Emily' place 0 @ 50;

speed: 24; "each picture is displayed 6 pixels apart."

shiftRate:4
```

CLASSES FOR OPERATING WINDOWS

The window operation is a useful feature in Smalltalk. Windows facilitate man-machine interface. A window requires the working of three types of classes: the application class such as **ClassBrowser** or **DiskBrower,** to synchronize panes; the **Pane** class to display the window on the screen; and the dispatching classes to process mouse and keyboard inputs. Each of the three types of classes contains several subclasses. The main functions of the three types of classes can be summarized, as follows:

- **Application** class
    1. Remember the current state
    2. Create panes
    3. Initialize contents of panes
    4. Carry out communication and synchronization
    5. Define menus for panes

- **Pane** Class, containing two subclasses (**TopPane**, and **SubPane**) to serve slightly different purposes:

    TopPane
    1. Display the window frame and evoke each **SubPane** to display its pane contents.
    2. Save, display, and highlight the window label.
    3. Activate the window and all subpanes
    4. Answer whether the window contains a certain point.
    5. Close the TopPane and invoke each Subpane to close itself.

    SubPane (with three subclasses, **Graph Pane**, **ListPane**, and **TextPane**)
    1. Display the pane frame.
    2. Activate itself.
    3. Answer whether the pane contains a certain point.
    4. Display a portion of its data in the pane.
    5. Scroll data in four directions.
    6. Make a selection on a piece of its data.
    7. Close itself.
    8. Dispatching classes such as **Dispatching**, **Prompter**, and **DispatchManager**.

- **Dispatch**
    1. Activate or deactivate the corresponding pane.
    2. Return the cursor to the top-left corner of its pane.
    3. Open or close the window.
    4. Cycle windows or panes in the window.

- **Prompter**
    1. Show the intended question.
    2. Edit the answer.

- **DispatchManager**
    1. Schedule all windows

The user generally needs to be concerned only with application classes because they are required to be written for each application. The **Pane**, dispatching classes and their subclasses are predefined building blocks in the system. The remaining discussion in this section concerns use of existing standard windows and creating of new windows.

Using Standard Windows

Standard windows can be used to perform the following tasks:

- Display and edit files on a given directory by opening a DiskBrowser Window.

- Display and edit the interrelationship of classes by opening a Class Hierarchy Browser .

- Examine and edit objects by opening an Inspector.

- Review and debug a program at the point of error by opening Walkback and Debug Windows.

Displaying and Editing a File

Files can be browsed on a disk drive to display and edit file by activating a Disk Browser Window.

A Disk Browser Window contains four panes, as shown in Figure 2.1:

- Directory hierarchy list pane, located in the upper-left corner, lists the names of all files in the directory selected.

- File list pane, located to the right of the directory hierarchy list pane, displays the files under the subdirectory selected in the directory hierarchy list pane.

- Contents (text) pane, located in the bottom of the window, displays the text of a selected file.

- Directory order pane, located between the directory hierarchy pane and the contents pane, contains a statement regarding the order of subdirections.

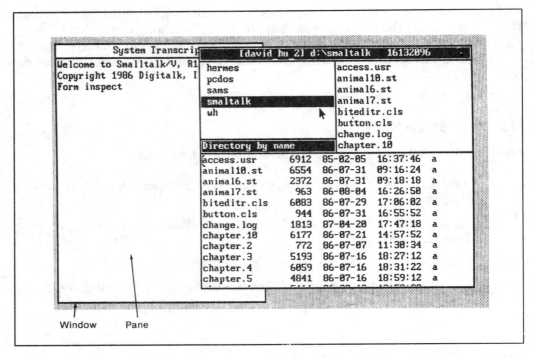

Figure 2.1   *The structure of a disk brower window.*

The following tasks can be performed to display and edit files:

- To open a Disk Browser Window:
    1. select **browse disk** on the system menu.
    2. input disk drive name at the prompter.
    3. size the window by fixing the upper left and bottom right corners.

- To select directory to browse:
    1. move the cursor into the directory list pane.
    2. press the right mouse button when the cursor is on top of the target directory.
    3. **remove**, to eliminate a subdirectory and its file from the disk.

4.   **update**, to browse another disk in the same drive, if it is a hard disk, it merely reinitiates the disk.

5.   **create**, to create a new directory as a subdirectory of the target directory.

6.   select the desired choice and press the right mouse button .

- To select a file to browse:

   1.   move the cursor into the file list pane (the top right hand pane).
   2.   press the left mouse button to select the target file.
   3.   press the right mouse button to display choice of file operation .
        remove, to eliminate the selected file
        rename, to change the file name
        copy, to duplicate the file in another location
        print, to print the selected file
        create, to generate a desired empty new file
   4.   Select the desired choice and press the right mouse button.

- To edit the contents of the file:

   The contents (text) pane shows the complete file for editing.   The procedure for editing a text pane discussed earlier in this chapter can be applied here.

- To display the directory:

   1.   move the cursor into directory order pane (between the directory list and text pane, see Figure 2.1).
   2.   press the left mouse button.
   3.   press the right mouse button to display the choice.
        data order, to order the files by data
        name order, to order the files by name
        size order, to order the files by size
   4.   press the left mouse button to select the desired choice.

Display and Edit the Interrelationships of Classes

A class Hierarchy Browser Window can be used to display and to edit the interrelationships of classes.

The class Hierarchy Browser in Figure 2.2, contains five panes:

- Class hierarchy list pane, located in the upper left, displays the names of all the classes in the system.

- Instance and class panes, located beneath method list pane, enable the user to select either the instance method or the class method, respectively.

- Method list pane, located to the right of the class hierarchy list pane, displays the methods for either class or instance that is selected in the instance or class pane.

- Content pane, located at the button of the window, displays the contents of the code selected.

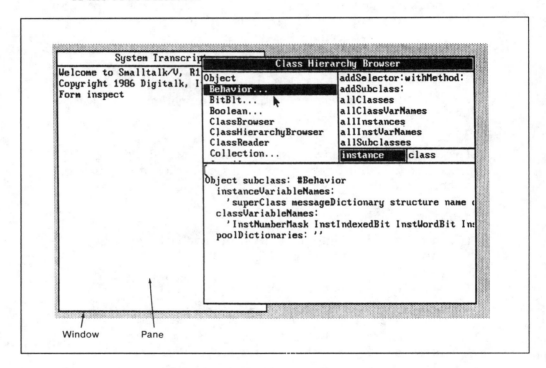

Figure 2.2   Sample class hierarchy browser window.

The following tasks can be performed to display and edit the interrelationships of classes:

- To open a class Hierarchy Browser Window:
    1. select **browse class** on the system menu.
    2. size the window.

- To select a class to display:
    1. Move the cursor into the class hierarchy list pane.
    2. Press the left mouse button when the cursor is on top of the target class.
    3. Press the right mouse button to display the following choices on the selected class.
        file out, to write the class definition and related data to a file with the class name plus the extension **.cls.**
        update, to update the class file
        Hide/show,to display the subclasses of the selected class and to hide those of other classes.
        add-subclass, to add a subclass
        browse , to display the contents of a class

- To add a subclass:
    1. Select the superclass from the class hierarchy list pane.
    2. Pop up the pane menu and select **add subclass**.
    3. Input the subclass name to the prompt.
    4. Select one of the following choices:
        named instance variable
        indexed instance variable
        word arrays
        byte arrays

- To browse a class:
    1. Select **browse** from the class hierarchy list pane (by pressing the right button when the cursor is in the class hierarchy list pane).
    2. Size the selected class browser window.
    3. Select methods to display, edit, or create.

- To change class definition — change the instance variables, class variables etc. of a class:

    1. Select the target class in the class hierarchy list pane to display the text in the contents pane.
    2. Edit the text in the contents pane.
    3. Select **save** from the contents pane menu (by pressing the right mouse button to display the choices).

- To remove classes:

    1. Confirm the name of the class to be removed.
    2. Evaluate the following expression in the text pane.

    ```
    nameOfClass removeFromSystem
    ```

- To display methods:

    1. Move cursor into either the instance or class pane as desired, and click the left mouse button.
    2. All of the methods show in the methods list. Move the cursor into the methods list and press the right mouse button to display the choices of method manipulation:
        remove, to remove a method
        new method, to add a new method
        sender, to search and display the methods that send a message with the selected message selector.
        implementers, to search and display the classes that implement the method of the selected message selector.

- To add a method:

    1. Select **new method** from the methods list pane.
    2. Edit an existing method or create a new method in the contents pane.
    3. Select **save** from the contents pane menu (by pressing the right mouse button to display all choices).
    4. Check whether the new method's name is added onto the methods list pane.

- To remove a method:

    1. Select **remove** from the methods list pane menu.
    2. Check whether the method name is deleted from the methods list pane.

- To modify a method:
    1. Select the target method in the methods list pane to display the code in the contents pane.
    2. Edit the code.
    3. Select **save** from the contents pane menu .

Examining and Editing Objects

An **inspector** window is opened to examine and change objects in the system; it is a low-level debugging helper. As shown in Figure 2.3, an inspector window has two panes: instance variable list and contents.

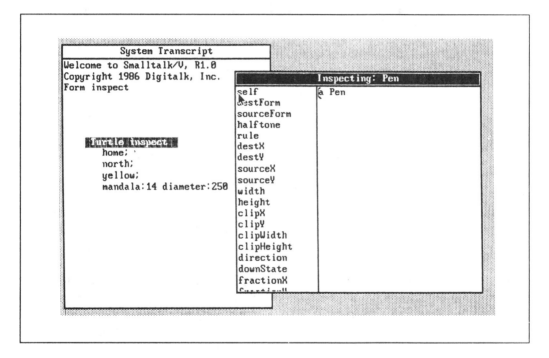

Figure 2.3   Sample inspector window.

The following tasks can be performed by using an inspector window:

- To open an inspector window to inspect an object other than a dictionary:
    1. Select the object to be inspected, such as a global variable, **Demo**.
    2. Evaluate the following expression, Demo inspect:

       ```
       Demo inspect
       ```

    3. Select a variable for inspection from the instance variable list.
    4. Edit or evaluate the text in the contents pane to examine the object.
    5. Select **inspect** from the variable list pane menu to open another inspect window.

- To open a dictionary inspector to inspect a dictionary:
    1. Select the dictionary to be inspected.
    2. Evaluate the following expression:

       ```
       NameOfDictionary Inspect
       ```

    3. Select one of the following choices from the list pane:
       remove, to remove a selected key
       inspect, to open another inspector window
       add, to add a new element to the dictionary

Reviewing and Debugging a Program

A **walkback** window and a **debug** window are provided to review and debug a program. When an error is detected, a walkback window pops up automatically. However, the user has to request a debug window by selecting a command from the walkback window menu. You can use the following sample program that is designed to draw a multi-mandala:

```
Turtle
home;
north;
yellow;
mandala: a5 diameter: 250
```

When the **show it** command from the text pane menu is selected, Smalltalk picks the obvious error **a** and puts a darkened "undefined" before it to indicate that **a** has been not defined. The error **a** is then charged to 1 because it was a typographical error. Following this correction, **do it** is clicked to rerun the mandala program. Another error is detected and this time a walkwindow, as shown in Figure 2.4, appears in the screen, partially overlapping the original window.

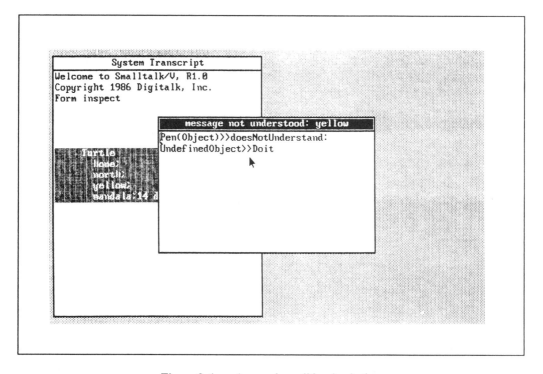

Figure 2.4   A sample walkback window.

The walkback window contains two panes: **label** (on the top) and **text** (on the bottom). The label describes the error for example, **message not understood: yellow** and the text pane contains the exhibition of the methods called (or messages sent) that led to the error in a reversed nest order, that is, the most recent send listed first. On each line of the text, the class of the receiver, (for example, **Pen**) is given and the class defining the method appears next in parentheses, **object**. The string follows the method and the symbol " > > " is the message selector, in this case, **doesNotUnderstand**. The message in the walkback window that **yellow** is an undefined variable. The user has to choose one of the following three actions to continue:

- If the walkback window has provided enough information for the user to locate the error, the user can then move the cursor over the top pane of the window, clip the right mouse button and select **close** to close the window and then correct the problem.

- Move the cursor over the text pane of the walkback window, press the right mouse button to select **resume,** if the walkback window occurred as a result of the programmer's intention, such as a control-breakinterrupt (by typing the break key) or a **halt** message. The walkback window closes and execution continues.

- Move the cursor over the text pane of the walkback window and select **debug** instead of **resume** because the user needs more information to locate the error.The walkback window closes automatically and is prompted for the two corners of the debug window.

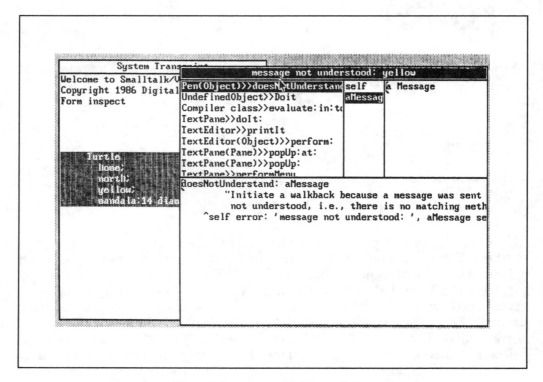

Figure 2.5   A sample debug window.

The debug window provides an expanded view of the walkback window in four panes, as shown in Figure 2.5:

- List pane (top left pane): report the error message in the walkback window and allow the user to select an errorline for further examination.

- Textpane(bottom pane): display the source code for the selected error method and allow the user to modify the method using the procedure described in the class Hierarchy Browser.

- Variable name pane (to right of the list pane):contains **self** representing receiver and the names of all arguments and temporary variables for the error line selected in the list pane. The user can click the right mouse button to open an inspector window to probe further on the object listed in this pane; for example, **self**.

- Variable value pane (to the right of the variable name pane): allows the user to edit the value of a variable that has been selected in the variable name pane.

Creating New Windows

The three elements for creating new windows are (1) creating pane windows, (2) connecting panes, and (3) customizing pane menus.

Creating Pane Windows

Two types of pane windows are created differently: prompt windows (prompters) and other pane windows, such as text panes. To create a prompter, evaluate the following expression:

```
Prompter prompt: 'Message you want.....?'
        default: 'yes,........'
```

A window will pop up with the **prompt**: argument as the window label (for example, "message you want....",) with the **default:** argument (for example, "yes,.......") shown below it.

Two approaches can be used to create a pane window, such as text pane. The first approach is to use the message **windowLabeled: frame:**, as follows:

```
PaneYouCreate :=
  TextEditor
    windowLabeled: 'pane you have created'
    frame( 0 @ 0 extent: 250 @ 200).
```

Note that **PaneYouCreate** is capitalized because a window is a global variable. **TextEdit** is used to provide the window with text editing capability. The message **windowLabeled: frame:** creates a rectangular area (0 @ 0 extent: 250 @ 200) on the screen with the label "Pane you have created."

The second approach is to use **openOn** or **open** as shown in Listing 2.1. The **openOn** message is sent to create a window having a toppane and a subpane. The message **topPane:** is sent to create **TopPane** that encompasses the entire window, as well as the label. The message **addSubpane** is used to add TextPane as a subpane to the TopPane. The dispatcher of the TopPane then is open to schedule the window , that is, to pick up the active pane.

Listing 2.1 Sample Program to Create a Window

```
openOn: aString

    "Create a single pane window with aString

    as its initial script."

    topPane

    inputString := aString.

    topPane := TopPane new label: 'WindowName:

    Toppane addSubpane: TextPane new.

    topPane dispatcher open scheduleWindow
```

Connecting Panes

A means of communicating between the panes is required. The following lines of code are added after **topPane addSubPane:** to connect the textpane to the top pane (the window):

```
(TextPane new
   model: self;
   name: #input).
```

These two additional messages are explained, as follows:

- **model: self**, instruct the textpane to send the message to the application class (**WindowName**)

- **name: #input**, give the name **#input** to the textpane and initialize the window to be initialized with the **input** message, such as:

```
input
"initialize inputPane with inputString"
^inputString
```

The window can be initialized by evaluating the following expression:

```
WindowName new openOn:'It is a new window.'
```

Customizing a Pane Menu

To customize a pane menu, the following expressions are required:

```
(inputPane := TextPane new

model: self;

name: #input;

menu: #inputMenu).
topPane dispatcher open scheduleWindow
```

The message **menu:** informs the window of receiving a methodcall, **inputMenu**, to create the menu for the input pane. The instance variable **inputPane** is assigned to **TextPane** new.

The **inputMenu** method needs to be defined to include a desired menu list. A sample menu list of five selections is shown, as follows:

```
inputMenu
        "Answer a Menu for the input Pane."
        ^Menu
         label:
           ('copy\cut\paste',
            'new Menu 1\new Menu 2') withCrs
         lines: #(3)
         selectors: #(copySelection cutSelection
          pasteSelection menu1Selection menu2Selection)
```

This sample method returns a menu that contains five selections. Each selection needs to be defined. In this case, the first three selections are standard TextEditor methods requiring no definition. However, the last two selections, **menu1Selection** and **menu2Selection**, need to be defined by the reader to meet the need of the application.

Listing 2.2 Sample program that combines a replay pane, input pane with menu selection, and a graph pane

```
openOn: aString
    "Create a sample window with a string
         as its initial script."
    topPane replyPane
    inputString := aString.
    topPane := TopPane new label: 'Sample window'.
    topPane addSubpane:
        (replyPane := TextPane new
         model: self;
         name: #reply;
         framingRatio: (0@0 extent: 2/3 @(1/4))).
    topPane addSubPane:
        (GraphPane new
         model: self;
```

continued...

```
        name: #graph:;
        framingRatio: (0 @ (1/4) extent: 2/3 @ (3/4))).
   topPane addSubpane:
      (inputPane := TextPane new
         menu: #inputMenu;
         model: self;
         name: #input;
         framingRatio: (2/3 @ 0 extent 1/3 @ 1)).
   topPane reframe:
   (Display boundingBox insetBy: 16@16).
   replayStream := replyPane dispatcher.
   topPane dispatcher openWindow scheduleWindow
```

More than one subpane can be created in a window. Listing 2.2 shows a sample program that combines one reply pane, one input with menu selection, and one graph pane. Note that the message **framingRatio** is used. This message defines the position and size of each pane relative to its window. Coordinates of the rectangle argument to **framingRatio:** are a fraction of the width or height of the window. For example, if the window rectangle is:

```
50 @ 100 extent: 200 @ 250
```

Then a framing ratio of (0 @ 0 extend: 2/3 @ 1/4) yields a rectangle of (50 @ 100 extent: 140 @ 40) by using the following calculation:

```
(50 @ 100) + (210 @ 160) * (0 @ 0))  extent:
            (210 @ 160) * (2/3 @ 1/4)
=> 50 @ 100 extent:140 @ 40
```

The window operation and menus are powerful in making a program user-friendly.

SUMMARY

- This chapter has focused on familiarizing the reader with distinctive Smalltalk expressions, classes and methods in manipulating data, graphics, and windows.

- Basic Smalltalk expressions may contain objects, messages, and variables. Simple Smalltalk programs are composed of these three elements.

- Objects are the basic building blocks of Smalltalk, analogous to pieces of data in other languages. The three elementary Smalltalk objects are integers, strings of characters, and arrays.

- In Smalltalk, a message is sent to an object to evaluate the object itself. Messages perform a task similar to that of function calls in other languages. Methods are the internal algorithms performed by an object after receiving a message. They represent the internal implementation of an object. A Smalltalk expression contains at least one object and a message.

- Expressions can be grouped together as a series and then evaluated as a single unit. Each expression except the last expression is separated from the next with a period. If all of the messages in the series are sent to the same receiver, they can be cascaded. The receiver is written once only, and each message (except the last) is terminated with a semicolon instead of a period.

- Smalltalk variables are containers for objects. The two types of variables used in Smalltalk are temporary variables and global variables. Temporary variables are declared after the program is executed. They are declared by enclosing them in pairs of vertical bars at the beginning of an expression series and their names must start with a lower case letter.

- Global variables are systemwide objects and are not automatically disposed of after a program has been executed; their use is not confined only to use in an expression. Global variable names always begin with an upper case letter.

- The concept of control structure and iteration in Smalltalk is fairly similar to that of other programming languages. Generally, a control structure consists of a series of testing expressions and conditional executions. An iteration is composed of indexing and looping statements.

- A basic program consists of a comment statement embraced by a pair of double quote marks (") as the title of the program, declaration of the temporary variables, and assignment of values and expressions (including control structures).

- The concept of classes is one of the most distinctive features of Smalltalk. Together with the other three concepts - - objects, messages, and methods - - it forms the basis of programming to solve problems.

- Classes describe data structures (objects), algorithms (methods) and external interface (messages). Each object is an instance of certain class. All objects in a class are similar because they share the same structure and respond to same class messages and methods. All classes begin with a capital letter.

- Classes form a hierarchy that consists of a root class, **Object**, and many subclasses. Subclasses may contain more layers of subclasses. Each class inherits the functionality of all its superclasses in the organization. Each class builds on its superclasses by adding its own methods and "instance variables" to characterize its behavior. Instance variables are accessible and belong only to their own objects and their own internal variables.

- Smalltalk makes available more than 100 classes to the user for selection, modification, and editing to meet the requirements of their applications. The major classes that serve as basic building blocks for most applications include:

    Magnitude
    Stream (Input/output)
    File and Directory (DOS System Interface)
    Collection
    Classes for Windows
    Classes for Graphics

- The magnitude class group defines objects that can be compared, measured, ordered, and counted, such as characters, numbers, dates, and times that are most frequently used.

- The **Stream** class is used for accessing files devices and internal objects as sequences of characters and is used to access messages to get or to put the next object at the current position. Stream is used for scanning input and writing edited output.

- Classes **File** and **Directory** together provide the programmer with a facility for obtaining files stored in a DOS directory. The most useful expression often combines messages from the classes to read a file that contains a Smalltalk program code as, follows:

```
(File Pathname: 'c:\Smalltalk\chapter7') fileIn
```

- Class **Collection** is the superclass of all the collection classes; and collections are the basic structures used to organize and to store objects in a group manner, for example, **Arrays** and **Strings**.

- Any subclass in class **Collection** generally provides the following capabilities to the user:
    1. Searching, adding, removing, accessing, and changing elements of a collection
    2. Iterating over the elements of a collection.

- Class **Dictionary** stores and retrieves objects with an external lookup key. A dictionary can be easily created using **Dictionary**.

- Smalltalk graphics are generated by bitmapped operations. Four classes are involved in bitmapped graphics: **Point**, **Rectangle**, **Form**, and **BitBlt**. Points are used to refer to a position of an individual dot within a bitmap. Rectangles are employed to denote areas in which a group of dots can be moved from one place to another. Dots are displayed on a monitor screen as colored pixels and stored internally as a bitmap that is contained in a form.

- Windows facilitate man-machine interface. A window requires the working of three types of classes: the application class, such as **ClassBrowser** or **DiskBrower**, to synchronize panes, the **Pane** class to display the window on the screen, and the dispatching classes to process mouse and keyboard inputs.

CHAPTER REFERENCES

Digitalk, Inc., "Smalltalk V/286: Tutorial and Programming Handbook", Los Angeles, CA, 1988.

Goldberg, A. & Robson, D., " *Smalltalk-80: the Language and Its Implementation*", Addison-Wisley, Reading, MA, 1983.

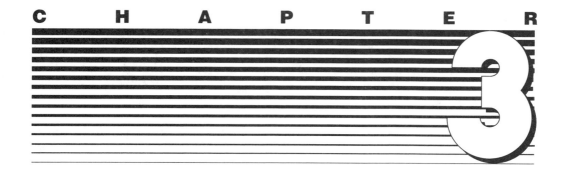

OBJECT-ORIENTED PROGRAMMING IN C++

C++ is an extension of C; the basic syntax and semantics of the two languages are the same. An experienced C programmer can apply their programming knowledge directly to C++ programming. As the need for stronger type checking, data abstraction, and class mechanisms (such as class inheritance) grows, C++ facilities supporting these programming activities can be mastered gradually. C++ retains the same interface facilities that correspond directly to computer hardware and enhance the facilities for designing interfaces among program modules.

C++ modules are compatible with C modules and can be linked freely so that existing C libraries may be used with C++ programs. Furthermore, C++ and C functions may be combined.

Unlike Smalltalk, however, C++ is not an interactive language; it is either compiled directly (using a compiler such as Zortech C++) or interpreted and then compiled (using interpreters such as Guideline C++).

This chapter highlights main C++ features in an ascending manner; C++ functions that are least different from C functions will be discussed first:

1. Program Organization
        Header and implementation files
        Comments

2. Lisp-like Functions
        Enumeration names
        Void
        Function prototype
        Overloading of function names
        Default arguments
        Reference parameters in function
        Unspecified number of parameters in function

3. Object-Oriented Programming Features
        Classes and data encapsulation
        Creating subclasses and inheritance
        Virtual functions and polymorphism

4. Comparing C++ with C

The application of C++ is discussed in Chapters 5, 6, 7, 8, 9, and 10.

PROGRAM ORGANIZATION

Header and implementation files and comments are discussed in this section.

Header and Implementation Files

Before using a C++ translator or compiler, you must prepare your source program (using any text editor) in two distinct types of source files:

- Header files, with extensions of either **.hpp** or **.h**
- Implementation files, with extensions of **.cpp**

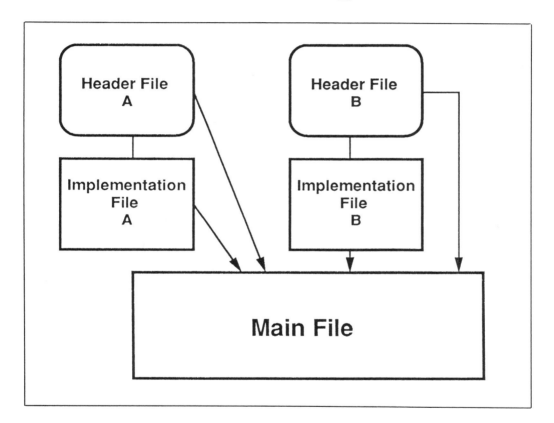

Figure 3.1   Source program files.

As shown in Figure 3.2, a header file includes the interface, a set of related classes, functions, and data type declarations that can be manipulated by other files. In a sense, a header file collects all information and operations on an object; a miniature user's guide may be included to explain (in comments, as discussed in the following section) the application of each function and examples may be provided. Like classes and methods in Smalltalk, a header file is often all that is available to a programmer or user (the source code for the implementation file is usually not supplied); although the source code is the natural place for the user to seek help in understanding how to use the functions. In the near future, when more programmers and developers have used C++, classes and methods on various specific applications similar to Bags, Dictionary, and Directory in Smalltalk will be available to C++ programmers to increase their programming productivity.

The implementation file manipulates the classes, functions, and other data types specified in the header file. Because C++ is an object-oriented language, it allows you to focus your attention on describing the objects on which you want to operate. Once you have clearly organized the objects, writing the implementation file is fairly straightforward.

Comments

Both // and /* can be used in C++ to indicate comments. The symbols // are used to signal a comment to the end of a line, and the older C-like comment delimiters, /* and */, are used to bracket a comment on a single line or over multiple lines.

LISP-LIKE FUNCTIONS

The term Lisp-like function is used loosely to indicate that a function is frequently used in Lisp-written expessions. Main C++ functions in this area include enumeration names, void, function prototype, overloading of function names, reference parameters in function, default arguments, and unspecified number of parameters in functions.

Enumeration Names

The declaration containing **typedef** allows users to define identifiers that can be used later as if they were of the type keyword:

```
typedef(right, middle, left)  mouse_button;
```

the above declaration introduces the user-defined type identifier, **mouse_button**. Any variables declared to be of this new type can have one value from the value set: right, middle, and left, such as the following:

```
typedef   struct key_operation
  {

    mouse_button   keyboard;

//...
//...
//...
};
```

This declaration is useful for providing convenience for value choice in multiple menu selections.

Void

In C++, **void** is a type indicating that a function does not return a value. Pointer variables may be declared to point to void for the purpose of passing pointers to functions that are not allowed to make assumptions about the type of the object, and for returning untyped objects from functions. This use of void is particularly powerful in providing menu-driven user interfaces. For example, the declaration (see Listing 3.1)

```
typedef   void (*menu_driven) ( );
```

defines a pointer to a function, menu_driven, that returns void and has no parameters. If there are five menu choices, (such as exit, input, output, disk, and ideo), the declaration:

```
menu_driven    menu[5];
```

defines an array of five functions and each specifies an operation. For this declaration to work, an assignment function is needed to load the array of menu functions by assigning the five function pointers to menu[0],...,menu[4].

Listing 3.1: Menu-Driven Applications

```
# include <stdio.h>
   typedef  void  (* menu_driven)  ( );

   menu_driven      menu[5];

Main ( )
{
extern void assign_fn ( );
extern void exit ( );
extern void input ( );
extern void print ( );
extern void ask_user ( );
extern void trace ( );

int choice;
// .
// .
// .
// .
}
void assign_fn ( )
{
menu[0] = exit           ;
menu[1] = input            ;
menu[2] = print            ;
menu[3] = ask_user ;
menu[4] = trace            ;
```

Function Prototype

Function prototyping specifies the parameters of a function within the parameter definition section of each function. This allows the compiler to perform run-time data type checking. Consequently, Function prototyping minimizes serious interface problems in passing data to functions. The following is an example:

```
void    function_name (char a, char b)
```

Overloading of Function Names

C++ allows a function name to be overloaded (redefined) within the same scope of functions if the specifier, **overload**, is given before the overloaded functions are declared. The following is an example:

```
#include <stdio.h>
overload pprint;
extern void pprint (int j)
extern void pprint (char* string)
//...
//...
//...

void pprint (int i)
{
// define pprint
}
void pprint (char* string)
{
// define pprint
}
```

Pprint is thus overloaded to allow printing of integers and strings. It can be further defined to print data sets, real numbers, or complex numbers.

Function name overloading is extremely important for intelligent object-oriented system development because it is heavily relied upon to connect classes with the inference engine to prepare for user queries (see Chapter 8 for examples).

Default Arguments, Reference Parameters in a Function, and Unspecified Numbers of Parameters in a Function

C++ features, such as default arguments, reference parameters in a function, and unspecified numbers of parameters in a function provide more efficient operations for programmers.

Default Arguments

C++ allows arguments in a function to have default values; however, arguments with default values must appear as the last set of arguments in the following function:

```
void default (int first, int second = 3, char third = 'a')
```

Reference Parameters in a Function

A reference in C++ acts as a name for an object. One use of references is to ensure that the address of an object, rather than the object itself, is passed to a function (this is also named **call by reference**). References allow the use of arithmetic operators on large objects, without excessive copying, when pointers cannot be used. A parameter can be declared as reference parameter by using the & operator as follows:

```
void decrement (int&  foo)

{ foo++ }

decrement (x);
```

Unspecified Number of Parameters in a Function

C++ allows functions to have an unspecified number of arguments by using ellipsis, ..., in the argument, such as the following:

```
int  printf (char* ...);
```

in the stdio.h. Calls to printf require at least one argument (a string). Note that argument checking is turned off when a function is declared to have an unspecified number of arguments.

OBJECT-ORIENTED PROGRAMMING CONCEPTS

The concept of classes in C++ is similar to that in Smalltalk. Adding classes and associated features makes C++ closer to an object-oriented language than C.

Object-oriented programming focuses on data to be manipulated rather than procedures performing the manipulating. The main task of writing a C++ program is dividing the problem into underlying data types (classes or subclasses) and the definition of the properties (method interface) of each of the classes and subclasses. The class or subclass variables correspond to physical or logical entities constituting the actual problem. C++ provides conveniences for creative class structures. Unlike Smalltalk, in which various classes for different purposes are available to the user (such as making directories and creating graphics) the C++ programmer must create their own. When more programmers have used C++, series of C++ class libraries may be made available by software developers. Classes and inheritance are the focus of the rest of this section.

Classes and Data Encapsulation

The class construct provides the basic foundation for object-oriented programming for C++. The class encapsulates the set of values and the associated methods for an object. These values or methods can be available completely or partially to the users, and they may be passed down completely or partially to subclasses. The class also provides a base for an inheritance hierarchy of data/knowledge representation.

The **struct** in C++ is a special case of a class with no protected section; that is, all data (the normal struct in C) or methods (functions) are available to every call.

Special features in the C++ class include: structure of a class (private, protected, and public sections), constructors and destructors, objects and messages, friends, overloading of operators, and function names in classes.

Structure of a Class

A class is generally constructed, as follows:

```
class   class_name
{
private :
   data and methods

// The data and methods that cannot be accessed
// directly by other classes

public  :
   data and methods
// The data and methods that can be accessed directly
// by other classes

protected :
   data and methods
// The data and methods that can be accessed only by
// children classes

};
```

Listing 3.2: A Sample Program Including "Public" Data

```
// textscro.h
#ifndef TextScroller_h
#define TextScroller_h

#include <InterViews/Text/textviewer.h>
#include <InterViews/scroller.h>
#include <InterViews/box.h>
#include <InterViews/world.h>
#include <InterViews/painter.h>
#include <InterViews/frame.h>
#include <InterViews/sensor.h>
#include <InterViews/interactor.h>

class KillBox : public Interactor {
    Bitmap      *picture;
    Interactor *victim;
public:
    KillBox(Interactor *i, Painter *p);
    ~KillBox();
    void Draw();
    void Redraw(Coord, Coord, Coord, Coord);
    void Handle(Event &);
};
```
continued...

```
class TextScroller : public Frame {
private:
    HScroller  *hs;
    VScroller  *vs;
    TextViewer *text;
public:
    TextScroller(Painter *p,int cols=COLS ,int rows=ROWS);
    ~TextScroller();
    TextViewer* Text() { return text; } ;
};


#define SCROLLERSIZE 16
#endif
```

Listing 3.2 shows a component class for building user-interface packages: **textscroller**. The class **KillBox** has methods **Draw, Redraw,** and **Handle** that are available to everybody and has **HScroller, VScroller** and **Textviewer** that can be used by the functions declared within the class.

Listing 3.3 shows another component class for user-interface: **messages** (bulletins) with data regarding the characteristics of the class. These data can be passed down to children classes and declared as offset, length, author, and subject. etc. These data or methods are not accessible to outside classes.

After the header file is completed, methods, also called **member functions** in C++ can be defined using the double colon (::). The syntax requires the class name followed by the double colon and the function name, as in the following example:

```
    void KillBox :: Draw ( ){
//...
//...
    }
```

Listing 3.3: A Sample Program to Show Inheritance

```
// message.h
#ifndef Message_h
#include "TextScroller.h"
class Message : public Interactor {
protected:
    long     offset;     // where in file the message is
    long     length;     // how long the message is
    char*    author;     // who wrote it
    char*    subject;    // what it's about
    char*    date; // when it was written
    char*    file; // where to read it from
    boolean  selected;   // cursor is here right now
    Painter* fgpainter,*bgpainter;
    boolean  seen; // read or seen
    boolean  deleted;    // has it been deleted?
public:
    Message(long, long, char*, Painter *p,boolean);
    ~Message();
    void    Draw();
    void    Redraw(Coord,Coord,Coord,Coord);
    void    Handle(Event &);

    TextScroller *Read();     // return a textscroller with message
    char* From() ;            // Who the message is from
    Message*    Add();        // add a message to the list
    char* FindHeader(char *); // find the specified header
field
    char* SaveHeader(char *); // stash away an eventual header
};
#define MESSAGEWIDTH 128
#endif
```

The above defines Draw ( ) for class KillBox, as shown in Listing 3.4.

Listing 3.4: A Sample Program in Which a Member Function is Declared For a Given Class

```
/* textscro.c
*/
#include "TextScroller.h"
#include <InterViews/border.h>
#include <InterViews/bitmap.h>
#include <InterViews/shape.h>

/*
** Data for the killbox
*/

#include "killbox.icon"

KillBox::KillBox(Interactor *i,Painter *p=stdpaint) {
    shape->Rect(killbox_width,killbox_height);
    shape->Rigid();
    output = p;
    picture = new Bitmap(killbox_bits,killbox_width,
      killbox_height);
    victim = i;
    Sensor *s = new Sensor(stdsensor);
    s->CatchButton(UpEvent,LEFTMOUSE);
    s->CatchButton(UpEvent,MIDDLEMOUSE);
    s->CatchButton(UpEvent,RIGHTMOUSE);
    s->CatchButton(DownEvent,LEFTMOUSE);
    s->CatchButton(DownEvent,MIDDLEMOUSE);
    s->CatchButton(DownEvent,RIGHTMOUSE);
    Listen(s);
}

KillBox::~KillBox() {
    delete picture;
}

void KillBox::Draw() {
    output->ClearRect(canvas,0,0,xmax,ymax);
    picture->Draw(canvas);
}

void KillBox::Redraw(Coord, Coord, Coord, Coord) {
    Draw();
}

void KillBox::Handle(Event &e) {
    Coord dummy;
    World *w;
```

continued...

```
      e.GetAbsolute(w,dummy,dummy);
      if (e.eventType == DownEvent) {
   picture->Invert();
   picture->Draw(canvas);
      }
      if (e.eventType == UpEvent) {
   w->Remove(victim);            // kill the bastard
      }
   }


   /*
   ** TextScroller: a TextScroller will scroll a given text both
   horizontally
   ** and vertically.
   */
   TextScroller::TextScroller(Painter *p = stdpaint,
            int cols = COLS,int rows = ROWS) : (p) {
      text   = new TextViewer(p,cols,rows);
      hs     = new HScroller(text,SCROLLERSIZE,nil,p);
      vs     = new VScroller(text,SCROLLERSIZE,nil,p);
      output = p;
      Insert(new VBox(
       new HBox(
            text,
            new VBorder(output),
              vs
       ),
       new HBorder(output),
       new HBox(
            hs,
            new VBorder(output),
            new KillBox(this,output)
       )
       )
      );
   }
```

An object can be declared as any class in the same manner an object is declared to be an integer or a real number. For example, **a** in Listing 3.5 is declared to be an inside_class that has been defined earlier. The methods defined in the public section (referred to as public functions) can be used by calling the class name followed with a period (.), the name of class type, two colons, and the name of the public function as follows:

```
      a.inside_class :: write ()
```

Listing 3.5: Initializing Classes Within a Class

```
// Program to illustrate the nesting of classes
#include <stdio.h>
class inside_class
{
   private
     int a;

   public:
     inside_class( int c ) { a = c; }
     void write ()  { printf( "\n%d", a); }
};

class outside_class
{
   private:
     int b;
     inside_class a;
public:
   outside_class( int c);
   void write()  { printf( "\n%d", b );  }
};

outside_class::outside_class(  int c) : a(10)
{
   b = c;
}

main()
{
   outside_class object( -12 );

object.write();
}
```

Constructors and Destructors

Constructors are used to automatically initiate objects at their point of declaration; destructors are called to automatically deallocate the storage occupied by a
class. As shown in Listing 3.2, the constructor KillBox has the same name as the
class itself where the class KillBox is initialized with **Interactor** and **Painter**.
Whereas, the tilde symbol (~) in front of KillBox immediately following the
constructor is a destructor that automatically deallocates the storage occupied by
the class. The destructor is used to release the storage in the heap contained by
the class.

Nesting of Classes and Their Initialization

C++ allows the nesting of classes; that is, a class contains one or more classes as its members either in the private or public section. As shown in Listing 3-5, the inside_class was first defined by giving a private member (int a) and two public members (constructor inside_class(int c) { a=c;} and method write()).

The outside_class is then created by declaring int b, inner_class a to be private members and the following objects to be public members:

- o   Constructor, outside_class (int c)
- o   write()
- o   write_inside_a which is a public member function of the inside_class.

The initialization of nested classes uses constructors slightly different from those for the simple class. For example, the variables inside the inside_class are initialized as follows:

```
inside_class (int c)  { a = c ; }
```

This example is shown in Listing 3-5. The class is declared to be initialized with a constructor for int a. If you want to assign the value of 10 to **a**, the following statement is required:

```
inside_class  (10)
```

To assign private data (**a**) in **inside_class** from **outside_class**, write the following:

```
outside_class :: outside_class (int c) : a(10)
{ b=c;}
```

The internal data object **a** is initialized by the contractor for class outsider_class. The constructor for the internal object is executed before those for the class containing the internal object. In general, a list of constructors is given after a colon. Each construction is separated by a comma if there is more than one data object. When a class containing internal data objects is deallocated by a destructor, the order of deallocation is reversed; therefore, the destructor of the class is executed before those for its internal data objects.

Friends

To benefit from the efficiency of object-oriented programming, data and methods must be defined within the same class; otherwise, a function call overhead is required because the private data and methods are available only within the class definition. These methods might be implemented in different classes. C++ provides programmers with a convenient facility, **friend**, to bypass this requirement.

Friend is used to declare a method in the private section of a class, an entire class, or a function to be accessible by a given class (friends of a given class). The following is an example:

```
class  friends_example
{
   friend char*     x:: list ( );
   friend class     y ;
   friend vector multiply (matrix &, vector &);
   //...
}
```

In the above example, method char* list () from class x, class y, and function vector multiply are all declared to be friends of class friends_example. A friend declaration can be inserted into either the private or public section of a class. The location of a declaration makes no difference in the program execution.

The declaration of friends releases the software engineer from the responsibility of consistently tracking the methods required for manipulating the underlying data for all potential situations. Friend increases code efficiency and computation speed by reducing the need of applying unnecessary methods in a class when the class is called.

Static Members

If every object in the class needs to share the same data, such as a corporate calendar, the corporate calendar can be declared as **static** in the class calendar :

```
class calendar {
//...
calendar*    next;
static calendar*    corporate_calendar;
void    appoint (int);
//...
};
```

Declaring corporate_calendar as static, assures that only one copy of corporate calendar exists. Corporate_calender can be called from outside of the class :

```
calendar :: corporate_calender
```

In a member function, static member is referenced in the same manner as other members. The use of static class members will help reduce the need for global variables.

Static members are like own slots. Copies are not made for every child entity.

Creating Subclasses (Derived Classes) and Inheritance

Subclasses can be created by using the inheritance feature of C++. Inheritance allows reuse of data and functions in the classes created by passing all or parts of them to children classes (that is, subclasses). This property is extremely useful in building intelligent systems and provides programmers with ready-made frame structures. In many object-oriented languages, such as Smalltalk, the property of inheritance forms the backbone of the entire programming environment, making available a sophisticated baseline class organization.

Each object-oriented language handles inheritance differently. C++ allows a children class to inherit or modify the methods of its parent class (sometimes, called member slots), such as the following :

- Add more methods not contained in the parent class (called own slots).

  In the current version of C++, a class can have only one parent. (Note that in Smalltalk, a class can have several parents (referred to as **multiple inheritance**). Unless specially authorized, a derived class cannot access the private data of its parent. This authorization can be granted by either of the following ways:

- A **friend** declaration: an entire subclass or given methods in a subclass can be declared as friends of the parent class.

- A **protected** mode: all class members can be declared as protected in the parent class. Protected members are hidden in the same way as private members, but they are accessible to subclasses, as shown in Figure 3-2.

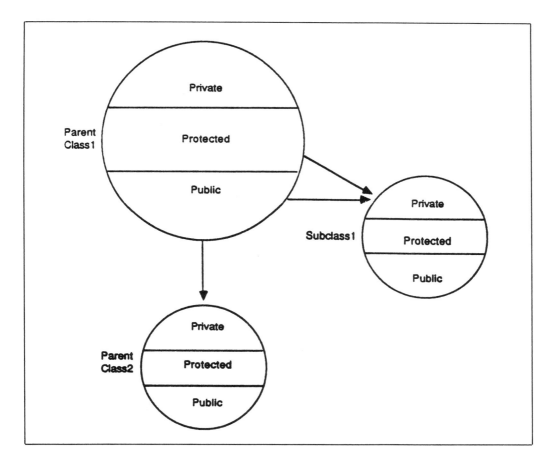

Figure 3.2   Inheritance of the three types of class members: public, protected, and private.

Figure 3.2 shows the inheritance of three types of class members: public, protected, and private. Information in both the public and protected types can be accessible to subclasses. In fact, the information in the public section of the parent class can be available to anyone.

A class is declared to be a subclass of a parent class as, follows:

```
class   parent_class1 ;
{
real    private1, private2 ;
public :
method1 ( )   {//...} ;
method2 ( )   {//...} ;
};
class   subclass_name: public  parent_class_name
{
//...
} ;
```

Every object of a subclass contains its own copy of the public data of its parent class and its own private data. The object of the subclass may not use the methods of the parent class in the header, unless one of the following situations applies:

1. The subclass includes these methods in its public section, for example,

```
class   subclass1 : parent_class1
{
public :
void    method1 ( )
{ parent_class1 :: method1 ( );
}
//...
};
```

In the above example, method1 is available to the objects in subclass1.

2. The subclass is defined with the following declaration (note the word **public** before the parent_class_name):

```
class subclass_name : public parent_class_name
{
//...
};
```

In the implementation phase (main program), however, subclasses can assess the methods (but not the private data) of the parent class, for example:

```
main ( )
{
parent_class1 x ;
        x.method1 ( );
subclass1   y ;
  y.parent_class1 :: method2( );};
```

Initializing a Subclass with a Parent Class Constructor

When a parent class includes a constructor for initialization, consider invoking this constructor in a subclass, since objects of each subclass contain a copy of the data from the parent class.

Objects of each subclass can initialize parent class data by using a constructor that contains all parameters required in the following order: first, parent class, second internal class (guests) members, and finally, the subclass last. For example, initialize five parameters, as shown in Listing 3.6:

1. Two parameters, X1 and X2, are for the private data of the parent class: private1 and private2

2. Two parameters, X3 and X4, are for the private data of guest member parent_class private 4.

3. One parameter, X5, is for the public data of the subclass private3.

Listing 3.6: Initializing a Subclass With a Parent Class Constructor

```
#include <stdio.h>

class parent_class1
{
   private :
     int private1, private2;

   public :
   parent_class (int X1, X2)
```

continued...

```
//....
};

class  subclass1 : parent_class1
{
   private :
   int private3;
   parent_class1 private4:

   public :
   subclass1 ( int X1, int X2, int X3, int X4, int X5 ) :
      (X1, X2), private4 (X3, X4)
   {
     private3 = X5;

   }
   //...
};
```

To initialize all five parameters, a constructor must be declared in the public section of the subclass as follows:

```
Subclass1  (int X1, int X2, int X3, int X4, int X5)
   : (X1, X2), private4 (X3, X4)
   {
   private4 = X5;
   }
```

Virtual Functions and Polymorphism

In C++, functions can be declared in a base (root) class and redefined in each subclass. (The compiler guarantees the correct correspondence between objects and functions). This feature is called **polymorphism**; it allows the programmer to send a message to an object without worrying about implementing the action in the system.

A virtual function must be declared in a parent class (or the class in which it is declared) by using the keyword **virtual** before the function definition. This keyword is used only once in the base class, and only a overloaded function name is used in the subsequent derived classes; However, not all subsequent subclasses, must declare and implement the virtual function. A virtual function can be used, even if no subclass will be derived,. Like function name overload, virtual functions use the function names repeatedly in subclasses and to slightly modify the content of the function, for example:

```
class parent_class1
{
protected
  int  version ;
public :
  parent_class1 ( ) { version = 1 ;}
  virtual void  print  ( )
  {
        printf ("\n  the parent class.  version%d," version):
  }
  };

class  subclass1 : public parent_class1
{ private :
  int  layer ;

public :
//...

void print ( )
{
  printf ("\nSubclass1  layer:%d.  version%d",layer,  version);
}
};
```

In the above example, the two print ( )'s are slightly different even though they use the same member function name.

COMPARING C++ WITH C

This section summarizes the advantages of C++ over C in programming. The three main strengths of using C++ are code efficiency, code security, and incremental code modification. These benefits result primarily from the three features of an object-oriented language.

Code Efficiency

In addition to the structure of classes with inheritance that may be used to organize, classify, and manage objects, the following two methods in C++ promote efficiency in code writing:

- Using virtual functions to avoid duplicated code for similar functions
- Using in-line function definition to avoid run-time overheads

As previously discussed, virtual functions are declared to overload function names in subclasses, for example:

```
    class OurFile {
  friend class InvFile;
  friend class SysFile;
  friend class VndFile;
  friend class CusFile;
  friend class SalFile;
  friend class CatFile;
private:
  char    fname[MAXFILENM];
  FILE    *fdatp;
public:
  OurFile(char fnm[]) { strcpy(fname,fnm); }
  ~OurFile();

  virtual int GetStuff() { ; }
  virtual int AddStuff() { ; }
  virtual int DelStuff() { ; }
  virtual int ChgStuff() { ; }
  virtual int SrchStuff() { ; }
};

class VSSFile : public OurFile {
public:
  VSSFile():(char[]);        // constructor
  ~VSSFile();                // destructor

  int  GetStuff(char[],struct VENDORDAT*); // get the data
  ......
};
```

If the "GetStuff" function were declared in base class **OurFile** as a regular, non-virtual function and inherited to subclass **VSSFile**, it would be required to be redefined with a new name in the subclass. Therefore, two separate functions have been created in the above example. However, if the function were declared to be virtual in the base class; the same function name could be redefined in subclasses without creating new names, as in the example.

In-line function definition is not a feature of OOP but an improvement of C++ over C. For example, function **strcpy** is defined in-line in the following sample code:

```
      class OurFile {
    friend class InvFile;
    friend class SysFile;
    friend class VndFile;
  private:
    char    fname[MAXFILENM];
    FILE    *fdatp;
  public:
    OurFile(char fnm[]) { strcpy(fname,fnm); }// in-
//  line definition
    ~OurFile();
    //......
  };
```

In-line definition provides a notational convenience of creating functions without a run-time overhead.

Data Security

Data may be defined as private in a class when access is only by its member functions; therefore, concern is not necessary about the security of data in a given class or the interference by functions in other classes. For example, because the FILE pointer "fdatp" of OurFile in an inventory system, Listing 1.3 is accessible only by its member functions, and the programmer doesn't need to worry about the OurFile inventory data being interfered with by other unauthorized data or functions.

Incremental Code Modification

Since C++ provides function name overloading, dealing with incremental code modification is much easier for C++ programs than for C programs. Listing 3-7 shows an example in both C and C++ for incremental code modification of a file management system.

Listing 3-7 Sample Code in C and C++ to Show Code Incremental Modification

```c
    /* 1)     Code in C */
/*name functions differently */

int  GetStuff(itcode,data)
char itcode[];
struct CUS_DAT* data;
{
  int   pos;
  FILE *fdatp;

  fdatp = fopen("CUSDAT", "rb");
  if(SrchStuff(itcode,&pos) != 0)
  {
     return FAIL;
  }
  fseek(fdatp,(long)(2+sizeof(struct CUS_DAT)*pos),0);
  fread((char*)data,sizeof(struct CUS_DAT),1,fdatp);

  return SUCCEED;
}

int  GetStuff1(itcode,data)
char itcode[];
struct INV_DAT* data;
{
  int   pos;
  FILE *fdatp;

  fdatp = fopen("INVDAT","rb");
  if(SrchStuff1(itcode,&pos) != 0)
  {
     return FAIL;
  }
  fseek(fdatp,(long)(2+sizeof(struct INV_DAT)*pos),0);
  fread((char*)data,dtblksiz,1,fdatp);

  return SUCCEED;
}


/*using "case" statements*/

int  GetStuff(itcode,flag)
char itcode[];
int  flag;
{
  int   pos;
  FILE *fdatp;
```

```
    struct CUS_DAT cusdata;
    struct INV_DAT invdata;

    switch(flag)
    {
      case CUSDAT:           //get the customer data
        fdatp = fopen("CUSDAT", "rb");
        if(SrchStuff(itcode,&pos) != 0)
        {
        return FAIL;
        }
        fseek(fdatp,(long)(2+sizeof(struct CUS_DAT)*pos),0);
        fread((char*)cusdata,sizeof(struct CUS_DAT),1,fdatp);
        return SUCCEED;
        break;

      case INVDAT:           //get the inventory data
        fdatp = fopen("INVDAT", "rb");
        if(SrchStuff1(itcode,&pos) != 0)
        {
        return FAIL;
        }
        fseek(fdatp,(long)(2+sizeof(struct INV_DAT)*pos),0);
        fread((char*)invdata,sizeof(struct INV_DAT),1,fdatp);
        return SUCCEED;
        break;
    }
}


// Code In C++

class IdxFile : public OurFile {
private:
  char      fidxname[MAXFILENM]; // index file
  FILE      *fidxp;          // index file id
  int       ixblksiz;      // the size of a index record
  int       dtblksiz;      // the size of a data record
  unsigned int Inv_Dat_N;    // # of data records
  struct INV_IDX *Inv_Idx;  // points to the index block
  struct INV_HDR Inv_Hdr;   // used for search index block
public:
  IdxFile(char[],int,int);   // constructor
  ~IdxFile();               // destructor

  int GetStuff(char[],struct INV_DAT*);// Get the inventory data
  int GetStuff(char[],struct CUS_DAT*);// Get the customer data

  ......
};
```

Assume when we initially designed the file management system, we were concerned with only one data type, that is, inventory data, struct INV_DAT. However, because of expansion, another data type (customer data, **CUS_DAT**) is also required, but the functions are pretty much the same as those used for the previous data type. In C, it is almost impossible to add another data type without changing a lot of codes using "case" statements as shown in the listing (lines after **/*using "case" statements*/**), or renaming the functions involved differently.

However, in C++ the programmer can avoid changing the function name while adding a new data type. For the same example, simply overload the function **"GetStuff"** and add a new parameter of data type "CUS_DAT", as follows:

```
int  GetStuff(char[],struct INV_DAT*);// Get the inventory
         //data
int  GetStuff(char[],struct CUS_DAT*);// Get the customer
         //data
```

SUMMARY

- C++ like Smalltalk is an object-oriented language, with the following features: information hiding, class inheritance, and function name overloading.

- The concept of classes in C++ is similar to Smalltalk. Adding classes and associated features makes C become an object-oriented language.

- Object-oriented programming focuses on data to be manipulated rather than on procedures performing the manipulating. The main task of writing a C++ program is determining the underlying data types (classes or subclasses) of the problem and defining the properties (method interface) of each class and subclass. The class or subclass variables correspond to physical or logical entities constituting the actual problem. C++ provides the conveniences for creative class structures.

- The class construct provides the basic foundation for object-oriented programming for C++. The class encapsulates the set of values and the associated methods for an object. These values or methods can be completely or partially available to other classes, and they may be completely or partially passed down to its subclasses. Class construct provides an inheritance-based hierarchy for data/knowledge representation.

- Classes with inheritance and function name overloading give C++ programmers great convenience in representing structured knowledge.

- The three main advantages of using C++ over C in programming are code efficiency, code security, and incremental code modification. These benefits result largely from three features of an object-oriented language.

CHAPTER REFERENCES

Stroustrup, B. *The C++ Programming Language*, Reading, MA: Addison-Wesley, 1986.

Zortech, Inc. "Zortech C++: Product Description," Arlington, MA, 1988.

Guidelines Software, Inc. "Guidelines C++: Installation Guide and Release Notes," Orinda, CA, 1988.

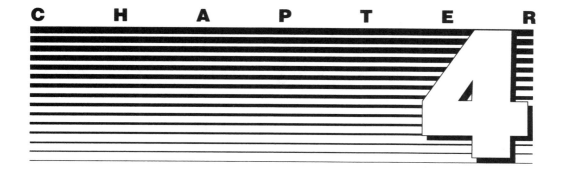

OBJECT-ORIENTED PROGRAMMING IN OBJECTIVE-C

The three major object-oriented languages presented in this book are Smalltalk, C++, and Objective C. Smalltalk is presented in Chapter 2, and C++ in Chapter 3. As shown in the discussion, Smalltalk is an interactive environment and "long" in providing friendly user-interface. However, Smalltalk is an environment, and all programs written in Smalltalk can live only in its environment, requiring too much resource. On the other hand, C++ is a basic language and "long" in providing programming convenience for building all the user-interface facilities available in Smalltalk. The only difficulty is that C++ needs to build most foundations (fortunately, they will be done in this book) before C++'s benefits can be realized by the user.

This chapter discusses the third OOP language, Objective-C, a language similiar to Smalltalk. Most facilities in Objective-C can be rewritten straightforwardly and even more efficiently in C++.

Objective-C is a hybrid programming language which "grafts" the Smalltalk features onto a C language rootstock. Mastering Smalltalk provides an understanding of Objective-C. The object is added as a new data type to those that C already provides. Another new operation is the message expression which handles binding at run-time, making no compile-time distinction between different kinds or classes of objects.

Because Objective-C is a superset of C, this superset is very different from the superset of C++. The programmer develops source files with a regular text editor, such as EMACS, compiles them to binary with the Objective-C compiler; stores them in libraries; links them; and tests them, similar to other compiled C codes (shown in Figure 4-1).

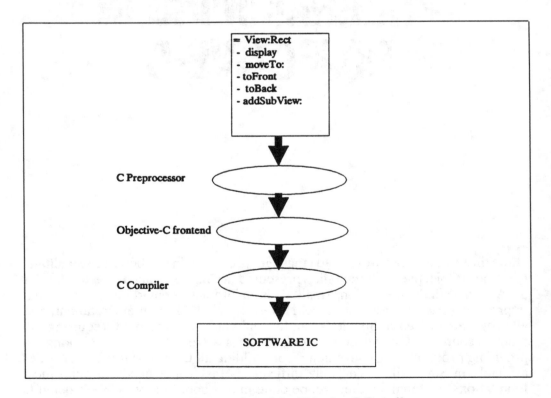

Figure 4.1   The structure of the Objective-C Compiler.

Like Smalltalk, the power of Objective-C lies in the specialized prepackaged classes that provide convenience to programmers. Consequently, for programmers to fully master the language, a good understanding of all classes and available methods is a must. This chapter is written assuming that the reader has read Chapter 2.

Objective-C is used as the prime language in Next computers offered by Next, Inc. (Palo Alto, California). The Next computer is a new generation of workstations designed for academia and laboratories.

This chapter provides only an introduction to the language with a focus on a brief comparison of the three OOP languages included in the book. The discussion includes 1) becoming familiar with Objective-C, 2) using Objective-C, and 3) comparison of Smalltalk, C++,and Objective-C.

BECOMING FAMILIAR WITH OBJECTIVE-C

Object identifier, message expression, factory object, class, and method are the five key words in Objective-C.

Object Identifiers

An object identifier or id is used to provide an unconditional access to an object without any restriction on access rights. The id must be unique for every object coexisting in the system at any one time. The physical address of the object in the memory is used as its identifier; a typedef statement is generated onto each file to define a new type, id. The ids are treated and used as freely as other C built-in data types, such as char, int, float, for example:

```
int engineStock ; // declare an integer
id engineObject;  // declare an object identifier
```

These two statements declare variable, engineStock, as an int type which can hold any integer value, and engineObject as an object identifier to hold an id for any kind of object. However, an id is a pointer, consuming a space wide enough to identify objects only, but not to store private data in the object itself.

Message Expressions

A message expression is a request for an object to execute a certain command by specifying the name of an action to be taken. This name is called the message selector. After the object has received the message, it "looks" up the selector and determines a series of things to implement the command. Message expressions are written as a pair of balanced square braces surrounding the receiver, selector, and arguments, such as:

```
[myObject doThis]
Example:
  [Pen new]
```

This message expression sends the unary message (which requires no arguments) **new** to object **Pen**; this expression can then be assigned to a variable:

```
Message expressions may be written as follows:
    myPen =[Pen new]
  [myObject doThis:arg1] or
    [myObject do:arg1 with:arg2 with:arg3 ...]
    Example:
    [totalPen add:myPen]
    [totalPen add:myPen with:yourPen with:hisPen]
```

These messages which take one or more arguments are called keyword expressions.

Factory Objects

Factory objects are the primal objects which are built at the time of compilation and assembled into memory by the loader. Every factory's name is a global variable and is treated the same as a class name in Smalltalk. The factory object name describes the class of the object they produce, such as **Pen**. An instance name always begins with a lower case letter, such as myPen.

Classes and Their Instances

A class is defined with a beginning of the "=" symbol which is followed by the name of the class and ends with a colon. The colon denotes that the following name is its superclass, as shown in Listing 4-1.

Listing 4.1: A Class Definition File for Class Animal

```
c1 = Animal: Object(Demo, Primitive)
c2  { unsigned int weight;}
c3  //.....
c4  //.....
c5  //.....
c6  =:    // symbol which ends a class definition
```

The new class name always begins with an upper-case character, and almost always has an existing class that is its superclass.

The only exception is the Object class, defined to be the root of all classes. The terms (Demo, Primitive) are the message groups used by this class to keep track of the return types of new methods one creates. The "Primitive" message group is provided by the Objective -C Library.

Classes are always bigger than their superclasses by having more detailed, specialized data than those of their superclasses. For example, class **Animal** is defined to be a subclass of class **object** ; and includes an additional variable **weight**. Class **Animal** is bigger than class **Object**.

A class is only an abstraction of a group of similar objects. New instances can be created by the factory object. Each instance of a class will share the same memory layout for the same field names and field types and use the same methods (code) in responding to messages. Differences for each individual object are described in the field's values. As shown in Figure 4-2, the individual object (for example, myPen) is made up of two parts: a private and a shared part.

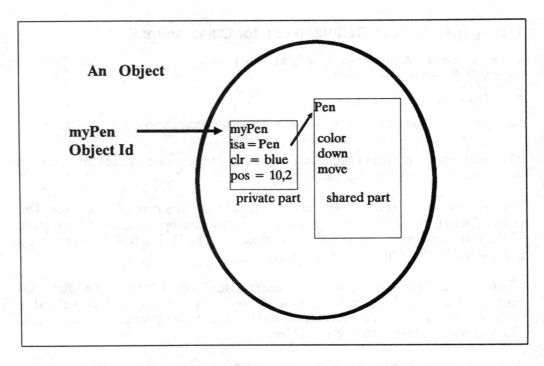

Fig. 4-2 : Private and shared parts of an object.

The private part stores the instance's specific data field, for example, **"BLACK"**, **"10, 20"**. The shared part holds the general information guiding the behavior of all the instance in the class, such as **"code"**, that is shared with other instances; this information may be inherited from the superclasses.

A class description file includes two types of variable declarations (instance and factory variables). Variable **weight** in statement c2 is an instance variable, which changes for each individual object in a class. A factory variable is a Smalltalk's class variable; in the current version, factory variables are simulated by using C global variables.

A " = :" symbol is used to denote the ending of a class definition.

Methods

A class description file may contain two types of methods: factory and instance methods.

Factory Methods

Factory methods produce impact on the class and its subclasses. They are able to define new factory objects and override inherited objects. They usually appear first in the class definition file. A plus sign "+" leads a factory method, followed by the name of the selector (shown in Listing 4-2), for example:

```
+create {
   id newInstance          // declare a local variable
   newInstance = [self new]; // create instance of Animal;
self                       // refer to class Animal
```

Listing 4-2: Creating A New Class—Animal—by using "Create"

```
//create a new Animal class by using superclass Object's 'new'
// method +create {
   id newInstance          // declare a local variable
   newInstance = [self new]; // create instance of Animal;
self                       // refers to class Animal
   [newInstance weight: 120];// set the weight
   [newInstance feature: "feathers"];// set the feature
   return newInstance;      // return the new instance
 }
```

The two important terms used in the factory method are "self" and "super". The term self is similar to the one used in Smalltalk; however, "super" is used only in Objective-C.

Self

The hidden variable "**self**" in the previous code performs a convenient and efficient way of programming. The variable "self" in the factory method refers to the factory class in which instances are created. "Self" is used to refer to the instance variable receiving the message in an instance method.

Super

"Super" is not a variable like "self"; it provides a way to circumvent an infinite recursion in which an inherited method is overridden with another similar method by the same name, such as "new" (see Listing 4-3):

```
    +new {      id newInstance // declare a local variable
    newInstance = [self new]; // create instance of Animal;
self
                            // refers to class Animal
```

Listing 4.3: An Infinite Recursion Involving "new"

```
 +new {      id newInstance // declare a local variable
    newInstance = [self new]; // create instance of Animal;
self
                            // refers to class Animal
    [newInstance weight: 120];// set the weight
    [newInstance feature: "feathers"];// set the feature
    return newInstance;       // return the new instance
 }
```

The above code would create an infinite loop because factory method "new" in class Animal used the same name as the factory name inherited from superclass Object. The only way to go around is to use "super" instead of "self" (Listing 4-4), as follows:

```
    +new {      id newInstance // declare a local variable
    newInstance = [super new];//create instance of Animal;super
                            // refers to superclass Object
```

Listing 4.4: Creating a New Instance Using "super"

```
    +new {      id newInstance // declare a local variable
    newInstance = [super new];//create instance of Animal;super
                            // refers to superclass Object
    [newInstance weight: 120];// set the weight
    [newInstance feature: "feathers"];// set the feature
    return newInstance;       // return the new instance   }
```

The above code performs the same function as the code shown in the previous section. Because many packaged methods are available such as "new" and "print-On" from the Objective-C Library, "super" is powerful for utilizing them properly.

Instance Methods

Instance methods affect only instance variables; they always begin with a minus sign, for example:

```
-weight: (int)aSize { // set the weight instance variable for
                      // an Animal object
       weight = aSize;
return self;          // return the value of weight }
```

USING OBJECTIVE-C

This section concerns the programming issues of using Objective- C, such as writing a main program and tracing methods.

WRITING A MAIN PROGRAM

As with C++, after all classes have been defined, a main program is written to test these new classes.

The main difference between a C program and an Objective-C program is that messages are sent before the beginning of the "main" statement, as shown in Listing 4-5.

Listing 4.5: A Main Program for Testing Animal and Cat Classes

```
m1=(Demo, Primitive)// declare the two message groups are used
m2                       // in this program
m3  @requires Animal, Cat; //declare the Animal and Cat are
m3.1                             //external classes
m4    id anAnimal, aCat;
m5
m6
m7  main ( arg1, arg2 )
m8  {     // create an instance of an Animal
m9    anAnimal = [Animal new];
m10   [aCat grow]; // grow the Cat
m11   }  // end of the main program m12
m13
m14   @classes ()
m15   @messages ()
```

The key points are summarized from the code in Listing 4-5 in the following order:

1. Declare the message groups for tracking new methods created in the program (as in m1).

2. Declare the external classes to be used in the program (as in m3, m4).

3. Send messages to create new instance and perform other tasks (as in m9, m10)

4. Request the Objective-C compiler to combine all classes and messages used in the program (as in m14, m15).

Tracing Methods

You can turn on the message trace flag to cause all the messages sent to be printed in order to know what is happening with the methods used in the program. Listing 4-6 shows a sample whose key elements are summarized, as follows:

- include <objc.h> in the include file (as in m0)

- declare an external file, BOOL msgFlag (as in m0.1)

- set up the message trace flag (as in m8.1, 8.2):

    m8.1 if (arg1 >1 && *arg[1]='t'

    m8.2   msgFlag = YES;

- when you run the program, enter
    animalDemo t

The runtime message system will print the trace statements of all the messages that have been sent in the program.

Listing 4.6: A Main Program for Testing Animal and Cat Classes with a Method Tracing

```
m0       #include <objc.h>
m0.1     extern BOOL msgFlag;
m0.2
m0.3
m1=(Demo, Primitive)// declare the two message groups are used
m2                       // in this program
m3  @requires Animal, Cat; //declare the Animal and Cat are
m3.1                          //external classes
m4   id anAnimal, aCat;
m5
m6
m7   main ( arg1, arg2 )
m8   {
m8.1  if (arg1 >1 && *arg[1]=='t'
m8.2     msgFlag = YES;
m8.3
m8.4          // create an instance of an Animal
m9   anAnimal = [Animal new];
m10  [aCat grow]; // grow the Cat
m11  }  // end of the main program
m12
m13
m14  @classes ()
m15  @messages ()
```

COMPARISON OF SMALLTALK, C++ AND OBJECTIVE-C

Because the three object-oriented languages, Smalltalk, C++, and Objective-C were developed at different times for various reasons and with varying degrees of resources, comparing them is fairly difficult. The following criteria are used for comparison (shown in Table 4-1):

- features (data encapsulation, inheritance, operator overloading)
- facility (interactive environment, binding time, garbage collection)
- programming flexibility
- efficiency
- portability
- convenience (library for classes and methods)

	Smalltalk	**C++**	**Objective-C**
Data encapsulation	yes	extensive	yes
Inheritance	multiple	single	single
Operator overloading	yes	yes	yes
Interactive environment	yes	no	no
Binding time	late	early/late	early/late
Garbage collection	yes	no	no
Programming flexibility	low	high	medium
Portability	low	high	medium
Efficiency	low	high	medium
Library(classes/methods)	yes	possible (by vendors)	yes

Table 4.1 Comparison of Smalltalk, C++, and Objective-C.

All three languages provide data encapsulation, inheritance, and operator over-loading. C++ has the most comprehensive data encapsulation where public, protected, and private data can be declared for various purposes of data usage. Smalltalk supplies programmers with multiple inheritance, a useful tool for programming time-constraint events, such as live cartoons.

Smalltalk is an interactive environment which provides garbage collection and late binding (dynamic binding); however, the environment is also a weakness of Smalltalk. Programs written in Smalltalk have to live in the environment, and are less efficient than C++ because of its overhead. The same is true for Objective-C, even though it is not a completely interactive environment. The portability for Smalltalk depends on the developer's resourcefulness, that is, whether the developer has extended the environment to the computing facility to be used. Since C++ has the least overhead, the programmer can build up only the environment needed to resolve problems.

Both Smalltalk and Objective-C provide an extensive library for classes and methods for programming convenience. Kernels of similar libraries written in C++ are discussed in this book and packages of the C++ libraries for user interface, such as iconic interface, menus, and windows, are available to the reader from Baldur Systems Corporation.

The three object-oriented languages in Chapters 2, 3 and 4 represent a small sample of these types of languages. Other object-oriented languages include:

- Flavors and Loops designed specially for organizing facts and knowledge regarding a problem domain in artificial intelligence .

- Actors for concurrent object-oriented programming.

- Object-Pascal, Modula-2 for hybrid conventional programming languages.

Most of these languages, for example, Flavors and Modula-2, were developed to serve a set of particular purposes for certain clients and require a steep learning curve. Because of this, the programmer needs to evaluate their strengths and weaknesses carefully before they are seriously adopted.

SUMMARY

- Objective-C is more similar to Smalltalk than to C+ +. Its facilities can be rewritten straightforwardly and even more efficiently in C+ +.

- Objective-C is a hybrid programming language which "grafts" the Smalltalk features onto a C language rootstock. It adds the object as a new data type to those that C already provides, and includes the message expression as a new operation. Objective-C handles binding at run-time, making no distinction between the time of compilation of different kinds or classes of objects.

- The object identifier, message expression, factory object, class, and method are the five key words in Objective-C.

- An object identifier or id is used to provide an unconditional access to an object without any restriction on access rights. It must be unique for every object coexisting in the system at any one time.

- A message expression is a request for an object to execute a certain command by specifying the name of an action to be taken. This name is called the message selector. The object receives the message, "looks" up the selector and determines a series of things to implement the command. Message expressions are written as a pair of balanced square braces surrounding the receiver, selector, and arguments.

- Factory objects are the primal objects built at compile-time and assembled into memory by the loader. The factory object name describes the class of the object they produce, such as **Pen.** An instance name always begins with a lower case letter, such as myPen.

- A class is defined with a beginning of the " = " symbol followed by the name of the class and ending with a colon. The colon denotes that the following name is its superclass.

- Classes are always bigger than their superclasses by having more detailed, specialized data than those of their superclasses. A class is only an abstraction of a group of similar objects. New instances can be created by the factory object.

- A class description file includes two types of variable declarations (instance and factory variables). A class description file may contain two types of methods, factory and instance methods.

- Factory methods produce impact on the class and its subclasses. They define new factory objects and override inherited objects. They usually appear first in the class definition file. A plus sign " + " leads a factory method, followed by the name of the selector.

- The two important terms used in the factory method are "self" and "super". The term self is similar to the one used in Smalltalk; however, "super" is used only in Objective-C.

- The hidden variable **"self"** performs a convenient and efficient way of programming. The variable "self" in the factory method refers to the factory class in which instances are created. "Self" is used to refer to the instance variable receiving the message in an instance method.

- "Super" is not a variable like "self"; it provides a way to circumvent an infinite recursion in which an inherited method is overridden with another similar method by the same name, such as "new", "printOn" from the Objective-C Library .

- Instance methods affect only instance variables; they always begin with a minus sign.

- As with C+ +, after all classes have been defined, a main program is written to test these new classes. The main difference between a C program and an Objective-C program is messages are sent before the beginning of the "main" statement.

- All three languages provide data encapsulation, inheritance, and operator overloading. C+ + has the most comprehensive data encapsulation. Public, protected, and private data can be declared for various purposeS of data usage.

- Both Smalltalk and Objective-C provide an extensive library for classes and methods for programming convenience. Kernels of this library in C++ are discussed in this book.

- The three object-oriented languages that have been discussed represent a small sample of these types of languages. Other object-oriented languages include: Flavors and Loops for organizing facts and knowledge regarding a problem domain in artificial intelligence, Actors for concurrent object-oriented programming, Object-Pascal, and Modula-2 for hybrid conventional programming languages.

CHAPTER REFERENCES

Cox, B. . *Object-Oriented Programming: an Evolutionary Approach*. Addison-Wesley., 1986.

Baldur Systems Corporation. C++ Object-Oriented Environment Libraries,. Hayward, CA 1989.

Moon, D. "Object-Oriented Programming with Flavors." Proceedings of OOPSLA , 1986.

Bobrow, D. G. and M. J. Stefik. "The LOOPS Manual," Technical Report, Xerox PARC., December 1983.

Agha, G. *Actors: A Model of Concurrent Computation in Distributed Systems*, Cambridge, MA: MIT Press, 1986.

Wirth, N. *Programming in Modula-2*, New York. Springer-Verlag, 1982.

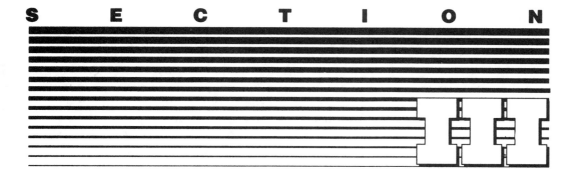

MAKING YOUR PROGRAMS FRIENDLY WITH OOP: USER INTERFACE ENVIRONMENT DESIGN

Section I introduces the concept and basics of OOP focusing on the strength of OOP; Section II presents the three most frequently mentioned OOP languages with a brief comparison of the three languages; and Section III focuses on the design of an object-oriented user-interface environment using C++.

The object-oriented environment is naturally suitable for user interface because in the environment, everything is an object: an icon, a mouse cursor, a menu, or even a window. Each object represents a series of operations beneath the symbol on the computer screen. The three main features of OOP, encapsulation, inheritance, and overloading, enable the programmer to design a friendly user-interface rapidly. Non-OOP can be used to program such an environment, but non-OOP requires considerably more resources. For example, through inheritance, OOP enables a programmer to program animation like a cartoonist. By designing the generic original picture as the root class and layering over sequential pictures to animate the movement, gradually changing a small portion of the picture (attributes).

Principles of a good, friendly user interface environment such as MacApp Desktop Interface can be applied in the design, and the Desktop Interface may be simulated to the degree suitable for the requirement of an individual program. This approach is particularly apparent when C++ is used to design an environment because of the freedom and facilities that C++ provides to the programmer. Unlike other OOP languages,such as Smalltalk or Objective-C, the programmer does not operate in a prefabricated environment, a programmer can use C++ and the kernels discussed in this section to create their own appropriate user-interface environment.

In designing an object-oriented user-interface environment, the programmer needs to observe the following basic principles:

- Use real-world metaphors and select concrete plain objects to represent operations.

   For example, use a representation of factory floor in a user-interface module of a computer-integrated manufacturing system, and use a desktop interface for an office automation system.

- Use the basic object-oriented pattern of **"object message(action) arguments ,"** such as "you write this page."

   For example, in a series of menus, a user can first select an object of interest and then select an action to be performed on the object in the second menu. All available actions for the selected objects are listed on the menu including "exit" and "previous" to allow the user to leave the system or to return to previous action, respectively. Further, the user can point at what they see. For example, the user can drag a pen icon to a color tray to pick a desirable color, paint a rectangular area, or make a circle with a mouse.

- Use simple, well-designed symbols or caricatures to convey precise meanings or actions to the intended users; use animation sparingly to draw users' attention to the current situation (such as the active window) on the screen.

- Allow the user to modify the look of their workspaces on the screen to some limited degree, so the programmer doesn't have to face the problem of designing a user-interface that pleases everyone.

These principles will be strickly adhered to in the design of user interface environment throughout the book.

This section consists of two chapters. Chapter 5 discusses the design of a text window that is best suited for portable , small applications in simple microprocessors. Chapter 6 presents the core design of graphical control interface that is more system-dependent (the sample programs are mainly tested for the IBM PC family). The Zortech C++ compiler is used to test programs written. The use of C++ features is discussed in detail in Chapter 5 and briefly in subsequent chapters.

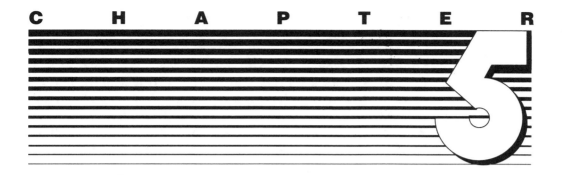

TEXT-WINDOW DESIGN WITH OBJECT-ORIENTED PROGRAMMING

Chapter 1 introduces the fundamentals of object-oriented programming; Chapters 2 and 4 present three object-oriented programming languages; and Chapter 5 discusses the design of text windows.

Physically, a window is a delimited area on the display screen that provides a viewport to data. Printable characters, graphic images, or both can be inputted. Accordingly, the two types of windows are text-mode window and bit-mapped windows. In the text-mode window (text window), only printable charaters can be displayed. However, the bit-mapped window can display both graphic images and printable characters.

Chapter 5 focuses on the first type of windows: text windows. Examples of text windows include the UNIX Curses Library and the C++ text window library presented in this chapter. Text-mode windows are particularly suitable for small applications running slow microprocessors. For example, The Curses Library is intended for use with display terminals connected through a low- to medium-bandwidth serial port to a host machine running the UNIX operating system.

Chapter 6 presents the other kinds of windows, bit-mapped winodw (graphical user interface). Examples of bit-mapped window systems include Smalltalk, Macintosh User Interface, Xerox PARC first "paperless" office, and X Windows, SunView on workstations, such as MicroVAX, and Sun. Graphical control interface design is quite system-dependent and requires relatively large memory because the design adopts a bit-mapping technique when making icons.

This chapter first presents the general requirements of a window and then concentrated the discussion on making text windows, including class TextWindow, member functions of class TextWindow, and a sample text window. The implementation is in Zortech C++ (see Appendix C for the Zortech variables and functions used in this book). Minor changes are needed to implement this TextWindow on other C/C++ compilers.

REQUIREMENTS OF A WINDOW

A window is a complex object which may require the following operations:

- Input/Output from the mouse and/or the keyboard
- Scrolling (up/down/left/right)
- Moving the output point
- Clearing selected areas of the screen
- Moving the window around the screen
- Putting attributes (BOLD, FLASHING) and colors onto the window
- Responding to mouse clicks and/or key strokes (events) on its controlling area
- Dragging a pane on the screen
- Overlaying panes to create an image of animation

Clearly, not every window will be implemented with all of these operations. The text window discussed will have most operations and can be improved by the reader with the source code provided. In many cases not every operation is required in a program. For example, the window of the calculator created in Chapter 6 does not require bold/flashing attributes.

Windows can be created through class TextWindow discussed in this chapter for the text-mode type. Windows can also be created using the basic classes presented in the next chapter for more sophisticated iconic types.

CLASS TEXTWINDOW

Class TextWindow is complex. TextWindow functions similarly to the WINDOW in the UNIX Curses Library and requires the following seven basic functions:

- Draw(): Accessing the video screen directly from a PC (personal computer) running MS-DOS is a straightforward matter since all output can be made directly on to the screen. This functionality is needed for other types of operating systems. Drawing is done by dumping the window image onto the appropriate place on the screen, and moving the cursor to indicate where the pointer is located.

- Constructor: This function allocates space for the image and sets up the default attributes, puts the cursor in the upper left hand corner and determines the monitor type.

- Destructor: This function frees the allocated space.

- Erasing: Clear() fills the window with ASCII spaces and the current attributes.

- Setting the attributes (with default parameter values).

- Input/Output: This function is performed with an operator overloading of "<<", similar to the usage in Bjarne Stroustrup's <stream.h> package. However, "<<" is a member function of the TextWindow class rather than being defined as class TextWindowBuf derived from Streambuf in <stream.h>. Although we have not taken advantage of this exiting class, the expression

```
win << "print this string";
```

states more clearly what the programmer intends than the other method.

- Moving cursor: The function can be done in two ways:

  - SetXY(), yet another inline member function to set cursor location.

  - Overloaded operator().

The overloaded operator() was chosen becuase moving the cursor is a very common operation performed in a window. Making it an operator on a window keeps the code "cleaner."

Compare

```
win.SetXY(xloc,yloc);
win << "How are you?";
```

with

```
win(xloc,yloc) << "How are you?";
```

If more than one type of operating system is considered for ultimate implementation of the window program, TextWindow may have to consider providing the following additional function:

- Redraw(): This function's operation on a window makes the terminal's output conform to the contents of the window. This resembles a buffering operation, accumulating output operations and then releasing them to the output device in a single "burst." Text that is added to a window won't appear until that window has been refreshed.

A sample header file for class TextWindow performing these basic functions is shown in Listing 5.1 and discussed in the following section.

Listing 5.1: Header File for Class TextWindow

```
#ifndef window_hpp
#define window_hpp

/*
** window.hpp
**
** Copyright 1989 Baldur Systems Corporation

//color definitions

typedef enum {
black + 0, blue, green, cyan, red, magenta, yellow, white
} color:

#define VIDEOSEG 0Xb800

class TextWindow {
protected:
int lastchar;
int wrapmode;
int nlmode;
int echomode;
int height,width,x,y,xoff,yoff;
char *winbuf;        //storage for window data
char attribute;       //current color
void mvCursor();
void echoC(char c);
char eatWhitespace();
public:
TextWindow(int,int,int,int);    //constructor
-TextWindow();        //destructor

virtual void Draw();       //reflects all changes

//output stuff to the TextWindow

    TextWindow &operator<<(const char *);
    TextWindow &operator<<(long a);
    TextWindow &operator<<(int a) {return *this<<(long)a;}
    TextWindow &operator<<(double a);
    virtual void Put(char c);          // put the character

// erase stuff in the TextWindow
    virtual void Clear();
    virtual void Scroll(int);
    virtual void DeleteChar();
```

continued...

```
    virtual void ClearEOL();
    virtual void ClearEOW();

// find out where we are, and what char is there, change posi
//tion

    void GetXY(int& xx,int& yy) { xx = x; yy = y; }
    void SetXY(int xx,int yy) { x = xx; y = yy; }
    void GetCh(char&,char&);
    void MoveWindow(int x, int y) { xoff = x; yoff = y; }
    TextWindow &operator()(int xx,int yy) { x = xx; y = yy;
return *this; }

// modes and attributes

    void EchoMode(){ echomode = 1;}
    void NoEchoMode()    { echomode = 0;}
    void NLMode()   { nlmode = 1; }
    void CRLFMode(){ nlmode = 0; }
    void WrapMode(){ wrapmode = 1; }
    void NoWrapMode()    { wrapmode = 0; }
    void SetAttribute(color fg=white,color bg=black,int in-
tens=0,int flash=0);

// input operations

    TextWindow &operator>>(char &);
    TextWindow &operator>>(long &);
    TextWindow &operator>>(int &i) {long l; *this>>l; i =
(int)l; return *this;}
    TextWindow &operator>>(double &);
    TextWindow &operator>>(char *);
    int GetString(char *,int,char ='\r');
    int Get();
    void UnGet(int c) { lastchar = c; }
};

// Inline functions

/*
** SetAttribute: all successive operations will use the colors
** set by this method. fg is the foreground color, bg is the
** background color, intens is used to determine whether the
** foreground color should be intensive or not, and flash is
**used
** to determine whether the foreground color should flash or
**not.
*/
```

continued...

```
inline void TextWindow::SetAttribute(color fg,color bg=black,
        int intens=0,int flash=0) {
    attribute = (flash?0x80:0)+(intens?0x8:0)+((char)
bg)*0x10+(char) fg;
}

extern TextWindow stdscr;

#endif
```

Class TextWindow has several protected data objects, such as last character, wrap mode, size of the window (Height, width), attribute, for example:

```
class TextWindow {
  protected:
    int lastchar;    // space for the last char
    int wrapmode;    // flag for wrapping around the the margin
    int nlmode;      // flag for a newline
    int echomode;    // flag for echoing
    int height,width,x,y,xoff,yoff; // window position
    char *winbuf;    // storage for window data
    char attribute; // current color
    void mvCursor();    // in mvcursor.cpp
    void echoC(char c); // in get.cpp
    char eatWhitespace(); // in oprs.cpp
```

Note that the current version of the Zortech compiler treats objects in the protected or the private area as if they were public and can be freely accessed.

TextWindow uses the functions constructor and destructor, and a few member functions, such as Draw(), operator < <, Clear(), Delete Line(), GetXY(), Echo-Mode, operator > >, SetAttribute() to perform the following operations:

- Allocate space for the window's image and set up default attributes

  ```
  TextWindow(int,int,int,int); // constructor
  ```

- Remove memory space

  ```
  ~TextWindow(); // destructor
  ```

- Dump the window image to the appropriate place on the screen

  `virtual void Draw();` // reflect all changes

- Note this function is declared virtual and thus can be overloaded by subclasses of TextWindow.

- Output data to the TextWindow

  For example:

  ```
  TextWindow &operator< <(const char *a);
  TextWindow &operator< <(long a);
  ```

- Erase stuff to the TextWindow

  For example,

  ```
  virtual void Clear() ;
  virtual void DeleteChar() ;
  ```

- All these methods are declared virtual and will be defined later.

- Find out where the output pointer is, and when char is there, change the position.

  For example:

  ```
  void Getxy (int& yy) { xx = x; yy = y; }
  void MoveWindow( int x, int y)  { xoff + x yoff = y; }
  TextWindow &operator() (int  xx, int  yy) {x = xx: y = yy;
  return *this }
  ```

- Set modes and attributes:

  For example:

  ```
  void  EchoMode(){ echomode = 1;}
  void WrapMode(){ wrapmode =1; }
  void SetAttributes (color fg = white, color bg = black, int
  ints = 0 int flash =0);
  ```

- Input operations

  For example:

  ```
  TextWindow &operator>>(char &);
  TextWindow &operator>>(long &);
  void UnGet(int c)  {lastchar = c;}
  ```

The TextWindow Constructor and Destructor

TextWindow uses its constructor to allocate space for a window x by y in size. The upper left corner of the window is located at (xo, yo). The constructor sets up the attributes and locates the cursor in the upper left hand corner of the window.

```
TextWindow::TextWindow(int x, int y, int xo, int yo)
{
width x; height = y;
xoff = xo; yoff = yo;
SetAttribute();                               //use
white on black
winbuf = new char[width*height*2]      // alloc space for char
// and attribute
Clear():
//clear the window
WrapMode();
EchoMode();
SetXY(0,0);
lastchar = -1;                                //
last char read
```

the destructor deallocates storage used for TextWindow image:

```
TextWindow:: ~TextWindow()
{ x = y = 0; mvCursor(); delete winbuf;}
```

Member Functions of Class TextWindow

Member functions provide methods for the class to manipulate its data objects. These methods are either defined in Listing 5-1 (as inline functions) or in Listing 5-2. Both private and public member functions are used in class TextWindow. The member functions will be outlined first and will be presented in detail in the subsequent section. The three private functions are:

```
void mvCursor();
void echoC(char c);
char eatWhitespace();
```

Note the convention of using lower case names for the private and protected members to distinguish them from the public members whose names start with an uppercase letter.

The public functions are numerous and can be classified into 6 categories:

- Draw the image of the window on the screen.

```
- Draw():
```

- Output stuff to the TextWindow.

```
- TextWindow &operator<<(const char *);
- TextWindow &operator<<(long a);
- TextWindow &operator<<(int a) {return *this<<(long)a;}
- TextWindow &operator<<(double a);
- Put(char c);
```

Overloaded function operator < < has been defined inline.

- Erase stuff in the TextWindow.

```
- Clear();
- Scroll(int);
   -  Delete Char();
- ClearEOL();
- ClearEOW();
```

- Find location, when character is there, and change position.

```
- GetXY(int& xx,int& yy) { xx = x; yy = y; }
- SetXY(int xx,int yy) { x = xx; y = yy; }
- GetCh(char&,char&);
- MoveWindow(int x, int y) { xoff = x; yoff = y; }
- TextWindow &operator()(int xx,int yy) { x = xx; y = yy;
return *this; }
```

All the above functions under this category have been defined inline.

- Set modes and attributes.

```
- EchoMode() { echomode = 1;}
-NoEchoMode()    { echomode = 0;}
-NLMode()    { nlmode = 1; }
-CRLFMode()     { nlmode = 0; }
-WrapMode()     { wrapmode = 1; }
```

```
-NoWrapMode() { wrapmode = 0; }
- SetAttribute(color fg=white,color bg=black,int in-
  tens=0,int flash=0);
```

All these functions under this category except SetAttribute() have been defined inline.

- Input operations.

```
-  TextWindow &operator>>(char &);
-  TextWindow &operator>>(long &);
-  TextWindow &operator>>(int &i) {long l; *this>>l; i =
     (int)l; return    this;}
-  TextWindow &operator>>(double &);
-  TextWindow &operator>>(char *);
-  int GetString(char *,int,char ='\r');
-  int Get();
-  UnGet(int c) { lastchar = c; }
```

The overloaded function operator> > has been defined inline for each individual case.

Listing 5-2 Implementation Files for Class TextWindow (Containing Many Separate Files)

```
#include <stream.hpp>

#include "window.hpp"

/*
** window.cpp
**
** Copyright 1989, Baldur Systems Corp.
*/

/*
** Window: constructor method;allocate space for the image of a
** window of size x by y, whose upper left corner is located at
** (xo,yo).
*/
```

continued...

```
Window::Window(int x,int y,int xo, int yo)
{
width =X; height = y;
xoff = xo;yoff = yo;
SetAttribute();
winbuf = new char [width*heiqht*2];

Clear();
WrapMode();
EchoMode();
SetXY(0,0);
lastchar =-1;
}
/*
** ~Window: destructor method; deallocates storage used for
**window
** image
*/

Window::~Window()
{
    x = y = 0;
    mvCursor();
    delete winbuf;
}
/*
** Draw(): draws the image of the window on the screen
*/

void Window::Draw()
{
    for (int i = 0; i  <height; ++i) { // iterate through rows
    poke(VIDEOSEG,(yoff+i)*160+xoff*2,// dump line to screen
    winbuf+width*i*2,width*2);
    }
    mvCursor(); // show cursor
}

/*
** Put(): put the character C in the current location of the
**window,
** and advance its current location according to modes
*/
```

continued...

```
void Window::Put(char c)
{
    char *p = winbuf+(x+y*width)*2;
    *p      = c;
    *(p+1) = attribute;
    if (++x> = width) {           // passed the right col?
    x = 0;
    if (!wrapmode) {         // if not wrapping, scroll
        ++y;
        if (y> = height) {
        y = height-1;
        Scroll(1);

 }
   }
    }
}

// stdscr: the default window

Window stdscr(80,25,0,0);


#include "window.hpp"

/*
** clear.cpp
**
*/

/*
** Clear(): clears the window, setting all characters to
**spaces,
** and all attributes to the current attribute
*/
void Window::Clear()
{
    for (register int i = 0; i  <width*height*2; )
    {
    winbuf[i++] = ' ';
    winbuf[i++] = attribute;
    }
}
```

continued...

```
#include "window.hpp"

/*
** cleareol.cpp
**
*/

/*
** ClearEOL(): erase the characters from the current output
**point
** to the end of this line
*/

void Window::ClearEOL()
{
    char *p = winbuf+(x+y*width)*2;
    for (int i = x; i  width; ++i) {
   *p++ = ' ';
   *p++ = attribute;
    }
}
}


#include "window.hpp"

/*
** cleareow.cpp
**
*/

/*
** ClearEOW(): erase the characters from the current position
** to the end of this window.
*/

void Window::ClearEOW()
{
    ClearEOL();      // clear this line first
    char *p = winbuf+((y+1)*width)*2;
   for (int i = y+1; i  <height; ++i) {
   for (int j = 0; j  <width; ++j) {
      *p++ = ' ';
      *p++ = attribute;
   }
    }
}
```

continued...

```
#include "window.hpp"

/*
** deletech.cpp
**
*/
/*
** Delete the character at the current position of the window,
** moving any characters to the right one step to the left and
** filling the rightmost character of the line with a blank
*/

void Window::DeleteChar()
{
    char *p = winbuf + (y*width + x)*2;

    for (int i = 0; i <(width - x - 1); ++i) {
    *p = *(p+2);
    ++p;
    *p = *(p+2);
    ++p;
    }
    *p++ = ' ';
    *p   = attribute;
}



#include <dos.h>
#include <bios.h>
#include "window.hpp"

/*
** get.cpp
**
*/

/*
** Get: get a single character from the window
*/
```

continued...

```
int Window::Get()
{    int c;

    if (lastchar != -1) {        // "ungotten" keystroke
    c = lastchar;
    lastchar = -1;
    } else {
    c = bioskey(0);              // wait for keystroke
    if (echomode) {
        echoC(c);
        Put(c);
    }
    }
    return (c & 0xFF) ? (c & 0xFF) : c;// if normal key, just
                                 // return 8-bit value.
                              // special keys, like F10,
                              // return 16-bit value
}


/*
** echoC(): echo the character c at the current output point
**of this
** window
*/

void Window::echoC(char c)
{
    union REGS r;

    mvCursor(); // move to right spot
    r.h.ah = 0x09;
    r.h.bh = 0;
    r.h.al = c;
    r.h.bl = attribute;
    r.x.cx = 1;
    int86(0x10,&r,&r);
}

#include <bios.h>
#include "window.hpp"

/*
** getstring.cpp
**
*/
```

continued...

```
/*
** GetString(): get a string from the keyboard.
** Note: it doesn't handle backspaces gracefully -- no input
**editing
**is possible
/*

int Window::GetString(char *buffer,int max,char haltchar)
{    while (max >0) {
   int c = bioskey(0);
   *buffer++ = (char) c;
   if ((char)(c & 0xFF) == haltchar)
       break;
   if (echomode) {
       echoC(c);
       Put(c);
       mvCursor();
   }
    }
    *buffer = '\0';
}




#include <dos.h>
#include "window.hpp"

/*
** mvcursor.cpp
**
*/

/*
** mvCursor(): move the cursor on the screen so that it
ap**pears located
** at the current output point of this window
*/

void Window::mvCursor()
{
    union REGS r;

    r.h.ah = 0x02;
    r.h.bh = 0;
    r.h.dl = xoff + x;
    r.h.dh = yoff + y;
  int86(0x10,&r,&r);
}
```

continued...

```
#include "window.hpp"

/*
** opls.cpp
**
** Output operations are performed by overloading the < <(Left-
Shift
** operator) and calling the appropriate function, depending
** on the argument type.
*/

/*
** String output*/

Window &Window::operator<<(const char *s)
{
    while (*s) {
    Put(*s++);
    }
    return *this;
}

/*
** Integer output
*/

Window &Window::operator<<(long a)
{
    if (a < 0)
  {
    Put('-');
    a = 0 - a;
    }
    static char buf[80];
    char *p = buf+sizeof (buf) -1;

    *p = '\0';
    do {
    *--p = a % 10 + '0';
    a /= 10;
} while (a != 0);
 while(*p);
    Put(*p++);
    }
    return *this;
}
/*
** Floating point output
*/
Window &Window::operator<<(double a)
{
    static char buf[80];
```

continued...

```
        sprintf(buf,"%lg",a);
        return *this << buf;
}


#include  <ctype..h>
#include  "window.hpp"

/*
** oprs.cpp
**
** Input operations are defined by overloading the >> operator
(RightShift)
** and calling with the appropriate argument type.
*/

/*
** Read a char from the window
*/

Window & Window::operator>>(char &c)
{
    c = Get();
    return *this;
}

/*
** Read a long integer from the window
*/

Window & Window::operator>>(long &l)
{
    char c;

    l = 0L;
    c = eatWhitespace();
    while (isdigit(c)) {
    l *= 10L;
    l += c - '0';
    c = Get();
}

    return *this;
}
```

continued...

```
char Window::eatWhitespace()
{
    char c = Get();
    while (c == '\t' || c == ' ') {
  c = Get();
    }
    return c;
}



#include  <string.h>
#include "window.hpp"

/*
** scroll.cpp
**
** Scroll the window the specified amount of lines. If lines
is negative,
** scrolling is performed "downwards". Scrolling 0 lines is a
no-op.
**
** WARNING: memmove() as defined in the Zortech library, is
capable
** of performing overlapping moves intelligently. This may not
be the
** case with other libraries.
*/

void Window::Scroll(int lines)
{
    if (lines == 0) {
  return;
    } else if (lines > 0) {         // scroll up
    if (lines < height) {         // actually have to scroll
        memmove(winbuf,winbuf+width*lines*2,(height-
lines)*width*2);
        char *p = winbuf + (height - lines) * width * 2;
        for (int i = 0; i < lines; ++i) {
      for (int j = 0; j < width; ++j) {
          *p++ = ' ';
          *p++ = attribute;
      }
        }
    } else {
        Clear();                    //
```

continued...

```
        }
        } else {                    // scroll down
    lines = 0 - lines;          // convert to abs value
    if (lines < height) {
        memmove(winbuf+width*lines*2,winbuf,(height-
lines)*width*2);
        char *p = winbuf;
        for (int i = 0; i < lines; ++i) {
     for (int j = 0; j < width; ++j) {
        *p++ = ' ';                 *p++ = attribute;
     }
        }
    } else {
        Clear();
    }
     }
}
```

Private Member Functions

Private member functions can be accessed by the public member functions of its class or its friend classes. The three private member functions for TextWindow, mvCursor(), echoC(), and eatWhitespace() are explained.

Function mvCursor() moves on the screen, the cursor appears located at the current output point of this window:

```
// mvcursor.cpp
void Window::mvCursor()

{
  union REGS r;
        r.h.ah = 0x02;
        r.h.bh = 0;
     r.h.dl = xoff + x;
     r.h.dh = yoff + y;
     int86(0x10,&r,&r); }
```

Function mvCursor() is system-dependent because it uses IBM PC interrupt service routines and the data structures provided in "dos.h" as shown in the include statements. REGS is a register structure type used by the int86() function.

The echoC() function echoes the character c at the current output point of this window (puts the character c on the screen):

```
#include <dos.h>
#include "window.hpp"

void Window::echoC(char c)
  {    union REGS r;
         mvCursor();                      //move to right spot
     r.h.ah = 0x09;
     r.h.bh = 0;
     r.h.al = c;
     r.h.bl= attribute;
     r.x.cx = 1;
     int86(0x10,&r,&r); }
```

EchoC() uses the previous function, mvCursor(), to move the cursor to current output position of the window and to put character c there. Like mvCursor(), echoC() is system-dependent and uses dos.h routines involving a BIOS interrupt, int86.

Function eatWhitespace() is used to get rid of "white" spaces which the user has not intended to occur while using get() input from the keyboard:

```
char Window::eatWhitespace()
  {
    char c = Get();
    while(c == '\t' || c == ' ') {    c = Get();
    }
    return c;
  }
```

Public Member Functions

This section presents the public member functions for TextWindow that have not been defined inline in the following five groups:

- Drawing the image of the window on the screen
- Outputting stuff to the TextWindow
- Erasing stuff in the textWindow.
- Setting modes and attributes.
- Inputting operations.

Drawing on the Screen

Function Draw() illustrates the image of the window on the screen by using the Zortech routine poke() to iterate through rows and dumplines of characters and attributes onto the screen. Finally, Function Draw() uses mvCursor to place the cursor where the output point is on the screen:

```
// window.cpp

void TextWindow::Draw()
{
   for (int i = 0; i <height; ++i){     // iterate through rows
   poke(VIDEOSEG,(yoff+i)*160+xoff*2,
    winbuf+width*i*2,width*2);    //dump line to screen
   }
   mvCursor();                  // show cursor }
```

Output Operations

Output operations for string and numerical (integer and floating point)outputs, are performed by overloading the "<<" (LeftShift operator)and calling the appropriate function, depending on the argument type:

```
#include "window.hpp"

/*
** opls.cpp
**
** String output
*/

Window &Window::operator<<(const char *s)
{
   while (*s) {    Put(*s++);
      }
   return *this;
}

/*
** Integer output
*/
```

continued...

```
Window &Window::operator<<(long a)
{
    if (a <0)
{
Put('-');
    a = 0 - a;
    }
    static char buf[80];
    char *p = buf+sizeof (buf)-1;

    *p = '\0';
    do {   *--p = a % 10 + '0';  a /= 10;
    }while (a != 0);
    while (*p) {     Put(*p++);
    }
    return *this;
}

/*

** Floating point output
*/

Window &Window::operator<<(double a)
  {
    static char buf[80];
        sprintf(buf,"%lg",a);
    return*this << buf;
  }
```

Function Put() is declared virtual and will be redefined later. Put()retrieves the character C in the current location of TextWindow using the current attribute, and advances character's current output location according to modes, such as wrap or scroll.

```
// in window.cpp

void TextWindow::Put(char c)
{
    char *p = winbuf+(x+y*width)*2;
    *p =c;
    *(p+1) = attribute;
    if (++x> = width) {            // passed the rightcol?
        x = 0;
```

continued...

```
    if (!wrapmode) {              // if not wrapping, scroll
      ++y;
       if (y> = height) {
          y = height-1;
          Scroll(1);
       }
     }
   }
}
```

Erasing Data in the TextWindow

The five functions for erasing data in the TextWindow include:
- Clear();
- Scroll(int);
- DeleteChar();
- ClearEOL();
- ClearEOW();

All these functions are declared virtual so they can be redefined to meet the need of each subclass inheriting them. These functions are discussed in this subsection. Function DeleteLine() can be useful but is not used in this chapter. Interested readers can define the function for their own use by modifying the code for DeleteChar().

Function Clear() clears the window by setting all characters to spaces, and all attributes to the current attribute:

```
#include "window.hpp"
  /*
 ** clear.hpp
 **
 */

void Window::Clear()
{
   for (register int i = 0; i  <width*height*2;)
   winbuff[i++] = ' ';
   winbuf[i++] = attribute;
   }
}
```

Scroll() uses memmove() and Clear() to allow the user to scroll the window the specified amount of lines. If argument lines are negative, scrolling is performed "downwards;" otherwise, scrolling is performed "upwards." Scrolling (zero) 0 lines is a no-operation. The code to accomplish this scrolling is, as follows:

```
#include <string.h>
#include "window.hpp"
/*
 ** scroll.cpp
*/
void Window::Scroll(int lines)
{
  if (lines == 0) {
   return;
   } else if (lines> 0) {       //scroll up
   if (lines < height) {        // actually have to scroll
      memmove(winbuf,winbuf+width*lines*2,(height-
lines)*width*2);
      char *p = winbuf + (height - lines) * width * 2;
      for (inti = 0; i < lines; ++i) {
    for (int j = 0; j < width; ++j) {
       *p++= ' ';
       *p++ = attribute;
   }
      }
   } else {
      Clear();                  // }
      } else {                  // scroll down
    lines = 0 - lines;
    if (lines <height) {        // convert to abs value
      memmove(winbuf+width*lines*2,winbuf,(height-
lines)*width*2);
      char *p = winbuf;
      for (int i = 0; i < lines; ++i) {
    for(int j = 0; j  <width; ++j) {
       *p++ = ' ';
       *p++ = attribute;
   }
      }
   } else {
      Clear();
   }
   }
}
```

Function memmove() in the above code is a Zortech defined routine; mem-move(0), as defined in the Zortech library, is capable of performing overlapping moves intelligently. This may not be the case in other implementations.

Function DeleteChar() eliminates the character at the current position of the window, moves any characters on the right one step to the left, and fills the rightmost character of the line with a blank:

```cpp
#include "window.hpp"
/*
 ** deletech.cpp
 */
void Window::DeleteChar()
{
    char*p = winbuf + (y*width + x)*2;
        for (int i = 0; i <(width -x - 1); ++i) {
    *p = *(p+2);
    ++p;
    *p = *(p+2);
    ++p;
    }
     *p++= ' ';
     *p    = attribute;
}
```

Function ClearEOL() erases the characters from the current output point to the end of the line:

```cpp
#include "window.hpp"
/*
** cleareol.cpp
**
*/
void Window::ClearEOL()
{
    char *p = winbuf+(x+y*width)*2;
    for (int i = x; i < width;++i) {      *p++ = ' ';
    *p++ = attribute;
    }
 }
```

Function ClearEOW() erases the characters from the current position to the end of the window:

```
#include "window.hpp"
/*
** cleareow.cpp
**
*/
void Window::ClearEOW()
{
    ClearEOL();                   // clear this line first
    char *p = winbuf+((y+1)*width)*2;
    for(int i = y+1; i  <height; ++i) {
    for (int j = 0; j <width; ++j) {
        *p++= ' ';
        *p++ = attribute;
    }
    }
}
```

Set Attributes

Function SetAttribute() is defined inline. All successive operations will use the colors set by this method:"fg" is the foreground color, "bg" is the background color, "intens"is used to determine whether the foreground color should be intensive or not, and "flash" is used to determine whether the foreground color should flash or not:

```
// defined in window.hpp

inline void TextWindow::SetAttribute(color fg,color bg=black,
            int intens=0,int flash=0)
{
 attribute =
(flash?0x80:0)+(itens?0x8:0)+((char)bg)*0x10+(char) fg;
}
```

Input Operations

Input operations are defined by overloading the > (RightShift) operator and calling input operations with the appropriate argument type, such as character, long integer, double real, and blank-terminated string. Functions eat-Whitespace(), Get() and GetString() may be employed in these operations.

```
#include <ctype.h>
#include "window.hpp"
/*
** oprs.cpp
**
*/

/*
** Read a char from the window
*/

Window & Window::operator>>(char &c)
 {
    c = Get();
    return*this;
}

/*
** Read a long integer from the window
*/

Window & Window::operator>(long &l)
{
    char c;
        l= 0L;
    c = eatWhitespace();
    while (isdigit(c)) {
    l *= 10L;
    l+= c - '0';
    c = Get();
    }
    return *this;
}
```

```
** Read a blank-terminated string from the window
*/

Window &Window::operator>>(char *p)
  {
    char c = eatWhitespace();
        while(isprint(c)) {
    *p++ = c;
    c = Get();
    }
    *p = '\0';
    return*this;
}
```

Function Get() enable one to get a single character from the window:

```
#include <dos.h>
#include <bios.h>
#include "window.hpp"

// get.cpp

int Window::Get()
{
    int c;

     if (lastchar != -1) {              // in-buffer keystroke
    c= lastchar;
    lastchar = -1;
    } else {
    c = bioskey(0); // waitfor keystroke
    if (echomode) {
        echoC(c);
        Put(c);
    }
    }
    return(c & 0xFF) ? (c & 0xFF) : c; // if normal key, just
                                        // return8-bit value.
                                     // special keys, like F10,
                                     // return 16-bitvalue
  }
```

Function GetString() gets a string from the keyboard; however, it doesn't handle backspaces gracefully -- consequently, no input editing is possible when Get-String() is used. Editing could be accomplished in a class derived from Text-Window, if desired.

```
#include <bios.H>
#include "window.hpp"

/*
** getstring.cpp
**
*/

int Window::GetString(char *buffer,int max,char haltchar)
{
    while (max  >0) {
    int c = bioskey(0);  *buffer++ = (char) c;
    if ((char)(c & 0xFF) == haltchar)
        break;
    if (echomode) {
        echoC(c);
        Put(c);
        mvCursor();
    }
    }
      *buffer = '\0';
}
```

A SAMPLE TEXTWINDOW

Listing 5-3 shows the code for a sample text window in which C++ features, such as declaring w, win2 to be a text window at different locations, using constructors to initialize windows, and employing member functions to reduce use of excessive variable names are exemplified extensively, for example:

```
w.SetAttribute(red,blue,1);
w.Clear();
win2.SetAttribute(green,white,1);
win2.Clear();
win2.Draw();
```

The resultant text window is demonstrated in Figure 5-1.

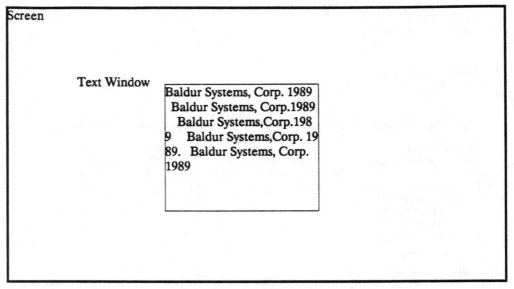

Fig. 5.1, a sample TextWindow.

SUMMARY

This chapter has focused on the design of the textwindow, consisting of four main sections, requirements of a window,class TextWindow, member functions of class TextWindow, and a sample text window.

- A window is a complex object. A window require the following basic operations:
  - Input/Output from the mouse and/or the keyboard
  - Scrolling (up / down / left / right)
  - Moving the output point
  - Clearing selected areas of the screen
  - Moving the window around the screen
  - Attributes(BOLD, FLASHING) and colors
  - Sensitive to mouse clicks (events) on its area

- Not every operation will be implemented in every window.
- A simple TextWindow class performing similarly to theWINDOW in the UNIX Cursor Library requires the following 7 basic functions:

  - Draw the screen

  - Constructor

  - Destructor

  -Clearing the screen

  - Setting attributes/modes

  -Input/Output

  - Moving cursor

- The overloaded operator() is chosen for input/output operations.
- Class TextWindow has a series of protected data objects,such as last character, wrap mode, size of the window (height, width),attribute.
- TextWindow uses its constructor and destructor, and a few member functions, such as Draw(), operator< <, Clear(), DeleteLine(),GetXY(), EchoMode, operator> >, SetAttribute() to perform the following operations:

  -Allocate space and set up default attribute .

  -Remove memory space.

  - Dump the window image to the appropriate place on the screen.

  -Output stuff to the TextWindow.

  -Erase stuff in the TextWindow .

  -Find the pointer's location when the character is there and change position .

  - Set modes and attributes.

  - Input operations.

- A sample text window is discussed to demonstrate the use of C+ + class features.

CHAPTER REFERENCES

Wetmore, Russ. MacApp 2.0 Viewedit User's Guide. Apple Computer, 1988.

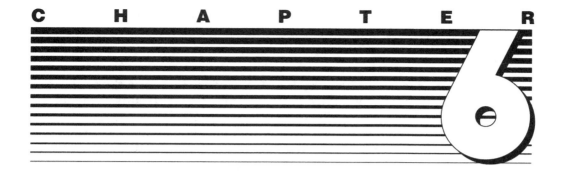

GRAPHICAL CONTROL INTERFACE DESIGN WITH OBJECT-ORIENTED PROGRAMMING

Chapter 5 discusses the design of a text-mode window which can accept only printable characters. This chapter presents a design of graphical user control (iconic user interface) environments. The strategies in designing graphical user control environments are encapsulation, code reusability, rapid prototyping iterative development, and hierarchical structure. While these strategies are derived from those of expert systems development, the sample programs and discussions throughout this book will follow them faithfully.

This chapter provides you with kernels of C++ codes that form the foundation for many graphical control interface designs. This chapter consists of the following elements: the hierarchy of the kernel classes of graphical control interface, nine kernel classes (Pen, Event, Pane, Bunch, Manager, Cursor, Sensor, Queue, and List), offspring classes (Icon, TextMessage, Display, and Menu), making sample icons, and making a sample calculator. The Zortech C++ compiler is used; the Zortech graphics variables and functions used in the book are listed in Appendix C.

THE HIERARCHY OF THE KERNAL CLASSES

 The nine kernel classes are Pen, Event, Pane, Bunch, Manager, Cursor, Sensor, Queue, and List. These classes can be used to build subclasses to serve a particular function in designing a graphical control interface environment. Figure 6-1 shows the organization of these classes. Unlike Smalltalk classes which belong to a tree structure, these nine classes do not have a common root origin.

```
               Pen
               Event

               Pane -|-- Bunch-|--- Manager

               Cursor
               Sensor
               List
               Queue
```

Figure 6-1 The organization of the nine   kernel classes for graphical control interface.

Classes Pen, Event, Cursor, Sensor, Queue, and List stand independently as the root classes even though much of the public data and methods in these classes can be shared among themselves. The only exception is class Pane which has a chain of subclasses:

```
Pane --- Bunch---- Manager
```

Table 6-1 The Purposes and Responsibilities of Kernel Classes for Graphical Control Interface

General Purpose	Class	Responsibility
Management	Manager	Overall control of the screen
Image Control	Pen	Control of the pen: color, position, etc.
	Pane	Control of panes
	Bunch	Bunching panes
Mouse Control	Event	Recordkeeping of events
	Cursor	Control of the cursor's shapes and movements
	Sensor	Catching the state of the mouse
Data Structure	Manager	The queue structure for event
	List	General list structure
	Queue	General queue structure

These classes can be classified into the following categories:

- general management: Manager

- image control: Pen, Pane Bunch

- mouse control: Event, Cursor, Sensor

- data structure: List, Queue

The responsibility of each class as shown in Table 6-1 includes:

- Manager: overall control of the screen, for example., image, event, mouse control

- Pen: control of the pen, such as color, and position, etc., and screen output operations.

- Pane: control of a pane

- Bunch: collection of panes including other bunches

- Event: describing events of the screen

- Cursor: control of the cursor's shapes and movements

- Sensor: catching the state of the mouse

- List: general list structure
- Queue: general queue structure

C++ is used to write these classes. Basic classes, such as Menu, can be created from these kernel classes.

PROGRAMMING THE NINE KERNAL CLASSES

This section discusses programming these kernel classes using C++. Although conventional programming languages can be used in writing kernel classes, they are not as convenient and efficient with respect to resources and time required. The order of discussion follows the sequence of classes appearing on Figure 6-1.

Pen

Class Pen is designed to control the pen status and movements on the screen, such as color, position, or mode (shown in Listing 6-1). Class Pen has the following private data to indicate its status:

- int mode // setting or XORing colors
- fg color t color //foreground color
- int linetype
- int x,y //(position)

Pen works closely with class Pane. Using its constructor and several member functions to work with Pane, Pen can be called to perform:

- Set color: SetColor(fg color t c) { color = c; }
- Set line pattern: SetLinePattern(int lp) { linetype = lp; }
- Set mode: SetMode(int m) { mode = FG_MODE_SET; }
- XOR mode: XorMode(int m) { mode = FG_MODE_XOR; }
- Move position to: MoveTo(Pane *,int, int);
- Plot a pane: Plot(Pane *,int,int);
- Write text to a pane: Text(Pane *,char *);

- Draw line in a pane: Line(Pane *,int,int,int,int);

- Draw a rectangle: Rect(Pane *,int,int,int,int);

- Fill a rectangle: FillRect(Pane *,int,int,int,int);

- Put an icon onto a pane: Put(Pane *,int,int,char *,int,int);

Note that several Zortech graphics functions, types, variables, and constants are used. Examples are fg_color_t, FG_MODE_SET, and FG_MODE_XOR which are quite system-specific.

Listing 6-1 Header File for Class Pen and Common Macros

//A. Header File for Class Pen

```
#ifndef pen_hpp
#define pen_hpp

/*
** pen.hpp
**
**
** History:
** Date    Why?
** ====    ====
** 89-May-18   Original code.
**
** Definition of the Pen class.
*/

#include <fg.h>

class Pane;

class Pen {
private:
    int mode;
    fg_color_t color;
    int linetype;
    int x,y;
public:
    Pen(fg_color_t c = FG_BLACK);
    void SetColor(fg_color_t c) { color = c; }
    void SetLinePattern(int lp) { linetype = lp; }
    void SetMode(int m) { mode = FG_MODE_SET; }
    void XorMode(int m) { mode = FG_MODE_XOR; }
    void MoveTo(Pane *,int, int);
```

continued...

169

```
    void Plot(Pane *,int,int);
    void Text(Pane *,char *);
    void Line(Pane *,int,int,int,int);
    void Rect(Pane *,int,int,int,int);
    void FillRect(Pane *,int,int,int,int);
    void Put(Pane *,int,int,char *,int,int);
};

#include "pane.hpp"

inline void Pen::MoveTo(Pane *paper, int xm,int ym)
{
    x = xm+paper->xoff; y = ym+paper->yoff;
}

inline void Pen::Plot(Pane *paper,int x,int y)
{
    msm_hidecursor();
    fg_drawdot(color,mode,~0,x+paper->xoff,y+paper->yoff);
    msm_showcursor();
}

inline void Pen::Text(Pane *paper,char *s)
{
    msm_hidecursor();
    fg_puts(color,mode,~0,FG_ROT0,x,y,s,paper->clipbox);
    msm_showcursor();
}

#endif
```

//B. Common Macros

```
#ifndef common_hpp
#define common_hpp

/*
** common.hpp
**
**
** History:
** Date    Why?
** ====    ====
** 89-May-15   Original code.
**
** Commonly used functions and macro definitions.
*/

#define max(x,y) (((x)>(y))?(x):(y))
#define min(x,y) (((x)<(y))?(x):(y))
#endif
```

Member functions, such as MoveTo, Plot, Text, Line, Rect, FillRect, and Put are either defined inline in the header file or in the implementation file (pen.cpp), as shown in Listings 6-1 and 6-2.

Listing 6-2 Implementation File for Class Pen

```
/*
** pen.hpp
**
**
** History:
** Date    Why?
** ====    ====
** 89-May-18   Original code.
**
** Constructor and member functions of the Pen class.
*/

#include "pen.hpp"
#include "common.hpp"

/*
** Constructor: define a pen with the color _c_ and always
overwriting
** whatever it draws on. The other possible mode is
FG_MODE_XOR, and
** can be selected with the XorMode() member function.
*/

Pen::Pen(fg_color_t c)
{
    color = c;
    mode = FG_MODE_SET;
    linetype = FG_LINE_SOLID;
}

/*
** Line(): draw a line on the pane _paper_
*/
```

continued...

```
void Pen::Line(Pane *paper,int x1,int y1,int x2,int y2)
{
    fg_line_t line;
    line[FG_X1] = paper->xoff+x1;
    line[FG_Y1] = paper->yoff+y1;
    line[FG_X2] = paper->xoff+x2;
    line[FG_Y2] = paper->yoff+y2;
    msm_hidecursor();
    fg_drawlineclip(color,mode,~0,linetype,line,paper->clip-
box);
    msm_showcursor();
}

/*
** Rect(): draw a rectangular outline on the pane _paper_
*/

void Pen::Rect(Pane *paper,int x1,int y1,int x2,int y2)
{
    fg_box_t box;

    box[FG_X1] = min(x1,x2)+paper->xoff;
    box[FG_X2] = max(x1,x2)+paper->xoff;
    box[FG_Y1] = min(y1,y2)+paper->yoff;
    box[FG_Y2] = max(y1,y2)+paper->yoff;
    msm_hidecursor();
    fg_drawbox(color,mode,~0,linetype,box,paper->clipbox);
    msm_showcursor();
}

/*
** FillRect(): draw a filled rectangle on the pane _paper_
*/

void Pen::FillRect(Pane *paper,int x1,int y1,int x2,int y2)
{
    fg_box_t box;
    box[FG_X1] = min(x1,x2)+paper->xoff;
    box[FG_X2] = max(x1,x2)+paper->xoff;
    box[FG_Y1] = min(y1,y2)+paper->yoff;
    box[FG_Y2] = max(y1,y2)+paper->yoff;
    msm_hidecursor();
    fg_fillbox(color,mode,~0,box);
    msm_showcursor();
}

/*
** Put(): put the pattern pointed to by _pat_ onto the pane
   _paper_
** at the location (x,y) relative to _paper_'s lower left hand
corner.
** The _pat_ pattern is _sx_ pixels wide by _sy_ pixels high.
```

continued...

```
*/

void Pen::Put(Pane *paper,int x, int y,char *pat,int sx,int sy)
{
    fg_box_t b;

    b[FG_X1] = b[FG_Y1] = 0;
    b[FG_X2] = sx-1;
    b[FG_Y2] = sy-1;
    msm_hidecursor();
    fg_drawmatrix(color,mode,~0,FG_ROT0,x+paper->xoff,y+paper-
>yoff, pat,b,paper->clipbox);
    msm_showcursor();
}
```

Note that in member function FillRect(), a set of macros for max() and min() are used to obtain appropriate coordinates: They are required by function fg_fillbox() in the Zortech graphics library.

```
void Pen::FillRect(Pane *paper,int x1,int y1,int x2,int y2)
{
    fg_box_t box;
    box[FG_X1] = min(x1,x2)+paper->xoff;
    box[FG_X2] = max(x1,x2)+paper->xoff;
    box[FG_Y1] = min(y1,y2)+paper->yoff;
    box[FG_Y2] = max(y1,y2)+paper->yoff;
```

Max() and Min() are defined in the B portion of Listing 6-1 (common.hpp):

```
#define max(x,y) (((x)>(y))?(x):(y))
#define min(x,y) (((x)<(y))?(x):(y))
```

These two macros will be used in many classes concerned with coordinates on the screen, such as Pen and Pane.

Event

Class Event performs a housekeeping job while working in conjunction with classes Manager and Pane. Class Event records the type of mouse and/or keyboard event that has occurred.

- Position x,y: position of the event
- Event Type: type or movement of the event, either from the mouse or the keyboard

- Mouse status: the status of the mouse
- Keyboard status: the status of the keyboard
- Pane on target: the pane in which the event occurred

Listing 6-3 Header File for Class Event

```
#ifndef event_hpp
#define event_hpp

/*
** event.hpp
**
**
** History:
** Date     Modificator     Why?
** ====     ===========     ====
** 89-May-02                Original code.
**
** Definition of the Event class.
*/

class Manager;
class Pane;

struct Event {
    int x,y;
    int eventType;
    int status;
    int key;
    Pane *target;
};

#define E_MOTION        0x01
#define E_LEFTDOWN      0x02
#define E_LEFTUP        0x04
#define E_RIGHTDOWN     0x08
#define E_RIGHTUP       0x10
#define E_CENTERDOWN    0x20
#define E_CENTERUP      0x40
#define E_KEY           0x80

#define B_LEFT          0x01
#define B_RIGHT         0x02
#define B_CENTER        0x04

#endif
```

Class Event also defines the detailed movements of the keyboard and the mouse:

1. for events on the screen

- E_MOTION   0x01
- E_LEFTDOWN   0x02
- E_LEFTUP   0x04
- E_RIGHTDOWN 0x08
- E_RIGHTUP   0x10
- E_CENTERDOWN 0x20
- E_CENTERUP   0x40
- E_KEY   0x80

2. for the mouse buttons

- B_LEFT   0x01
- B_RIGHT   0x02
- B_CENTER   0x04

These definitions will then be utilized in the member functions of class Manager, such as:

```
void Manager::Read(Event &e)
{
e.status = msm_getstatus(&e.x,&e.y);
e.y = fg_displaybox[FG_Y2] - e.y;   // convert to right coords
    while (e.status == oldEvent.status && e.x == oldEvent.x &&
       e.y == oldEvent.y && !bioskey(1)) {
    e.status = msm_getstatus(&e.x,&e.y);
    e.y = fg_displaybox[FG_Y2] - e.y;// convert to right coords
    }
    Pane *p;
    e.eventType = 0;

    if (!(oldEvent.status & B_LEFT) && (e.status & B_LEFT)) {
       e.eventType |= E_LEFTDOWN;       // button pressed
    } else if ((oldEvent.status & B_LEFT) && !(e.status &
B_LEFT)) {
```

continued...

```
      e.eventType |= E_LEFTUP;          // button released
      }
 //.....
}
```

More details on the above code will be discussed in class Manager.

Pane

Class Pane provides a restricted area for Pen to operate. Pen is allowed access to Pane's private data and member functions to draw icons or write text by declaring (in Listing 6-4):

```
class Pane {
protected:
      friend class Pen;    // Pens are allowed access
                           // to  Pane's privates
```


Listing 6-4 Header File for Class Pane

```
#ifndef pane_hpp
#define pane_hpp

/*
** pane.hpp
**
**
** History:
** Date    Why?
** ====    ====
** 89-May-10   Original code.
** 89-Jun-18   Code rewritten to fit class Bunch better
**
** Class definition of the Pane class.
*/

#include <fg.h>
#include "event.hpp"
#include "list.hpp"

class Pen;

class Pane {
protected:
```

continued...

```
    friend class Pen;          // Pens are allowed access
                          // to Pane's Privates
    int    xoff;              // offset from lower left
    int    yoff;                // corner of screen
    int    xrel;              // offset from lower left
    int    yrel;              // corner of parent Bunch
    fg_box_t     clipbox;        // pane's area on screen
    void    clear(fg_color_t);  // clear the pane
    int    xmax,ymax;          // maximal local coordinates
public:
    Pane();
    virtual void Configure();      // set up the clipbox
    virtual void Draw();        // Draw yourself
    virtual void Handle(Event &);   // handle the event
    int    Inside(int,int);      // are abs coords inside Pane?
    void        Flush() {fg_flush();}   // flush pending
graphics ops.
};

#include "pen.hpp"

inline void Pane::clear(fg_color_t c)
{
    Pen p(c); p.FillRect(this,0,0,xmax,ymax);
}

/*
** Inside(): return 1 if the point x,y is inside the pane's
** screen area.
*/

inline int Pane::Inside(int x,int y)
{
    return (x >= xrel && x <= (xrel+xmax) && y >= yrel && y <=
(yrel+ymax));
}

/*
** PaneList: a list of panes
*/

class PaneList : public List {
public:
    PaneList();
    void Append(Pane *n) { List::Append((void *)n); }
    void Insert(Pane *n) { List::Insert((void *)n); }
    void Delete(Pane *n) { List::Delete((void *)n); }
};


inline PaneList::PaneList()
{}
#endif
```

Most often, more than a Pane is required in an application. Panes are bunched together; this collection of Panes is called Bunch. As discussed before, class Bunch is the subclass of Pane. A given pane is identified by two sets of coordinates: one set relates to the screen, one set relates to the Bunch pane in which the given pane "lives" (shown in Figure 6-2).

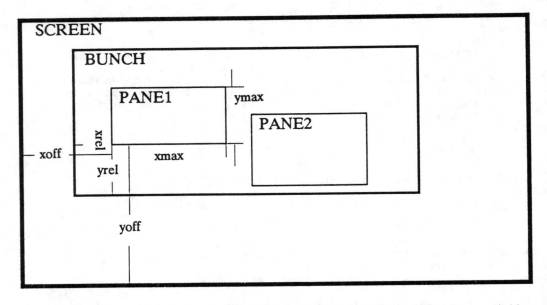

Figure 6-2 *The two sets of coordinates required to identify the position of a given pane (with respect to Bunch and Screen).*

The two sets of coordinates are located in the protected area:

```
int   xoff;                    // offset from lower left
int   yoff;                    // corner of screen
int    xrel;                   // offset from lower left
int   yrel;                    // corner of the parent Bunch
fg_box_t   clipbox;            // pane's area on screen
void   clear(fg_color_t);      // clear the pane
int   xmax,ymax;               // maximal local coordinates
```

Note in the above code, the "clipbox" is declared to be a type of coordinate box of **fg_box_t** (a Zortech variable type). The clipbox will be normalized before being passed to the graphics functions. Function Clear() is used to clear the area of the pane immediately after the pane has been created. A set of maximal local coordinates is required to specify the size of the pane.

The three essential methods in a Pane are Configure(), Draw(), and Handle(). The three methods are located in the shared area of the class:

```
public:
    Pane();
    virtual void Configure();          // set up the clipbox
    virtual void Draw();          // Draw yourself
    virtual void Handle(Event &);      // handle the event
    int     Inside(int,int);       // are abs coords inside Pane?
    void          Flush() {fg_flush();} // flush pending
graphics ops.
};
```

These three methods are overloaded by a declaration of "virtual," so that the same operator names can be redefined. In addition to these methods, a constructor and two non-virtual member functions, are also needed (Listing 6-5):

- Constructor: does nothing. A class derived from Pane should minimally assign values to xmax and ymax, to give the pane a shape.

  ```
  Pane::Pane()
  {
  }
  ```

- Configure(): is a virtual function and sets up the pane's clipping box so that all graphics operations will be clipped correctly. In particular, configure makes sure that nothing happens *outside* the screen.

```
void Pane::Configure()
{
        clipbox[FG_X1] = max(xoff,fg_displaybox[FG_X1]);
        clipbox[FG_Y1] = max(yoff,fg_displaybox[FG_Y1]);
        clipbox[FG_X2] = min(xoff+xmax,fg_displaybox[FG_X2]);
        clipbox[FG_Y2] = min(yoff+ymax,fg_displaybox[FG_Y2]);
}
```

- Handle(): is an empty virtual function. The behavior of each derived class from Pane is defined through the appropriate redefinition of Handle().

```
void Pane::Handle(Event &)
{
    }
```

- Draw(): is an empty virtual function. The behavior of each derived class from Pane is defined through the appropriate redefinition of Draw().

```
  void Pane::Draw()
{

  }
```

- Inside(): makes sure the things Drawn or Handled are within the boundary of the Pane; returns 1 if the point x,y relative to the pane's enclosing Bunch is inside the Pane's screen area.

```
  inline int Pane::Inside(int x,int y)
    {
return (x >= xrel && x <= (xrel+xmax) && y >= yrel&& y <=
  (yrel+ymax));
    }
```

- Flush(): flushes pending graphics operations

```
    void            Flush() {fg_flush();}
```

Listing 6-5   Implementation File for Class Pane

```
/*
** pane.cpp
**
**
** History:
** Date    Why?
** ====    ====
** 89-May-10  Original code.
**
** Constructor and member functions of the Pane class.
*/

#include "pane.hpp"
#include "common.hpp"

/*
** Constructor: does nothing. A class derived from pane should
**minimally
** assign values to xmax and ymax, to give the interactor a
**shape
*/
Pane::Pane()
{
}


/*
** Configure(): set up the pane's clipping box so that all
**graphics
** operations will be clipped correctly. In particular, make
**sure that
** nothing happens *outside* the screen.
*/

void Pane::Configure()
{
    clipbox[FG_X1] = max(xoff,fg_displaybox[FG_X1]);
    clipbox[FG_Y1] = max(yoff,fg_displaybox[FG_Y1]);
    clipbox[FG_X2] = min(xoff+xmax,fg_displaybox[FG_X2]);
    clipbox[FG_Y2] = min(yoff+ymax,fg_displaybox[FG_Y2]);
}

void Pane::Handle(Event &)
{
    /* virtual function. Each derived class from pane defines
**its own
    ** behavior through the appropriate redefinition of
Hand**le() and
    ** Draw()
    */
}
```

continued...

```
void Pane::Draw()
{
    /* virtual function. Each derived class from pane defines
**its own
    ** behavior through the appropriate redefinition of
Hand**le() and
    ** Draw()
    */
}
```

PaneList

Class Pane also includes a class, PaneList, for operating on a list of Panes. PaneList is a subclass of List and inherits its three operations: Append(), Insert(), and Delete ()(in Listing 6-4):

```
class PaneList : public List {
public:
    PaneList();
    void Append(Pane *n) { List::Append((void *)n); }
    void Insert(Pane *n) { List::Insert((void *)n); }
    void Delete(Pane *n) { List::Delete((void *)n); }
};
inline PaneList::PaneList()
{}
```

Bunch

Class Bunch allows the organization of Panes into any type of grouping desired. Bunch is a subclass of Pane. Bunch has a subclass, Manager. Class Manager is allowed access to Bunch's data by declaring "friend" (Listing 6-6):

```
class Bunch : public Pane {
    friend class Manager;
```

Note with the current version of the Zortech compiler, "friends" can be put in the private or the public area.

Listing 6-6 Header File for Class Bunch

```
#ifndef bunch_hpp
#define bunch_hpp

/*
** bunch.hpp
**
**
** History:
** Date    Why?
** ====    ====
** 89-May-10   Original code.
**
** Class definition of the Bunch class.
*/

#include "pane.hpp"

class Bunch : public Pane {
    friend class Manager;
protected:
    PaneList paneList;    // list of all the panes in the bunch
    Pane *find(int,int);    // find member pane at coordinates
public:
    Bunch();
    ~Bunch();
    virtual void Insert(Pane *,int,int); // insert pane at coor-
dinates
    virtual void Remove(Pane *);// remove pane from bunch
    void Draw();            // draw all the panes
    void Configure();      // determine the clipbox of this bunch
    void Raise(Pane *);
    void Lower(Pane *);
    void Handle(Event &);
};

#endif
```

Because Bunch organizes a collection of Panes, the private data in Bunch are the list of all the Panes in the Bunch and the member function locating the Member Pane at the coordinates given.

```
protected:
    PaneList paneList;   // list of all the panes in the bunch
    Pane *find(int,int); // find member pane at coordinates
```

The member function, find(), locates the pane where the event occurred (if any) and returns a pointer to the Pane where the event occurred.

```
Pane *Bunch::find(int x,int y)
{
    ListIterator it(paneList);
    Pane *p,*target = this;        // default target is the
                          // Bunch background
    while (p = (Pane *)it()) {
if (p->Inside(x,y)) {
        target = p;
    }
    }
    return target;
}
```

Seven public methods are available in Bunch:

```
public:
    virtual void Insert(Pane *,int,int); // insert pane at
coordinates
    virtual void Remove(Pane *);  // remove pane from bunch
    void Draw();           // draw all the panes
    void Configure();    // determine the clipbox of this bunch
    void Raise(Pane *);
    void Lower(Pane *);
    void Handle(Event &);
```

Among these methods, the functions of Configure(), Draw(), and Handle() are inherited from superclass Pane, but they are redefined (overloaded) in this class. Note their definitions in Pane are empty. The seven methods are defined as follows (in Listing 6-7):

- Configure(): determines how large the bunch is and propagates any changes to lower level Panes.

```
void Bunch::Configure()
{
    int x1,y1,x2,y2;
    ListIterator iter(paneList);

    Pane::Configure();
    Pane *p;

    while (p = (Pane *)iter()) {
p->xoff = xoff + p->xrel;
p->yoff = yoff + p->yrel;
p->Configure();
    }
}
```

- Draw(): tells all the component Panes to redraw themselves. The drawing order is from the first Pane in the list to the last. Consequently, panes toward the beginning of the list will be overlaid by Panes toward the end of the list.

```
void Bunch::Draw()
{
    ListIterator wi(paneList);
    Pane *p;

    while (p = (Pane *)wi()) {
   p->Draw();
    }
}
```

- Insert(): inserts a Pane into the world. This Pane will appear superimposed on any other Panes of the Bunch, since it will be the last Pane to be drawn.

```
void Bunch::Insert(Pane *p,int x,int y)
{
    p->xoff = xoff + x;    // xoff, yoff is offset
    p->yoff = yoff + y;    // relative to global screen
    p->xrel = x;           // xrel, yrel is offset
    p->yrel = y;           // relative to this bunch
    p->Configure();        // set up proper clipbox
    paneList.Append(p);        // append the paneList
}
```

- Raise(): move the Pane _p_ to the end of the Pane list, so that the Pane will appear superimposed on all other Panes.

```
void Bunch::Raise(Pane *p)
{
    paneList.Delete(p);
    paneList.Append(p);
}
```

- Lower(): moves the Pane _p_ to the beginning of the Pane list, so that the Pane will appear "below" all other Panes when the Bunch is redrawn.

```
void Bunch::Lower(Pane *p)
{
    paneList.Delete(p);
    paneList.Insert(p);
}
```

* Remove(): removes the Pane _p_ from the display. Note that the Pane could be reinserted with Bunch::Insert() at a later time.

```
void Bunch::Remove(Pane *p)
{
    paneList.Delete(p); //delete the space occupied by _p_
}
```

* Handle() finds the right pane and records the event.

```
void Bunch::Handle(Event &e)
{
    Pane *p = find(e.x,e.y);

    if (p != this) {
    e.x -= xrel;
    e.y -= yrel;
    p->Handle(e);
    }
}
```

Listing 6-7 Implementation File for Class Bunch

```
#include "bunch.hpp"
#include "common.hpp"

/**/
#include <stdio.h>
/**/

/*
** bunch.cpp
**
**
** History:
** Date    Why?
** ====    ====
** 89-Jun-18   Original code.
```

continued...

```
**
** Bunch constructor and member functions
*/


Bunch::Bunch()
{
}

Bunch::~Bunch()
{
    ListIterator wi(paneList);
    Pane *p;

    while (p = (Pane *)wi()) {
    delete p;
     }
}
/*
** Configure(): Determine how large the bunch is, propagate
**any changes to
** lower level panes (if any).
*/

void Bunch::Configure()
{
    int x1,y1,x2,y2;
    ListIterator iter(paneList);

    Pane::Configure();
    Pane *p;

    while (p = (Pane *)iter()) {
    p->xoff = xoff + p->xrel;
    p->yoff = yoff + p->yrel;
    p->Configure();
     }
}
/*
** Draw(): Tell all the component panes to redraw themselves.
**The drawing
** order is from the first pane in the list to the last. That
**means
** that panes towards the beginning of the list will be
**overlaid
** by panes towards the end of the list.
*/
```

continued...

```
void Bunch::Draw()
{
    ListIterator wi(paneList);
    Pane *p;

    while (p = (Pane *)wi()) {
    p->Draw();
    }
}

/*
** Insert(): insert a pane into the world. This pane will
**appear
** superimposed on any other panes of the bunch, since it will
** be the last pane to be drawn.
*/

void Bunch::Insert(Pane *p,int x,int y)
{
    p->xoff = xoff + x;          // xoff, yoff is offset
    p->yoff = yoff + y;          // relative to global screen
    p->xrel = x;                 // xrel, yrel is offset
    p->yrel = y;                 // relative to this bunch
    p->Configure();              // set up proper clipbox
    paneList.Append(p);
}

/*
** Raise(): move the pane _p_ to the end of the pane list,
** so that the pane will appear superimposed on all other
**panes.
*/

void Bunch::Raise(Pane *p)
{
    paneList.Delete(p);
    paneList.Append(p);
}

/*
** Lower(): move the pane _p_ to the beginning of the pane
**list,
** so that the pane will appear "below" all other panes when
**the
** Bunch is redrawn.
*/
```

continued...

```
void Bunch::Lower(Pane *p)
{
    paneList.Delete(p);
    paneList.Insert(p);
}


/*
** Remove(): remove the pane _p_ from the display. Note that
**the
** pane could be reinserted with Bunch::Insert() at a later
**point.
*/

void Bunch::Remove(Pane *p)
{
    paneList.Delete(p);             // occupied by _p_
}


/*
** find(): find the pane on which the event occurred (if any)
** Returns a pointer to the pane on which the event occurred.
If the
** event happened on no window, the event is reported to the
** Bunch.
*/

Pane *Bunch::find(int x,int y)
{
    ListIterator it(paneList);
    Pane *p,*target = this;        // default target is the
                                   // Bunch background

    while (p = (Pane *)it()) {
    if (p->Inside(x,y)) {
        target = p;
    }
    }
    return target;
}

/*
** Handle
*/

void Bunch::Handle(Event &e)
{
    Pane *p = find(e.x,e.y);

    if (p != this) {
    e.x -= xrel;
    e.y -= yrel;
    p->Handle(e);
    }
}
```

Manager

Class Manager performs the task of general management for the graphical control interface environment. To be displayed on the screen, a pane must be inserted either directly or indirectly (by inserting it's parent Bunch) into the Manager.Class Manager is a subclass of Bunch. Access to private data is not allowed, although the function uses information from Classes, Pane, Event, and Bunch.

The background color, location of previous mouse poll, and previous Pane are the private data for Manager:

```
class Manager : public Bunch {
protected:
    fg_color_t background; // Background color
    Event oldEvent;        // location of prev mouse poll
    Pane *oldpane;         // previous pane
```

Listing 6-8 Header File for Class Manager

```
#ifndef manager_hpp
#define manager_hpp

/*
** manager.hpp
**
**
** History:
** Date     Why?
** ====     ====
** 89-May-01   Original code.
** 89-Jun-15   Rewritten as if derived from Pane.
** 89-Jun-18   Rewritten as if derived from Bunch.
**
** Definition of the Manager class.
*/

#include <stdio.h>
#include "pane.hpp"
#include "event.hpp"
#include "bunch.hpp"

class Manager : public Bunch {
protected:
    fg_color_t background;   // Background color
    Event oldEvent;          // location of prev mouse poll
    Pane *oldpane;           // previous pane
```

continued...

```
public:
    Manager();
    ~Manager();
    void Configure();
    void Init(fg_color_t b = FG_BLACK);
    void Read(Event &);      //read one event
    void Clear();
    void Remove(Pane *);
};

#endif
```

The Manager constructor is activated to create a Manager if and only if there is
no other active manager, and to initialize a pointing device (mouse) if there is one
available. The Manager destructor is used also to delete all Panes, to reset the
graphics screen and the mouse handler. Manager has five public methods:

```
public:
    Manager();
    ~Manager();
    void Configure();
    void Init(fg_color_t b = FG_BLACK);
    void Read(Event &);      //read one event
    void Clear();
    void Remove(Pane *);
```

These methods serve various purposes and are defined/redefined if overloaded,
as follows:

- Configure(): makes sure that Manager always covers the entire screen.

  ```
  void Manager::Configure()
  {
      clipbox[FG_X1] = fg_displaybox[FG_X1];
      clipbox[FG_X2] = fg_displaybox[FG_X2];
      clipbox[FG_Y1] = fg_displaybox[FG_Y1];
      clipbox[FG_Y2] = fg_displaybox[FG_Y2];
  }
  ```

- The clipbox variable is a member inherited from the pane.

- Init(): displays mouse pointer (after background has been painted)

```
void Manager::Init(fg_color_t b)
{
    background = b;
    Clear();
    msm_showcursor();
    msm_setareax(fg_displaybox[FG_X1],fg_displaybox[FG_X2]);
    msm_setareay(fg_displaybox[FG_Y1],fg_displaybox[FG_Y2]);
}
```

Functions such as msm_setareax are Zortech mouse functions.

- Read(): determines whether an event has occurred from either the mouse or the keyboard, and if so, the location is registered where the event happened.

```
void Manager::Read(Event &e)
{
    e.status = msm_getstatus(&e.x,&e.y);
    e.y = fg_displaybox[FG_Y2] - e.y; // convert to right coords
     while (e.status == oldEvent.status && e.x == oldEvent.x &&
        e.y == oldEvent.y && !bioskey(1)) {
    e.status = msm_getstatus(&e.x,&e.y);
e.y = fg_displaybox[FG_Y2] - e.y; // convert to right coords
    }
    Pane *p;
    e.eventType = 0;

    if (!(oldEvent.status & B_LEFT) && (e.status & B_LEFT)) {
        e.eventType |= E_LEFTDOWN;          // button pressed
    } else if ((oldEvent.status & B_LEFT) && !(e.status &
B_LEFT)) {
        e.eventType |= E_LEFTUP;          // button released
    }

    if (!(oldEvent.status & B_RIGHT) && (e.status & B_RIGHT)) {
    e.eventType |= E_RIGHTDOWN;          // button pressed
    } else if ((oldEvent.status & B_RIGHT) && !(e.status &
B_RIGHT)) {
    e.eventType |= E_RIGHTUP;          // button released
    }
```

continued...

```
    if (!(oldEvent.status & B_CENTER) && (e.status & B_CEN-
TER)) {
    e.eventType |= E_CENTERDOWN;   // button pressed
    } else if ((oldEvent.status & B_CENTER) && !(e.status &
B_CENTER)) {
    e.eventType |= E_CENTERUP;         // button released
    }

    if (e.x != oldEvent.x || e.y != oldEvent.y) {// cursor
moved
    e.eventType |= E_MOTION;
    }

    oldEvent.status = e.status;
    oldEvent.x      = e.x;
    oldEvent.y      = e.y;

    if (bioskey(1)) {            // key events waiting
    e.key = bioskey(0);          // read the key event
    if (e.key & 0xFF) {          // "normal" key pressed?
        e.key &= 0xFF;           // yes: get rid of scan code
    }
    e.eventType |= E_KEY;
    }

    e.target = find(e.x,e.y);           // find the pane on which
                    // the event occurred
    e.x -= e.target->xoff;      // convert to local
    e.y -= e.target->yoff;            // coordinates
}
```

- Clear(): fills the screen with the color specified by the member function, background.

```
    void Manager::Clear()
    {
        fg_fillbox(background, FG_MODE_SET, ~0, fg_displaybox);
    }
```

- Remove(): clears the Pane's background area and draws all the Panes.

```
    void Manager::Remove(Pane *p)
    {
        p->clear(background);
        Bunch::Remove(p);
        Draw();
    }
```

Listing 6-9 Implementation File for Class Manager

```
#include "manager.hpp"
#include <fg.h>

/*
** manager.cpp
**
**
** History:
** Date    Why?
** ====    ====
** 89-May-02   Original code.
** 89-May-18   Added the Init() member function.
**
** Constructor and member functions of the Manager class.
*/

static int nmanagers = 0;
/*
** Constructor: create a manager if and only if there is no
other active
** manager. The optional argument _b_ specifies the background
color of the
** screen (default is black).
** The msm_init() called is used to initialize a pointing
device if
** there is one available. fg_init_all() is the Zortech Flash-
Graphics
** library call that puts the display in high-resolution
graphics
** mode (if possible).
** Finally, the mouse driver is informed of the eventHandler.
All subsequent
** mouse events will be handled by the function eventHandler.
*/

Manager::Manager()
{
    if (nmanagers++) {
fputs("manager error: more than one active manager\n",stderr);
exit(1);
    }
    if (msm_init() != -1) {
fputs("manager error: no pointing device available\n",stderr);
    exit(1);
    }
    if (fg_init_all() == FG_NULL) {
```

continued...

```
fputs("manager error: couldn't open graphics port\n",stderr);
exit(1);
    }
    Configure();
    xoff = yoff = 0;
}

/*
** Manager destructor: deletes all panes, resets the graphics
screen and
** the mouse handler.
*/

Manager::~Manager()
{
    ListIterator wi(paneList);
    Pane *p;

    while (p = (Pane *)wi()) {
    delete p;
    }
    --nmanagers;
    fg_term();
    msm_term();
}
/*
** Init(): display mouse pointer (after background has been
painted)
*/

void Manager::Init(fg_color_t b)
{
    background = b;
    Clear();
    msm_showcursor();
    msm_setareax(fg_displaybox[FG_X1],fg_displaybox[FG_X2]);
    msm_setareay(fg_displaybox[FG_Y1],fg_displaybox[FG_Y2]);
}

/*
** Configure(): the manager is always the entire screen
*/

void Manager::Configure()
{
    clipbox[FG_X1] = fg_displaybox[FG_X1];
    clipbox[FG_X2] = fg_displaybox[FG_X2];
    clipbox[FG_Y1] = fg_displaybox[FG_Y1];
    clipbox[FG_Y2] = fg_displaybox[FG_Y2];
}
```

continued...

```
/*
** Clear(): fills the screen with the color specified by the
** member function _background_
*/

void Manager::Clear()
{
    fg_fillbox(background, FG_MODE_SET, ~0, fg_displaybox);
}

/*
** Remove(): removing a pane results in its background area
being cleared,
** followed by a drawing of all the panes
*/

void Manager::Remove(Pane *p)
{
    p->clear(background);
    Bunch::Remove(p);
    Draw();
}

/*
** Read(): Determine whether an event has occurred, and if so,
register
** its location (where it happened)
*/

void Manager::Read(Event &e)
{
    e.status = msm_getstatus(&e.x,&e.y);
    e.y = fg_displaybox[FG_Y2] - e.y;// convert to right coords
    while (e.status == oldEvent.status && e.x == oldEvent.x &&
       e.y == oldEvent.y && !bioskey(1)) {
    e.status = msm_getstatus(&e.x,&e.y);
    e.y = fg_displaybox[FG_Y2] - e.y;// convert to right coords
    }
    Pane *p;
    e.eventType = 0;

    if (!(oldEvent.status & B_LEFT) && (e.status & B_LEFT)) {
        e.eventType |= E_LEFTDOWN;        // button pressed
    } else if ((oldEvent.status & B_LEFT) && !(e.status &
B_LEFT)) {
    e.eventType |= E_LEFTUP;          // button released
    }
```

continued...

```
   if (!(oldEvent.status & B_RIGHT) && (e.status & B_RIGHT)) {
e.eventType |= E_RIGHTDOWN;          // button pressed
   } else if ((oldEvent.status & B_RIGHT) && !(e.status &
B_RIGHT)) {
   e.eventType |= E_RIGHTUP;         // button released
   }

   if (!(oldEvent.status & B_CENTER) && (e.status & B_CEN-
TER)) {
   e.eventType |= E_CENTERDOWN;   // button pressed
   } else if ((oldEvent.status & B_CENTER) && !(e.status &
B_CENTER)) {
   e.eventType |= E_CENTERUP;         // button released
   }

   if (e.x != oldEvent.x || e.y != oldEvent.y) {// cursor
moved
   e.eventType |= E_MOTION;
   }

   oldEvent.status = e.status;
   oldEvent.x    = e.x;
   oldEvent.y    = e.y;

   if (bioskey(1)) {            // key events waiting
e.key = bioskey(0);         // read the key event
if (e.key & 0xFF) {         // "normal" key pressed?
   e.key &= 0xFF;           // yes: get rid of scan code
}
e.eventType |= E_KEY;
   }

   e.target = find(e.x,e.y);         // find the pane on which
            // the event occurred
   e.x -= e.target->xoff;     // convert to local
   e.y -= e.target->yoff;           // coordinates
}
```

Cursor

Class Cursor controls the display device cursor's shape and movements. Class Cursor is a root class without any subclasses. Cursor has two private data sets (image and hot spot) and one public method, Set(), as shown in Listing 6-10:

```
class Cursor {
protected:
    int image[IMAGESIZE];
    int hotx,hoty;
public:
    Cursor(int *,int *,int, int);
    void Set();
};
```

Listing 6-10 Header File for Class Cursor

```
#ifndef cursor_hpp
#define cursor_hpp

/*
** cursor.hpp
**
**
** History:
** Date    Why?
** ====    ====
** 89-May-15   Original code.
**
** Header file for the Cursor class.
*/

#define   IMAGESIZE 32

class Cursor {
protected:
    int image[IMAGESIZE];
    int hotx,hoty;
public:
    Cursor(int *,int *,int, int);
    void Set();
};

#endif
```

The Cursor constructor and method Set() are used to set the cursor of the display device. The constructor copies the bitmaps that represent the cursor's image into the _image_ member variable and defines the location of the "hot spot". Due to the physical constraint of IBM PCs and MS-DOS, the "hot spot" is relative to the upper left corner of the pointer image, and each pixel offset must be in the range of -16 to +16. In display modes 4 and 5, the horizontal offset must be an even number (*Microsoft Mouse Programming Reference Guide,* Microsoft Press, 1989, p. 598).

Method Set() establishes the shape of the graphics display device pointer to the cursor pattern discussed above (Listing 6-11):

```
void Cursor::Set()
{
    msm_setgraphcur(hotx,hoty,image);
}
```

This is accomplished by calling the Microsoft Mouse driver interrupt (0x33 hexadecimal) with the AX, BX, CX and ES:DX registers of the 80x86 set appropiately (see Microsoft Mouse Guide for details).

Listing 6-11 Implementation File for Class Cursor

```
#include "cursor.hpp"
#include "common.hpp"
/*
** cursor.cpp
**
**
** History:
** Date   Why?
** ====   ====
** 89-May-15  Original code.
**
** Constructor and function to set the cursor of the display
device
*/

/*
** Constructor: copy the bitmaps that represent the cursor
** image into the _image_ member variable and define the loca-
tion
** of the "hot spot".
**
*/

Cursor::Cursor(int *and,int *xor, int x, int y)
{
    memcpy(image,and,IMAGESIZE);
    memcpy(image+(IMAGESIZE>>1),xor,IMAGESIZE);
    hotx = x; hoty = y;
}
```

continued...

```
/*
** Set(): set the graphics display device pointer shape to the
** this cursor pattern.
**
*/

void Cursor::Set()
{
    msm_setgraphcur(hotx,hoty,image);
}
```

Sensor

Class Sensor is a simple root class whose main function is to catch signals. Sensor
has a private data, mask, and two public methods, Catch() and Ignore(), shown in
Listing 6-12, as follows:

```
class Sensor {
private:
    int mask;
public:
    Sensor() { mask = 0; }
    void Catch(int signal) { mask |= signal; } // when there
// is signal
    void Ignore(int signal) { mask &= ~signal; } // when there
// is no signal
```

Listing 6-12 Header File for Class Sensor

```
#ifndef sensor_hpp
#define sensor_hpp

/*
** sensor.hpp
**
**
** History:
** Date   Why?
** ====   ====
** 89-May-02   Original code.
**
** Definition of the Sensor class.
*/
```

continued...

```
class Sensor {
private:
    int mask;
public:
    Sensor() { mask = 0; }
    void Catch(int signal) { mask |= signal; }
    void Ignore(int signal) { mask &= ~signal; }
};

#endif
```

A sensor could be used to "filter" out signals that are not used by a given pane.

List

Class List performs the role of a general list manager and a list iterator. Class List consists of three classes: 1_node, List, and ListIterator. Class 1_node is a linked list node and used by the general data structure classes, such as List and Queue.

Class 1_node is a "friend" of List, ListIterator, and Queue; and has two private pointers to list nodes, and *next and *data to indicate the position of the nodes. It uses the constructor to initialize the pointers (in Listing 6-13).

```
class 1_node {
    friend class List;
    friend class Queue;
    friend class ListIterator;
private:
    1_node *next;
    void  *data;
public:
    1_node(void *d,1_node *n = 0) { data = d; next = n; }
};
```

Class List is a friend of ListIterator and uses 1_node to perform insert, append, and delete of the list. List has a pointer to the first of the linked list nodes. It also has three virtual functions doInsert(), doAppend(),and doDelete(). The constructor of List is used to initialize the head to be zero, thereby making an empty list and defines three methods inline: Insert(), Append(), and Delete().

```
class List {
    friend class ListIterator;
protected:
    l_node *head;
    virtual l_node *doInsert(void *d,l_node *n) { return new
l_node(d,n); }
    virtual l_node *doAppend(void *d,l_node *n);
    virtual l_node *doDelete(void *d,l_node *n);
public:
    List() { head = 0; }
    ~List();
    void Insert(void *d) { head = doInsert(d,head); }
    void Append(void *d) { head = doAppend(d,head); }
    void Delete(void *d) { head = doDelete(d,head); }
};
```

Listing 6-13 Header File for Class List

```
#ifndef list_hpp
#define list_hpp

/*
** list.hpp
**
**
** History:
** Date    Why?
** ====    ====
** 89-May-15   Original code.
**
** Class definition of a general list manager and list
**iterator.
*/

/*
** l_node: a linked list node. Used by the general data
**structure
** classes.
*/

class l_node {
    friend class List;
    friend Queue;
    friend class ListIterator;
private:
    l_node *next;
    void   *data;
public:
    l_node(void *d,l_node *n = 0) { data = d; next = n; }
};
```
continued...

202

```
class List {
    friend class ListIterator;
protected:
    l_node *head;
    virtual l_node *doInsert(void *d,l_node *n) { return new
l_node(d,n); }
    virtual l_node *doAppend(void *d,l_node *n);
    virtual l_node *doDelete(void *d,l_node *n);
public:
    List() { head = 0; }
    ~List();
    void Insert(void *d) { head = doInsert(d,head); }
    void Append(void *d) { head = doAppend(d,head); }
    void Delete(void *d) { head = doDelete(d,head); }
};

class ListIterator {
    l_node *ptr;
public:
    ListIterator(List& l) { ptr = l.head; }
    void *operator()() {
    void *p = ptr ? (ptr->data) : 0 ;
    ptr = ptr ? ptr->next : 0;
    return p;
    }
};

#endif // list_hpp
```

The three pointer functions, doInsert(), doAppend(), and doDelete() are defined separately. The function doInsert() is defined inline, as shown above. The remaining two functions are defined, as follows in Listing 6-14:

```
l_node *List::doAppend(void *d,l_node *n)
{
    if (n == 0) {
    return new l_node(d);
    } else {
    n->next = doAppend(d,n->next);
    return n;
    }
}
l_node *List::doDelete(void *d,l_node *n)
{
    if (n == 0) {                    // item not found
    return 0;
    } else if (n->data == d) {       // item found!
    l_node *tail = n->next;
    delete n;
```

continued...

```
    } else if (n->data == d) {        // item found!
  l_node *tail = n->next;
  delete n;
  return tail;
    } else {
  n->next = doDelete(d,n->next);
  return n;
    }
}
```

Listing 6-14 Implementation File for Class List

```
#include "list.hpp"

/*
** list.hpp
**
**
** History:
** Date    Why?
** ====    ====
** 89-May-02   Original code.
**
** Constructor and member functions of the List class
*/
l_node *List::doAppend(void *d,l_node *n)
{
    if (n == 0) {
  return new l_node(d);
    } else {
  n->next = doAppend(d,n->next);
  return n;
    }
}

l_node *List::doDelete(void *d,l_node *n)
{
    if (n == 0) {                // item not found
  return 0;
    } else if (n->data == d) {        // item found!
  l_node *tail = n->next;
  delete n;
  return tail;
    } else {
  n->next = doDelete(d,n->next);
  return n;
    }
}
```

continued...

```
List::~List()
{
    l_node *victim;

    while (head) {
    victim = head;
    head = head->next;
    delete victim;
    }
}
```

Queue

Class Queue is a general queue manager. Class Queue is also a root class, using data from class List. The function contains private data on the head and the tail of the queue and two operators to add elements to the queue at the tail and to remove elements from the head of the queue (see Listing 6-15).

```
class Queue {
private:
    l_node *head;
    l_node *tail;
public:
    Queue();
    void operator<<(void *); // add an element to the queue
    void operator>>(void * &); // remove an element from the
queue
```

Listing 6-15 Header File for Class Queue

```
#ifndef queue_hpp
#define queue_hpp

/*
** queue.hpp
**
**
** History:
** Date    Why?
** ====    ====
** 89-May-15   Original code.
**
** Class definition of a general queue manager.
*/

#include "list.hpp"
```

continued...

```
class Queue {
private:
    l_node *head;
    l_node *tail;
public:
    Queue();
    void operator<<(void *); // add an element to the queue
    void operator>>(void * &); // remove an element from the
queue
};


/*
** Constructor: initially the queue is empty
*/

inline Queue::Queue() { head = tail = 0; }

#endif
```

The two operators for Queue are defined in Listing 6-16.

Listing 6-16 Implementation File for Class Queue

```
#include "queue.hpp"

/*
** queue.hpp
**
**
** History:
** Date   Why?
** ====   ====
** 89-May-15   Original code.
**
** Constructor and member functions of the Queue class
*/

/*
** <<: put an element into the queue, i.e. at the tail.
*/
void Queue::operator<<(void *d)
{
    register void *n = new l_node(d);
```

continued...

```
    if (head == 0) {        // empty queue
head = tail = n;
    } else {
tail->next = n;
tail = tail->next;
    }
}

/*
** >>: get an element from the queue, i.e. at the head. If the
queue
** is empty, a NULL pointer is returned in d.
*/

void Queue::operator>>(void *&d)
{
    if (head == 0) {        // empty queue
d = 0;        // returning 0 means "no data available"
    } else if (head == tail) { // all but empty
d = head->data;
delete head;
head = tail = 0;
    } else {
register l_node *victim = head;
d = head->data;
head = head->next;
delete victim;
    }
}
```

Offspring Classes

The kernel classes provide a good foundation to build offspring classes suitable for application needs. Four generic classes useful for making icons, menus, and prompt messages are provided in this section: Icon, TextMessage, Display, and Menu. These classes are subclasses of Pane, as shown in the following underlined classes:

```
              |-- Manager
Pane -|-- Bunch |-- Menu
      |--_Icon
      |-- TextMessage
      |--_Display
```

The overall hierarchy of the kernel classes plus these four offspring classes (they are thereafter called the basic classes, as shown in Figure 6-3 with offspring classes underlined.

```
Pen
Event

                    --- Manager
Pane -|-- Bunch-|---_Menu
      |--_Icon
      |-- TextMessage
      |--_Display
Cursor
Sensor
List
Queue
```

Figure 6-3 The organization of the basic classes for graphical control interface.

All four offspring classes perform image control duty as follows:

- image control: Pen, Pane [Bunch (Menu),Icon, TextMessage, Display]

The general purposes and responsibilities for all classes discussed are shown in Table 6-2. The structure of the four individual offspring classes are discussed below. The users can make their own offspring classes based on the basic classes.

Table 6-2 The Purposes and Responsibilities of Fourteen Basic Classes for Graphical Control Interface

General Purpose	Class	Responsibility
Management	Manager	Overall control of the screen
Image Control	Pen	Control of the pen: color, position, etc.
	Pane	Control of panes
	Bunch	Bunching panes
	Icon	Control of image
	Menu	Controlling user selection
	TextMesage	Showing prompt messages
	Display	Interactive text-editing
Mouse Control	Event	Recordkeeping of events
	Cursor	Control of the cursor's shapes and movements
	Sensor	Catching the state of the mouse
Data Structure	List	General list structure
	Queue	General queue structure

Icon

Class Icon controls a bit-mapped image on the screen. Icon is a subclass of Pane. Icon uses private pattern and foreground and background colors to make an image on the screen. Two public member functions are required: Icon() and Draw(); both functions are defined inline. Note that Draw() is a virtual function in Pane and overloaded in Icon.

```
inline void Icon::Draw()
{
    background->FillRect(this,0,0,xmax,ymax);
    foreground->Put(this,0,0,pattern,xmax+1,ymax+1);
}
```

In Draw(), messages are sent to background and foreground to perform FillRect() and Put(), respectively (Listing 6-17).

Listing 6-17 Header File for Class Icon

```
#ifndef icon_hpp
#define icon_hpp

class Icon : public Pane {
protected:
    char *pattern;
    Pen *foreground,*background;
public:
    Icon(char *,int,int,int,int);
    void Draw();
};

inline Icon::Icon(char *p,int fg,int bg,int wi,int he) {
    pattern = p;
    xmax = wi-1; ymax = he - 1;
    foreground = new Pen(fg);
    background = new Pen(bg);
}

inline void Icon::Draw()
{
    background->FillRect(this,0,0,xmax,ymax);
    foreground->Put(this,0,0,pattern,xmax+1,ymax+1);
}

#endif
```

TextMessage

Class TextMessage allows the prompt message, rather than icons as in Icon, to be shown on the screen. TextMessage is a subclass of Pane, inheriting Pane's methods and data objects, and uses information from Bunch. TextMessage uses Pen's foreground and background pointers to indicate its location, puts the prompt message on the location, and determines whether the message is complete, as follows (see Listing 6-18):

```
class TextMessage : public Pane {
    Pen *foreground,*background;
    char *message;
    int done;
```

The Class TextMessage constructor is used to set up the Pane for accepting messages and contains three methods in the public area.

```
public:    TextMessage(char *,int,int);
    void Draw();
    void Run();
    void Handle(Event &);
```

Both Draw() and Handle() are virtual functions redefined in this class to meet its particular need for handling text messages. Method Run() is a new method which is defined:

```
void TextMessage::Run()
{
    Event e;
    extern Manager m;
    while (!done) {
    m.Read(e);
    if (e.target != 0) {
        e.target->Handle(e);
    }
    }
}
```

Run() is used to determine whether the message is complete. If the message is not complete, Run() reads the message into the Pane.

Listing 6-18 Header File for Class TextMessage

```
// textmessage.hpp
// (c) Copyright 1989 Baldur Systems Corp.
//
#include "bunch.hpp"
#include "pane.hpp"

class TextMessage : public Pane {
    Pen *foreground,*background;
    char *message;
    int done;
public:
    TextMessage(char *,int,int);
    void Draw();
    void Run();
    void Handle(Event &);
};
```

Display

Display depicts the window where the current value is displayed. As a subclass of Pane Display inherits methods and data objects from Pane and some methods from Bunch.

Display receives the value and background and foreground colors of Pen from Class Pane. The Display uses its constructor to clear the display and set up the Pens to paint the display. Class Display has seven public methods which have been redefined in this area class to meet Display need (see Listing 6-19):

- Display(): create a 20-char wide display

- void Draw(): draw the display

- void Erase(): erase a character

- void Add(char): add a character

- char *Get(): get the value out of the display

- void Put(char *): put a value into the display

- void Handle(Event &): handle keystrokes

Listing 6-19 Header File for Class Display

```
//
// display.hpp
// (c) Copyright 1989 Baldur Systems Corp.
//

/*
** Display is the window in which the current value is dis-
played
*/
#include "bunch.hpp"
#include "pane.hpp"

class Display : public Pane {
    char value[20];          // buffer for value
    Pen *background,*foreground;  // background and foreground
colors
public:
    Display();               // create a 20-char wide display
    void Draw();             // draw the display
    void Erase();            // erase a character
    void Add(char);          // add a character
    char *Get();             // get the value out of the display
    void Put(char *);        // put a value into the display
    void Handle(Event &);    // handle keystrokes
};
```

Menu

Class Menu provides the control of user selection. Class Menu is a subclass of Bunch. Class Menu also includes another class, MenuItem, a subclass of Pane. Menu uses objects from four other classes (see Listing 6-20):

```
#include "bunch.hpp"
#include "pane.hpp"
#include "manager.hpp"
#include "menu.hpp"
```

Class Menu keeps the number of items, and selection status as private:

```
class Menu : public Bunch {
protected:
    int  nitem;              //number of items
    int  selcflg;            //keep the selection exclusive
    int  done;
```

The Class Menu constructor is used to set the status flag as zero (done =0;) and four public methods to manipulate objects:

```
public:
    Menu();
    virtual void Do(char*);   //do the operation
    void Draw();   //how to draw menus
    void Run();     //control the execution of the Menu
    void SetStatus(int);   //set the status flag for the menu
```

The source of these methods comes from different classes:

- void Menu::Do(char*)

  ```
  A virtual function. Each derived class defines its own
  behavior through the appropriate redefinition of Do()
  ```

- void Menu::Draw(), comes from class Bunch,

```
    Bunch::Draw(); // draw the entire menu items defined on
//this bunch
```

- void Menu::Run(), Similar to the Run() in TextMessage, but redefined in this class,

```
{
    Event e;
    extern Manager m;
    extern int exitflg;

    while (!done)   //check user click on "end" or not
    {
    m.Read(e);  //read in an event
    Pane *temp = find(e.x,e.y); // check click on which menu item
    if((temp != this) && (e.eventType & E_LEFTDOWN))
    {
        e.target->Handle(e);   //yes, do as it means
        if(exitflg == 1)
      done = 1;
    }
      }
}
```

continued...

- void Menu::SetStatus (int status) Defined in this class as follows:

```
{
    done = status;
}
```

Class MenuItems is a subclass of Pane, and contains two private objects: toggle and itemtext:

```
class MenuItem : public Pane {
protected:
    int    toggle;        // toggle the color
    char   *itmtext;      // menu item text
```

MenuItems uses two methods for menu item manipulation:

```
public:
    virtual void Draw();
    virtual void Handle(Event&);
```

Both methods are virtual functions and will be defined later in the subclasses of MenuItem:

- void MenuItem::Draw()

```
{
    /* A virtual function. Each derived class defines its own
    ** behavior through the appropriate redefinition of
**Draw()
    */
}
```

- void MenuItem::Handle(Event&)

```
{
    /* a virtual function. Each derived class defines its own
    ** behavior through the appropriate redefinition of
**Handle() and
    ** Draw()
    */
}
```

Listing 6-20 Header File for Class Menu

```
//
// Menu.hpp
// (c) Copyright 1989 Baldur Systems Corp.
//

class Menu : public Bunch {
protected:
    int    nitem;            //number of items
    int    selcflg;        //keep the selection exclusive
    int    done;
public:
    Menu();
    virtual void Do(char*);        //do the operation
    void Draw();
    void Run();
    void SetStatus(int);
};

//
// Menuitems
//
class MenuItem : public Pane {
protected:
    int    toggle;           // toggle the color
    char   *itmtext;         // menu item text
public:
    virtual void Draw();
    virtual void Handle(Event&);
};
```

MAKING ICONS

Making an icon is fairly straightforward. The six classes required to make an icon are, as follows:

```
#include "pen.hpp"
#include "icon.hpp"
#include "bunch.hpp"
#include "pane.hpp"
#include "manager.hpp"
#include "textmesg.hpp"
```

continued...

The user needs to follow a three-step procedure:

1. Create/modify a special pattern of a 16 x 16 bit grid which models the real-world object.

2. Create/modify a new class, for example specialIcon, the subclass of Icon, to indicate how to manipulate the subject icon.

3. Write a main program to print it out on the screen or a laser printer.

A sample program to make an icon for Chinese "Large" is shown in Listing 6-21 and explained below.

Listing 6-21 Sample Icon for Chinese Character "Large"

```
#include "pen.hpp"
#include "icon.hpp"
#include "bunch.hpp"
#include "pane.hpp"
#include "manager.hpp"
#include "textmesg.hpp"

/*
** large.cpp
**
**
** History:
** Date    Why?
** ====    ====
** 89-May-02   Original code.
** 89-May-28   Chinese "Large" character added to demo.
**
** Test program for "large".
*/

Manager m;
```

continued...

```
static char specialpattern[] = {
    0x00,0x00,
    0x03,0x00,
    0x03,0x00,
    0x03,0x00,
    0x03,0x00,
    0x3f,0xfc,
    0x03,0x00,
    0x03,0x00,
    0x02,0x80,
    0x02,0x80,
    0x04,0x40,
    0x80,0x20,
    0x70,0x1c,
    0,0,0,0,0,0
};

/*
** specialIcon: class derived from Icon. It has a
*/

class specialIcon : public Icon {
public:
    specialIcon(int,int);
    void Handle(Event &);
};

specialIcon::specialIcon(int d,int e) : (specialpat-
tern,d,e,16,16)
{
}

void specialIcon::Handle(Event &e)
{
    if (e.eventType & E_LEFTDOWN) {
    Pen *temp = background;
    background = foreground;
    foreground = temp;
    Draw();
    TextMessage* t = new TextMessage("Hit the left mouse but-
ton",FG_BLACK,FG_HIGHLIGHT);
        m.Insert(t,e.x+xoff,e.y+yoff);
    t->Draw();
    t->Run();
    m.Remove(t);
    delete t;
    }
}
```

continued...

```
main()
{
    char foo[80];
    specialIcon *s1 = new specialIcon(FG_BLACK,FG_HIGHLIGHT);
    specialIcon *s2 = new specialIcon(FG_HIGHLIGHT,FG_BLACK);

    m.Init(FG_BLACK);
    m.Insert(s1,200,200);
    m.Insert(s2,210,210);
    m.Draw();
    Event e;
    do {
    m.Read(e);
    if (e.target != 0) {
        e.target->Handle(e);
    }
    } while (e.key != 'q');
}
```

Creating a Special Pattern of an Icon

Assume a size of two-byte icon is desired, and a Chinese character "Large" is used to demonstrate the procedure. "Large" is partitioned to 16 x 16 tiny squares and represented in bit by the following pattern:

```
static char specialpattern[] = {
    0x00,0x00,
    0x03,0x00,
    0x03,0x00,
    0x03,0x00,
    0x03,0x00,
    0x3f,0xfc,
    0x03,0x00,
    0x03,0x00,
    0x02,0x80,
    0x02,0x80,
    0x04,0x40,
    0x80,0x20,
    0x70,0x1c,
    0,0,0,0,0,0
};
```

For example, the second row is represented by:
```
        0x03,0x00,
```

because boxes 2-g, and h are one, and the other boxes are zero.   The same principle applies for row 3:
```
        0x03,0x00,
```

This special pattern has to be made for each individually different icon. For the structure of the pattern, see the Zortech C++ manual.

Creating Class SpecialIcon

Class specialIcon is derived from class Icon. SpecialIcon takes the special pattern created and displays a bit-mapped image of the real-world object. The specialIcon constructor is used to prepare enough icon space in accordance with the special pattern.

```
class specialIcon : public Icon {
public:
    specialIcon(int,int);
    void Handle(Event &);
};

specialIcon::specialIcon(int d,int e):(specialpattern,d,e,16,16)
{
}
```

The specialIcon class has no other data object other than a public method, Handle() which is redefined in this class to handle iconic image input, text messages and their appearance on the screen.

```
void specialIcon::Handle(Event &e)
{
    if (e.eventType & E_LEFTDOWN) {
    Pen *temp = background;
    background = foreground;
    foreground = temp;
    Draw();
    TextMessage* t = new TextMessage("Hit the left mouse but-
ton",FG_BLACK,FG_HIGHLIGHT);
        m.Insert(t,e.x+xoff,e.y+yoff);
    t->Draw();
    t->Run();
    m.Remove(t);
    delete t;
    }
}
```

Writing a Program to Print an Icon on the Screen or a Laser Printer

A main() program is written to select the background and foreground color of the icon and the location on the screen where the icon and other text messages will appear:

```
main()
{
    char foo[80];
    specialIcon *s1 = new specialIcon(FG_BLACK,FG_HIGHLIGHT);
    specialIcon *s2 = new specialIcon(FG_HIGHLIGHT,FG_BLACK);

    m.Init(FG_BLACK);
    m.Insert(s1,200,200);
    m.Insert(s2,210,210);
    m.Draw();
    Event e;
    do {
    m.Read(e);
    if (e.target != 0) {
        e.target->Handle(e);
    }
    } while (e.key != 'q');

}
```

If an HP laser printer is used to print the icon, the program HPDUMP.EXE is used, as follows:

- Insert System("hpdump") into the main program immediately after Draw()

A sample printout for Chinese "Large" is shown in Figure 6-4.

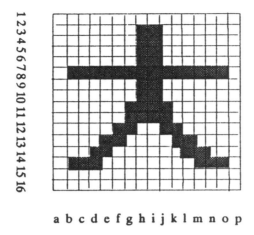

Figure 6-4. A printout of the Chinese character "Large"

Figure 6-5 A sample printout of the Chinese character "Large"

continued...

Making Another Similar Icon

To make another similar icon, for example, the icon "hand", the user need only change the special pattern to model the real hand shape.

```
static char specialpattern[] = {
    0x00,0x00,
    0x01,0x00,
    0x05,0x40,
    0x05,0x50,
    0x05,0x50,
    0x05,0x50,
    0x15,0x50,
    0x15,0x50,
    0x15,0x50,
    0x1F,0xF0,
    0x1F,0xF0,
    0x1F,0Xf0,
    0X1F,0xF0,
    0x1F,0xF0,
    0x0F,0xE0,
    0x00,0x00,
};
```

The resultant printout is shown in Figure 6-5-A.

Figure 6-5 -A A printout of icon "hand".

MAKING A CALCULATOR

The icons in the previous section do not take inputs from the keyboard; the keyboard accepts commands from the left button of the mouse.   This section demonstrates an example icon which combines inputs from both the mouse and the keyboard.

Four classes are required to build a live calculator and will take two numbers from the keyboard to perform four functions: addition(+), subtraction (-), multiplication (*), and division (/).

```
#include "bunch.hpp"
#include "pane.hpp"
#include "manager.hpp"
#include "display.hpp"
```

A three-step procedure is needed to write this sample program (Listing 6-22):

> 1. Create a new class, CalcButton, derived from Pane to design a calculator and all the appropriate buttons .
>
> 2. Create another new class, Calculator, derived from Bunch to bring Calcbutton and Display together in a group.
>
> 3. Write a main() program which sets up a Manager, a Calculator and reads events until the user hits "q" (quit).

The three steps are discussed below, separately.

Listing 6-22 Sample Program for Making a Calculator

```
#include "bunch.hpp"
#include "pane.hpp"
#include "manager.hpp"
#include "display.hpp"

/*
** calc.cpp
**
**
** History:
** Date    Why?
** ====    ====
** 89-Jun-19   Original code.
**
** Calculator demo program
*/
```
continued...

```
class Calculator;

/*
** All the buttons on the calculator are CalcButtons
*/

class CalcButton : public Pane {
private:
    Calculator *target;       // the target calculator
    char symbol[2];           // this button's symbol (+,-,&c)
    Pen *foreground;          // foreground and background colors
    Pen *background;
public:
    CalcButton(Calculator *, char); // create a button with sym-
bol
    void Draw();              // draw itself
    void Handle(Event &);     // Handle any clicks
};

/*
** Calculator class: it is a bunch of CalcButtons and display
*/

class Calculator : public Bunch {
    Display *display;         // the calculator display
    double  accumulator;      // accumulator has the running total
    char    pendingOperation; // next operation to be performed
    Pen     *color;           // gray color
public:
    Calculator();             // construct the calculator
    void Do(char);            // obey a button command
    void Draw();              // draw the calculator
    void Operate(double);     // perform an operation with the arg.
};

/*
** Calcbutton constructor: make a button with the symbol _c_
and
** a pointer to the calculator _t_ it operates upon.
*/

CalcButton::CalcButton(Calculator *t, char c)
{
    target = t;
    *symbol = c;              // string of length 1 (+ the \0)
    *(symbol+1) = '\0';
    xmax = ymax = fg_charbox[FG_Y2];   // size of the button is
'square'
    foreground = new Pen(FG_LIGHT_WHITE);
    background = new Pen(FG_BLACK); // colors are white and
black
}
```

continued...

```
/*
** Draw(): drawing is trivial; paint a black box, then draw a
white
** character on top of it.
*/

void CalcButton::Draw()
{
    background->FillRect(this,0,0,xmax,ymax);
    foreground->MoveTo(this,3,0);
    foreground->Text(this,symbol);
    Flush();
}

/*
** Handle(): if the user clicks the Left mouse on me, tell the
calculator
** that I got clicked
*/
void CalcButton::Handle(Event &e)
{
    if (e.eventType & E_LEFTDOWN) {
    target->Do(*symbol);
    }
    Draw();
}

/*
** symbols[]: an array of symbols used for the calculator keys
*/

char symbols[21] = ".0C/ 123*=456-c789+";


/*
** calculator constructor: creates a calculator, with twenty
buttons
** and a display.
*/

Calculator::Calculator()
{
    accumulator = 0.0;        // calculator's initial value is 0
    CalcButton *b;            // temp. variable

#define XSEP 10
#define YSEP 4
```

continued...

```
/** OK: we set up an array of 4 X 5 buttons **/

    for (int row = 0; row < 4; row++) {
    for (int col = 0; col < 5; col++) {
        b = new CalcButton(this,symbols[row*5+col]);
        Insert(b,30 + (b->xmax + XSEP)*col,YSEP + (b->ymax +
YSEP)*row);
    }
    }

    display = new Display();
    Insert(display,0,(b->ymax + YSEP) * 5);
    xmax = display->xmax;  // make sure that the bunch overlaps
            // all the panes inside it
    ymax = (b->ymax + YSEP) * 5 + display->ymax + YSEP;
    color = new Pen(FG_GRAY);      // the calculator is Gray
}

/*
** Draw(): Draw the calculator gray background
*/

void Calculator::Draw()
{

    color->FillRect(this,0,0,xmax,ymax); // first draw gray
rectangle
    Bunch::Draw();        // then overlay it with the buttons &
}           // display

/*
** Do(): execute a button command
*/

void Calculator::Do(char op)
{
    double atof(char *);

    if (isdigit(op) || op == '.') { // a valid digit
    display->Add(op);        // add it to the
    } else {
    switch (op) {
      case '':              // backarrow? Erase!
        display->Erase();
        break;
      case '=':              // Equals?
        char buf[80];
        Operate(atof(display->Get()));// get whatever we have in
        the
        sprintf(buf,"%lf",accumulator);// display, operate on it
```

continued...

```
      display->Put(buf);      // and then display it on the
      display->Draw();       // screen.
      display->Put("");       // we're ready for next op.
      pendingOperation = 0;
      break;
   case '+':case'-':case'*':case'/': // see above.
      Operate(atof(display->Get()));
      sprintf(buf,"%lf",accumulator);
      display->Put(buf);
      display->Draw();
      display->Put("");
      pendingOperation = op;
      break;
   case 'C':case 'c':       // clear the accumulator
      display->Put("");
      display->Draw();
      accumulator = 0.0;
      break;
   }
  }
}

/*
** Operate(): take the argument and operate upon it depending on
** the previous value of the accumulator. After Operate() accumulator
** has a new value
*/
void Calculator::Operate(double d)
{
    switch (pendingOperation) {
      case '+':
   accumulator += d;
   break;
      case '-':
   accumulator -= d;
   break;
      case '*':
   accumulator *= d;
   break;
      case '/':
   if (d != 0.0) accumulator /= d;
   break;
      default:
   accumulator = d;
   break;
    }
}
```

continued...

```
/*
** Main program: set up a manager, set up a calculator, read
events until
** user hits 'q'
*/

main()
{
    Manager m;
    m.Init(FG_BLUE);
    Calculator* c = new Calculator();
    m.Insert(c,100,100);
    m.Draw();
    Event e;
    do {
    m.Read(e);
    if (e.target != 0) {
        e.target->Handle(e);
    }
    } while (e.key != 'q');
}
```

Creating CalcButton

Class CalcButton, a subclass of Pane, makes buttons for the calculator. A CalcButton has a private pointer to the Calculator to which it belongs, as well as, the operation symbols (+, -, *, /, c) and the background and foreground colors:

```
class Calculator;

class CalcButton : public Pane {
private:
    Calculator *target;     // the target calculator
    char symbol[2];         // this button's symbol (+,-,&c)
    Pen *foreground;        // foreground and background colors
    Pen *background;
```

The CalcButton constructor is used to create buttons with symbols for the Calculator. CalcButton's two methods, Draw(), and Handle(), are redefined in this class:

```
public:
    CalcButton(Calculator *, char); // create a button with sym-
bol
    void Draw();            // draw itself
    void Handle(Event &e); // Handle any clicks from the user
```

The constructor and two methods are explained, as follows:

- Calcbutton constructor: makes a button with the character c and a pointer to the calculator t it operates upon:

```
CalcButton::CalcButton(Calculator *t, char c)
```

- Draw(): drawing is trivial; paint a black box, then draw a white character on top of it.

```
  void CalcButton::Draw()
{
  background->FillRect(this,0,0,xmax,ymax);
  foreground->MoveTo(this,3,0);
  foreground->Text(this,symbol);
  Flush();
}
```

- Handle(): if the user clicks the left mouse, tells the calculator that it receives a click

```
void CalcButton::Handle(Event &e)
{
   if (e.eventType & E_LEFTDOWN) {
   target->Do(*symbol);
   }
   Draw();
}
```

Creating Class Calculator

Class Calculator is derived from Bunch to bring classes CalcButton and Display together. The data object and methods are, as follows:

```
class Calculator : public Bunch {
    Display *display;        // the calculator display
    double  accumulator;    // accumulator has the running total
    char    pendingOperation;// next operation to be performed
    Pen     *color;         // gray color
public:
    Calculator();           // construct the calculator
    void Do(char);          // obey a button command
    void Draw();            // draw the calculator
    void Operate(double);   // perform an operation
//with the arguments.
```

continued...

The constructor and three methods (redefined in this class shown in Listing 6-22) are briefly explained, as follows:

- Calculator constructor: creates a calculator, with an array of 4 x 5 (twenty) buttons and a display.

```
Calculator::Calculator()
{
    accumulator = 0.0;          // calculator's initial value is 0
    CalcButton *b;              // temp. variable
#define XSEP 10
#define YSEP 4

/** OK: we set up an array of 4 X 5 buttons **/

    for (int row = 0; row < 4; row++) {
    for (int col = 0; col < 5; col++) {
        b = new CalcButton(this,symbols[row*5+col]);
        Insert(b,30 + (b->xmax + XSEP)*col,YSEP + (b->ymax +
YSEP)*row);
    }
    }

    display = new Display();
    Insert(display,0,(b->ymax + YSEP) * 5);
    xmax = display->xmax;      // make sure that the bunch overlaps
            // all the panes inside it
    ymax = (b->ymax + YSEP) * 5 + display->ymax + YSEP;
    color = new Pen(FG_GRAY);      // the calculator is Gray
}
```

- Draw(): draws the calculator gray background.
- Do(): executes a button command.
- Operate(): takes the argument and operates upon the argument, depending on the previous value of the accumulator. After Operate(), the accumulator will have a new value.

See Listing 6-22 for detailed definitions of these methods.

Writing a Main Program to Print a Calculator

The main program is written to set up a Manager, a Calculator, and read events until the user hits quit, 'q.'

```
main()
{
    Manager m;
    m.Init(FG_BLUE);
    Calculator* c = new Calculator();
    m.Insert(c,100,100);
    m.Draw();
    Event e;
    do {
  m.Read(e);
  if (e.target != 0) {
     e.target->Handle(e);
  }
    } while (e.key != 'q');
}
```

A printout of a calculator with readout of the last computation is shown in Figure 6-6. This calculator as presently designed does not take consecutive operations, such as (3+6)*7/2; instead, it takes one operation at a time.

For readers who are interested in seeing a more sophisticated menu selection refer to Chapter 9.

(Insert Fig.6-6 A printout of a calculator with readout of the last computation)

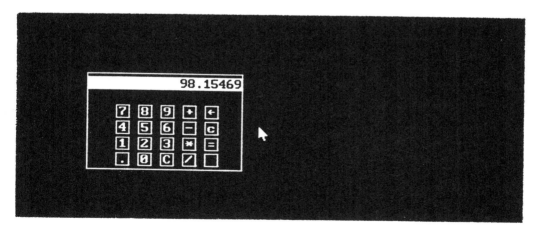

Figure 6-6 A printout of a calculator with a readout of the last calculation.

SUMMARY

- This chapter has presented a design of graphical user control (iconic user interface) environments. The strategies in designing graphical user control environments are encapsulation, code reusability, rapid prototyping iterative development, and hierarchical structure.

- This chapter provides the user with kernels of C++ codes that form the foundation for many graphical control interface designs.

- The nine kernel classes are Pen, Event, Pane, Bunch, Manager, Cursor, Sensor, Queue, and List. These classes then can be used to build their subclasses to serve a particular function in designing a graphical control interface environment. While Smalltalk classes belong to a tree structure, these nine classes do not have a common root origin.

- Classes Pen, Event, Cursor, Sensor, Queue, and List stand independently as the root classes even though much of the public data and methods in these classes can be shared among themselves. The only exception is class Pane which has a chain of subclasses: Pane --- Bunch---- Manager.

- These kernel classes can be classified into the following categories: general management: Manager; image control: Pen, Pane [Bunch]; mouse control: Event, Cursor, Sensor; data structure: List, Queue.

- The responsibility of each of the nine kernel classes includes:
  -Manager: overall control of the screen, for example, image, event, mouse control.

  -Pen: control of the pen, such as color, position, mode.
  - Pane: control of a pane.

  - Bunch: collection of similar panes.

  - Event: describing events of the screen.

  - Cursor: control of the cursor's shapes and movements.

  - Sensor: catching the state of the mouse.

  -- List: general list structure.

  - Queue: general queue structure.

- C++ is used to write these classes. Offspring classes such as Menu and Icon are created from these kernel classes.

- Icon, TextMessage, Display, and Menu are four offspring classes which perform image control duty.

- The responsibility of the four offspring classes are:

  - Icon: Control of image

  - Menu: Controlling user selection

  - TextMessage: Showing prompt messages

  - Display: Interactive text-editing

- Sample icons for Chinese "Large" and handshapes are made using classes: Pen, Icon, Bunch, Pane, Manager, and TextMessage.

- A sample calculator is made using classes: Bunch, Pane, Manager, and Display.

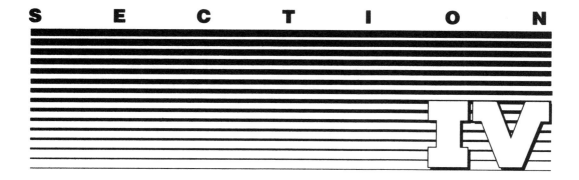

MAKING YOUR PROGRAMS INTELLIGENT WITH OOP

The class structure provided in C++ enables a programmer to represent organized knowledge/data conveniently. This new dimension provides a program with the capability of capturing rule-of-thumb or heuristic expert knowledge (called expert system technology). Programs embedded with expert system technology may enable the user to acquire the judgmental knowledge of experts, such as geologists, doctors, lawyers, bankers, or insurance underwriters.

Expert system technology is merely a new software technique that will make programs more powerful and friendly. By integrating expert systems technology, these programs are empowered with reasoning capability (to obtain new facts from existing ones), query ability (to obtain data and explain to the user the reasons behind a decision), and user conveniences (such as error checking, natural language templates).

Because C++ doesn't allow dynamic defining of data at runtime, an expert system shell may be used to rapidly prototype, test, and refine the structure of the expert system in response to a real world problem. After the prototype has been approved, C++ can then be employed to represent the hierarchical data and knowledge to be prepared for final delivery to multiple computer environments.

In this part, expert system technology is first introduced, C++ is used to represent structured objects/data/knowledge. The focus is on the use of object- oriented programming in representing knowledge for the subsequent deriving of knowledge from expert systems. Readers who are interested in details of expert systems or artificial intelligence are referred to other publication (*C/C++ for Expert Systems*, Management Information Source, Inc, 1989).

Chapter 7 presents knowledge representation and organization in C++, and Chapter 8 discusses deriving knowledge using object rules.

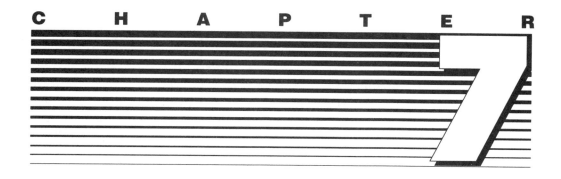

REPRESENTING AND ORGANIZING STRUCTURED KNOWLEDGE/DATA USING OOP(C++)

$\mathbf{O}$bject-oriented programming (OOP) can be used to build expert systems conveniently. OOP in conjunction with expert system technology provides programmers with a new capability for incorporating symbolic representation of facts, data, and heuristic knowledge in their conventional software packages.

Expert systems are different from conventional software programs that provide access to computer capability in arithmetic power and different from decision support systems that provide access to computer capability in distributing information. Expert systems capture and distribute the human expert's expertise in making judgments under various conditions. They "clone" experts by capturing knowledge that is perishable, scarce, vague, and difficult to apply, distribute, or accumulate. Expert systems afford cost-effective services in areas that require symbolic processing of knowledge and rules-of-thumb judgmental problem- solving methods. An initial application of expert systems was in the diagnosis and treatment of human physical disorders; the basic purpose of these systems was to determine what the symptoms indicate and what remedial treatment was appropriate.

Expert system technology is one of the most successful branches of artificial intelligence (AI). Other branches of AI include robotics, voice recognition and synthesis, and vision. Expert system technology started to emerge as a potent force in 1977 when Professor Feigenbaum of Stanford University presented an insight that the problem-solving power of a computer program comes from the knowledge of a given domain it processes, not just from the programming techniques and formalism it contains. However, the author's experience indicates that the programming techniques and formalism may also determine the eventual destiny of an expert system.

This chapter presents the basics of expert system technology and then the representation and organization of knowledge in OOP/C++. It includes basic concepts of expert systems, building frame structures to represent structured knowledge, methods to design frame structures, and implementation of the frame structure with C++.

BASIC CONCEPTS OF EXPERT SYSTEMS

The structure of an expert system resembles a conventional software program, as shown in Figure 7-1. The major components of an expert system are knowledge base, inference engine, user interface mechanism (including explanation facility), and data. Major components of conventional programs are data (or data base), code, interpreter/compiler, and sparse user interface mechanism, but the interpreter/compiler is not obvious to the user. Expert systems are capable of symbol processing, inferring, and explaining.

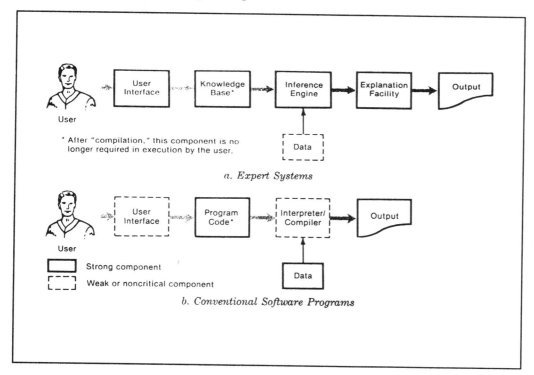

Figure 7.1   Expert systems vs. conventional software programs

In terms of terminology used, expert systems can be considered an advanced form of programming. The terminology of expert systems can be mapped on a one-to-one basis to that of software programs as shown in Table 7-1. For example, a knowledge base of an expert system that contains rules (likely IF-THEN rules) and facts matches the program (code) of a software program. However, a knowledge base is not correspondent to a data base. A knowledge base is executable but not a data base. A data base can only be queried and updated.

Like an interpreter that evaluates a program in the source code and executes the statements, the inference engine takes the statements in a knowledge base and executes them because it contains search control and substitution mechanisms. AI/ES languages such as Lisp, Prolog, and Smalltalk can be used to build an empty package of the knowledge base, inference engine, and user-interface. This package is called an expert system shell or tool. Expert system shells that are used to build expert systems are high-level programming languages with many unconventional conveniences such as explanation and tracing facility.

One-to-One Correspondence in Expert System and Software Program Technologies

Expert_Systems	Software_Programs
Knowledge base	Program
Inference engine	Interpreter
Expert system tool/shell	Programming language
Knowledge engineers	Software engineers/programmer-analysts

Table 7.1

Knowledge Base

The programmer can use three types of knowledge to build expert systems: (1) rules of thumb, (2) facts and relations among components, and (3) assertions and questions. To represent these types of knowledge in the knowledge base, three methods are used:

- Rules to represent rules of thumb
- Frames to represent structured facts and relations
- Logic to represent assertions and queries

All these types can be represented with objects in an OOP such as C++. We will first introduce the concepts but focus on frames in this chapter. Rules and queries will be discussed in Chapter 8.

Rules

Rules are conditional sentences; they are expressed in the form:

IF (premise) FACT 1, FACT 2, ...

THEN (conclusion) FACT 9, FACT 10, ...

For example, If the rule of "starts per month" is as follows:

IF (the number of motor starts per month exceed 20 times)

THEN (increase the operational potential of the motor)

Frames or Units

A frame is also called a unit which contains the hierarchies of objects (components), the attributes of objects that can be assigned, inherited from other frames, or computed through procedures or other computer programs. The attributes are filled in the "slots" of a frame. Figure 7-2 shows a sample unit.

```
┌─────────────────────────────────────────────────────────────┐
│              Sample Frame in ASD_Advisor                      │
│  Frame name:      ASD Adjustable Frequency AC Drive           │
│  Installed to:    Induction motor                             │
│  Inherited from:  ASD                                         │
│  Created by:      6-30-86                                      │
│  Modified by:     7-5-86                                       │
│                                                               │
│  Slot:   Capacity                                             │
│          Type: Real number, value: 0 to 1000 hp               │
│  Slot:   Main component                                       │
│          Type: Alphanumeric, value: INVERTERS                 │
│  Slot:   Usage                                                │
│          Type: Alphabet, value: (Inherited from ASD it is a kind │
│          of ASD)                                              │
│  Slot:   Economics                                            │
│          Type: Real number, value: (Computed from            │
│          PROCEDURE = ECONOMICS)                               │
│  Slot:   Operation                                            │
│          Type: Logic, value: (Rule 5a)                        │
└─────────────────────────────────────────────────────────────┘
```

Figure 7.2 A Sample Unit or Frame.

Logic

Logic expressions consist of predicates and values to assess facts of the real world. A predicate is a statement concerning an object such as:

```
kind-of (adjustable-Frequency-AC-Drive, ASD)
```

The above predicate may be interpreted as an adjustable-frequency AC drive, is a kind of ASD (adjustable speed drive). The object may be either a constant or a variable that may change over time. A predicate may have one or more arguments that are the objects it describes. In the example of ASD_Advisor, the other kind of logic expression is appropriate for asking questions such as the following:

```
      ? - (Indicator_Matrix, X) :- company (X), ASD (X),
economics        (X, excellent).
```

The question can be interpreted as: indicate all possible ASD installations in a given company that can be implemented with only induction motors which are considered to possess excellent economic potential.

Inference Engine

Once the knowledge base is completed, execution can begin through a reasoning mechanism and search control to solve problems. The most common reasoning method in expert systems is the application of the following simple logic rule (also called *modus ponens*):

```
IF A is true, and IF A THEN B is true, then B is true
```

```
The implication of this simple rule is that:
```

```
    IF B is not true, and IF A THEN B is true, A is not true
```

```
Another implication of the simple logic rule is that
```

```
    Given:        IF A, THEN B and
                  IF B,THEN C
    Conclusion:   IF A, THEN C.
```

In other words, IF A is true, THEN we can conclude C is also true.

These three simple reasoning principles are used to examine rules, facts, and relations in expert systems to solve problems. However, to minimize the reasoning time, search control methods are used to determine where to start the substitution process and to choose which rule to examine next when several rules are conflicting at the same point. The two main methods of search are forward and backward chaining. These two methods of chaining may be combined in use in an expert system for maximum efficiency of search control.

Forward Chaining

When the rule interpreter is forward chaining, if premise clauses match the situation, then the conclusion clauses are asserted. For example, in the rule of starts per month, if the real situation matches the premise (that is, the number of motor starts per month exceeds 20), the operational potential of ASDs to the motor will increase. Once the rule is used or "fired," the rule will not be used again in the same search; however, the fact concluded as the result of that rule's firing will be added to the knowledge base. This cycle of finding a matched rule, firing it, and adding the conclusion to the knowledge base will be repeated until no more matched rules are available.

Backward Chaining

Backward chaining mechanism attempts to prove the hypothesis from facts. If the current goal is to determine the fact in the conclusion (hypothesis), then it is necessary to determine whether the premises match the situation. For example,

- Rule One:

```
IF you lose the key and
   gas tank is empty

THEN the car is not running
```

- Rule Two:

```
IF the car is not running and
   you have no cash

THEN you are going to be late
```

```
Fact One: you lost the key

Fact Two: the gas tank is empty
```

For instance, to prove the hypothesis that "you are going to be late," given the facts and rules in the knowledge base (Facts 1 and 2, Rules 1 and 2), apply a backward chaining to determine whether the premises match the situation. Rule 2, containing the conclusion, would be fired first to determine whether the premises match the fact. The knowledge base does not contain the facts in the premises of Rule 2, "the car is not running" and "you have no cash," therefore "the car is not running" becomes the first subgoal. Rule 1 will be fired to determine whether the premises "you lost the key" and "gas tank is empty" match the facts. Because Facts 1 and 2 in the knowledge base match the premise of Rule 1, the subhypothesis is proven. However, the system still has to prove that "you have no cash." This information is neither in the knowledge base nor in the rules since no rule is related to it. The system will then ask the user "IS IT TRUE THAT: you have no cash?" If the answer is "yes," then the second subgoal is satisfied; therefore, the original hypothesis is proven, concluding that "you are going to be late."

Man-Machine Interface

The man-machine interface mechanism produces dialogue between the computer and the user. The current expert system may be equipped to use templates, "menus," mice, or natural language. The expert system may include an explanation module to allow the user to challenge and examine the reasoning process underlying the system's answers. User-interface facilities such as windows, menus, icons are discussed in Chapters 5 and 6.

Uncertainty of Knowledge

Rules obtained from human experts are sometimes uncertain; they described some rules as "maybe," "sometimes," "often," or "not quite certain about the conclusion." The user needs methods to handle these types of uncertain statements. Expert systems like human experts draw inferences based on incomplete information such as unavailable, unknown, or uncertain information. Unavailable or unknown information is resolved by allowing rules to fail if the information needed is critical in evaluating the premise, i.e., the information needed is a condition (IF) statements connected by AND. When IF statements are connected by OR, the absence of one or more statements will not affect the outcome of the rule.

Often the reliability of knowledge inserted into the knowledge base is questionable, an important aspect to expert systems is the ability to represent facts that are not guarenteed to be 100% accurate. The probability of a fact being true is called the fact's Certainty. In most expert systems, the factor number is between 0 and 1, where 0 represents no confidence in the fact, while 1 represents complete trust in the validity of the fact. For example, the user msy assign a CF of 1.0 to:

"IBM is a company"

and perhaps a CF of 0.5, representing 50% surety, to:

"IBM is the best company" .

The CF is an integral part of any fact and is always displayed to the user along with any display of the fact.

"IBM is a company" [CF = 1.0]

"IBM is the best company" [CF = 0.5]

Certainty factors for facts can be established in either of two ways: first, the source of the fact, generally the user, supplies a certainty factor for the fact; second, an expert system uses rules to compute the certainty factor. Any fact NOT assigned a certainty factor is assumed to have a factor of 1.0.

Building Frame Structures

Knowledge which resides in an expert system provides the power of that system. Because knowledge is often abstract and ambiguous, a well-specified language for encoding this knowledge becomes essential. This language is called *knowledge representation languaage* and may employ one or a combination of frames, rules, and logic to represent fact explicitly. OOP can be used as a powerful language to represent knowledge, particularly, the frame structure.

A frame is called a "unit" or "schema" in some AI tools, such as KEE (distributed by IntelliCorp.). A frame structure can provide the expert/specialist with a uniform set of representation services for complex data collections or data bases. A frame is more than a structure that is used in other computer languages such as "C" or Pascal. A frame is a generalized structure containing spaces (called slots). These spaces can be filled with information describing various aspects of that structure, in addition to that slot's value. For example, the slots can contain a default value, a restriction of value to be added, a procedure activated to compute a needed value, or a rule activated when certain conditions are met. Furthermore, a frame is a *generalization* hierarchy whose information is inherited from its parent class. This section discusses the fundamental assumptions and advantages/disadvantages.

Fundamental Assumptions

A fundamental assumption about the frame representation language is that frames can be used to unify and denote a loose collection of objects, for example, related ideas, concepts, facts, and experiences. Frames can be linked into a classification system. Each frame represents a class of objects that is connected to a parent class (called superclass) or a child class (called subclass). A frame contains slots that can be filled with other expressions such as frames, names, identifiers, specifications, relationships between slots, or procedural attachment. Both declarative knowledge ("knowing that" such as facts, relationships and procedural knowledge) and ("knowing how" such as when to do something and the method to do it) can be represented in a frame.

The operation of classifications is one basic reasoning method, i.e., the property of an object in the superclass which does not specify a restriction will be passed down to the object in the subclass. Through this operation, we can apply a whole set of specific knowledge in a particular class to objects in the downstream classes. The user can also guide the search for specific facts about the object in the frame, or make assumptions about properties that must be true for the entire class of frames without checking specific slots.

Advantages/Disadvantages

The advantage lies in the powerful features of a frame, such as default values, declarative knowledge, and procedural attachments. These features are available to experts and specialists for extracting knowledge. In particular, the concept of classification system is analogous to the real world structure of facts and organization. The user relates the concept of frame to daily activities. Properties, relationships, and events can be easily fitted into slots of an object from conditions and situations; restrictions can be attached to the slots to trigger a sequence of actions by the program.

Two difficulties arise in the design of a frame structure. First, the theoretical foundation of the frame assuming that both declarative and procedural knowledge can be contained cost-effectively in the frame requires further research. Second, the implementation of frames in the context of class deserves attention. Class structure of a frame allows the users to change the order of hierarchy and to create subclasses or superclasses to any given class. However, because of inheritance features of frames, special care is needed when a superclass is inserted into an existing classification system to ensure that the properties of slots are properly passed down to subclasses. Because a frame can be attached to a slot, the depth and number of layers of the frame can become infinite and thus prohibit an efficient search in consultation.

Methods to Design Frame Structures

To design a frame structure that will provide classification and inheritance, four essential elements are required: class, unit (entity, or end-class), slot, and inheritance. Note "unit" is a term that can refer to both *class* units and *entity* units. Some systems do not make such a marked distinction between a class and its instances (entities). This treatment is less efficient, but allows for incremental refinement of knowledge. The functions of these elements are described briefly as follows:

- Class: provides a hierarchical structure through an inheritance tree with links (nodes), so we may locate a frame by traversing, either subclass (child) or superclass (parent) links.

- Unit: provides an organization to host slots that will be used to store both declarative and procedural information on a given subject.

- Slot: provides a data structure to hold information regarding a particular attribute of a unit, that is certainty factors and inheritance.

- Inheritance modes that will either enable or disable a class to inherit value and default value from the parent class (superclass) and pass the value and default value to the child class (subclass).

The relationships among the four elements are discussed in Chapter 1 (Figure 1-1) where class contains another class, a unit, or a slot. Depending on whether the value of the slots can be passed down to those of the subclass, slots can be classified as member slots or own slots:

- Member slots: the value of the slot will be inherited by those of the subclass.

- Own slots: the whole slot and the value of the slot.

C++ may be used to build most of these features. This chapter discusses the programming of the four elements.

Class

A class is a set of closely related objects that share the same attributes. The initial class is always the basic class that is the root class of any classes; every other class created thereafter is a subclass of the root class, as shown in Figure 7-3. A class can have slots that will be inherited by subclasses, other classes, or units. The values in the slots of the basic class will also be inherited by all classes.

C++ has a readily available capability for implementing these features into a frame structure. The two difficulties in using C++ to build a frame structure are non-dynamic defining of data during runtime and inflexibility of class hierarchy. Because C++ provides no dynamic defining to allow the user to define problem structures at runtime. When using C++ to create a frame structure, the user needs to know in advance the complete structure of the problem which normally cannot be known before a prototype is completed and tested. A compromise is to use an expert system shell to build an expert system prototype, test and refine the prototype until satisfied, and then use C++ to structure the final system for delivery.

The second problem is more difficult to deal with under the current implementation of C++. Ideally, classes should be implemented in such a way as to allow any change of class structure to be easily incorporated. While creating the root class, the user makes a mistake; class 0 for example, should be the root class instead of class 1. As shown in Figure 7-3, the frame structure should provide the user with facility to change the hierarchy of a class. Another example is the subclass 112 shown in the same illustration. Users find allowing a subclass to have two parent classes is a difficult task.

Due to the current implementation of C++, we will discuss a simplified version of class hierarchy with the following assumptions:

- Classes are not distinguished from units, that is, the structures for classes and units are similar.

- A class can have only a parent class (superclass) with as many child classes (subclasses) as desired; the parent class is the root class.

- Hierarchy of a class cannot be changed easily. When it is changed, care will be given to detailing the attributes that can be inherited.

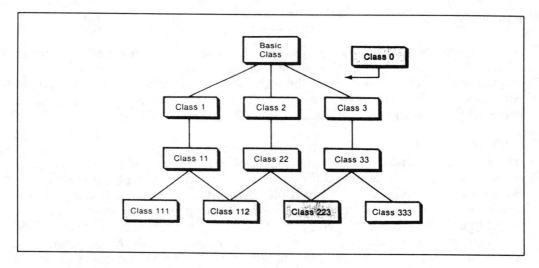

Figure 7.3 A Frame Structure

Unit (Entity)

For clarity, sometimes "entity" is used rather than "unit", both are exchangable in this discussion. Unit structure is similar to the class structure, except that a unit is like a table storing all data regarding characteristics of specific object but a unit cannot have any subclasses.

Slot and Inheritance

A slot is an object that holds information regarding a particular attribute of a unit. A unit can have as many slots as desired. The primary items of information include:

- Slot Name: name of the slot.

- Slot Value: value given by the user.

- Slot Type-Restriction: value is restricted that can be inputted for this slot.

- Slot Source: Source of inheritance for the attribute.

- Slot Destination: destination for the attribute.

- Slot Default-value: value used, if no value is given.

- Slot Certainty: confidence level the user feels about the information.

- Slot Prompt: tool for the user to enter value.

- Slot Documentation: method to document the purpose and function, etc. of the slot.

- Slot Assertable?: determination whether the value of the slot can be asserted.

Slot name and value are self-explanatory. **Slot type-restriction** is used to restrict the value of the slot that can be accepted when input by the user. The type restriction of the slot value, can be restricted by:

- Expression: the value can be any expression

- Number: the value can be any number

- String: the value can be any string

- Boolean: the value must be yes or no

- (member (<atom>*)): the value must be one of the atoms in the list
- (predicate <predicate>): the value must satisfy the lisp predicate
- (class <classname>) : the value must be an entity of classclassname
- Name: the value must be a name

Slot source and **slot destination** are used for inheritance to indicate the original unit of the slot and the destination of the slot (the destination is either :own or :member). **Slot default value** is used if the user does not input a value. **Slot certainty** indicates the confidence level that the user feels about inputting the value. For the purpose of probability calculation, the value is selected to range between zero and one. **Slot prompt** allows the user to input value. Using a more sophisticated tool, a procedure name can be input to compute the appropriate value. The procedure is called a method or a demon. Additionally, this procedure can be implemented in the rule structure. **Slot documentation** is provided for the user to input desirable information regarding the slot for the future user. **Slot assertable?** is either yes or no. Activating slot assertable allows the value to be asserted for future reasoning. If the slot is nonassertable, when reasoning is evoked, the information the slot contains will not be checked; it is considered merely a document.

All of the slot features may not be needed in a specific domain, depending on the requirement of an application. The user may need to tailor the slot features for each applications.

IMPLEMENTATION OF THE FRAME STRUCTURE WITH C++

As discussed before, because C++ is not dynamic-defining, the user may not be able to use it to create run-time classes. The following steps are required to build an applications knowledge representation in C++:

1. Use an expert system tool to prototype, test, and refine the structure of the problem.

2. Pertinent to a specific application domain, draw a class hierarchical chart similar to Figure 7-4.

3. For each class which appears in the organizational chart, define the slot data structure; for each class at the lowest layer, such as HAYWARD-INV, STANFORD-CUSTS, link all entities into a tree for efficient searches in querying the expert system

4. For the private slots, define the member functions that manipulate these slots' values, i.e. get_slot_value(), set_slot_value(), and print_slot_value().

5. For the relationship between parent and children classes, use the C++ inheritance mechanism to define the inheritance. For example, the relation between class 1 and class 11 in Figure 7-3 can be defined as:

```
class_11: Public class_1 /* .... */
```

An inventory control system may be used as an example to demonstrate how C++ is used to represent frame knowledge.

Inventory Control System-- An Example

The Inventory Control System (ICS) discussed in Chapter 1 is recapitulated to serve a demonstration purpose.

```
Object---KNOWLEDGE-SOURCE
            |-HOST
            -LOCATION--WAREHOUSE
                    -DEALER
            -INVENTORY--WAREHOUSE-INV--SAN-FRAN-INV
                    |-DEALER-INV--STANFORD-INV
                                    |-PALO-ALTO-INV
                                    |-HAYWARD-INV
            -CUSTOMER--STANFORD-CUSTS
                    |-PALO-ALTO-CUSTS
                    |-HAYWARD-CUSTS
            -SALES-RECORDS--SAN-FRAN-SALES-RECORDS
```

Figure 7-4 The Class Structure for the Inventory Control System

Assume Figure 7-4 represents the object structure of an automobile dealership. The dealer wishes to gather information from the dealer warehouse database and other dealers. Currently, to obtain information about the availability or price of a part, the dealer is required to:

- find the Part ID number the warehouse uses for the part to order.

- call the warehouse and request information about availability or pricing
- wait 2-3 days for the request to be processed and a reply initiated.

In addition to this procedure, there are two problems associated with the responsibilities of the warehouse.

- warehouse personnel must be familiar with dBASE III, and Lotus 1-2-3
- information requested may be inaccurate due to processing lag times or inaccuracies associated with a high volume of requests.

An expert system tool, IQ-200, is first used to rapid-prototype the ICS (a description of IQ-200 is presented in Appendix B). The five tasks required to build this ICS are, as follows:

1. uses structures called OBJECTS to represent groups of information, such as an inventory on a specific part in the warehouse.
2. uses structures called KNOWLEDGE-SOURCES to represent the various sources of information, such as a warehouse dBASE III program files.
3. uses structures called RULES to serve as guidelines for making decisions based upon the information in other objects or on a Host.
4. uses a REASONING SYSTEM (an inference engine) to derive information from the Knowledge Source Objects.
5. uses structures called HOSTS to represent the location of information from external sources (the phone number and login procedures of the warehouse computers) and to interface with them.

This chapter concentrates at representing structured knowledge (items 1 and 2), Chapter 8 presents examples of rules (item 4) and inferencing (item 5), and Chapter 10 examines intelligent interface with various data bases (item 5).

The sample application stores the inventory of parts in dBASE III files. The warehouse file we will use is fairly simple. Below is a sample listing of the dBASE file WARE.DBF:

Record#	NAME	CIL	OIL	COST	DISCOUNT	MIN_ORD	ORDER_TIME
1	oil_pump	20	30	50.00	0.00	2	21
2	oil_pan	10	50	15.00	0.00	2	21
3	cooling_fan	2	23	45.00	0.00	1	28
4	fan_belt	10	45	8.00	1.00	5	14
5	battery	30	50	22.00	5.00	5	14
6	headlight	50	50	20.00	3.00	41	4
7	parking_brake	28	30	17.50	0.00	1	21
8	distributor	30	23	80.00	0.00	1	28
9	spark_plug	100	120	0.50	0.10	20	14
10	tire	100	125	80.00	10.00	4	28
11	fuel_pump	20	25	45.00	0.00	1	28
12	ignition_coil	30	31	25.00	0.00	1	28

As the listing show, the warehouse contains inventories on 12 different parts. Selecting the first part as a example, indicates:

Record#	NAME	CIL	OIL	COST	DISCOUNT	MIN_ORD	ORDER_TIME
1	oil_pump	20	30	50.00	0.00	2	21

This dBASE III record describes the inventory on a part called OIL_PUMP:

```
Current Inventory Level (CIL)   20
Optimal Inventory Level (OIL)   30
Cost       $50.00
Discount         $ 0.00
Minimum Order Quantity (MIN_ORD)   2
Days Until Delivery (ORDER_TIME)   21
```

Information will be discussed from four of the fields for each part:: the CIL, OIL, COST, and DISCOUNT.

For the inventory control system, a number of inventories for automobile parts will be tracked. An inventory of a part consists of the part's name, its current inventory level (CIL), the optimal inventory level of the part (OIL), the cost of the part, and an optional discount. (The Min_Ord and Order_Time fields will not be used in the following examples.) Thus, as a sample inventory of Battery:

```
Name:   Battery
CIL: 30
OIL: 50
COST:   22.00
DISCOUNT: 5.00
```

To store this information, we will create an object called an ENTITY with SLOTS called Name, Cil, Oil, Cost, and Discount (thus an ICS Entity corresponds to a dBASE record, ICS Slots correspond to dBASE fields). Each of these Slots has a VALUE that is limited by a CONSTRAINT which defines the type of value the VALUE can assume. For this entity, we have slot values of (constraints are in brackets)

```
Battery{:NAME}
30 {:INTEGER}
50 {:INTEGER}
22.00  {:NUMBER}
5.00 {:NUMBER}
```

However, since there are many parts, more than one of the above inventories will be created. The creation of many entities can be simplified by creating a CLASS object grouping of all the inventories together. Assuming this class object is called PARTS, a tree structure will be created similar to

```
Object---PARTS
     {Battery-Parts, Distributor-Parts, ...}
```

[Note: Object is the root of the tree structure.]

The class PARTS contained many specific parts, such as, Battery-Parts, and several slots: NAME, CIL, OIL, COST, and DISCOUNT.

Converting the ICS Frame Representation into C++

The class structure for the inventory control system is shown in Figure 7-4. Listing 7-1 shows a C++ implementation of the class structure. The subprograms for individual classes shown in Figure 7-4 and their associated slots are self-explanatory.

The objective of Listing 7-1 is to translate the hierarchy of the dealership inventory relationship shown in Figure 7-4 into a C++ class structure. The root (base) class is the basic class with four subclasses: location, inventory, customer, and sales-records. These four classes are declared to be friend classes, so their data and methods may be shared. Their own data and methods are subsequently declared.

The subclasses of these four classes and the child classes of the subclasses (e.g. Stanford_inventory) are further declared.

Listing 7-2 exhibits the programs that initialize classes by using constructors and define member functions in the classes shown in Listing 7-1, such as

```
Inv* location::get_slot_value2()
{
   Inv* temp = NULL;
```

Listing 7-1 The Inventory Control System Class Structure in C+ +

```
/****************************************************************
**************
       This header file defines the knowledge representation
data structure
   in the inventory control system in C++.
   Inventory Control System class structure :

   Object
          |
   ------------------------------------------------------
      |               |              |             |
   Location_Class  Inventory_Class  Customer_Class
Sales_Records_Class    |                     |             |
   ----------        |        -------------- ------------
sf_sales_record_class
    |         |        |          |       |           |
  Warehouse  Dealer  WH_Inv   DL_Inv  ST_Cus      HY_Cus
                       |         |
       SF_Inv      --------
          |            |
        ST_Inv     HY_Inv


****************************************************************
**/
/*
**   icsclass.h
**
**Copyright 1989, Baldur Systems Corp.
**   Define each class.
**
**   Date:      8/6/89
*/ Revised for the Zortech implementation


/*-------------------------------define class-----------*/

class basic_class {
   friend class   location;
   friend class   inv;
   friend class   cust;
   friend class   sales_records;
};
```

continued...

```
/*-------------------------------------------cust class-------*/

class cust : public basic_class {
   char_slot        *dealer;
   char_slot        *name;
   char_slot        *part;
   int_slot         *number;
   char_slot        *order_date;
   char_slot        *time;
   friend class st_cust;
   friend class hayward_cust;
public:
   cust();
   ~cust() { delete dealer; delete name; delete part;
         delete order_date; delete number; delete time;
      }    /*destructor*/
   void  set_slotval();                      /*set the slot value*/
   Cust* get_slotval();                        /*get the slot value*/
   void  prn_value();
};

/*-------------------------------------------st_cust class---*/
/*Inheritance from class cust
*/

class st_cust : public cust {};


/*-------------------------------------------inv class------
-*/

class inv : public basic_class {
   char_slot     *name;                   /*part name*/
   int_slot      *cil;                    /*current inv level*/
   int_slot      *oil;                    /*optimal inv level*/
   friend class dealer_inv;
   friend class warehs_inv;
public:
   inv();
   ~inv() { delete name; delete cil; delete oil;}
   void set_slotval();
   Inv* get_slotval();
   void prn_value();
};


/*-------------------------------------------dealer_inv class-----
*/
/*Inherited from class inv
*/
class dealer_inv : public inv {};
```

continued...

```
/*----------------------------------------st_inv class--------
*/
/*Inherited from class dealer_inv
*/
class st_inv : public dealer_inv {};


/*---------------------------------------warehs_inv class-----
*/
/*Inherited from class inv
*/

class warehs_inv : public inv {
   double slot    *cost;
   double slot    *discount;
   int slot       *min_order;
   char slot      *order_time;
public:
   warehs_inv();
   ~warehs_inv() { delete order_time; delete cost;
           delete min_order; delete discount;}
   void set_slotval1();
   Ware_Inv* get_slotval1();
   void prn_value1();
};


/*-----------------------------------------sf_inv class-----
*/
/*Inheritance from class warehs_inv
*/

class sf_inv : public warehs_inv {};


/*--------------------------------------------location
class-----------*/
class location : public basic_class {
   char slot         *address;            /*address of the
location*/
   char slot         *phone;              /*phone number of
the loc*/
   class  invent : public inv {} *invntory;   /*inventory sub-
class*/
   friend class dealer;
   friend class warehs;
public:
   location();
   ~location() {  delete address; delete phone;}
   void set_slotval();                    /*set the slot value*/
   Loc* get_slotval1();                   /*get the address,
phone*/
```

continued...

```
    Inv* get_slotval2();                    /*get the subclass inventory
value*/
    void prn_value();
};



/*-------------------------------------------------dealer
class-----------*/
/*Inherited from class location
*/

class dealer : public location {
    class  custmers : public cust {} *custm;
public:
    dealer() { custm = new custmers;}
    ~dealer() { delete custm;}
    void set_cust_slotval();
        Cust* get_cust_slotval();
    void prn_cust_slotval();
};



/*-------------------------------------------sales_records
class-------*/
class sales_records : public  basic_class {
    int slot         *sale_number;
    char slot         *date;
    char slot      *part;
    int slot      *number_sold;
    double slot         *cost;
    double slot    *total_sale;
    char slot       *sold_to;
    friend class sf_sales_records;
public:
    sales_records();
        ~sales_records() { delete date; delete part;
                    delete sold_to; delete sale_number;
                delete number_sold; delete cost;
            delete total_sale;}
    void set_slotval();
    Sales_Rec* get_slotval();
    void prn_value();
};



/*-------------------------------------------sf_sales_records
class--*/
/*Inherited from class sales_records
*/
```

continued...

```
class sf_sales_records : public sales_records {};


/*--------------------------------------------------warehs
class---------*/
/*Inherited from class location
*/

class warehs : public location {
   class  sales_recs : public sales_records {} *sales_rec;
public:
   warehs() {sales_rec = new sales_recs;}
   ~warehs() { delete sales_rec;}
   void set_sales_recs_slotval();
       Sales_Rec* get_sales_recs_slotval();
};


/*
**   ics.h
**
**   Define the overloaded functions which are used in building
**    KB.
**   Date:      8/6/89
**
*/


#define    FAIL           0
#define    SUCCEED        1


struct slot_node {         /*slot node used in the slot list*/
   char      name[15];
   slot_node*    next;
};

struct cls_slot {
   char              name[15];
   slot_node*        sllist;
};


/*--------------------------------------------------For ICS
-------------*/
/*
**   Define each class node and entity node structure for the
**   leaves of the class tree.
**   Because C++ is compiler language instead of intepreter
**   language,
```

continued...

```
**   it is impossible to dynamically define the data structure
in **   run time.
*/


/*
** st_cust class
*/
struct stcust_etynd {                    /*st_cust class entity
node*/
    char            name[15];
    st_cust*                  entity;
    stcust_etynd*             next;
};

struct stcust_class {                     /*st_cust class node*/
    char            name[15];
    slot_node*                slist;
    stcust_etynd*             elist;
};


/*
** st inv  class
*/
struct stinv_etynd {                  /*st_inv class entity node*/
    char            name[15];
    st_inv*                   entity;
    stInv_etynd*              next;
};

struct stinv_class {                   /*st_inv class node*/
    char            name[15];
    slot_node*                slist;
    stinv_etynd*              elist;
};


/*
** san francisco inv  class
*/
struct sfinv_etynd {                  /*sf_inv class entity node*/
    char            name[15];
    sf_inv*                   entity;
    sfInv_etynd*              next;
};

struct sfinv_class {                   /*sf_inv class node*/
    char            name[15];
    slot_node*                slist;
    sfinv_etynd*              elist;
};


/*
**   warehouse class
```

continued...

```
*/
struct warehs_etynd {
   char            name[15];
   warehs*                 entity;
   warehs_etynd*           next;
};

struct warehs_class {
   char            name[15];
   slot_node*       slist;
   warehs_etynd*        elist;
};

/*
**   dealer class
*/
struct dealer_etynd {
   char            name[15];
   dealer*                 entity;
   dealer_etynd*           next;
};

struct dealer_class {
   char            name[15];
   slot_node*       slist;
   dealer_etynd*        elist;
};

/*
**   sf_sales_records class
*/
struct sfsalrec_etynd {
   char            name[15];
   sf_sales_records*       entity;
   sfsalrec_etynd*         next;
};

struct sfsalrec_class {
   char            name[15];
   slot_node*       slist;
   sfsalrec_etynd*       elist;
};

/*--------------------------------Overload define-----------*/
/*
** The best way to generalize the routines.
*/
overload addslot_clsnd;
void addslot_clsnd(cls_slot*,stcust_class*);     /*for st_cust
class*/
void addslot_clsnd(cls_slot*,stinv_class*);      /*for st_inv
class*/
```

continued...

```
void addslot_clsnd(cls_slot*,sfinv_class*);        /*for sf_inv
class*/
void addslot_clsnd(cls_slot*,warehs_class*);       /*for warehs
class*/
void addslot_clsnd(cls_slot*,dealer_class*);       /*for dealer
class*/
void addslot_clsnd(cls_slot*,sfsalrec_class*);     /*for
sf_sales_rec class*/

overload addety_clsnd;
void addety_clsnd(char*,st_cust*,stcust_class*); /*for st_cust
class*/
void addety_clsnd(char*,st_inv*,stinv_class*);     /*for st_inv
class*/
void addety_clsnd(char*,sf_inv*,sfinv_class*);     /*for sf_inv
class*/
void addety_clsnd(char*,warehs*,wareha_class*);    /*for warehs
class*/
void addety_clsnd(char*,dealer*,dealer_class*);    /*for dealer
class*/
void addety_clsnd(char*,sf_sales_records*,sfsalrec_class*);
/*for sf_sales_rec class*/

overload p_entity_name;
void p_entity_name(stcust_etynd*);         /*for st_cust class*/
void p_entity_name(stinv_etynd*);          /*for st_inv class*/
void p_entity_name(sfinv_etynd*);          /*for sf_inv class*/
void p_entity_name(warehs_etynd*);         /*for warehs class*/
void p_entity_name(dealer_etynd*);          /*for dealer class*/
void p_entity_name(sfsalrec_etynd*);         /*for sf_sales_rec
class*/

overload p_clsnode;
void p_clsnode(stcust_class*);             /*for st_cust class*/
void p_clsnode(stinv_class*);              /*for st_inv class*/
void p_clsnode(sfinv_class*);              /*for sf_inv class*/
void p_clsnode(warehs_class*);             /*for warehs class*/
void p_clsnode(dealer_class*);             /*for dealer class*/
void p_clsnode(sfsalrec_class*);           /*for sf sale rec class*/
              overload f_entity_node;
st_cust* f_entity_node(char*,stcust_class*);  /*for st_cust
class*/
st_inv*  f_entity_node(char*,stinv_class*);   /*for st_inv
class*/
sf_inv*  f_entity_node(char*,sfinv_class*);   /*for sf_inv
class*/
warehs*  f_entity_node(char*,warehs_class*);  /*for warehs
class*/
dealer*  f_entity_node(char*,dealer_class*);  /*for dealer
class*/
sf_sales_records*  f_entity_node(char*,sfsalrec_class*);
/*for sf_sale class*/
```

continued...

```
                   overload f_all_entities;
stcust_etynd* f_all_entities(stcust_class*);   /*for st_cust
class*/
stinv_etynd* f_all_entities(stinv_class*);     /*for st_inv
class*/
sfinv_etynd* f_all_entities(sfinv_class*);     /*for sf_inv
class*/
warehs_etynd* f_all_entities(warehs_class*);   /*for warehs
class*/
dealer_etynd* f_all_entities(dealer_class*);   /*for dealer
class*/
sfsalrec_etynd* f_all_entities(sfsalrec_class*);   /*for sf sal
rec class*/
                   overload f_e_w_s;
stcust_etynd* f_e_w_s(char*,char*, stcust_class*);   /*for
st_cust class*/
stinv_etynd* f_e_w_s(char*,char*, stinv_class*);   /*for st_inv
class*/
sfinv_etynd* f_e_w_s(char*,char*,sfinv_class*);  /*for sf_inv
class*/
warehs_etynd* f_e_w_s(char*,char*, warehs_class*);  /*for
warehs_inv class*/
dealer_etynd* f_e_w_s(char*,char*,dealer_class*);  /*for
dealer_inv class*/
sfsalrec_etynd* f_e_w_s(char*,char*,sfsalrec_class*);  /*for
sf sales_records class*/



/*
**   slotdef.h
**
**   Define the slot structure
**   Date:    8/6/89
*/

struct char_slot {                          /*the slot value is
char*/
   char     slot_name[15];
   char     slot_value[15];
};

struct double_slot {                        /*the slot value is
double*/
   char     slot_name[15];
   double      slot_value;
};

struct int_slot {                           /*the slot value is
int*/
   char     slot_name[15];
   int      slot_value;
};
```

continued...

```
#define     SLOTNAME      15
#define     SLOTVALUE     15
#define     SLOT_END      "END"


/*
**     parse.h
**
**     Define the structure used in parsing query.
**     Date:     8/6/89
**
*/


#define     CASE1     1     /*C and E are instantiated without
slot*/
#define     CASE2     2     /*C is instantiated but E isn't without
slot*/
#define     CASE3     3     /*C and E are instantiated with slot
var*/
#define     CASE4     4     /*C is instantiated but E isn't with
slot var*/
#define     CASE5     5     /*C and E are instantiated with slot
constant*/
#define     CASE6     6     /*C is instantiated but E isn't with
slot constant*/
#define     CASE7     7     /*entity is instantiated and class
isn't*/
#define     ZERO      0
#define     ONE       1
#define     TWO       2
#define     THREE     3
#define     FOUR      4
#define     FIVE      5
#define     SIX       6
#define     SEVEN     7
#define     EIGHT     8


/*
**     tempstru.h
**
**This header file defines some structures for inputting and
**     outputting
**     the class slot data.
**
**     Include:     Location,Inventory,Customer
**     Date:        7/22/89
*/
```

continued...

```
struct Loc {                                    /*location*/
   char_slot       *address;        /*address of the loca-
tion*/
   char_slot       *phone;              /*phone number of the
loc*/
};


struct Inv {                                    /*inventory*/
   char_slot       *name;           /*part name*/
   int_slot        *cil;            /*current inventory
level*7
   int_slot        *oil;            /*optimal inventory
level*7
};


struct Cust {                                   /*customer*/
   char_slot            *dealer;
   char_slot            *name;
   char_slot            *part;
   int_slot             *number;
   char_slot            *order_date;
   char_slot            *time;
};

struct Sales_Rec {                      /*sales records*/
   int_slot        *sale_number;
   char_slot       *date;
   char_slot       *part;
   int_slot     *number_sold;
   double_slot *cost;
   double_slot *total_sale;
   char_slot    *sold_to;
};

struct Ware_Inv {                       /*warehouse inventory*/
   double_slot      *cost;
   double_slot          *discount;
   int_slot     *min_order;
   char_slot        *order_time;
};
```

Listing 7-2 The ICS Class Constructors and Member Functions

```
/*
**   icskb0.cpp
**   Define the member functions of each class.
**
**   Date:     8/6/89
*/

#include "stream.hpp"
#include "string.h"
#include "slotdef.h"
#include "tempstru.h"
#include "icsclass.h"


/*---------------------------------------cust_class----*/

cust::cust()
{
    strcpy(dealer->slot_name,"dealer");
    strcpy(dealer->slot_value,"");
    strcpy(name->slot_name,"name");
    strcpy(name->slot_value,"");
    strcpy(part->slot_name,"part");
    strcpy(part->slot_value,"");
    strcpy(number->slot_name,"number");
    number->slot_value = 0;
    strcpy(order_date->slot_name,"order_date");
    strcpy(order_date->slot_value,"");
    strcpy(time->slot_name,"time");
    strcpy(time->slot_value,"");
}

Cust* cust::get_slotval()                    /*get the slot value*/
{
    Cust* temp = new Cust;

    strcpy(temp->dealer->slot_value,dealer->slot_value);
    strcpy(temp->dealer->slot_name,dealer->slot_name);
    strcpy(temp->name->slot_value,name->slot_value);
    strcpy(temp->name->slot_name,name->slot_name);
    strcpy(temp->part->slot_value,part->slot_value);
    strcpy(temp->part->slot_name,part->slot_name);
    temp->number->slot_value = number->slot_value;
    strcpy(temp->number->slot_name,number->slot_name);
    strcpy(temp->order_date->slot_value,order_date->slot_value);
    strcpy(temp->order_date->slot_name,order_date->slot_name);
    strcpy(temp->time->slot_value,time->slot_value);
    strcpy(temp->time->slot_name,time->slot_name);
    return temp;
}
```

continued...

```
void cust::set_slotval()                        /*set the slot value*/
{


    cout << "\n" << dealer->slot_name << ":   ";
    cin >> dealer->slot_value;
         cout << name->slot_name << ":   ";
    cin >> name->slot_value;
         cout << part->slot_name << ":   ";
    cin >> part->slot_value;
         cout << number->slot_name << ":   ";
    cin >> number->slot_value;
         cout << order_date->slot_name << ":   ";
    cin >> order_date->slot_value;
         cout << time->slot_name << ":   ";
    cin >> time->slot_value;
}


void cust::prn_value()
{
    cout << "\n" << dealer->slot_name << ": " << dealer-
>slot_value;
    cout << "   " << name->slot_name << ": " << name->slot_value;
    cout << "   " << part->slot_name <<  ": "<< part->slot_value;
    cout << "   " << number->slot_name <<  ": " << number-
>slot_value;
    cout << "   " << order_date->slot_name << ": " << order_date-
>slot_value;
    cout << "   " << time->slot_name << ": " << time->slot_value;
}


/*----------------------------------------inv_class----*/


inv::inv()
{
    strcpy(cil->slot_name,"cil");
    cil->slot_value = oil->slot_value = 0;
    strcpy(oil->slot_name,"oil");
    strcpy(name->slot_name,"name");
    strcpy(name->slot_value,"");
}
```

continued...

```
void inv::set_slotval()
{
   cout << "\n" << name->slot_name << ":   ";
   cin >> name->slot_value;
   cout << cil->slot_name << ":   ";
   cin >> cil->slot_value;
   cout << oil->slot_name << ":   ";
   cin >> oil->slot_value;
}


Inv* inv::get_slotval()
{
   Inv* temp = new Inv;

   strcpy(temp->name->slot_name,name->slot_name);
   strcpy(temp->name->slot_value,name->slot_value);
   strcpy(temp->cil->slot_name,cil->slot_name);
   temp->cil->slot_value = cil->slot_value;
   strcpy(temp->oil->slot_name,oil->slot_name);
   temp->oil->slot_value = oil->slot_value;
   return temp;
}

void inv::prn_value()
{
   cout << "\n" << name->slot_name << ": "<< name->slot_value;
   cout << "   " << cil->slot_name << ":   " << cil->slot_value;
   cout << "   " << oil->slot_name << ":   " << oil->slot_value;
}


/*-------------------------------------------warehs_inv class-
----*/

warehs_inv::warehs_inv()
{
   strcpy(cost->slot_name,"cost");
   cost->slot_value = 0.0;
   strcpy(discount->slot_name,"discount");
   discount->slot_value = 0.0;
   strcpy(min_order->slot_name,"min_order");
   min_order->slot_value = 0;
      strcpy(order_time->slot_name,"order_time");
         strcpy(order_time->slot_value,"");

}
```

continued...

```
void warehs_inv::set_slotval1()
{
    cout << "\n" << cost->slot_name << ":  ";
    cin >> cost->slot_value;
    cout << discount->slot_name << ":  ";
    cin >> discount->slot_value;
    cout << min_order->slot_name << ":  ";
    cin >> min_order->slot_value;
    cout << order_time->slot_name << ":  ";
    cin >> order_time->slot_value;
}

Ware_Inv* warehs_inv::get_slotval1()
{
    Ware_Inv* temp = new Ware_Inv;

    strcpy(temp->cost->slot_name,cost->slot_name);
    temp->cost->slot_value = cost->slot_value;
    strcpy(temp->discount->slot_name,discount->slot_name);
    temp->discount->slot_value = discount->slot_value;
    strcpy(temp->min_order->slot_name,min_order->slot_name);
    temp->min_order->slot_value = min_order->slot_value;
    strcpy(temp->order_time->slot_name,order_time->slot_name);
    strcpy(temp->order_time->slot_value,order_time->slot_value);
    return temp;
}

void warehs_inv::prn_value1()
{
    cout << "\n" << cost->slot_name << ":  "<< cost->slot_value;
    cout << "  " << discount->slot_name << ":  " << discount-
>slot_value;
    cout << "  " << min_order->slot_name << ":  " << min_order-
>slot_value;
    cout << "  " << order_time->slot_name << ":  " << order_time-
>slot_value;
}

/*------------------------------------------------loca-
tion class-------------*/
location::location()
{
    strcpy(address->slot_name,"address");
    strcpy(address->slot_value,"");
    strcpy(phone->slot_name,"phone");
    strcpy(phone->slot_value,"");
    invntory = new invent;
}
```

continued...

```
void location::set_slotval()
{
    cout << "\n" << address->slot_name << ":   ";
    cin >> address->slot_value;
    cout << phone->slot_name << ":   ";
    cin >> phone->slot_value;
    invntory->set_slotval();
}

Loc* location::get_slotval1()
{
    Loc* temp = new Loc;

    strcpy(temp->address->slot_name,address->slot_name);
    strcpy(temp->address->slot_value,address->slot_value);
    strcpy(temp->phone->slot_name,phone->slot_name);
    strcpy(temp->phone->slot_value,phone->slot_value);
    return temp;
}

Inv* location::get_slotval2()
{
    Inv* temp = new Inv;

    temp = invntory->get_slotval();
    return temp;

}


void location::prn_value()
{
    cout << "\n" << address->slot_name << ":   " << address->slot_value;
    cout << " " << phone->slot_name << ":" << phone->slot_value;
    invntory->prn_value();   /*print out the subclass inventory value*/
}


/*---------------------------------------------------------
dealer_class-------*/


void dealer::set_cust_slotval()
{
    custm->set_slotval();
}

Cust* dealer::get_cust_slotval()
{
```

continued...

```
    Cust* temp = new Cust;

    temp = custm->get_slotval();
    return temp;
}

void dealer::prn_cust_slotval()
{
    custm->prn_value();
}

/*-----------------------------------------------------
warehs_class------*/

void warehs::set_sales_recs_slotval()
{
    sales_rec->set_slotval();
}

Sales_Rec* warehs::get_sales_recs_slotval()
{
    Sales_Rec* temp = new Sales_Rec;

    temp = sales_rec->get_slotval();
    return temp;
}


/*----------------------------------sales_records class--*/


sales_records::sales_records()
{
    strcpy(sale_number->slot_name,"sale_number");
    sale_number->slot_value = 0;
    strcpy(number_sold->slot_name,"number_sold");
    number_sold->slot_value = 0;
    strcpy(date->slot_name,"date");
    strcpy(date->slot_value,"");
    strcpy(part->slot_name,"part");
    strcpy(part->slot_value,"");
    strcpy(sold_to->slot_name,"sold_to");
    strcpy(sold_to->slot_value,"");
    strcpy(cost->slot_name,"cost");
    strcpy(total_sale->slot_name,"total_sale");
    cost->slot_value = total_sale->slot_value = 0.0;
}
```

continued...

```
void sales_records::set_slotval()
{
   cout << "\n" << sale_number->slot_name << ":   ";
   cin >> sale_number->slot_value;
   cout << date->slot_name << ":   ";
   cin >> date->slot_value;
   cout << part->slot_name << ":   ";
   cin >> part->slot_value;
   cout << number_sold->slot_name << ":   ";
   cin >> number_sold->slot_value;
   cout << cost->slot_name << ":   ";
   cin >> cost->slot_value;
   cout << total_sale->slot_name << ":   ";
   cin >> total_sale->slot_value;
   cout << sold_to->slot_name << ":   ";
   cin >> sold_to->slot_value;
}

Sales_Rec* sales_records::get_slotval()
{
   Sales_Rec* temp = new Sales_Rec;

   strcpy(temp->sale_number->slot_name,sale_number->slot_name);
   temp->sale_number->slot_value = sale_number->slot_value;
   strcpy(temp->date->slot_name,date->slot_name);
   strcpy(temp->date->slot_value,date->slot_value);
   strcpy(temp->part->slot_name,part->slot_name);
   strcpy(temp->part->slot_value,part->slot_value);
   strcpy(temp->number_sold->slot_name,number_sold->slot_name);
   temp->number_sold->slot_value = number_sold->slot_value;
   strcpy(temp->cost->slot_name,cost->slot_name);
   temp->cost->slot_value = cost->slot_value;
   strcpy(temp->total_sale->slot_name,total_sale->slot_name);
   temp->total_sale->slot_value = total_sale->slot_value;
   strcpy(temp->sold_to->slot_name,sold_to->slot_name);
   strcpy(temp->sold_to->slot_value,sold_to->slot_value);
   return temp;
}


void sales_records::prn_value()
{
   cout << "\n" << sale_number->slot_name << ":  " << sale_number->slot_value;
   cout << "   " << date->slot_name << ":  " << date->slot_value;
   cout << "   " << part->slot_name << ":  " << part->slot_value;
   cout << "   " << number_sold->slot_name << ":  " << number_sold->slot_value;
   cout << "   " << cost->slot_name << ":  " << cost->slot_value;
   cout << "   " << total_sale->slot_name << ":  " << total_sale->slot_value;
   cout << "   " << sold_to->slot_name << ":   " << sold_to->slot_value;
}
```
continued...

```
/*
** Building  slot name lists and their initializations
**
**   icskb1.cpp
**   Define some funtions which  will be used for initializa-
tion.
**   Date:     8/6/89
*/

#include <stream.hpp>
#include <string.h>
#include "slotdef.h"
#include "tempstru.h"
#include "icsclass.h"
#include "ics.h"

extern stcust_class* STCUST_CLASS;       /*st_cust class node*/
extern stinv_class*  STINV_CLASS;        /*st_inv class node*/
extern sfinv_class*  SFINV_CLASS;        /*sf_inv class node*/
extern warehs_class* WAREHS_CLASS;       /*warehs class node*/
extern dealer_class* DEALER_CLASS;       /*dealer class node*/
extern sfsalrec_class* SFSALREC_CLASS;   /*sf sale rec class
node*/


/*
**   C++ does not support the dynamic defining of the data
**    structure.
**   In order to do  reasoning in an object- oriented
**    knowledge base, the
**   developer should initialize each class name, the slot
**   names which defined
**   in the class definition before starting reasoning .
*/
/*
** Make up the slot name list of the class
** Genaric function.
*/

cls_slot* make_up_cls_slot(char *clsname,char* slot[])
{
   cls_slot* temp = new cls_slot;
   int i = 0;

   strcpy(temp->name,clsname);
   temp->sllist = NULL;
   while(strcmp(slot[i],SLOT_END))
   {
     slot_node*  temp1 = new slot_node;
     strcpy(temp1->name,slot[i]);
     temp1->next = temp->sllist;
     temp->sllist = temp1;
     i++;
```
continued...

```
    }
    return temp;
}


/*
**   Insert a slot name list into the class node.
**   Overloaded functions.
*/

/*for sf_inv class*/
void addslot_clsnd(cls_slot* c,stcust_class* s)
{
    /* The following are same for different class.
 Overloaded!!*/
    strcpy(s->name,c->name);
    s->slist = c->sllist;
}

/*for sf_inv class*/
void addslot_clsnd(cls_slot* c,sfinv_class* s)
{
    /*...... same as above ....*/
}

/*for st_inv class*/
void addslot_clsnd(cls_slot* c,stinv_class* s)
{
    /*...... same as above ....*/
}

/*for warehs class*/
void addslot_clsnd(cls_slot* c,warehs_class* s)
{
    /*...... same as above ....*/
}

/*for dealer class*/
void addslot_clsnd(cls_slot* c,dealer_class* s)
{
    /*...... same as above ....*/
}

/*for sf sale rec class*/
void addslot_clsnd(cls_slot* c,sfsalrec_class* s)
{
    /*...... same as above ....*/
}
```

continued...

```
/*-  Thisis not a generic  function-------------*/
/*
** Initialize the class node.
*/

void initstcustcls()            /*for st_cust class*/
{
   STCUST_CLASS = new stcust_class;

   STCUST_CLASS->slist = NULL;
   STCUST_CLASS->elist = NULL;
}

void initstinvcls()             /*for st_inv class*/
{
   STINV_CLASS = new stinv_class;

   STINV_CLASS->slist = NULL;
   STINV_CLASS->elist = NULL;
}

void initsfinvcls()             /*for sf_inv class*/
{
   SFINV_CLASS = new sfinv_class;

   SFINV_CLASS->slist = NULL;
   SFINV_CLASS->elist = NULL;
}


void initwarehscls()            /*for warehs class*/
{
   WAREHS_CLASS = new warehs_class;

   WAREHS_CLASS->slist = NULL;

   WAREHS_CLASS->elist = NULL;
}

void initdealercls()            /*for dealer class*/
{
   DEALER_CLASS = new dealer_class;

   DEALER_CLASS->slist = NULL;
   DEALER_CLASS->elist = NULL;
}

void initsfsalreccls()            /*for sf sale rec class*/
{
```

continued...

```
      SFSALREC_CLASS = new sfsalrec_class;

      SFSALREC_CLASS->slist = NULL;
      SFSALREC_CLASS->elist = NULL;
}


/*
** Linking entity nodes into a tree structure for query
**
**   icskb2.cpp
**   Define some utility functions which are used to build  the
**KB.
**   Date:    8/6/89
*/


#include <stream.hpp>
#include <string.h>
#include "slotdef.h"
#include "tempstru.h"
#include "icsclass.h"
#include "ics.h"



/*---------------------------------------------Class Node---------
-----------*/
extern stcust_class* STCUST_CLASS;  /*st_cust class node*/
extern stinv_class*  STINV_CLASS;   /*st_inv class node*/
extern sfinv_class*  SFINV_CLASS;   /*sf_inv class node*/
extern warehs_class* WAREHS_CLASS;  /*warehs class node*/
extern dealer_class* DEALER_CLASS;  /*dealer class node*/
extern sfsalrec_class* SFSALREC_CLASS;  /*sf sale rec class
node*/

/*
**   Insert the entity into the class node
**   Overloaded function.
*/

/*For st cust class*/
void addety_clsnd(char* ename,st_cust* s,stcust_class* s1)
{
    stcust_etynd* temp = new stcust_etynd;

    /* The following are same for different class.  Overloaded!!*/
    strcpy(temp->name,ename);
    temp->entity = s;
    temp->next = s1->elist;
    s1->elist = temp;
}
```

continued...

```
/*For st inv class*/
void addety_clsnd(char* ename,st_inv* s,stinv_class* s1)
{
    stinv_etynd* temp = new stinv_etynd;

    /*......  same as above ....*/

}

/*For sf inv class*/
void addety_clsnd(char* ename,sf_inv* s,sfinv_class* s1)
{
    sfinv_etynd* temp = new sfinv_etynd;

    /*......  same as above ....*/

}

/*For warehs class*/
void addety_clsnd(char* ename,warehs* s,warehs_class* s1)
{
    warehs_etynd* temp = new warehs_etynd;

    /*......  same as above ....*/
}

/*For dealer class*/
void addety_clsnd(char* ename,dealer* s,dealer_class* s1)
{
    dealer_etynd* temp = new dealer_etynd;

    /*......  same as above ....*/
}

/*For dealer class*/
void addety_clsnd(char* ename,sf_sales_records* s,sfsal-
rec_class* s1)
{
    sfsalrec_etynd* temp = new sfsalrec_etynd;

    /*......  same as above ....*/
}
/*
**  p slot name
**  Generic function.
*/
void p_slot_name(slot_node* c)
{
```

continued...

```
    slot_node* temp;

    temp = c;
    cout << "\n" << "SLOT NAME :   ";
    while(temp != NULL)
    {
      cout <<  temp->name << "    ";
      temp = temp->next;
    }
}

/*
**   p out entity.
**   Overloaded functions
*/

/*For st cust class*/
void p_entity_name(stcust_etynd* ety)
{
    stcust_etynd* temp;

    /* The following are same for different class.  Overloaded!!*/
    temp = ety;
    cout << "\n" << "ENTITIES:   ";
    while(temp != NULL)
    {
      cout << "\n" << temp->name << ":";
      temp->entity->prn_value();
      temp = temp->next;
    }
}
}

/*For st inv class*/
void p_entity_name(stinv_etynd* ety)
{
    stinv_etynd* temp;

    /*...... same as above ....*/
}

/*For sf inv class*/
void p_entity_name(sfinv_etynd* ety)
{
    sfinv_etynd* temp;

    /*...... same as above ....*/
}
```

continued...

```
/*For dealer class*/
void p_entity_name(dealer_etynd* ety)
{

   /*......  same as above ....*/
}

/*For warehs class*/
void p_entity_name(warehs_etynd* ety)
{

   /*......  same as above ....*/
}

/*For sfsalrecord class*/
void p_entity_name(sfsalrec_etynd* ety)
{

   /*......  same as above ....*/
}

/*
**  p out class node.
**  Overloaded functions
*/

/*For st cust class*/
void p_clsnode(stcust_class* st)
{
   /* The following are same for different class.  Overloaded!!*/
   cout << "\n" << "ClASS NAME:  " << st->name;
   p_slot_name(st->slist);
   p_entity_name(st->elist);
}

/*For st inv class*/
void p_clsnode(stinv_class* st)
{
   /*......  same as above ....*/
}

/*For sf inv class*/
void p_clsnode(sfinv_class* st)
{
   /*......  same as above ....*/
}

/*For warehs class*/
void p_clsnode(warehs* st)
```

continued..

```
{
    /*...... same as above ....*/}

/*For dealer class*/
void p_clsnode(dealer_class* st)
{
    /*...... same as above ....*/
}

/*For sf sale rec class*/
void p_clsnode(sfsalrec_class* st)
{
    /*...... same as above ....*/
}
```

SUMMARY

- An expert system mimics experts or specialists in a specific field, for example, medicine, computer configuration.

- The principal components of these current systems are knowledge base, inference engine, and man-machine interface.

- The knowledge base contains facts and rules that embody an expert's expertise.

- Knowledge which resides in an expert system provides the power of that system. Because knowledge is often abstract and ambiguous, a well-specified language for encoding this knowledge becomes essential. This language is called *knowledge representation language*. The knowledge representation language may employ any one or a combination of frames, rules, and logic to represent fact explicitly.

- Frame structures are also called "unit" or "schemas" in some AI tools, such as KEE. A frame structure can provide the expert/specialist with a uniform set of representation services for complex data collections or data bases. A frame is more than a structure that is used in other computer languages such as "C" or Pascal. A frame is a generalized property one list that contains spaces (called slots) to specify more than property value. For example, the slots can in turn contain a default value, a restriction of value to be added, a procedure activated to compute a needed value, or a rule activated when certain conditions are met. Furthermore, a frame is a *generalization* hierarchy inheriting information is inherited from the frame superclass.

- OOP/C++ provides a readily available facility for implementing a frame structure. The two difficulties in using C++ to build a frame structure are non-dynamic defining and inflexibility of class hierarchy. Because C++ provides no dynamic defining when using C++ to create a frame structure, the complete structure of the problem needs to be known in advance. This information normally cannot be known before a prototype is completed and tested. A compromise is to use an expert system shell: to build an expert system prototype, test and refine the prototype until satisfied, and then use C++ to structure the final frame structure for delivery.

CHAPTER REFERENCES

Feigenbaum, E. A. "The Art of Artificial Intelligence: Themes and Case Studies." Conference Proceedings of the International Joint Conference on Artificial Intelligence. 1014-1029. 1977.

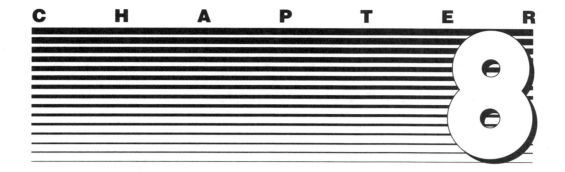

DERIVING KNOWLEDGE
AND DATA

This chapter focuses on deriving knowledge and data in an object-oriented fashion from an expert system   using rules and the inference engine.   Rules and the inference engine, as introduced briefly in Chapter 8, empowers an expert system with a reasoning mechanism and search control to derive knowledge and query the knowledge base.

The most common reasoning method in expert systems is the application of the following simple logic rule (discussed in Chapter 7 and recited below):

IF A is true, and IF A THEN B is true, then B is true.

The implication of this simple rule is that:
    IF B is not true, and IF A THEN B is true, A is not true .

Another implication of the simple logic rule is that

    Given: IF A, THEN B and IF B THEN C

    Conclusion: IF A, THEN C.

In other words, IF A is true, THEN we can conclude C is also true. Clearly, rules need to be developed first to indicate how to derive knowledge, and then reasoning and search methods built, so solutions can be obtained efficiently.

This chapter examines the following topics building a rule structure, methods to implement rule structure, designing an inference engine (forward chaining, backward chaining, and search strategy), and querying the ICS, as an example.

BUILDING RULE STRUCTURES

Rule structures are also called "production rules", "production systems," or "rule-based systems," which are the most used, and simplest form of knowledge representation. In this form of knowledge representation, heuristic knowledge or experience is expressed. Fundamental assumptions, and advantages/disadvantages are discussed.

Fundamental Assumptions

A rule structure in its simple form consists of templates that enable programmers or experts/specialists to input if-then rules to build expert systems. The five fundamental assumptions about the rule structure are: acceptance of rule formalism, modus ponems, limited interaction between factors in rules, limited attributes of a given object, and common understanding between various users.

Acceptance of rule formalism by the user or the expert/specialist is the most important assumption. Experts/specialists must be able to transform their knowledge into rules, that is, they can recognize and then formalize chunks of their knowledge and experience and express them in rules. Unfortunately, not every field will support this assumption. Rule formulation appears to require a field which has attained a certain level of formalization, yet has not achieved a thorough, scientific formalization of the problem solving process.

Fields that are inclined to accept rules in representing knowledge generally have a broadly recognized set of conceptual primitive factors and a minimum understanding of basic processes, such as diagnosis, or configuration. Building rule structures assumes that the IF-THEN format of rules is sufficiently simple, expressive, and intuitive that it can provide a useful knowledge representation language for use by experts to express their knowledge. However, for the rule structure to be useful in representing knowledge, their simple modus ponems chaining must appear natural enough that a user can readily identify with it.

Limited interaction between factors in rules entails two assumptions: (a) only a small number of factors (about six clauses) in the premise may be considered simultaneously to trigger an action in the consequence, (b) the presence or absence of each of these clauses can be determined without adverse effects on the others, and (c) the clauses of rule premise connected by AND/OR can be set up toward nonconflicting subgoals, so action clauses in the consequence will not depend on the order of collecting evidence.

Limited number of attributes for a given object and limited number of objects will prevent the exponential growth in search time for the expert system when the number of rules in the knowledge base grows considerably. Thus newly acquired rules will reference only to established attributes of a given object and the use of these rules will not cause further branching because the attributes appearing in the premises of these rules already will have been traced.

Common understanding between various users assures that the same representation language is communicative between different classes of users, that is, the domain experts who "train" the expert system, and the naive users who possess little knowledge of the expert system but use the system to gain knowledge. It can be assumed that common understanding is feasible.

Advantages and Disadvantages

The advantages of the rule structure are in three areas: modular coding, ease in explanation, and ease in knowledge acquisition.

Each rule in the rule structure is a simple conditional statement consisting of the premise with a limited number of conditional clauses, and the action containing one or more conclusions. Each statement is modular and independent of each other. Such modular coding provides an easy way to identify contradiction and subsumption in the knowledge base by examination of premises and conclusions. Individual rules can be manipulated to facilitate automatic detection and correction of undesirable interactions among rules.

Since rules are retrieved only when they are relevant to a specific goal (that is, the goal appears in their action part), the addition of new rules becomes easy: the premise and action parts of rules can be systematically scanned to search the desired goals. The rules can then be added to the appropriate internal lists according to the parameters found in their actions. These rules can simply be added to the rule set in the knowledge base without changing other rules since rules in the knowledge base are relatively independent, that is, one rule never directly calls another. This advantage is particularly significant when one compares an addition of rules to the addition of a new procedure to a typical FORTRAN program.

Ease in explanation is another benefit; inquiries of an expert system can be answered by retrieving rules whose premise and action (consequence) contain the relevant items. Then the reason for these actions can be easily explained by tracing the passage of rules fired. Explanation evokes the tracing of the consultation process in searching through an AND/OR goal tree. In general, inquiries are of two types : <u>HOW</u> a conclusion is reached and <u>WHY</u> a question is asked. In <u>HOW</u> type inquiries, rules are traced from the top down, as shown in Figure 8-1a. For example, if we ask the expert system, "<u>HOW</u> is C11 obtained?" the system will answer that C11 is obtained because of:

Rule A and B1

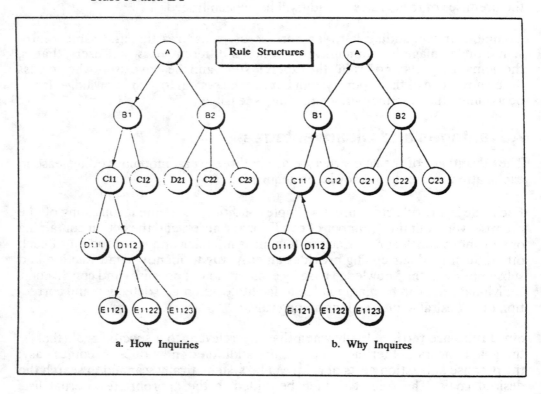

Figure 8-1--Rule Tracing: How and Why.

However, in <u>WHY</u> type inquiries, rules are traced from the bottom up ,as shown in Figure 8-1. If we ask "<u>WHY</u> C11 is obtained ?", the answer will be:

Rule E1121 and D112

Ease of knowledge acquisition lies in the fact that rules are a reasonably intuitive way of expressing chunks of inferential knowledge and experience that are significant without the prerequisite of acquaintance with any programming language. Writing a complete set of rules, may be impossible; however, the rule structure provides a capability for incremental improvement of competence in response to new research that produces new results and modifications of old principles and rules. The rule structure further facilitates the explanation of errors in the conclusion process. This tracing facility supplies the expert with subsequent clues for fixing errors and a set of expectations about the form and content of the anticipated correction.

The disadvantages of the rule representation language include inflexibility of rule expression, sequence of rules, and insufficient power. Inflexibility of rule expression, that is, a predetermined format reduces the freedom of expressing the experts' knowledge and experience and at times appears difficult to the naive user.

Furthermore, all contextual information must be stated explicitly in the premise and the consequence in order to meet the requirement of modularity. This requirement often results in rules with long and complicated premises that entail many subgoals. Rules are inflexible and cannot learn from mistakes. Determining which rules to add or change may be difficult when trying to receive correct behavior of the expert system.

Sequence (correct ordering) of rules affects the efficiency of production systems in consultation. The requirement of correct sequence for either backward or forward chaining means substantive effort is needed in arranging rules to meet the appropriate sequence.

The rule structure provides insufficient power for expressing complex, large, or dynamic concepts because rules are simple conditional statements. In particular, mapping a sequence of events to a set of rules has at times proven extremely difficult. Goal directed chaining may require excess human effort to structure the appropriate sequence for large chunks of knowledge that can not be subdivided easily into separate pieces.

IMPLEMENTATION OF RULE STRUCTURES

The two primary components of a rule are the PREMISE and the CON-CLUSION. The premise is the condition under which the rule is said to "fire;" it is a proposition that is not assumed to be true given an unknown environment, whose truth value will be occasionally evaluated. The conclusion of the rule is the result of firing the rule; it is a proposition that will be become true when the rule fires. For example:

> Premise (IF):(todays-date "7/28/89")
>
> Conclusion (THEN):(todays-day Friday)

When a rule is ATTEMPTED, the expert system needs to find a fact in the knowledge base that complies with the conditions of the premise. Using the previous example, if the knowledge base contained the fact:
> (todays-date "7/28/89"),

then the rule would fire upon being attempted and
> (todays-day Friday)

would be put in the knowledge base. If the fact in the premise did not appear in the knowledge base, then nothing would happen and the rule would not fire.

The firing of a rule frequently affects the knowledge base through the addition or modification of facts. A rule is affected by its certainty. The certainty of these new facts is determined by a combination of:

- the certainty of the facts used to fire the rule and
- the certainty of the rule itself.

In general, the attributes of a rule enabling the user to extract knowledge may include:

- Rule premise
- Rule conclusion
- Rule action
- Rule explanation
- Rule certainty
- Rule askable?

Rule premise provides the facility to record the premise of a rule. The premise can contain conjunctive (**and**) and disjunctive (**or**) phrases: **Rule premise** can be a logical expression.

Rule conclusion is the rule's "then" part; and can contain conjunctive and disjunctive phrases and logical expression.

Rule action indicates the set of action to be taken if the rule is invoked.

Rule explanation explains the rule and uses the English language to describe why the rule is true.

Rule certainty indicates the likelihood of the conclusion given the premise is true. This attribute represents the degree of confidence in a rule or a fact. In determining the confidence factor of a conjunction of rules or facts, the minimum confidence factor is given. For a disjunction, the maximum confidence factor is used. Once the confidence factor of the premise of a rule is determined, then the confidence factor of the conclusion is calculated. The product of the confidence level the premise, the rule and of the rule **Rule askable?** indicates whether the user can provide the premise of the rule when the system cannot determine the premise internally.

To implement a rule structure is relatively straightforward, as shown in Listing 8-1. The sample program in the listing contains the following features:

- reads rules as they appear in the following order:

  a) the IF part.

  b) the THEN part.

  c) the certainty factor.

- adds rules to the rule data base.

- locates and prints rules when they are requested and deletes rules that have been fired.

Listing 8-1 Sample Program for the Rule Structure

```
/*
** Rule.h
*/

typedef struct _rule {
  char *name;                 /* the name of the rule */
  cons *premise;              /* the premise predicates */
  cons *conclusion;           /* the conclusion predicate */
  double certainty;           /* the certainty of this rule */
  struct _rule *next;          /* the next rule in the database */
} rule;

extern rule *make_rule();
extern rule *delete_rule();
extern rule *find_rule();
extern void add_rule();
extern void kill_rule();
extern void print_rule();
extern void printall_rules();

extern rule *RuleDatabase;        /* pointer to all rules */

/*
****************************************************************
***

**
** Rule.c
*/
/*
**
** (new format of rules)
*/



#include "stdio.h"
#include "cons.h"
#include "rule.h"

rule *RuleDatabase = NULL;        /* pointer to all rules */

/*
** read_rule(): reads the rule from the standard input. Rules
**look like
** this:
** Rule-name IF (pred*) THEN pred
** E.g:
** Fuel-rule-1 IF ((fuel-level low)) THEN (out-of-fuel)
*/
```

continued...

```
rule *read_rule()
{   rule *rp;
  cons *pp;

  if (rp = (rule *) malloc(sizeof (rule))) {
    pp = lread(C_FILE,stdin);          /* first the name */
    rp->name = pp->car.s;       /* save the name */
    free(pp);                /* junk the cons */
    pp = lread(C_FILE,stdin);          /* get the 'IF' */
    if (strcmpi(pp->car.s,"IF")) {      /* not if? */
      free(rp);                  /* not a rule! */
      killcons(pp);
      return NULL;
    }
    killcons(pp);             /* get rid of it */
    rp->premise = lread(C_FILE,stdin);
    pp = lread(C_FILE,stdin);          /* get the 'THEN' */
    if (strcmpi(pp->car.s,"THEN")) {      /* not then? */
      killcons(rp->premise);      /* not a rule! */
      killcons(pp);
      free(rp);
      return NULL;
    }
    killcons(pp);             /* get rid of 'then' */
    rp->conclusion = lread(C_FILE,stdin);
    pp = lread(C_FILE,stdin);           /* lastly, the certainty */
    rp->certainty = atof(pp->car.s);
    killcons(pp);             /* junk the certainty */
    rp->next = NULL;
  }
  return rp;
}

/*
** _add_rule(): adds the rule _rp_ to the database _dbp_
*/

static rule *_add_rule(rp,dbp)
rule *rp,*dbp;
{
  rule *rp2 = dbp;

  if (dbp == NULL) {
    return rp;
  }
  while (rp2->next) {
    rp2 = rp2->next;
  }
  rp2->next = rp;
  return dbp;
}
```

continued...

```
/*
** add_rule(): adds the rule _rp_ to the RuleDatabase
*/
void add_rule(rp)
rule *rp;
{
   RuleDatabase = _add_rule(rp,RuleDatabase);
}

rule *delete_rule(rp,dbp)
rule *rp,*dbp;
{
  rule *rrp;

  if (dbp == NULL) {
    return NULL;
  } else if (rp == dbp) {
    rrp = dbp->next;
    kill_rule(rp);
    return dbp->next;
  } else {
    dbp->next = delete_rule(rp,dbp->next);
    return dbp;
  }
}

/*
** find_rule: find rule by name
*/

rule *find_rule(s,dbp)
char *s;
rule *dbp;
{
  if (dbp == NULL) {
    return NULL;
  } else if (!strcmp(s,dbp>name)) {
    return(dbp);
  } else {
    return find_rule(s,dbp>next);
  }
}

void kill_rule(rp)
rule *rp;
{
   killcons(rp>premise);
   killcons(rp>conclusion);
   free(rp);
}
void print_rule(rp)
rule *rp;
{
```

continued...

```
  printf("Name: %s\nPremise: ",rp->name);
  lprint(rp->premise,C_FILE,stdout);
  printf("\nConclusion: ");
  lprint(rp->conclusion,C_FILE,stdout);  printf("\nCertainty:
%g\n",rp->certainty);
}
void printall_rules(rule_base)
rule *rule_base;
{
  rule *db = rule_base;

  while (db != NULL) {
    print_rule(db);
    db = db->next;
  }
}
```

INVENTORY CONTROL SYSTEM RULES

Rules are used to create new data for the ICS that are not available in the knowledge base. For example, rule objects will be created using the information in the classes and entities created in Chapter 7 to calculate new information. One useful piece of information is the cost of a part to a potential customer. This value is the true cost of the part. The value is calculated by subtracting any applicable discounts from the cost of the part by creating a rule that calculates the true cost of any part:

> Rule: TRUE-COST
>
> PREMISE:
>
> The cost of ?entity is ?cost
>
> AND
>
> The discount of ?entity is ?discount
>
> AND
>
> ?cost - ?discount = ?true-cost
>
> CONCLUSION:
>
> The true-cost of ?entity is ?true-cost.

In obtaining this rule, two pieces of information are needed to find a part's true cost: Cost and Discount. Since the entity to be used is unknown, (many entities will be used), the unknown terms of the statement are given variables:

"The Cost of ?ENTITY is ?COST"

"The Discount of ?ENTITY is ?DISCOUNT"

Note that the variable "?ENTITY" is used twice in the premise of the rule to find the Cost and Discount of the same entity, and once the variable "?ENTITY" is bound to a particular entity, to assure the programmer of using the same variable. This technique of using the same variable names is the most common method used to relate two or more separate statements. To simply combine statements, we use the logical AND and OR operators.

Once the Cost and Discount of the Entity is found, subtract the two to find the true cost. If these values are found (the PREMISE portion of the rule is TRUE), then store this information (the CONCLUSION portion of the rule). The processes of searching, calculating, and storing are done by the inference engine . For this particular example, the Reasoning System performs the following steps:

1. Since the premise is an AND statement, an attempt is made to match EVERY English expression to make the Premise TRUE.

2. An attempt is made to match the first expression, "The Cost of ?ENTITY is ?COST", by:

   - finding a match with the first entity that has a Cost slot.

   - binding the ?ENTITY variable to the name of that entity.

   - binding ?COST to the value of the Cost slot of that entity.

3. If a true sentence is found, the reasoning system continues to match with the second statement:

"The Discount of ?ENTITY is ?DISCOUNT", by:

   - binding ?DISCOUNT to the value of the Discount slot in the same entity named by the previously bound variable ?ENTITY.

4. Then, if the second statement has matched, the reasoning system attempts to match the third statement:

"?COST - ?DISCOUNT = ?TRUE-COST", by:

   - evaluating the bound values of the ?COST and ?DISCOUNT variables using subtraction.

   - binding ?TRUE-COST to the value returned.

5. Finally, the successful rule can "fire" since the premise of the rule is TRUE. When the rule fires, the conclusion of the rule (True-Cost ?entity ?true-cost) is asserted by:

- substituting the values of the previously bound variables and asserting the statement in the knowledge base for future use.

A rule has been defined as given a part entity, a cost value and a discount value, the true cost of the part entity can be calculated, and the value in the knowledge base for later use.

To create the rule, enter the name, premise, and conclusion of the rule, as specified above. Upon completion the menu should appear, as follows:

Specify Rule to Create
Rule name:TRUE-COST

Explanation:

Premise (in English):

The COST of ?ENTITY is ?COST

AND

The DISCOUNT of ?ENTITY is ?DISCOUNT

AND

?COST - DISCOUNT = ?TRUE-COST

Conclusion (in English):

The TRUE-COST of ?ENTITY is ?TRUE-COST
Certainty:1.0

As another example, create a rule that does not store new information into the knowledge base, nevertheless, will give information about the existing entity objects.

To determine if a part is available in a certain quantity, compare the current inventory level of the part to a requested number of parts. Again, the rule is made as powerful as possible by using variables for the specific part of information that is needed:

Rule: AVAILABLE

PREMISE:

"Entity ?ENTITY is-a PARTS with CIL = ?CIL

AND

continued...

?NUMBER   ?CIL"

CONCLUSION:

"There are ?NUMBER ?ENTITY Available"

This rule will be used only for QUERYING. Given a number and an entity name in the form of "There are **number entity-name Available**", the rule will attempt to compare the current inventory level with the number specified. A query for this information will notify the user of the results of this attempt.

Now create the rule as usual:

Rule name:AVAILABLE

Rule Set:BASIC-RULE-SET

Explanation:

Premise (in English):

ENTITY ?ENTITY IS-A PARTS WITH CIL = ?CIL

and

?NUMBER   ?CIL

Conclusion (in English):

There are ?NUMBER ?ENTITY AVAILABLE

Certainty:1.0

Has rule fired?:NO

Meta Rules

In implementing a rule, the rule can be designated as: a forward chaining rule that can be used in forward chaining only, a backward chaining rule that can be employed in backward chaining only, and a bidirectional rule that can be called upon in both chaining directions. This feature is called **Meta Level** or rule set (class).

An even more advanced concept is the meta-level rule that is a rule describing the feature of all rules in a given rule set. Meta-level rule is called meta-rule, and refers to object rules by description rather than by name. Meta rules express strategies for using other knowledge in rules, frames, or other sources in the knowledge base. These strategies invoke subsequent rules in a situation where more than one chunk or source of knowledge may be applicable. For example, given a problem solvable by either a forward chaining search through rules first, or a tree search through the frame structure, meta rule might indicate which approach to take. Meta rule makes a decision based on the characteristics of the problem domain and other specifications of the desired solution, such as speed of search and accuracy of solution.

Meta rule makes a conclusion about other rules by deductions. The likely use of certain groups of rules is determined as well as partial ordering among subsets of rules or among rule sets. However, a meta-rule makes conclusions about rule classes in rule groups, but does not indicate circumstances under which some rule classes are invalid.

Implementing meta rules requires only a minor change to the control structure, that is, before the system retrieves the entire classes of rules relevant to the current goal, all relevant meta-rules are examined. These meta-rules are invoked first to determine the likely utility and relative ordering of rule classes and rules. As a result, the search space can be pruned or the branches of the search tree can be reordered to increase system efficiency.

C++ is efficient in grouping meta-rule structure because of its class structure.

Designing An Inference Engine

An inference engine can be simple or complicated, depending on the structure of the knowledge base. For example, if the knowledge base consists of simple rules (no rule set structured) and facts, a forward chaining will suffice. However, for a knowledge base that consists of structured frames and rules and unstructured logic (facts, data, and variables), both sophisticated forward and backward chaining with developed search strategy may be required. For simplicity, the main elements of an inference engine will be discussed: forward chaining, backward chaining, justification, and search strategy.

Forward Chaining

Forward chaining is simply an interactive program performing a loop of substitution. This rule steps through the rule list until a rule is found whose promise matches the fact or situation. The rule will be used or "fired" to assert a new fact. A rule is used only once and will not be used again in the same search; however, when a fact is found as the result of firing a rule, then that fact will be added to the knowledge base. This cycle of finding a matched rule, firing the rule, and adding the conclusion to the knowledge base will be repeated until no more matched rules are found. Variations of the simple forward chaining form can be suggested to enrich the inference mechanism. The implementation of a simple forward chaining form then will be discussed, as well as, a variation of the form.

Implementation Of A Simple Forward Chaining

Forward chaining is used to assert a fact that matches the premise of a rule and can be applied to determine further facts.

The detailed procedure for forward chaining is as follows:

1. A fact is asserted.
2. The fact matches the premise of a rule.
3. The system computes the substitution that unifies the fact and the premise.
4. The substitution is applied to the conclusion of the rule.
5. This result is asserted, and is available for further forward chaining.
6. Repeat steps 1 through 5.

Sample programs of **forward-chain** can be obtained from Reference 1.

Enhancement Of The Simple Forward Chaining

The simple forward chaining form can be enhanced in two ways: (1) by using a conflict resolution method (a tie breaking procedure) to select one of the eligible rules when the premises of more than one rule match the fact, and (2) by considering the combination of conjunctive and disjunctive propositions in the premise or conclusion.

The first enhancement includes two features: (1) to discard those rules that would add only duplicates to the knowledge base and (2) to execute a conflict resolution method to select one of the eligible rules. The enhanced procedure is as follows:

1. Make eligible all rules whose premise unifies with the fact.
2. Substitute the premises.
3. Discard the rules whose conclusion would have a nullifying effect.
4. Stop, if no eligible rules remain.
5. Use a conflict resolution method to select one of the eligible rules if more than one rule is eligible.
6. Locate the conclusion proposition to the knowledge base.
7. Repeat the previous six steps.

The procedure is not much different from that in the previous section, however, all eligible rules are first stored in the group of **eligible-rules**, and then, a conflict resolution method will indicate the way these rules are to be selected. If no other methods are preferred, a first-in-last-out method is used to break ties among all eligible rules.

Combination of conjunctive premises is discussed in backward chaining. The same principles can be applied in forward chaining.

Backward Chaining

When the user queries whether a certain fact is true, backward chaining reasoning is used. There is a rule determining the query from known information in the knowledge base or from answers given by the user.

In other words, backward chaining attempts to prove the hypothesis from facts. If the current goal is to determine the fact in the conclusion (hypothesis), then backward chaining reasoning is necessary to determine whether the premises match the situation. The example discussed in Chapter 7 is recited to show the logic of backward chaining:

> Rule One:
>
> IF you lose the key and gas tank is empty
>
> THEN the car is not running.
>
> Rule Two:
>
> IF the car is not running and
>
> you have no cash
>
> THEN you are going to be late
>
> Fact One: you lost the key.
>
> Fact Two: the gas tank is empty.

For instance, to prove the hypothesis that "you are going to be late," given the facts and rules in the knowledge base (Facts 1 and 2, Rules 1 and 2), backward chaining may be applied to determine whether the premises match the situation.

Rule 2, containing the conclusion, fires first to determine whether the premises match the fact. Because the knowledge base does not contain the facts in the premises of Rule 2, "the car is not running" and "you have no cash," "the car is not running" becomes the first subgoal. Rule 1 then fires to assert whether the premises "you lost the key" and "gas tank is empty" match the facts. Because the facts (Facts 1 and 2) in knowledge base match the premise of Rule 1, the subhypothesis is proven.

However, the system still is proving the "you have no cash," because this knowledge is not contained in the knowledge base and cannot be asserted through rules, since no rule is related. The system then will ask the user "IS IT TRUE THAT: you have no cash?" If the answer is "yes," then the second subgoal is satisfied and the original hypothesis is proven, concluding that "you are going to be late."

In summary the procedure for backward chaining is, as follow:

1. A request is made to achieve a fact (the goal).

2. The goal does not match any known fact.

3. The goal matches the conclusion of a rule.

4. The system computes the substitution that unifies the goal with the conclusion.

5. The substitution is applied to the premise of the rule.

6. This result becomes a new goal of the system.

7. This new goal can:

   - Match a fact in the knowledge base.

   - Match a conclusion of a rule, leading to further backward chaining.

   - Ask the user for the needed information.

   - Fail, then the original goal fails.

9. Repeat steps 1 through 7.

Coding for backward chaining is fairly complicated. Sample programs for backward chaining can be obtained from Reference 1.

Search Strategy

The three common search strategies are depth-first, breadth- first, and best-first. Each of the three strategies uses a slightly different approach to search for the target solution.

Depth-first Search

In the discussion of forward and backward chaining, an implied search strategy, depth-first, has been used. To explain the concept of depth-first search certain terms are defined. In both forward and backward chaining, there is always a starting point (either a fact or a goal). The starting point is called the root node. There are choices (branch nodes) after the starting point and more subbranches at each branch as the matching and substitution process goes along. This decision process is called a **tree** since every branch has a unique parent with only one exception (the root node).

Listing 8-2 Sample Programs to Search and Query the Knowledge Base in the ICS

```
/*
** icskb3.cpp
**
** Contains:
** 1). f_entity_node(entity_name,class_node).
**      where:
**    entity_name: is the entity name which you try to find data.
**    class_node: is the class which the entity belongs to.
**        return:
**    entity data(slot data).
**        e.g.    f_entity_node("lisa_hu",STCUST_CLASS) -
**lisa_hu slot data
**
** 2). f_all_entities(class_node).
**      where:
**    class_node: is the class.
**        return: all entities which belong to that class.
**        e.g.    f_all_entities(STCUST_CLASS) - "lisa_hu",
"david_hu", etc.
**
** 3). f_e_w_s(class_node,slot_name,slot_value).
**      where:
**    class_node: is the class name.
**    slot_name:  is the slot name you try to f.
**    slot_value: is the value of this slot.
**        return: all entities of that class with specified
**slots.
**        e.g.    f_all_entities_w_s(STCUST_CLASS,"dealer","val
**lejo").
**
*/

#include "stdis.h"
#include "string.L"
#include "slotdef.h"
#include "tempstru.h"
#include "icsclass.h"
#include "ics.h"

/*-------------------------------------------Class Node---------
-----------*/
extern stcust_class* STCUST_CLASS;   /*st_cust class node*/
extern stinv_class*  STINV_CLASS;    /*st_inv class node*/
extern sfinv_class*  SFINV_CLASS;    /*sf_inv class node*/
extern warehs_class* WAREHS_CLASS;   /*warehs class node*/
extern dealer_class* DEALER_CLASS;   /*dealer class node*/
extern sfsalrec_class* SFSALREC_CLASS;  /*sf sale rec class
node*/
```

continued...

```
/*
**   find the entity from the KB
**   Overloaded function.
*/

/*for st_cust class*/
st_cust* f_entity_node(char* s,stcust_class* sl)
{
    stcust_etynd* temp1;

    /* The following are same for different class. Overloaded!!*/
    temp1 = sl->elist;
    while(strcmp(s,temp1->name) && temp1 != NULL)
    {
      temp1 = temp1-next;
    }
    if(temp1 == NULL)
    {
      cout << "\n" << "Not such entity !";
      return NULL;
    }
    else
    {
      return temp1->entity;
    }
}

/*for st_inv class*/
st_inv* f_entity_node(char* s,stinv_class* sl)
{
    stinv_etynd* temp1;

    /*...... same as above ....*/
}

/*
** for sf_inv class
*/
sf_inv* f_entity_node(char* s,sfinv_class* sl)
{
    sfinv_etynd* temp1;

    temp1 = sl->elist;
    while(strcmp(s,temp1->name) && temp1 != NULL)
    {
      temp1 = temp1-next;
    }
    if(temp1 == NULL)
    {
      cout << "\n" << "Not such entity !";
      return NULL;
    }
}
```

continued...

```
    else
    {
      return temp1->entity;
    }
}
/*
** for warehs class
*/
warehs* f_entity_node(char* s,warehs_class* sl)
{
    warehs_etynd* temp1;

    temp1 = sl->elist;
    while(strcmp(s,temp1->name) && temp1 != NULL)
    {
      temp1 = temp1->next;
    }
    if(temp1 == NULL)
    {
      cout << "\n" << "Not such entity !";
      return NULL;
    }
    else
    {
      return temp1->entity;
    }
}
/*
** for dealer class
*/
dealer* f_entity_node(char* s,dealer_class* sl)
{
    dealer_etynd* temp1;

    temp1 = sl->elist;
    while(strcmp(s,temp1->name) && temp1 != NULL)
    {
      temp1 = temp1->next;
    }
    if(temp1 == NULL)
{
      cout << "\n" << "Not such entity !";
      return NULL;
    }
    else
    {
      return temp1->entity;
    }
}

/*
** for sf sale rec class
```

```
*/
sf_sales_records* f_entity_node(char* s,sfsalrec_class* sl)
{
    sfsalrec_etynd* templ;

    templ = sl->elist;
    while(strcmp(s,templ->name) && templ != NULL)
    {
      templ = templ->next;
    }
    if(templ == NULL)
    {
      cout << "\n" << "Not such entity !";
      return NULL;
    }
    else
    {
      return templ->entity;
    }
}


/*
**   find  all the entities
**   Overloaded function.
*/

/*for st_cust class*/
stcust_etynd* f_all_entities(stcust_class* sl)
{
    /* The following are same for different class. Overloaded!!*/
    return sl->elist;
}

/*for st_inv class*/
stinv_etynd* f_all_entities(stinv_class* sl)
{
    /*...... same as above ....*/
}

/*for sf_inv class*/
sfinv_etynd* f_all_entities(sfinv_class* sl)
{
    /*...... same as above ....*/
}

/*for warehs class*/
warehs_etynd* f_all_entities(warehs_class* sl)
{
    /*...... same as above ....*/
}

/*for dealer class*/
dealer_etynd* f_all_entities(dealer_class* sl)
```
continued...

```
{
    /*...... same as above ....*/
}

/*for st_sales_records class*/
sfsalrec_etynd* f_all_entities(sfsalrec_class* sl)
{
    /*...... same as above ....*/
}

/*
**   find all the entities with specified slots
**   Overloaded function.
*/

/*for st_cust class*/
stcust_etynd* f_e_w_s(char* slot_nm, char*
slot_val,stcust_class* sl)
{
    /* The following are same for different classes. Overloaded!!*/
    stcust_etynd* tmp2;
    tmp2 = NULL;
    slot_node*  temp1;
    temp1 = sl->slist;
    while(strcmp(slot_nm,temp1-name) && temp1 != NULL)
    {
        temp1 = temp1->next;
    }
     if(temp1 == NULL)
     {
        cout << "\n" << "This class has not this slot name !";
        return NULL;
     }
     else
     {
        stcust_etynd* temp;
        temp = sl->elist;

        extern stcust_etynd*
make_up_etylist(stcust_etynd*,stcust_etynd*);
        while(temp != NULL)
        {
          Cust*   tpm;
        tpm = temp->entity->get_slotval();
          if(!strcmp(slot_nm,"dealer"))
        {
            if(!strcmp(tpm->dealer->slot_value,slot_val))
            {
                stcust_etynd* tpp = new stcust_etynd;
                strcpy(tpp->name,temp->name);
                tpp->entity = temp->entity;
                tpp->next = NULL;
                tmp2 = make_up_etylist(tmp2,tpp);
            }
```

continued...

```
        }
        if(!strcmp(slot_nm,"name"))
        {
            if(!strcmp(tpm->name->slot-value,slot_val))
              make_up_etylist(tmp2,temp);
        }
        if(!strcmp(slot_nm,"part"))
        {
            if(!strcmp(tpm-part-slot-value,slot_val))
              make_up_etylist(tmp2,temp);
        }
        if(!strcmp(slot_nm,"order_date"))
        {
            if(!strcmp(tpm->order_date->slot_value,slot_val))
              make_up_etylist(tmp2,temp);
        }
        if(!strcmp(slot_nm,"time"))
        {
            if(!strcmp(tpm->time-slot_value,slot_val))
              make_up_etylist(tmp2,temp);
        }
        temp = temp->next;
          }
        }
        return tmp2;
}

stinv_etynd* f_e_w_s(char* slot_nm, char*
slot_val,stinv_class* sl)
{
    /*...... same as above ....*/
}

sfinv_etynd* f_e_w_s(char* slot_nm, char*
slot_val,sfinv_class* sl)
{
    /*...... same as above ....*/
}

warehs_etynd* f_e_w_s(char* slot_nm, char*
slot_val,warehs_class* sl)
{
    /*...... same as above ....*/
}

dealer_etynd* f_e_w_s(char* slot_nm, char*
slot_val,dealer_class* sl)
{
    /*...... same as above ....*/
}

sfsalrec_etynd* f_e_w_s(char* slot_nm, char* slot_val,sfsal-
rec_class* sl)
{
```

continued...

```
    /*...... same as above ....*/
}
/*
** The same for other classes for f_e_w_s().
*/


stcust_etynd* make_up_etylist(stcust_etynd* el1,stcust_etynd*
el2)
{
    /* The following are same for different class. Overloaded!!*/
    el2->next = el1;
    el1 = el2;
    return el1;
}


/*
**   icsparse.cpp
**
**   check_entity_pred_syntax()
**
**   Checks if the class name and the slot names are valid, but
**NOT ENTITY name
**   (It could be a remote entity from a ks)
**   If class-must-be-inst is nil, lets the class-name be var-
**term.
**In this case,
**   however, there may be no slot-specs.
**
**   Ex1.   (entity ?x is-a ?y with slot_name = slot_value)
**   Ex2.   (entity ?x is-a ?y)
**
**   Date:        8/3/89
**
*/

#include "stream.hpp"
#include "string.h"
#include "parse.h"


#define FAIL        0
#define QYMAX       8
#define WDMAX       30

char query_word[QYMAX][WDMAX];

int check_entity_pred_syntax(char* x)
{
    int i;
```

continued...

```
    extern int parse_query(char*);
    i = parse_query(x);

    if( i < THREE || i > SEVEN)
    {
      cout << "\n" << "Bad number of terms";
      return FAIL;
    }
    if(strcmp(query_word[ZERO],"entity"))   /*1st term not entity*/
    {
      cout << "\n" << "entity is expected in beginning";
      return FAIL;
    }
    if(strcmp(query_word[TWO],"is-a"))    /*3rd term not is-a*/
    {
cout << "\n" << "is-a connector is expected";
      return FAIL;
    }
    char  class_name[20];
    char entity_name[20];
    strcpy(class_name, query_word[THREE]);
    strcpy(entity_name, query_word[ONE]);
    extern int varp(char*);
    if(varp(class_name) && i  3)
    {
        cout << "\n" << "No slots can be specified when class_name
is a variable";
        return FAIL;
    }
    if(varp(class_name) && !varp(entity_name))
    {
      return CASE7;
    }
    if(!varp(class_name) && !varp(entity_name) && i == THREE)
    {
      return CASE1;
    }
    if(!varp(class_name) && varp(entity_name) && i == THREE)
    {
      return CASE2;
    }
    if(!varp(class_name) && !varp(entity_name) && i == SEVEN &&
!varp(query_word[SEVEN]))
    {
      return CASE5;
    }
    if(!varp(class_name) && varp(entity_name)
        && i == SEVEN && varp(query_word[SEVEN]))
    {
      return CASE4;
    }
    if(!varp(class_name) && varp(entity_name)
        && i == SEVEN && !varp(query_word[SEVEN]))
```

continued..

```
    {
      return CASE6;
    }
    if(!varp(class_name) && !varp(entity_name)
       && i == SEVEN && varp(query_word[SEVEN]))
    {
      return CASE3;
    }
}

int parse_query(char* pred)
{
    int i=0;
    int j,k;
    while(*pred == '(' || *pred == ' ')
      pred++;
    while(*pred != ')'){
      j=0;
      while(*pred != ' ')
          query_word[i][j++]=*pred++;
      query_word[i][j] = '\0';
      pred++;
      i++;
    }
    return --i;
}

int varp(char* s)
{
    if(*s == '?')
       return 1;
    return 0;
}
```

In a depth-first search, as illustrated in Figure 8-2, the search starts from X down to A, B, and C. Only the left most child of each node is examined. If it is not the desired node, the process goes down to the next level and picks the leftmost child of that node, always moving downward. If the search reaches the bottom level without finding the desired choice, the process returns to the last node where there was a choice. Then the downward motion is repeated. For example, if the target node for search is k2 in Figure 8-2, the depth-first strategy will take a great effort to reach the node of k2 because the process has to go through almost all nodes, down from X to C, returning from C to B and moving down again to D, returning to A, descending to E and F to get to K2.

The depth-first search entails a recursive procedure. The recursion occurs by moving down one tree branch and then by moving across all the branches. This recursion is implemented in both forward and backward chaining programs discussed before.

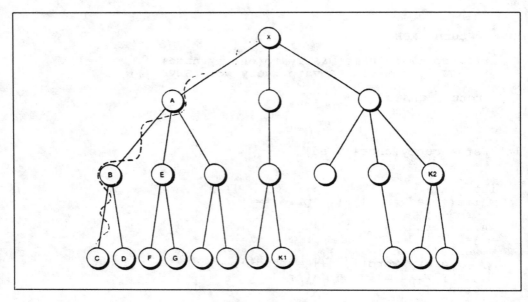

Figure 8.2 Depth-first search

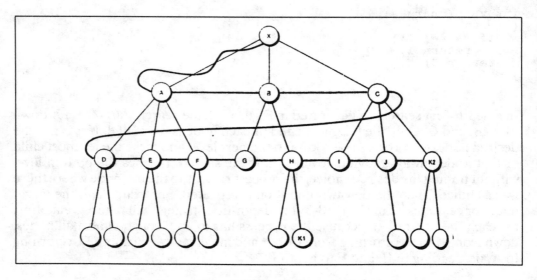

Figure 8.3 Breadth-first search

Breadth-first Search and Best-first Search

In breadth-first search, movement is performed level by level, the process examines all the nodes on the same level one by one. If the target node is not found, then the process looks at nodes on the next level, as shown in Figure 8-3.

Listing 8-3 Programs to Inintialize Slots and Test Knowledge Representation

```
/*
**    icsmain.cpp
**
**    This program is to implement the connction between
Knowledge Base which
**    is made up of objects and the query about the KB. There
are some steps
**    required before doing such kind of reasoning.
**
**    The steps are:
**    1) define the class. e.g. structs.h.
**    2) define the kb. e.g. kbstruct.h.
**    3) do the query.
**
**    The query's format is:
**          (entity ?x is-a ?y with slot_name = ?z)
**
**    Date:     8/5/89
**
*/
#include "stdis.h"
#include "string.h"
#include "slotdef.h"
#include "tempstru.h"
#include "icsclass.h"
#include "ics.h"
#include "parse.h"

#define MAXQUERY     60


/*
**    Because C++ does not support the dynamic defining of the
data structure.
**    In order to do reasoning in an object-oriented knowledge
base, the
**    developer should initialize each class name, the slot
names which defined
**    in the class definition before doing the reasoning.
*/
```
continued..

```
/*--------------------------------------------Class Node----------
-----------*/
stcust_class* STCUST_CLASS;          /*st cust class node*/
stinv_class*  STINV_CLASS;           /*st inv class node*/
sfinv_class*  SFINV_CLASS;           /*sf inv class node*/
warehs_class* WAREHS_CLASS;          /*warehs class node*/
dealer_class* DEALER_CLASS;          /*dealer class node*/
sfsalrec_class* SFSALREC_CLASS;      /*sf sale rec class node*/


/* initialization for each class' slots as follows.
** the SLOT_END must be added at the end of each initializa-
tion.
*/

/*for cust class*/
char* cust_slot[7] = { "dealer", "name", "part", "number",
"order_date",
        "time", SLOT_END};

/*for inv class*/
char* inv_slot[4] = { "name", "cil", "oil", SLOT_END};

/*for warehs class*/
char* warehs_inv_slot[8] = { "name", "cil", "oil", "cost",
"discount",
            "min_order", "order_time", SLOT_END};
/*for location class*/
char* loc_slot[3] = { "address", "phone", SLOT_END};

/*for sales record class*/
char* salrec_slot[8] = { "sale_number", "date", "part", "num-
ber_sold", "cost",
            "total_sale", "sold_to", SLOT_END};
/*----------------------------------------------------------------
------------*/


main()
{
   cls_slot* temp1;
   extern void initstcustcls();
   extern void initstinvcls();
   extern void initsfinvcls();
   extern cls_slot* make_up_cls_slot(char*,char*[]);

/*For st_cust*/
  initstcustcls();
  char *temp;
  temp = "st_cust";
        temp1 = make_up_cls_slot(temp, cust_slot);
  addslot_clsnd(temp1,STCUST_CLASS);
```
continued...

```
/*For entity creating and setting for st_cust*/
   st_cust* jan_stephen = new st_cust;
   char* te;
   te = "jan_stephen";
   addety_clsnd(te,jan_stephen,STCUST_CLASS);

   st_cust* lisa_hu = new st_cust;
   addety_clsnd("lisa_hu",lisa_hu,STCUST_CLASS);


   cout << "\n" << "Enter Jan Stephen's Data, Please";
   jan_stephen-set_slotval();
   cout << "\n" << "Enter Lise Hu's Data, Please";
   lisa_hu-set_slotval();

   p_clsnode(STCUST_CLASS);

/*-------------------------------------------------do some
queries------*/
   char x[MAXQUERY];
   cout << "\nEnter query: ";
   gets(x);
   int i;
   extern int check_entity_pred_syntax(char*);
   i = check_entity_pred_syntax(x);

   extern char query_word[8][30];
   char* class_name;
   class_name = query_word[THREE];

   switch (i)
   {
         case CASE1:

     if(!strcmp(class_name,"st_cust"))
     {
       stcust_class* x;
       st_cust* y;
       x = STCUST_CLASS;
       y = f_entity_node(query_word[ONE],x);
       if ( y != NULL)
          cout << "\nQuery is true!";
       else
          cout << "\nQuery is not true!";
     }
     if(!strcmp(class_name,"st_inv"))
     {
stinv_class* x;
       st_inv* y;
       x = STINV_CLASS;
       y = f_entity_node(query_word[ONE],x);
       y-prn_value();
```

continued...

```
    }
    if(!strcmp(class_name,"sf_inv"))
    {
       sfinv_class* x;
       sf_inv* y;
       x = SFINV_CLASS;
       y = f_entity_node(query_word[ONE],x);
       y-prn_value();
    }
    if(!strcmp(class_name,"warehs"))
    {
       warehs_class* x;
       warehs* y;
       x = WAREHS_CLASS;
       y = f_entity_node(query_word[ONE],x);
       y-prn_value();
    }
    if(!strcmp(class_name,"dealer"))
    {
       dealer_class* x;
       dealer* y;
       x = DEALER_CLASS;
       y = f_entity_node(query_word[ONE],x);
       y-prn_value();
    }
    if(!strcmp(class_name,"sfsalrec"))
    {
       sfsalrec_class* x;
       sf_sales_records* y;
       x = SFSALREC_CLASS;
       y = f_entity_node(query_word[ONE],x);
       y-prn_value();
    }
       break;

          case CASE2:
if(!strcmp(class_name,"st_cust"))
    {
       stcust_class* x;
       stcust_etynd* y;
       x = STCUST_CLASS;
       y = f_all_entities(x);
       p_entity_name(y);
    }
    if(!strcmp(class_name,"st_inv"))
    {
       stinv_class* x;
    stinv_etynd* y;
    x = STINV_CLASS;
    y = f_all_entities(x);
    p_entity_name(y);
    }
    if(!strcmp(class_name,"sf_inv"))
```

continued...

```
      {
        sfinv_class* x;
        sfinv_etynd* y;
        x = SFINV_CLASS;
        y = f_all_entities(x);
        p_entity_name(y);
      }
      if(!strcmp(class_name,"warehs"))
      {
        warehs_class* x;
        warehs_etynd* y;
        x = WAREHS_CLASS;
        y = f_all_entities(x);
        p_entity_name(y);
      }
      if(!strcmp(class_name,"dealer"))
      {
        dealer_class* x;
        dealer_etynd* y;
        x = DEALER_CLASS;
        y = f_all_entities(x);
        p_entity_name(y);
      }
      if(!strcmp(class_name,"sfsalrec"))
      {
        sfsalrec_class* x;
        sfsalrec_etynd* y;
        x = SFSALREC_CLASS;
        y = f_all_entities(x);
        p_entity_name(y);
      }
        break;
          case CASE6:

      if(!strcmp(class_name,"st_cust"))
      {
        stcust_class* x;
        stcust_etynd* y;
        x = STCUST_CLASS;
        char* s1;
        char* s2;
        s1 = query_word[FIVE];
        s2 = query_word[SEVEN];
        y = f_e_w_s(s1,s2,x);
        p_entity_name(y);
      }
if(!strcmp(class_name,"st_inv"))
      {
        stinv_class* x;
        stinv_etynd* y;
        x = STINV_CLASS;
        char* s1;
        char* s2;
```

continued...

```
        s1 = query_word[FIVE];
        s2 = query_word[SEVEN];
        y = f_e_w_s(s1,s2,x);
        p_entity_name(y);
    }
    if(!strcmp(class_name,"sf_inv"))
    {
        sfinv_class* x;
        sfinv_etynd* y;
        x = SFINV_CLASS;
        char* s1;
        char* s2;
        s1 = query_word[FIVE];
        s2 = query_word[SEVEN];
        y = f_e_w_s(s1,s2,x);
        p_entity_name(y);
    }
    if(!strcmp(class_name,"warehs"))
    {
        warehs_class* x;
        warehs_etynd* y;
        x = WAREHS_CLASS;
        char* s1;
        char* s2;
        s1 = query_word[FIVE];
        s2 = query_word[SEVEN];
        y = f_e_w_s(s1,s2,x);
        p_entity_name(y);
    }
    if(!strcmp(class_name,"dealer"))
    {
        dealer_class* x;
        dealer_etynd* y;
        x = DEALER_CLASS;
        char* s1;
        char* s2;
        s1 = query_word[FIVE];
        s2 = query_word[SEVEN];
        y = f_e_w_s(s1,s2,x);
        p_entity_name(y);
    }
    if(!strcmp(class_name,"sfsalrec"))
    {
        sfsalrec_class* x;
        sfsalrec_etynd* y;
        x = SFSALREC_CLASS;
        char* s1;
        char* s2;
        s1 = query_word[FIVE];
        s2 = query_word[SEVEN];
        y = f_e_w_s(s1,s2,x);
        p_entity_name(y);
    }
        break;
        }
}
```

The same example of searching for K2 is used to compare the difference in efficiency. Because K2 is on the third level, the search process will have to examine only 10 nodes to reach K2, in comparison with 19 nodes in the depth-first search. Whether the breadth-first search is more efficient than the depth-first search depends on the location of the target node. Consequently, the user sometimes makes a good guess about the distance of the target node from the current node and selects the shortest path leading to the target node. This strategy is called best-first search.

The two elements required in best-first are (1) complete ordering of the paths and (2) a method to determine the distance remaining between the current node and the target node. In theory, the ordering of the paths can be undertaken by using **Sqrt**. The straight-line distance between the target node and the current node can be used as the starting point if their locations can be identified. The straight line distance is estimated, as follows:

Distance = SQRT ((N1-X) (N1-X) + (N2-Y) (N2-Y))

when (N1, N2) is the target node position, and the X-Y coordinate is the current node on a travel map. The implementation of breadth-first and best-first search into the forward and backward chaining programs requires a careful estimation of the tradeoff between complexity and efficiency for the actual application of the expert system and tool.

ICS FOR KNOWLEDGE/DATA

The Inventory Control System discussed in the previous chapter is used as an example. The warehouse data are repeated here for the reader's convenience.

Record#	NAME	CIL	OIL	COST	DISCOUNT	MIN_ORD	ORDER_TIME
1	oil_pump	20	30	50.00	0.00	2	21
2	oil_pan	10	50	15.00	0.00	2	21
3	cooling_fan	2	23	45.00	0.00	1	28
4	fan_belt	10	45	8.00	1.00	5	14
5	battery	30	50	22.00	5.00	5	14
6	headlight	50	50	20.00	3.00	41	4
7	parking_brake	28	30	17.50	0.00	1	21
8	distributor	30	23	80.00	0.00	1	28
9	spark_plug	100	120	0.50	0.10	20	14
10	tire	100	125	80.00	10.00	4	28
11	fuel_pump	20	25	45.00	0.00	1	28
12	ignition_coil	30	31	25.00	0.00	1	28

As can be seen from the listing, the warehouse contains inventories on 12 different parts. The first part is an example to refresh the concept of expert systems discussed in Chapter 7:

Record#	NAME	CIL	OIL	COST	DISCOUNT	MIN_ORD	ORDER_TIME
1	oil_pump	20	30	50.00	0.00	2	21

This dBASE III record describes the inventory on a part called OIL_PUMP:

Current Inventory Level (CIL)	20
Optimal Inventory Level (OIL)	30
Cost	$50.00
Discount$	0.00
Minimum Order Quantity (MIN_ORD)	2
Days Until Delivery (ORDER_TIME)	21

Assume for convenience these parts are classified into two class groups: electrical_accessory, engine_accessory, and braking_parts, as shown in Figure 8-4.

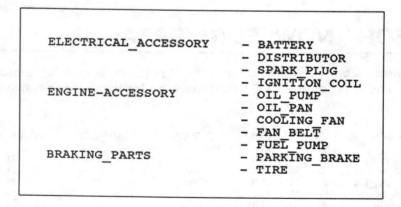

```
ELECTRICAL_ACCESSORY          - BATTERY
                              - DISTRIBUTOR
                              - SPARK_PLUG
                              - IGNITION_COIL
ENGINE-ACCESSORY              - OIL_PUMP
                              - OIL_PAN
                              - COOLING_FAN
                              - FAN_BELT
                              - FUEL_PUMP
BRAKING_PARTS                 - PARKING_BRAKE
                              - TIRE
```

Figure 8-4   Class structure of WARE.DBF.

The sample programs to search and query the knowledge base of the ICS are shown in Listing 8-2 and 8-3.

This knowledge base can be queried in many ways by using simple words such as "object", "is_a", "?x", and "with", as follows:

- To verify whether an object is a member of a class,

    the format is:

    (object object_name is_a class_name)

    Examples:

    a) To verify whether object "battery" is a member of class "electrical_accessory" by:

    (**object** battery is_a electrical_accessory) = yes

    b) To determine if part headlight is a member of class engine_accessory by:

    (object headlight is_a engine_accessory) = no

- To request information on the membership of a class,

    the format is:

    (object ?x is-a class_name)

    Example:

    c) To request all the members of class braking_parts by

    (object ?x is_a braking_parts) = (parking_brake tire)

- To request information on the attributes of an object,

    the format is:

    (object object_name is_a class_name with slot_name = ?x)

Note that in the above statement, "with" is used together with "object" and "is_a" to denote the relationship between "slot_name = ?x" and the rest of the statement.

Example:

d) To query information on current inventory level (CIL) of oil_pump by:

(object oil_pump is_a engine_accessory with CIL= ?x)= 20

- To request information that meet certain requirements,

    the format is:

  (object ?x is_a electrical_accessory with slot_name =number)

    Example:

    e) To query for all the parts in class electrical_accessory which have the same optimal inventory control level of 50

    (object ?x is_a electrical_accessory with OIL=50)

        = (battery headlight)

More sophisticated queries can be accomplished for requesting specific information derived from the knowledge base if one obtains appropriate rules from experts/specialists. For example, rules regarding optimal inventory control for a given Mazda dealer can be, as follows:

- Maximum_satisfaction

    -Engine.delivery $\leq 10\_$days

    -Fuel_pump.delivery $\leq 2\_$days

- Minimum-cost

    -Delivery $\leq 5\_$days

    -Terms $\leq 30\_$days

    -Order-size $\geq 5\_$pieces

Let us use the formats discussed to write some of these rules. The rule class for these rules is REGULAR-ORDERING. The final goal can be expressed as follows:

IF (AND (Maximum_Satisfaction is True) (Minimum_cost is True))

THEN (Inventory_Control is successful)

The subgoal of Maximum_Satisfaction can then be expressed as follows:

IF (AND (the Engine.Delivery of all WAGON is $\leq 10\_$days)
  (the Delivery of Fuel_Pump is $\leq 5\_$days)
THEN (Maximum-Satisfaction is True)

Note the difference in expression for Engine.Delivery and Fuel_Pump delivery. The engine.delivery is a slot of a class, WAGON, which is inherited by all of its subclasses, but Fuel_Pump.Delivery is a slot of a unit, Fuel_Pump. The subgoals of minimum cost can be expressed in a similar manner by the reader. More detail would be needed under each of the subgoals we have discussed, so rules on the relationship of all activities in the operations of the MAZDA_PARTS inventory are fully represented.

SUMMARY

- This chapter has examined building a rule structure, designing an inference engine,(forward chaining, backward chaining, and search strategy) and querying the ICS, as an example.

- Rule structures are also called "production rules", "production systems," or "rule-based systems," and are the most used, and simplest form of knowledge representation. In this form of knowledge representation, heuristic knowledge or experience is expressed.

- The simplest from of a rule structure consists of templates that enable programmers or experts/specialists to input if-then rules to build expert systems. The five fundamental assumptions about the rule structure are acceptance of rule formalism, modus ponems, limited interaction between factors in rules, limited attributes of a given object, and common understanding between various users.

- The two primary components of a rule are the PREMISE and the CONCLUSION. The premise is the condition the rule "fires"; the premise is not assumed to be true given an unknown environment, whose truth value is occasionally evaluated. The conclusion of the rule is the result of firing the rule. The premise is a proposition that will be become true when the rule fires.

- Rules are used to create new data that are not available in the knowledge base. For example, rule objects will be created to use the information in the classes and entities created in Chapter 7 to calculate new information.

- The inference engine empowers an expert system with rules in conjunction with a reasoning mechanism and search control to derive knowledge.

- An inference engine may be involved in forward chaining, backward chaining, justification, and search strategy.

- Forward chaining is simply an interactive program that performs a loop of substitution. Forward Chaining steps through the rule list until it finds a rule whose promises match the fact or situation. The rule then will be used or "fired" to assert a new fact.

- A backward chaining reasoning is employed when the user makes a query about whether a certain fact is true, and there is a rule that can determine the query from known information in the knowledge base or from answers given by the user.

- Backward chaining attempts to prove the hypothesis from facts. If the current goal is to determine the fact in the conclusion (hypothesis), then it is necessary to determine whether the premises match the situation.

- The three common search strategies are depth-first, breadth- first, and best-first. Each of the three strategies uses a slightly different approach to search for the target solution.

- In both forward and backward chaining, there is always a starting point (either a fact or a goal). The starting point is called the root node. There are choices (branch nodes) after the starting point and more subbranches at each branch as the matching and substitution process goes along. This decision process is called a tree since every branch has a unique parent with only one exception (the root node).

- In a depth-first search, the search starts from top to bottom. Only the left most child of each node is examined. If the node is not the desired node, the process goes down to the next level and picks the leftmost child of that node, always moving downward. If the bottom level is reached without finding the desired choice, the process returns to the last node where there was a choice. Then the downward motion is repeated. The depth-first search entails a recursive procedure where the recursion occurs for moving down one tree branch and then moving across all the branches. This recursion is implemented in both forward and backward chaining programs ,as discussed before.

- In breadth-first search, movement is performed level by level, the process examines all the nodes on the same level one by one. If the target node is not found, then the process looks at those on the next level. Consequently, the user sometimes makes a good guess about how far the target node is from the current node and selects the shortest path leading to the target node. This strategy is called best-first search.

- The ICS knowledge base can be queried in many ways by using simple words, such as "object", "is_a", "?x", and "with", as follows:

   -To verify whether an object is a member of a class,

   the format is:

   (object object_name is_a class_name)

- More sophisticated queries can be accomplished for requesting specific information derived from the knowledge base if the user obtains appropriate rules from experts and specialists.

CHAPTER REFERENCES

Baldur Systems Corp., "C/C++ Expert Systems Library," Hayward, CA 94545

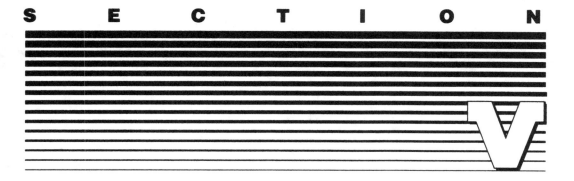

OBJECT-ORIENTED APPLICATIONS

Section I introduces the concepts of object-oriented programming, Section II describes the three main object-oriented languages, Section III discusses how to make a program user-friendly by incorporating the object-oriented environment, Section IV examines the uses of object-orient programming to make programs intelligent, and Section V assesses object-oriented applications.

This section presents two chapters. Each chapter shows a distinctive application. Chapter 9 adopts an object-oriented environment to an existing C program. Using classes discussed in Chapters 5 and 6, Chapter 9 demonstrates integrating icons, menus, and mouse operations into a C program and thus makes a Smalltalk- or MacApp window-like (Macintosh) interface for the program. Chapter 10 discusses object-oriented applications to data bases by integrating elements presented in Chapters 5, 6 , 7, 8 and 9.

325

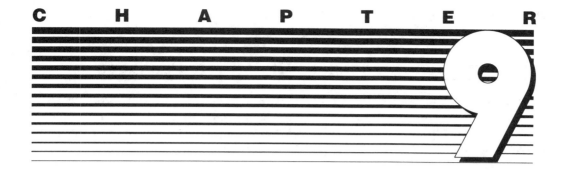

ADOPTING AN OBJECT-ORIENTED ENVIRONMENT TO YOUR PROGRAMS

This chapter presents methods and examples of adopting an object- oriented environment to a C program by using the basic classes discussed in Chapters 5 and 6. A prominent area of an object-oriented environment is improving user interface with existing, conventional software packages. Inclusion of an appropriate amount of windows, icons, and menus will make a software program easier to be accepted. The object-oriented environment provided in this text makes this inclusion fairly straightforward.

Improving User-friendliness Of Software Packages

Depending on the complexity of the software package, programs can be significantly improved and made more user friendly by incorporating an object-oriented environment. Acting as a facade where standard graphical interface can be established for the user, the object-oriented environment can:

- Identify where the user is anytime and anywhere .

- Allow the user to exit anytime and anywhere.

- Employ many layers of windows with icons and menus including systems commands.

- Provide the user with a choice of meaningful implied actions for both icons and menus.

- Ask the user whether to proceed or cancel the action in progress

All of these features do not need to be implemented extensively into a conventional software program because "more is not necessarily better." The intensity of these features depends on the sophistication of the user and on the required tasks of the conventional program.

A GENERAL PROCEDURE FOR BUILDING A FRIENDLY USER INTERFACE IN OOP (C+ +)

To bring the user-friendliness of Smalltalk- or MacApp window-like (Macintosh) graphical interface into your programs, the following three steps are recommended:

1. Build a "facade" of the existing software program to act as an interface manager using the basic classes, for example, Icon, Menu, Pen, and Bunch.

2. Develop an icon library to host meaningful specialized icons for a given domain problem, using Icon and other related classes.

3. Builds a file class group to interface icons and menus with relevant existing files, using programs such as C+ +/C.

Each of the three components of the user interface package, as shown in Figure 9-1, performs specified tasks to make the user feel at ease while using a software program.

An appropriate combination of the above three components will enable you to design an interface where desirable layers of windows can be built. Each window consists of as many panes as needed with active menus and icons that can be activated for selection of alternatives by the user.

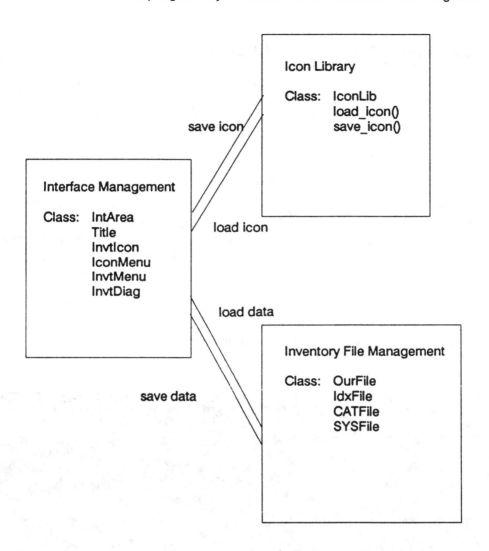

Figure 9.1 Three main groups of the OOP user Interface classes for an Inventory Accounting System.

BUILDING A PROGRAM FACADE

The four class groups required to build a facade for a software package include:

1. Title: provides system information around the outskirts of the screen.

2. DiagBox: provides user dialog boxes.

3. InvtMenu: provides menu items for the user to select.

4. InvtIcon: provides icon items for the user .

An existing Inventory Accounting System is used to demonstrate feasibility and as an example to test the concept. However, the use of a special domain example does not limit the usefulness of this approach. The sample programs included can be modified without substantial effort for most programs.

Class Group Title

Class group Title enables the user to organize, decorate the screen, and to arrange various panes, such as Time, Date, Logo on the screen.

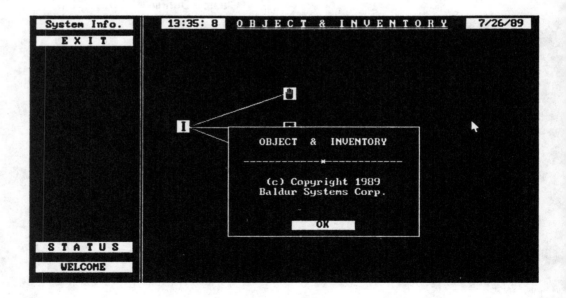

Figure 9-2. A Desired Layout of the Inventory Accounting System Notice.

For instance, Title may be designed to decorate the screen into a layout that provides the following information, as appeared on Figure 9-2.

- Title of the system, that is, "OBJECT & INVENTORY"
- Date
- Time
- System Information, for example, "CONTINUE" , "Exit"
- Status of operations, for example, "WELCOME," "ADD,"

the following classes need to be included in the Title class group:

- Title: to organize all the panes used to decorate the screen.
- TitlePane: the pane for the title .
- DatePane: the pane for the date.
- TimePane: the pane for the current time.
- InfoWin: the pane for system information.
- StatusWin: the pane for operation status.
- ExitPane: the pane to provide an exit any time .
- DividLine: the pane to provide a line that divides the system control and the interface areas.

The structure of these classes is shown in Listing 9-1.

Except class Title, which is a subclass of Bunch, all other five classes are a subclass of Pane. All these classes are fairly similar: all use the constructor to initialize the class to the initial status of the inventory accounting system, such as "EXIT," "STATUS", as shown in Figure 9-2; the classes all use Draw() to fill in the pane. However, each Draw() is defined slightly different to accommodate the need of each class, see Listing 9- 2. For example, the Draw() for class InfoWin is, as follows:

```
//
//InfoWin::Draw()
//Draw the system information window
//
```

Listing 9.1: Header File for Class Group Title

```
//
// Title.hpp
//
//
// Display the Title header file
//

class InfoDiagBox;

//
// Title class
//
class Title : public Bunch {
    Pen *background,*foreground;
public:
    Title();
    void Draw();
};

//
// TimePane class
//
class TimePane : public Pane {
    char *tme;
    Pen *background,*foreground;
public:
    TimePane();
    void Draw();
};

//
//DatePane class
//
class DatePane : public Pane {
    char *date;
    Pen *background,*foreground;
public:
    DatePane();
    void Draw();
};
continued...
```

```
//
//TitlePane class
//
class TitlePane : public Pane {
    char *text;
    Pen  *background,*foreground;
public:
    TitlePane(char*);
    void Draw();
};
////DividLine class
//
class DividLine : public Pane {
    Pen  *foreground;
public:
    DividLine();
    void Draw();
};

//
//StatusWin class
//
class StatusWin : public Pane {
    Pen *foreground,*background;
    char *text;
public:
    StatusWin();
    void Draw();
    void SetText(char*);
};

//
//InfoWin class
//
class InfoWin : public Pane {
protected:
    InfoDiagbox  *target;
    Pen *foreground,*background;
public:
    InfoWin(InfoDiagbox*);
    void Draw();
    void Handle(Event&);
```

continued..

```
};
//
// Exit Pane
//
class ExitPane : public Pane {
    Pen *foreground,*background;
public:
    ExitPane();
    void Draw();
    void Handle(Event&);
};
void InfoWin::Draw()
{
    background->FillRect(this,0,0,xmax,ymax);
    foreground->MoveTo(this,(15-strlen("System Info."))*8/2,0);
    foreground->Text(this,"System Info.");
}
```

Classes StatusWin and InfoWin require additional methods to accept text (Set-Text()) and to show system information when the user clicks the button (Hand-le()), respectively. Both methods are straightforward. For example, Handle() is defined, as follows:

```
//
//InfoWin::Handle()
//If someone clicks on me, show the system information
//
void InfoWin::Handle(Event &e)
{
    extern Manager m;

    if(e.eventType & E_LEFTDOWN)
    {
    m.Insert(target,250,100);
    target->Draw();
    target->Run();
    target->SetStatus(0);
    m.Remove(target);
    m.Draw();
    }
}
```

Listing 9.2: Implementation File for Class Group Title

```
//
// title.cpp
//
// Inventory screen decoration program
//
#include "stream.hpp"
#include "invntory.inc"
#include "invntfil.hpp"

#include "bunch.hpp"
#include "pane.hpp"
#include "manager.hpp"
#include "icon.hpp"
#include "diagbox.hpp"
#include "title.hpp"
#include "time.h"


//
// InfoWin constructor
//
InfoWin::InfoWin(InfoDiagbox *id)
{
    target = id;
    foreground = new Pen(FG_BLACK);
    background = new Pen(FG_GREEN);
    xmax = 15*8;
    ymax = fg_charbox[FG_Y2];
}

//
//InfoWin::Draw()
//Draw the System information window
//
void InfoWin::Draw()
{
    background->FillRect(this,0,0,xmax,ymax);
    foreground->MoveTo(this,(15-strlen("System Info."))*8/2,0);
    foreground->Text(this,"System Info.");
}
//
```

continued...

```
//InfoWin::Handle()
//If someone clicks on me, show the system information
//
void InfoWin::Handle(Event &e)
{
    extern Manager m;

    if(e.eventType & E_LEFTDOWN)
    {
    m.Insert(target,250,80);
    target->Draw();
    target->Run();
    target->SetStatus(0);
    m.Remove(target);
    m.Draw();
    }
}
//
//StatusWin constructor
//
StatusWin::StatusWin()
{
    text = "WELCOME";
    foreground = new Pen(FG_BLACK);
    background = new Pen(FG_YELLOW);
    xmax = 15*8;
    ymax = 3*fg_charbox[FG_Y2];
}
//
//StatusWin::SetText()
//Set the content to be shown on status window
//
void StatusWin::SetText(char* txt)
{
    text = txt;
}


//
//StatusWin::Draw()
//
void StatusWin::Draw()
{
continued...
```

```
background->FillRect(this,0,0,xmax,fg_charbox[FG_Y2]);
background->FillRect(this,0,2*fg_charbox[FG_Y2],xmax,3*fg_charbox[FG_Y2]);
Pen *temp = new Pen(FG_RED);
temp->MoveTo(this,(15-strlen("S T A T U S"))*8/2,2*fg_charbox[FG_Y2]);
temp->Text(this,"S T A T U S");
foreground->MoveTo(this,(15-strlen(text))*8/2,0);
foreground->Text(this,text);
}


//
//DividLine constructor
//
DividLine::DividLine()
{
    foreground = new Pen(FG_HIGHLIGHT);
    xmax = 8;
    ymax = fg_displaybox[FG_Y2];
}

//
//DividLine::Draw()
//Draw the line between the interface area and the control area
//
void DividLine::Draw()
{
    foreground->MoveTo(this,3,0);
    foreground->Line(this,3,0,3,ymax);
    foreground->Line(this,6,0,6,ymax);
}

//
//ExitPane constructor
//
ExitPane::ExitPane()
{
    foreground = new Pen(FG_YELLOW);
    background = new Pen(FG_RED);
    xmax = 15*8;
    ymax = fg_charbox[FG_Y2];
}
```

continued...

```
//
// ExitPane::Draw()
//
void ExitPane::Draw()
{
    background->FillRect(this,0,0,xmax,ymax);
    foreground->MoveTo(this,(xmax-8*strlen("E X I T"))/2,0);
    foreground->Text(this,"E X I T");
}


//
// ExitPane::Handle()
//
void ExitPane::Handle(Event &e)
{
    extern Manager m;
    extern int genflg;
    extern CATFile *CFile;
    extern IdxFile *InvIdx;
    extern SYSFile *SFile;
    extern DeleDiagbox *dd;

    if(e.eventType & E_LEFTDOWN)
    {
    dd->SetText("Save the changes??");
    m.Insert(dd,250,50);
    dd->Draw();
    dd->Run();
    if(dd-GetFlag() == OKFLAG)
    {
        delete(InvIdx);    //save the inv. file
        delete(CFile);     //save the cat. file
        delete(SFile);     //save the sys. file
    }
    genflg = EXIT;
    }


}
```

continued...

```
//
// Constructor for TDPane
//
TimePane::TimePane()
{
    tme = NULL;
    background = new Pen(FG_HIGHLIGHT);
    foreground = new Pen(FG_BLACK);
    xmax = 10*8;
    ymax = fg_charbox[FG_Y2];
}

//
// Draw() for TDPane
//
void TimePane::Draw()
{
    struct tm *t;
    time_t ltime;
    time(&ltime);
    t = localtime(&ltime);
    char buf[20],buf1[5];
    buf[0] = buf1[0] = NULL;
    sprintf(buf1,"%2d",t->tm_hour);
    strcat(buf,buf1);
    strcat(buf,":");
    sprintf(buf1,"%2d",t->tm_min);
    strcat(buf,buf1);
    strcat(buf,":");
    sprintf(buf1,"%2d",t->tm_sec);
    strcat(buf,buf1);
    strcpy(tme,buf);
    background->FillRect(this,0,0,xmax,ymax);
    foreground->MoveTo(this,8,0);
    foreground->Text(this,tme);
    Flush();
}

//
//DatePane constructor
//
DatePane::DatePane()
```

continued...

```
{
    date = NULL;
    background = new Pen(FG_HIGHLIGHT);
    foreground = new Pen(FG_BLACK);
    xmax = 10*8;
    ymax = fg_charbox[FG_Y2];
}
//
//DatePane::Draw()
//Get the current date and show the date
//
void DatePane::Draw()
{
    struct tm *t;
    time_t ltime;
    time(&ltime);
    t = localtime(&ltime);
    char buf[20],buf1[5];
    buf[0] = buf1[0] = NULL;
    sprintf(buf1,"%2d",t->tm_mon+1);
    strcat(buf,buf1);
    strcat(buf,"/");
    sprintf(buf1,"%2d",t->tm_mday);
    strcat(buf,buf1);
    strcat(buf,"/");
    sprintf(buf1,"%2d",t->tm_year%100);
    strcat(buf,buf1);
    strcpy(date,buf);

    background->FillRect(this,0,0,xmax,ymax);
    foreground->MoveTo(this,8,0);
    foreground->Text(this,date);
}


//
// TitlePane constructor
//
TitlePane::TitlePane(char *txt)
{
    text = txt;
    background = new Pen(FG_LIGHT_BLUE);
    foreground = new Pen(FG_HIGHLIGHT);
```

continued..

```
    xmax = strlen(text)*8;
    ymax = fg_charbox[FG_Y2];
}

//
//TitlePane::Draw()
//
void TitlePane::Draw()
{
    background->FillRect(this,0,0,xmax,ymax);
    foreground->MoveTo(this,0,0);
    foreground->Text(this,text);

    Pen *tep = new Pen(FG_GREEN);
    tep->MoveTo(this,8,0);
    tep->Line(this,0,0,xmax,0);
    tep->Line(this,0,2,xmax,2);

    Flush();
}

//
// Title constructor
//
Title::Title()
{
    TimePane *t;
    DatePane *d;
    TitlePane *tp;

    t = new TimePane();
    Insert(t,0,0);
    tp = new TitlePane("O B J E C T  &  I N V E N T O R Y");
    Insert(tp,t->xmax+16,0);
    d = new DatePane();
    Insert(d,t->xmax+tp->xmax+5*8,0);
    xmax = t->xmax+tp->xmax+d->xmax;
    ymax = fg_charbox[FG_Y2];
}

//
//Title::Draw()
```

continued...

```
//
void Title::Draw()
{
    Bunch::Draw();
}

//
// invmain.cpp
//
#include "stream.hpp"
#include "invntory.inc"
#include "register.inc"
#include "invntfil.hpp"

#include "bunch.hpp"
#include "pane.hpp"
#include "manager.hpp"
#include "icon.hpp"
#include "invticon.hpp"
#include "intarea.hpp"
#include "invtmenu.hpp"
#include "diagbox.hpp"
#include "invtdiag.hpp"
#include "iconlib.hpp"
#include "iconmenu.hpp"
#include "title.hpp"
#include "time.h"
//------------------------------------------------------------------------
char *menutext[7] = { "END","ADD","DELETE","CHANGE","VIEWING","REPORT","  M
E N U"};
//------------------------------------------------------------------------
Manager m;
int exitflg = 0;
int genflg = 0;
InvtIcon *curic;
InvtMenu *mnu = new InvtMenu(7,menutext);
IconLib *iclib = new IconLib("icon.lib");
IconMenu *icnmnu = new IconMenu();
InvtDiagbox *db = new InvtDiagbox();
CataDiagbox *ctdb = new CataDiagbox();
SysDiagbox *sysdb = new SysDiagbox();
InfoDiagbox *id = new InfoDiagbox();
```

continued...

```
DeleDiagbox *dd = new DeleDiagbox();
ErrorDiagbox *ed = new ErrorDiagbox();
//-------------------------------------------Invntory data file
//invntory index file
IdxFile *InvIdx = new IdxFile("baldur.dat","baldur.idx","baldur.del",
            sizeof(struct INV_IDX),sizeof(struct INV_DAT));
CATFile *CFile = new CATFile("baldur.cat"); //Category file
SYSFile *SFile = new SYSFile("baldur.sys"); //system args. file
//-------------------------------------------------------------
main()
{
   m.Init(FG_LIGHT_BLUE);
   Title *t = new Title();
   StatusWin *sw = new StatusWin();
   ExitPane *ep = new ExitPane();
   InfoWin *iw = new InfoWin(id);
   DividLine *dl = new DividLine();
   IntArea *ia = new IntArea();
   m.Insert(sw,1*8,fg_charbox[FG_Y2]);
   m.Insert(dl,135,0);
   m.Insert(t,165,fg_displaybox[FG_Y2]-fg_charbox[FG_Y2]-3);
   m.Insert(ia,175,0);
   m.Insert(iw,1*8,fg_displaybox[FG_Y2]-fg_charbox[FG_Y2]-4);
   m.Insert(ep,1*8,fg_displaybox[FG_Y2]-3*fg_charbox[FG_Y2]);

   m.Draw();
   Event e;
   do {
   m.Read(e);
   if(e.target!=0)
   {
       e.target->Handle(e);
   }
   } while(genflg != 1);
}


void ErrorProc(char *info)
{
    extern ErrorDiagbox *ed;
    extern Manager m;
```

continued...

343

```
        ed->SetInfo(info);
        m.Insert(ed,200,10);
        ed->Draw();
        ed->Run();
        ed->SetStatus(0);
        m.Remove(ed);
}
```

Class Group DiagBox

Class group DiagBox allows inputs from the keyboard and the buttons and displays output results on the screen. The DiagBox class group includes five subclasses and three other relevant classes, see Listing 9-3:

- Subclasses

    InvtDiagBox: a Dialog Box for input/output (I/O) of inventory data .

    CataDiagBox: a Dialog Box for I/O of inventory category.

    InfoDiagBox: a Dialog Box for I/O of system status.

    SysDiagBox: a Dialog Box for I/O of system parameters.

    DeleteDiagBox: a Dialog Box asking the user whether to proceed (OK) or to cancel (CANCEL).

- Relevant classes

    DiagItems: a class to accept dialog items.

    CtlItems: a class to control mouse buttons.

    Display: a class to display, discussed in Chapter 6.

Listing 9.3: Header File for Class Group DiagBox

```
//
// diagbox.hpp
//
//
// Dialog box header file
//
#define CRT_RET 13
#define BACKSPACE '\b'
#define DTY_FLAG 1
#define CLN_FLAG 0
#define INTDIGIT 1
#define CHARDIGIT 0
#define OK        "  OK"
#define CANCEL    "CANCEL"
#define OKFLAG     1
#define CANCELFLAG 0


//
// '!' icon
//
static char splicon[] = {
    0x00,0x00,
    0x03,0xC0,
    0x03,0xC0,
    0x03,0xC0,
    0x03,0xC0,
    0x03,0xC0,
    0x03,0xC0,
    0x03,0xC0,
    0x03,0xC0,
    0x03,0xC0,
    0x03,0xC0,
    0x00,0x00,
    0x00,0x00,
    0x03,0xC0,
    0x03,0xC0,
    0x00,0x00,
};

//
```

continued...

```
// Diagbox
//
class Diagbox : public Bunch {
protected:
    int  done;
public:
    virtual void Draw();
    virtual void Do(char*);
    void Run();
    void SetStatus(int);
};


//
// System Information Dialog box
//
class InfoDiagbox : public Diagbox {
protected:
    Pen   *foreground,*background;
public:
    InfoDiagbox();           //diagbox constructor
    void Draw();
    void Do(char*);
};
//
// Error Information Dialog box
//
class ErrorDiagbox : public Diagbox {
protected:
    char  *info;
    Pen   *foreground,*background;
public:
    ErrorDiagbox();           //diagbox constructor
    void Draw();
    void Do(char*);
    void SetInfo(char*);      // set the error info.
};


//
// Delete item confirmation dialog box
//
class DeleDiagbox : public Diagbox {
    int   okcancel;           //flag for "ok" or "cancel"
```

continued...

```
    char   *text;
protected:
    Pen    *foreground,*background;
public:
    DeleDiagbox();          //diagbox constructor
    void Draw();
    void Do(char*);
    int  GetFlag() { return okcancel; }
    void SetText(char*);    //set the text
};

//
// DiagItems
//
class DiagItem : public Pane {
protected:
    char      *itmtext;        // menu item text
    Pen       *background,*foreground;
public:
    DiagItem(char*,int,int);
    void Draw();
};

//
// Control buttons
class CtlItem : public Pane {
    Diagbox *target;
    char  *itmtext;
    Pen   *foreground,*background;
public:
    CtlItem(Diagbox*,char*,int,int);
    void Draw();
    void Handle(Event&);
};

//
// invtdiag.hpp
//
// Invntory Dialog box header file
//
//
// Inventory diagbox for data I/O
```

continued..

```
//
class InvtDiagbox : public Diagbox {
private:
    Pen         *foreground,*background;
    char            itmcd[15];       //place for the item code
    struct INV_DAT invtdata;     //place for the data I/O
    PaneList    dsplyList;        // list of all the displays
public:
    InvtDiagbox();               //diagbox constructor
    void Draw();
    void Do(char*);
    void PutCatCd(int);          //set the cat. code
    void PutTx(char);            //set the tax. code
    void PutInvDat();
    void SetItmCd(char x[]) { strcpy(itmcd,x);}// set the item code
    void SetInvDt();             // set the inventory data
    char *GetItmCd() { return itmcd; }  // get the inventory item code
    struct INV_DAT *GetInvDat() { return &invtdata; }// get the inventory data
    void Clear();
};


//
// Category item diagbox for data I/O
//
class CataDiagbox : public Diagbox {
private:
    Pen         *foreground,*background;
    struct CATCODE catadata;     //place for the data I/O
    PaneList    dsplyList;        // list of all the displays
public:
    CataDiagbox();               //diagbox constructor
    void Draw();
    void Do(char*);
    void PutCatDat();
    void PutId(int);             // set the category id
    void PutDesc(char*);         // set the Category desc.
    void SetCatDt(char*);        // set the Category data
    struct CATCODE *GetCataDat(){ return &catadata; }// get the Category data
    void Clear();
};


//
// System args. diagbox for data I/O
//
class SysDiagbox : public Diagbox {
private:
    Pen         *foreground,*background;
    struct SYSTEMARG sysdata;        //place for the data I/O
    PaneList    dsplyList;        // list of all the displays
```
continued...

```
public:
    SysDiagbox();          //diagbox constructor
    void Draw();
    void Do(char*);
    void PutSysDat();
    struct SYSTEMARG *GetSysDat() { return &sysdata; }// get the system data
    void Clear();
};
```

Class DiagBox is a subclass of Bunch with four public methods:

```
class DiagBox : public Bunch {
protected:
    int  done;
public:
    virtual void Draw();
    virtual void Do(char*);
    void Run();
    void SetStatus(int);
};
```

Draw() and Do() are declared virtual and will be defined later in each subclass to meet the class's operational needs. Run() and SetStatus() are defined, as follows:

```
//
void DiagBox::Run()
{
    Event e;
    extern Manager m;

    while (!done)                   //whether clicked on control
                                    //  buttons or not
    {
    m.Read(e);                      //not yet, read in the event
    Pane *temp = find(e.x,e.y); //find where the event happened
    if((temp!=this) && e.eventType&E_LEFTDOWN || //constrained on
//DiagBox
        (temp!=this) && e.eventType&E_KEY)
    {
        e.target->Handle(e);        //tell the corresponding object
                                    //on which the event happened
    }
    }
}
```

continued...

```
//
//DiagBox::SetStatus()
//Used to set the status flag
//
void DiagBox::SetStatus(int status)
{
    done = status;
}
```

Listing 9-4 Implementation File for Class Group DiagBox

```
//
// diagbox.cpp
//
// Dialog box program
//
#include "bunch.hpp"
#include "pane.hpp"
#include "manager.hpp"
#include "diagbox.hpp"
#include "icon.hpp"


//
// DiagItem constructor
//
DiagItem::DiagItem(char *text,int fg,int bg)
{
    itmtext = text;         //item text
    foreground = new Pen(fg);     //foreground & background colors
    background = new Pen(bg);
    xmax = 15*8;            //x max length 15 char long
    ymax = fg_charbox[FG_Y2];   //y max length 1 char high
}

//
// DiagItem Draw()
// Draw the diaglog text on the bunch
//
void DiagItem::Draw()
{
    background->FillRect(this,0,0,xmax,ymax);
    foreground->MoveTo(this,xmax-strlen(itmtext)*8,0);
    foreground->Text(this,itmtext);     //show the text
    Flush();
}
```

continued...

```
//
// CtlItem constructor
// The diagbox control button objects
//
CtlItem::CtlItem(Diagbox *d,char *text,int fg,int bg)
{
    target = d;              //the diagbox to which the control goes
    itmtext = text;      //text on the button
    foreground = new Pen(fg);  //foreground & background colors
    background = new Pen(bg);
    xmax = 10*8;            //length of the button
    ymax = fg_charbox[FG_Y2];    //hight of the button
}


//
// CtlItem Draw()
// Draw the control buttons
//
void CtlItem::Draw()
{
    background->FillRect(this,0,0,xmax,ymax);
    foreground->Rect(this,0,0,xmax,ymax);
    foreground->MoveTo(this,2*8,1);
    foreground->Text(this,itmtext);
    Flush();
}



//
//CtlItem Handle()
//Do what needs to be done when someone clicks on me
//
void CtlItem::Handle(Event &e)
{
        if (e.eventType & E_LEFTDOWN) //check if the left button is clicked
    {
        target->Do(itmtext);  //yes, tell Diagbox to do something

    }
}
```

continued...

```
//
//InfoDiagbox constructor
//System information diagbox constructor
//
InfoDiagbox::InfoDiagbox()
{
    done = 0;
    foreground = new Pen(FG_BLACK);
    background = new Pen(FG_HIGHLIGHT);
    xmax = 30*8;
    ymax = 11*fg_charbox[FG_Y2];
    CtlItem *c = new CtlItem(this,OK,FG_BLACK,FG_HIGHLIGHT);   //insert a con-
trol button
    Insert(c,xmax/3,8);
}


//
//InfoDiagbox::Draw()
//Draw the information diagbox
//
void InfoDiagbox::Draw()
{
    background->FillRect(this,0,0,xmax,ymax);
    foreground->MoveTo(this,(xmax-8*strlen("OBJECT & INVENTORY"))/2,ymax-
2*fg_charbox[FG_Y2]);
    foreground->Text(this,"OBJECT & INVENTORY");
    foreground->MoveTo(this,(xmax-8*strlen("------------*------------
"))/2,ymax-3*fg_charbox[FG_Y2]);
    foreground->Text(this,"------------*------------");
    foreground->MoveTo(this,(xmax-8*strlen("\(c\) Copyright 1989"))/2,ymax-
6*fg_charbox[FG_Y2]);
    foreground->Text(this,"\(c\) Copyright 1989");
    foreground->MoveTo(this,(xmax-8*strlen("Baldur Systems Corp."))/2,ymax-
7*fg_charbox[FG_Y2]);
    foreground-T>ext(this,"Baldur Systems Corp.");
    Bunch::Draw();
}


//
//InfoDiagbox::Do()
//Receiving the control from the control buttons, and set the status flag
//
void InfoDiagbox::Do(char *dummy)
{
    done = 1;        //set the flag as "done"
}
```
        continued...

```
//
//ErrorDiagbox constructor
//Error information diagbox constructor
//
ErrorDiagbox::ErrorDiagbox()
{
    done = 0;
    foreground = new Pen(FG_BLACK);
    background = new Pen(FG_YELLOW);
    xmax = 35*8;
    ymax = 5*fg_charbox[FG_Y2];
    CtlItem *c = new CtlItem(this,OK,FG_BLACK,FG_HIGHLIGHT);
//insert a control button
    Insert(c,xmax/3,8);
}


//
//ErrorDiagbox::Draw()
//Draw the error information diagbox
//
void ErrorDiagbox::Draw()
{
    background->FillRect(this,0,0,xmax,ymax);
    foreground->MoveTo(this,(xmax-8*strlen(info))/2,ymax-2*fg_charbox[FG_Y2]);
    foreground->Text(this,info);
    Bunch::Draw();

}


//
//ErrorDiagbox::Do()
//Receiving the control from the control buttons, and set the status flag
//
void ErrorDiagbox::Do(char *dummy)
{
    done = 1;        //set the flag as "done"
 }
```

continued...

```
//
//ErrorDiagbox::SetInfo()
//Set the error info
//
void ErrorDiagbox::SetInfo(char *erinfo)
{
    info = erinfo;
}



//
//DeleDiagbox constructor
//Delete information diagbox constructor
//
DeleDiagbox::DeleDiagbox()
{
    done = 0;
    foreground = new Pen(FG_BLACK);
    background = new Pen(FG_HIGHLIGHT);
    xmax = 30*8;
    ymax = 6*fg_charbox[FG_Y2];
    CtlItem *c;
    c = new CtlItem(this,OK,FG_BLACK,FG_YELLOW);   //insert a control button
    Insert(c,xmax/4-c->xmax/2,8);
    c = new CtlItem(this,CANCEL,FG_BLACK,FG_YELLOW);   //insert a control buttor
    Insert(c,3*xmax/4-c->xmax/2,8);

}



//
//DeleDiagbox::Draw()
//Draw the information diagbox

//

void DeleDiagbox::Draw()

{
    background->FillRect(this,0,0,xmax,ymax);
    Pen *temp = new Pen(FG_LIGHT_BLUE);
    temp->FillRect(this,3*8,4*fg_charbox[FG_Y2],6*8,5*fg_charbox[FG_Y2]+4);
    temp = new Pen(FG_HIGHLIGHT);
    temp->Put(this,(3+1/2)*8,4*fg_charbox[FG_Y2]+2,splicon,2*8,2*8);
```

continued...

```
    foreground->MoveTo(this,((xmax+3*8)-8*strlen(text))/2,ymax-2*fg_char-
box[FG_Y2]);
    foreground->Text(this,text);
    Bunch::Draw();
}


//
//DeleDiagbox::Do()
//Receiving the control from the control buttons, and set the status flag
//
void DeleDiagbox::Do(char *op)
{
    if(!strcmp(op,OK))
    okcancel = OKFLAG;        //click on "ok"
    else
    okcancel = CANCELFLAG;     //click on "cancel"
    done = 1;
}


//
//DeleteDiagbox::SetText()
//set the info.
//
void DeleDiagbox::SetText(char *info)
{
    text = info;
}



//
//Diagbox::SetStatus()
//Used to set the status flag
//
void Diagbox::SetStatus(int status)
{
    done = status;
}
```

continued...

```
//
//Diagbox::Run()
//Control focuses on the diagbox until someone clicks on the control button
//
void Diagbox::Run()
{
    Event e;
    extern Manager m;

    while (!done)          //whether someone has clicked on
// control buttons or not
    {
    m.Read(e);           //not yet, read in the event
    Pane *temp = find(e.x,e.y); //find where the event happened
    if((temp!=this) && e.eventType&E_LEFTDOWN || //constrained on diagbox
        (temp!=this) && e.eventType&E_KEY)

    {
        e.target->Handle(e);  //tell the corresponding
//object on which the event happened
    }
    }
}


//
//Diagbox::Draw()
//Draw the dialog box
//
void Diagbox::Draw()
{
    /* virtual function; each derived from Pane; will define its own
    ** behaviour through the appropriate redefinition of Handle() and
    ** Draw()
    */

}


//
//Diagbox::Do()
//
void Diagbox::Do(char*)
```

continued...

```
{

    /* virtual function; each derived from Pane; will  define its own
    ** behaviour through the appropriate redefinition of Handle() and
    ** Do()
    */

}

//
// invtdiag.cpp
//
// Invntory Dialog box program
//

#include "invntory.inc"
#include "register.inc"
#include "invntfil.hpp"

#include "bunch.hpp"
#include "pane.hpp"
#include "manager.hpp"
#include "diagbox.hpp"
#include "invtdiag.hpp"
#include "icon.hpp"
#include "invticon.hpp"


char diagtext[12][20] = { "QTY. ONORDER:","QTY. ONHAND:","REORDER
LEVEL:","LOCATION:","VENDOR:","CATEGORY CODE:","UNIT COST:","TAX:","SALE's
PRICE:","UNIT:","ITEM CODE:","DESCRIPTION:"};

char catatext[4][20] = { "COST:","SALES:","DESCRIPTION:","ID:"};

char systext[10][20] = { "RCPT. PRT:","INVOC. PRT:","FIN. CHG.RATE:","TAX
RATE:","ZIPPER CODE:","PHONE NO:","CITY:","STATE:","STORE NAME:","ADDRESS:"};




//
// InvtDiagbox constructor
// Specific diagbox for inventory data I/O
//
InvtDiagbox::InvtDiagbox()
```

```
{
    DiagItem *d;
    CtlItem  *c;
    Display  *dp;

    done = 0;                   //init the status
    foreground = new Pen(FG_PURPLE);

    for(int row = 0; row  <6; row++) //insert the diagbox's contents
    for(int col = 0; col  <2; col++)
    {
        d = new DiagItem(diagtext[row*2+col],FG_HIGHLIGHT,FG_BLACK);
        Insert(d,(d->xmax+15*8)*col,(d->ymax+2)*row+3*8);
        dp = new Display(row+col,CHARDIGIT);
        Insert(dp,(d->xmax)*(col+1)+dp->xmax*col,(d->ymax+2)*row+3*8)
        dsplyList.Insert(dp);
    }
    xmax = 2*(d->xmax+dp->xmax);     //get the length of the diagbox
    ymax = (d->ymax+4)*6+30;        //get the hight of the diagbox
    c=new CtlItem(this,OK,FG_BLACK,FG_HIGHLIGHT);//insert the control buttons
    Insert(c,xmax/4,0);
    c = new CtlItem(this,CANCEL,FG_BLACK,FG_HIGHLIGHT);
    Insert(c,3*xmax/5,0);


}

//
//InvtDiagbox::Draw()
//Draw the inventory diagbox
//
void InvtDiagbox::Draw()
{
    Pen *tmp = new Pen(FG_PURPLE);
    tmp->FillRect(this,0,0,xmax,ymax);
    Pen *temp = new Pen(FG_HIGHLIGHT);
    char *title;
    title = "I N V E N T O R Y   D A T A";
    temp->MoveTo(this,(xmax-strlen(title)*8)/2,ymax-fg_charbox[FG_Y2]-2);
    temp->Text(this,title);
    Bunch::Draw();          //draw all the objects defined on this bunch
}
```

continued...

```
//
//InvtDiagbox Do()
//Receiving the control from the control button, and do what you want to do
//
void InvtDiagbox::Do(char *op)
{
    ListIterator iter(dsplyList);
    Display *p;
    char *dt[12];          // '12', number of fields

    int i = 0;
    if(!strcmp(op,OK))      //clicked on "OK"
    {
    while (p = (Display *)iter()) {
        dt[i++] = p->Get();
    }
    strcpy(itmcd,dt[1]);    //set the item code
    extern void copyData(char*[],struct INV_DAT*);
    copyData(dt,&invtdata);
    }
    else
    {
    while (p = (Display *)iter()) {
        p->Clear();
    }
    }
    done = 1;               //set the status as already done
}

//
// Auxilliary function for setting the inventory data for displaying
//
void InvtDiagbox::SetInvDt()
{
    extern IdxFile *InvIdx;

    InvIdx->GetStuff(itmcd,&invtdata);
}
```

continued...

```
//
// Clear all the displays
//
void InvtDiagbox::Clear()
{
    ListIterator iter(dsplyList);
    Display *p;

    while(p = (Display *)iter())
    p->Clear();
}

//
//InvtDiagbox::PutTx()
//
void InvtDiagbox::PutTx(char tx)
{
    ListIterator iter(dsplyList);
    Display *p;
    char buf[20];

    int i;
    for(i=0;i;i++)
    p = (Display *)iter();
    p = (Display *)iter();
    sprintf(buf,"%c",x);
    p->Put(buf);
}

//
//InvtDiagbox::PutCatCd()
//
void InvtDiagbox::PutCatCd(int x)
{
    ListIterator iter(dsplyList);
    Display *p;
    char buf[20];
```

continued...

```
    int i;
    for(i=0;i;i++)
  p = (Display *)iter();
   p = (Display *)iter();
   sprintf(buf,"%d",x);
   p->Put(buf);
}

//
// Auxilliary function for copying the data to the display screen
//
void InvtDiagbox::PutInvDat()
{
    ListIterator iter(dsplyList);
    Display *p;
    char buf[20];

    p = (Display *)iter();
    p->Put(invtdata.desc);

    p = (Display *)iter();
    p->Put(itmcd);

    p = (Display *)iter();
    p->Put(invtdata.unit);

    p = (Display *)iter();
    sprintf(buf,"%lf",invtdata.price);
    p->Put(buf);

    p = (Display *)iter();
    sprintf(buf,"%c",invtdata.tax);
    p->Put(buf);

    p = (Display *)iter();
    sprintf(buf,"%lf",invtdata.cost);
    p->Put(buf);

    p = (Display *)iter();
    sprintf(buf,"%d",invtdata.catcod);
    p-P>ut(buf);

    p = (Display *)iter();
    p-Put(invtdata.vendor);
```

```
    p = (Display *)iter();
    p->Put(invtdata.locat);

    p = (Display *)iter();
    sprintf(buf,"%d",invtdata.relevl);
    p->Put(buf);

    p = (Display *)iter();
    sprintf(buf,"%d",invtdata.qtyonhnd);
    p->Put(buf);

    p = (Display *)iter();
    sprintf(buf,"%d",invtdata.qtyonodr);
    p->Put(buf);
}


//
// CataDiagbox constructor
// Specific diagbox for Category data I/O
//
CataDiagbox::CataDiagbox()
{
    DiagItem *d;
    CtlItem  *c;
    Display  *dp;

    done = 0;              //init the status
    foreground = new Pen(FG_PURPLE);
    for(int row = 0; row  <2; row++) //insert the diagbox's contents
    for(int col = 0; col  <2; col++)
    {
        d = new DiagItem(catatext[row*2+col],FG_HIGHLIGHT,FG_BLACK);
        Insert(d,(d->xmax+15*8)*col,(d->ymax+2)*row+3*8);
    }
    dp = new Display(0,INTDIGIT);   //insert "sals" display
    Insert(dp,(d->xmax),3*8);
    dsplyList.Insert(dp);

    dp = new Display(1,INTDIGIT);    //insert "cost" display
    Insert(dp,(d->xmax)*2+dp->xmax,3*8);
    dsplyList.Insert(dp);
```

continued...

```
    dp = new Display(1,CHARDIGIT);     //insert "desc" display
    Insert(dp,(d->xmax),(d->ymax+2)+3*8);
    dsplyList.Insert(dp);

    dp = new Display(2,INTDIGIT);      //insert "id" display
    Insert(dp,(d->xmax)*2+dp->xmax,(d->ymax+2)+3*8);
    dsplyList.Insert(dp);


    xmax = 2*(d->xmax+dp->xmax);      //get the length of the diagbox
    ymax = (d->ymax+4)*3+30;       //get the hight of the diagbox
    c=new CtlItem(this,OK,FG_BLACK,FG_HIGHLIGHT);//insert the control buttons
    Insert(c,xmax/4,0);
    c = new CtlItem(this,CANCEL,FG_BLACK,FG_HIGHLIGHT);
    Insert(c,3*xmax/5,0);


}

//
//CataDiagbox::Draw()
//Draw the inventory diagbox
//
void CataDiagbox::Draw()
{
    Pen *tmp = new Pen(FG_PURPLE);
    tmp->FillRect(this,0,0,xmax,ymax);
    Pen *temp = new Pen(FG_HIGHLIGHT);
    char *title;
    title = "C A T E G O R Y   D A T A";
    temp->MoveTo(this,(xmax-strlen(title)*8)/2,ymax-fg_charbox[FG_Y2]-2);
    temp->Text(this,title);
    Bunch::Draw();       //draw all the objects defined on this bunch
}

//
//CataDiagbox Do()
//Receiving the control from the control button, and do what you want to
//
void CataDiagbox::Do(char *op)
{
    ListIterator iter(dsplyList);
    Display *p;
    char *dt[4];        // '4', number of fields
```

continued...

```
    int i = 0;
    if(!strcmp(op,OK))      //clicked on "OK"
    {
while (p = (Display *)iter()) {
    dt[i++] = p->Get();
}
extern void copyCTData(char*[],struct CATCODE*);
copyCTData(dt,&catadata);
    }
    else
    {
while (p = (Display *)iter()) {
    p->Clear();
}
    }
    done = 1;              //set the status as already done
}

//
// Auxilliary function for setting the inventory data for displayin
//
void CataDiagbox::SetCatDt(char *x)
{
    extern CATFile *CFile;
    CFile->GetStuff(atoi(x),&catadata);
}

//
// Clear all the displays
//
void CataDiagbox::Clear()
{
    ListIterator iter(dsplyList);
    Display *p;

    while(p = (Display *)iter())
    p->Clear();
}
```

continued...

```
//
// Auxilliary function for displaying Category id
//
void CataDiagbox::PutId(int x)
{
    ListIterator iter(dsplyList);
    Display *p;
    char buf[20];

    p = (Display *)iter();
    sprintf(buf,"%d",x);
    p->Put(buf);
}

//
// Auxilliary function for displaying Category Desc
//
void CataDiagbox::PutDesc(char *x)
{
    ListIterator iter(dsplyList);
    Display *p;

    p = (Display *)iter();
    p = (Display *)iter();
    p->Put(x);
}

//
// Auxilliary function for copying the data to the display screen
//
void CataDiagbox::PutCatDat()
{
    ListIterator iter(dsplyList);
    Display *p;
    char buf[20];

    p = (Display *)iter();
    p = (Display *)iter();
    p->Put(catadata.desc);
    p = (Display *)iter();
    sprintf(buf,"%ld",catadata.sals);
```

continued...

```
        p->Put(buf);
        p = (Display *)iter();
        sprintf(buf,"%ld",catadata.cost);
        p->Put(buf);
}



//
// SysDiagbox constructor
// Specific diagbox for Category data I/O
//
SysDiagbox::SysDiagbox()
{
    DiagItem *d;
    CtlItem  *c;
    Display  *dp;

    done = 0;                //init the status
    foreground = new Pen(FG_PURPLE);

    for(int row = 0; row  5; row++) //insert the diagbox's contents
    for(int col = 0; col  2; col++)
    {
        d = new DiagItem(systext[row*2+col],FG_HIGHLIGHT,FG_BLACK);
        Insert(d,(d->xmax+15*8)*col,(d->ymax+2)*row+3*8);
        dp = new Display(row+col,CHARDIGIT);
        Insert(dp,(d->xmax)*(col+1)+dp->xmax*col,(d->ymax+2)*row+3*8)
        dsplyList.Insert(dp);

    }


    xmax = 2*(d->xmax+dp->xmax);    //get the length of the diagbox
    ymax = (d->ymax+4)*5+30;      //get the hight of the diagbox
    c=new CtlItem(this,OK,FG_BLACK,FG_HIGHLIGHT);//insert the control buttons
    Insert(c,xmax/4,0);
    c = new CtlItem(this,CANCEL,FG_BLACK,FG_HIGHLIGHT);
    Insert(c,3*xmax/5,0);


}

//
//SysDiagbox::Draw()
```

```
//Draw the inventory diagbox
//
void SysDiagbox::Draw()
{
    Pen *tmp = new Pen(FG_PURPLE);
    tmp->FillRect(this,0,0,xmax,ymax);
    Pen *temp = new Pen(FG_HIGHLIGHT);
    char *title;
    title = "S Y S T E M   D A T A";
    temp->MoveTo(this,(xmax-strlen(title)*8)/2,ymax-fg_charbox[FG_Y2]-2);
    temp->Text(this,title);
    Bunch::Draw();        //draw all the objects defined on this bunch
}


//
//SysDiagbox Do()
//Receiving the control from the control button, and do what you want to do
//
void SysDiagbox::Do(char *op)
{
    ListIterator iter(dsplyList);
    Display *p;
    char *dt[10];          // '10' number of fields

    int i = 0;
    if(!strcmp(op,OK))     //clicked on "OK"
    {
    while (p = (Display *)iter()) {
        dt[i++] = p->Get();
    }
    extern void copySysData(char*[],struct SYSTEMARG*);
    copySysData(dt,&sysdata);
    }
    else
    {
    while (p = (Display *)iter()) {
        p->Clear();
    }
    }
    done = 1;              //set the status as already done
}
```

```
//
// Clear all the displays
//
void SysDiagbox::Clear()
{
    ListIterator iter(dsplyList);
    Display *p;

    while(p = (Display *)iter())
    p->Clear();
}


//
// Auxilliary function for copying the data to the display screen
//
void SysDiagbox::PutSysDat()
{
    ListIterator iter(dsplyList);
    Display *p;
    char buf[20];

    extern SYSFile *SFile;
    struct SYSTEMARG *temp;
    temp = SFile->GetSysArg();

    p = (Display *)iter();
    p->Put(temp->ivhdr.storadd);
    p = (Display *)iter();
    p->Put(temp->ivhdr.storid);
    p = (Display *)iter();
    p->Put(temp->ivhdr.storsta);
    p = (Display *)iter();
    p->Put(temp->ivhdr.storcty);
    p = (Display *)iter();
    p->Put(temp ->ivhdr.storphn);
    p = (Display *)iter();
    p->Put(temp->ivhdr.storzip);
    p = (Display *)iter();
    sprintf(buf,"%lf",temp->txrat);
    p->Put(buf);
```

continued...

368

```
    p = (Display *)iter();
    sprintf(buf,"%lf",temp->finrat);
    p->Put(buf);
    p = (Display *)iter();
    p->Put(temp->ivprtr);
    p = (Display *)iter();
    p->Put(temp->rcvprtr);
}


//
// Auxilliary function for copying the inventory item data
//
void copyData(char *dt[],struct INV_DAT* idata)
{
    double atof(char *);

    strcpy(idata->desc,dt[0]);
    strcpy(idata->unit,dt[2]);
    idata->price = atof(dt[3]);
    idata->cost = atof(dt[5]);
    idata->tax = *dt[4];
    strcpy(idata->vendor,dt[7]);
    idata->catcod = atoi(dt[6]);
    strcpy(idata->locat,dt[8]);
    idata->relevl = atoi(dt[9]);
    idata->qtyonhnd = atoi(dt[10]);
    idata->qtyonodr = atoi(dt[11]);
}


//
// Auxilliary function for copying the Category data
//
void copyCTData(char *dt[],struct CATCODE *idata)
{
    strcpy(idata->desc,dt[1]);
    idata->sals = atol(dt[2]);
    idata->cost = atol(dt[3]);
}
```

continued...

```
//
// Auxilliary function for copying the system arguments
//
void copySysData(char *dt[],struct SYSTEMARG *idata)
{
    double atof(char *);

    strcpy(idata->ivhdr.storadd,dt[0]);
    strcpy(idata->ivhdr.storid,dt[1]);
    strcpy(idata->ivhdr.storsta,dt[2]);
    strcpy(idata->ivhdr.storcty,dt[3]);
    strcpy(idata->ivhdr.storphn,dt[4]);
    strcpy(idata->ivhdr.storzip,dt[5]);
    idata->txrat = atof(dt[6]);
    idata->finrat = atof(dt[7]);
    strcpy(idata->ivprtr,dt[8]);
    strcpy(idata->rcvprtr,dt[9]);
}

//
//   phncvt
//   Convert a number string to telephone format
//

void phncvt(sstrng,dstrng)

char sstrng[];          /* in: the source number string      */
char dstrng[];          /* ot: the phone formated string     */

{
    int len;

    if ((len=strlen(sstrng)) == 10)
    {
        dstrng[0] = '(';
        strncpy(&dstrng[1],sstrng,3);
        dstrng[4] = ')';
        strncpy(&dstrng[5],&sstrng[3],3);
        dstrng[8] = '-';
        strcpy(&dstrng[9],&sstrng[6]);
    } else if (len == 7)
```

continued...

```
    {
        strncpy(dstrng,sstrng,3);
        dstrng[3] = '-';
        strcpy(&dstrng[4],&sstrng[3]);
    } else
        strcpy(dstrng,sstrng);
}

//
//InvtDiagBox::Draw()
//Draw the inventory DiagBox
//
void InvtDiagBox::Draw()
{
    Pen *tmp = new Pen(FG_PURPLE);
    tmp->FillRect(this,0,0,xmax,ymax);
    Pen *temp = new Pen(FG_HIGHLIGHT);
    char *title;
    title = "I N V E N T O R Y   D A T A";
    temp->MoveTo(this,(xmax-strlen(title)*8)/2,ymax-fg_char-
box[FG_Y2]-2);
    temp->Text(this,title);
    Bunch::Draw();        //draw all the objects defined on this bunch
}

//
//InfoDiagBox::Draw()
//Draw the information DiagBox
//
void InfoDiagBox::Draw()
{
    background->FillRect(this,0,0,xmax,ymax);
    foreground->MoveTo(this,(xmax-8*strlen("OBJECT & INVEN-
TORY"))/2,ymax-2*fg_charbox[FG_Y2]);
    foreground->Text(this,"OBJECT & INVENTORY");
    foreground->MoveTo(this,(xmax-8*strlen("------------*------
------"))/2,ymax-3*fg_charbox[FG_Y2]);
    foreground->Text(this,"------------*------------");
    foreground->MoveTo(this,(xmax-8*strlen("\(c\) Copyright
1989"))/2,ymax-6*fg_charbox[FG_Y2]);
    foreground->Text(this,"\(c\) Copyright 1989");
```

continued...

```
    foreground->MoveTo(this,(xmax-8*strlen("Baldur Systems
Corp."))/2,ymax-7*fg_charbox[FG_Y2]);
    foreground->Text(this,"Baldur Systems Corp.");
    Bunch::Draw();
}


//
//DeleDiagBox::Draw()
//Delete the DiagBox
//
void DeleDiagBox::Draw()
{
    background->FillRect(this,0,0,xmax,ymax);
    Pen *temp = new Pen(FG_LIGHT_BLUE);
    temp->FillRect(this,3*8,4*fg_charbox[FG_Y2],6*8,5*fg_char-
box[FG_Y2]+4);
    temp = new Pen(FG_HIGHLIGHT);
    temp-Put(this,(3+1/2)*8,4*fg_char-
box[FG_Y2]+2,splicon,2*8,2*8);
    foreground->MoveTo(this,(xmax-8*strlen("Are you
sure??"))/2,ymax-2*fg_charbox[FG_Y2]);
    foreground->Text(this,"Are you sure??");
    Bunch::Draw();
}
```

All the three Draw()'s perform different tasks. For example, when InfoDiag-Box::Draw() is called, the white rectangle with the text "OBJECT & INVEN-TORY" and the copyright notice will appear, as shown in Figure 9-1.

Class InvtDiagBox, the following two methods are required to receive data from the conventional program:

```
void PutInvDat(); // copy the inventory data onto the screen
void SetInvDt();  // set the inventory data for displaying
```

These two functions are defined in Listing 9-4.

The two relevant classes in DiagBox, DiagItem and CtlItem are both a subclass of Pane and include similar data objects and methods. Both use Draw() to fill in the Pane; however, CtlItem includes Handle() to process events from the mouse buttons. These methods are defined in Listing 9-2.

Figure 9-3 shows a resultant screen of using the DialogBox class group.

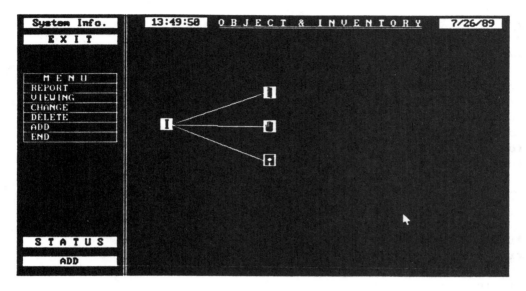

Figure 9-3. A Screen Resulting from the Use of the DiagBox Class Group.

Class Group InvtMenu

Class Group InvtMenu enables you to program menus with icons for the user to select. Specific applications can be created for menus and icons on a case by case situation.

Class Group InvtMenu includes the following classes:

- InvtMenu, a subclass of Menu
- InvtMenuItm, a subclass of MenuItem
- IconMenu, a subclass of Menu
- IconMenuItm, a subclass of MenuItem

The structure of all these classes are shown in Listing 9-5.

Both InvtMenu and IconMenu are a subclass of Menu and may inherit member functions from Menu. These functions are similar; both use Do() to activate the corresponding work implied in the item being clicked:

Listing 9.5: Header File for Class Group InvtMenu

```
//
// invtmenu.hpp
//
//
//InvtMenu head file
//
#define RPT 5        //click on "report"
#define VIW 4        //click on "view"
#define CHG 3        //click on "change"
#define DEL 2        //click on "delete"
#define ADD 1        //click on "add"


#include "bunch.hpp"
#include "pane.hpp"
#include "manager.hpp"
#include "icon.hpp"
#include "menu.hpp"


//
//Inventory Menu class
//
class InvtMenu : public Menu {     //icon operation menu
    int   opflg;                   //flag for deleting or adding
    char *icpat;            //added icon pattern
    int   icid;            //added icon id
public:
    InvtMenu(int,char*[]);
    void Do(char*);        //do what user wanted
    int  GetOpFlg();        //get the opflg
    void SetOpFlg(int);     //set the opflg
    char *GetIcPat();       //get the added icon pat.
    int  GetIcId();        //get the added icon id
};
```

continued...

```
//
//Inventory menu item class
//
class InvtMenuItm : public MenuItem {
protected:
    InvtMenu    *target;
    Pen *foreground,*background;
    Pen *frg1,*bkg1;
public:
    InvtMenuItm(InvtMenu*,char*);
    void Draw();
    void Handle (Event&);
};
```

```
  // InvtMenu::Do()
  // Do the corresponding work for the item being clicked
  //
  void InvtMenu::Do(char *op)
  {
      char c;
      extern Manager m;

      c = *op;
      extern int exitflg;
      exitflg= 0;
      StatusWin *temp;
      temp = (StatusWin*)m.find(10*8,2*fg_charbox[FG_Y2]);
      extern DeleDiagbox *dd;
      switch(c)
      {
    case 'A' : //click on "ADD"
        temp->SetText("ADD");
      opflg = ADD;
      break;
    case 'D' :      //click on "DELETE"
       temp->SetText("DELETE");
       dd->SetText("Are you sure??");
       m.Insert(dd,250,50);
       dd->Draw();
       dd->Run();
```

continued...

```
        if(dd->GetFlag() == OKFLAG)
            opflg = DEL;
              dd->SetStatus(0);
      m.Remove(dd);
      m.Draw();
      break;
   case 'C':   //click on "CHANGE"
      temp->SetText("CHANGE");
      opflg = CHG;
      break;
   case 'R':   //click on "REPORT"
      temp->SetText("REPORT");
      opflg = RPT;
      break;
        case 'V':   //click on "VIEWING"
      temp->SetText("VIEWING");
      opflg = VIW;
      break;
   case 'E':   //click on "END"
      temp->SetText("END");
      break;
   }
   done = 1;
   temp->Draw();
}


//IconMenu::Do()
//Doing the work which was implied by the icon item
//
void IconMenu::Do(int x,char *y)
{
   icid = x;          //record the clicked icon pattern
   ictext = y;        //record the clicked icon text
   done = 1;          //end of selection
}
```

For example, InvtMenu::Do() activates a list of the "STATUS" window alternatives, such as "ADD," "DELETE," "CHANGE," for the user to click. Once "ADD" is clicked, the corresponding series of designated tasks will pop up in the interface area for the user to act upon further, as shown in Figure 9-3. On the other hand, IconMenu uses Do() in conjunction with class InvtIcon to show menus with meaningful icons see Figure 9-4 for sample icon menu items.

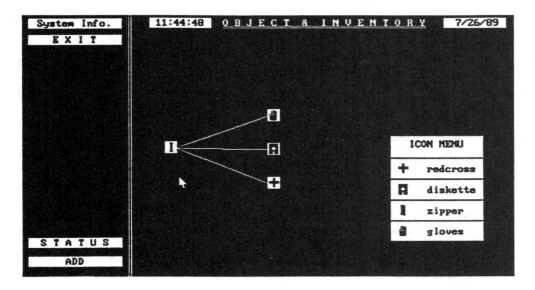

Figure 9-4. Sample Icon Menus.

Listing 9.6: Implementation Files for Class Group InvtMenu

```
//
// invtmenu.cpp
//
//InvtMenu program
//
#include "invntory.inc"
#include "invtmenu.hpp"
#include "title.hpp"
#include "diagbox.hpp"

//
// InvtMenuItm constructor
//
InvtMenuItm::InvtMenuItm(InvtMenu *im,char *txt)
{
    target = im;
    itmtext = txt;        // set the menu item text
    xmax = 15*8;          // menu item width
```

continued...

```
    ymax = fg_charbox[FG_Y2];    // menu item hight
    foreground =  new Pen(FG_BLACK);   //foreground & background colors
    background = new Pen(FG_YELLOW);
    bkg1 = new Pen(FG_GREEN);   // color used for showing being clicked

}

//
// InvtMenuItm::Draw()
// Draw the menu item
//
void InvtMenuItm::Draw()
{
    background->FillRect(this,0,0,xmax,ymax);
    foreground->Rect(this,0,0,xmax,ymax);
    foreground->MoveTo(this,10,0);
    foreground->Text(this,itmtext);
    Flush();
}


//
// InvtMenuItm::Handle()
// if the user clicks the Left mouse on me, tell the menu
// that I get clicked
//
void InvtMenuItm::Handle(Event &e)
{
    if(e.eventType & E_LEFTDOWN)
    {
        Pen *temp = background;  //change the color for showing being
        background = bkg1;             //clicked
        bkg1 = temp;
        Draw();
        target->Do(itmtext);
        Pen *temp1 = background; //change back the color
        background = bkg1;
        bkg1 = temp1;
        Draw();
    }
}
```

continued...

```
//
//InvtMenu constructor
//
InvtMenu::InvtMenu(int n,char *mntext[])
{
    nitem = n;
    selcflg = 0;
    InvtMenuItm *itm;

    done = 0;
    for(int i = 0; i  >nitem-1; i++) //insert the menu items
    {
    itm = new InvtMenuItm(this,mntext[i]);
    Insert(itm,0,(itm->ymax+2)*i);
    }
    itm = new InvtMenuItm(this,mntext[i]);
    Insert(itm,0,(itm->ymax+2)*i);
    xmax = itm->xmax;
    ymax = (itm->ymax+2)*n;
}


//
// InvtMenu::Do()
// Do the corresponding work for the item being clicked
//
void InvtMenu::Do(char *op)
{
    char c;
    extern Manager m;

    c = *op;
    extern int exitflg;
    exitflg= 0;
    StatusWin *temp;
    temp = (StatusWin*)m.find(10*8,2*fg_charbox[FG_Y2]);
    extern DeleDiagbox *dd;
    switch(c)
    {
    case 'A' : //click on "ADD"
        temp->SetText("ADD");
```

continued...

```
          opflg = ADD;
          break;
     case 'D' :         //click on "DELETE"
          temp->SetText("DELETE");
          dd->SetText("Are you sure??");
          m.Insert(dd,250,50);
          dd->Draw();
          dd->Run();
          if(dd->GetFlag() == OKFLAG)
               opflg = DEL;
                dd->SetStatus(0);
          m.Remove(dd);
          m.Draw();
          break;
     case 'C':   //click on "CHANGE"
          temp->SetText("CHANGE");
          opflg = CHG;
          break;
     case 'R':   //click on "REPORT"
          temp->SetText("REPORT");
          opflg = RPT;
          break;
            case 'V':  //click on "VIEWING"
          temp->SetText("VIEWING");
             opflg = VIW;
             break;
          case 'E':   //click on "END"
             temp->SetText("END");
             break;
          }
        done = 1;
        temp->Draw();
}

//
// InvtMenu::GetOpFlg()
// get the opflg
//
int InvtMenu::GetOpFlg()
{
     return opflg;
}
```

continued...

```
//
// InvtMenu::SetOpFlg()
// reset the opflg
//
void InvtMenu::SetOpFlg(int x)
{
    opflg = x;
}


//
// InvtMenu::GetIcPat()
// Get the added icon pattern
//
char *InvtMenu::GetIcPat()
{
    return icpat;
}

//
// InvtMenu::GetIcId()
// Get the added icon id
//
int InvtMenu::GetIcId()
{
    return icid;
}

//
// iconmenu.hpp
//
// IconMenu head file
//
//
// Icon menu class
//
class IconMenu : public Menu {
    char *icpatt;         // clicked icon pattern
    int  icid;            //clicked icon id
    char *ictext;         //clicked icon text
```

continued...

```
public:
    IconMenu();
    void Do(int,char*);
    char *GetIcPat();        // get the clicked icon pattern
    int  GetIcId();       // get the clicked icon id;
    char *GetIcTxt();        // get the clicked icon text;
    void Draw();
};

//
// Icon menu item class
//
class IconMenuItm : public MenuItem {
protected:
    IconMenu     *target;       //target to which the control passed
    int          iconid;        //icon index in the icon lib
    char         *itmtext;      //text associated with icon
    char         *iconpattern;   //icon pattern
    Pen          *foreground,*background; //colors
    Pen          *icnfg,*icnbg;
    Pen          *frg1,*bkg1;
public:
    IconMenuItm(IconMenu*,char*,char*,int);
    void Draw();
    void Handle(Event&);
};




//
// iconmenu.cpp
//
// IconMenu program
//
#include "bunch.hpp"
#include "pane.hpp"
#include "manager.hpp"
#include "icon.hpp"
#include "menu.hpp"
#include "iconlib.hpp"
#include "iconmenu.hpp"
```

continued...

```
//
//IconMenuItm constructor
//
IconMenuItm::IconMenuItm(IconMenu *im,char *txt,char *icnpat,int icid)
{
    target = im;
    iconid  = icid;       //icon index
    itmtext = txt;        //associated menu item text
    iconpattern = icnpat; //the icon associated
    xmax = 15*8;          //width of each item
    ymax = 2*fg_charbox[FG_Y2];
    foreground = new Pen(FG_BLACK);
    background = new Pen(FG_YELLOW);
    icnfg = new Pen(FG_YELLOW);
    icnbg = new Pen(FG_RED);
    bkgl = new Pen(FG_GREEN);
}
//
//IconMenuItm::Draw()
//
void IconMenuItm::Draw()
{
    icnbg->FillRect(this,0,0,5*8,ymax);
    icnfg->Put(this,3/2*8,fg_charbox[FG_Y2]/2,iconpattern,16,16);
    background->FillRect(this,5*8,0,xmax,ymax);
    foreground->MoveTo(this,6*8,fg_charbox[FG_Y2]/2);
    foreground->Text(this,itmtext);
    Flush();
}
//
//IconMenuItm::Handle()
// if the user clicks the Left mouse on me, tell the menu
// that I get clicked
//
void IconMenuItm::Handle(Event &e)
{
    if(e.eventType & E_LEFTDOWN)
    {
        target->Do(iconid,itmtext);            //tell the menu to remeber me
    }
}
```

continued...

```
//
//IconMenu constructor
//
IconMenu::IconMenu()
{
    char *icpat,*icnam;
    IconMenuItm *itm;
    extern IconLib *iclib;
    int i = 0;

    while(1)          //load all the icons from the icon library
    {
    icpat = new char[ICONLEN+1];
    icnam = new char[ICONNMLEN+1];
    if((iclib->load_icon(icpat,icnam,i)) == FAIL) //hit the end
         break;                         //yes
    itm = new IconMenuItm(this,icnam,icpat,i);         //no
    Insert(itm,0,(itm->ymax+2)*i);
    i++;
     }

    nitem = i;      //# of items in the menu
    selcflg = 0;
    done = 0;
    xmax = itm->xmax;
    ymax = (itm->ymax+2)*(i+1);
}


//
//IconMenu::Do()
//Doing the work which is implied by the menu item
//
void IconMenu::Do(int x,char *y)
{
    icid = x;        //record the clicked icon pattern
    ictext = y;      //record the clicked icon text
    done = 1;        //end of selection
}
//
//IconMenu::Draw()
//
```

continued...

```
void IconMenu::Draw()
{
    Pen *temp = new Pen(FG_HIGHLIGHT);
    Pen *temp1 = new Pen(FG_BLACK);
    temp->FillRect(this,0,ymax-2*fg_charbox[FG_Y2]-2,xmax,ymax);
    temp1->MoveTo(this,(xmax-8*strlen("ICON MENU"))/2,ymax-3/2*fg_char-
 box[FG_Y2]);
    temp1->Text(this,"ICON MENU");
    Bunch::Draw();
}

//
//IconMenu::GetIcPat()
//Get the clicked icon pattern
//
char *IconMenu::GetIcPat()
{
    return icpatt;
}

//
//IconMenu::GetIcId()
//Get the clicked icon id
//
int IconMenu::GetIcId()
{
    return icid;
}


//
//IconMenu::GetIcTxt()
//Get the clicked icon text
//
char *IconMenu::GetIcTxt()
{
    return ictext;
}
```

InvtMenuItm and IconMenuItm are used to draw the corresponding menu item when the menu is clicked by the user. These functions are a subclass of InvtMenu and IconMenu, respectively; their structures are similar, using the same methods, Draw() and Handle(), to draw and to handle the events from the left button. However, Draw() and Handle() are defined slightly different to meet the needs of these two classes, see the appropriate codes in Listing 9-6 for the differences.

Class Group InvtIcon

Class group InvtIcon is used to make icons for providing users with icon selection. When an icon is chosen, appropriate actions will be taken by the computer.

Class group InvtIcon includes the following classes:

- InvtIcon: inventory icons representing the files and actions underneath.
- IntArea: a manager class to control user interface area through icons.
- IconConn: a connection line class to connect icons into a "tree" type.
- InvList: a class used to link a list of inventory items (objects).
- CataList: a class used to link a list of inventory categories.

The structure of these classes are shown in Listing 9-7.

Listing 9.7: Header File for Class Group InvtIcon

```
//
// invticon.hpp
//
// Inventory icon header file
//

class IntArea;

static char Invicon[] = {
    0x00,0x00,
    0x00,0x00,
    0x03,0xE0,
    0x01,0xc0,
    0x01,0xc0,
    0x01,0xc0,
    0x01,0xc0,
    0x01,0xc0,
    0x01,0xc0,
    0x01,0xc0,
    0x01,0xc0,
    0x01,0xc0,
    0x01,0xc0,
    0x03,0xE0,
    0x00,0x00,
    0x00,0x00,
    };
//
// InvtIcon: class derived from Icon.
// Inventory item icon
//
class InvtIcon : public Icon {
protected:
    int        type;        //root, cat. & invnt item type
    int    status;
    IntArea    *target;
    char    itmcode[15];
    char    *pat;
    struct CATCODE catdt;
    Pen *newfgcolor,*newbgcolor;
```

continued...

```
public:
    InvtIcon(int,char[],char*,IntArea*,int,int);
    void Handle(Event &);
    void SetStatus(int);
    int  GetType();
    char *GetItmCode();
    int  GetCatDtFF();
    struct CATCODE *GetCatDt() { return &catdt; }
};
//
// Icon connection line class
//
class IconConn : public Pane {
protected:
    int x0,y0;
    int x1,y1;
    Pen *foreground,*background;
public:
    IconConn(int,int,int,int);
    void Draw();
};
```

Class InvtIcon connects icons to the actual inventory categories and items. It is a subclass of Icon, specialized for the inventory accounting system. Icons created under this class are meaningfully related to real world inventory items, such as automobiles and pumps. InvtIcon has a series of protected data concerning the status and operation of the icons and their associated files:

```
class InvtIcon : public Icon {
protected:
    int         type;          //root, cat. & invnt item type
    int    status;
    IntArea     *target;
    char    itmcode[15];
    char    *pat;
    struct CATCODE catdt;
    Pen *newfgcolor,*newbgcolor;
```

The constructor of Class InvIcon is used along with eight methods, for example, Handle(), SetStatus(), GetItmCode(), and GetCatDtFF(), to manipulate these items to perform tasks in inventory accounting:

```
public:
    InvtIcon(int,char[],char*,IntArea*,int,int);
    void Handle(Event &);
    void SetStatus(int);
    int  GetType();
    char *GetItmCode();
    int  GetCatDtFF();
    struct CATCODE *GetCatDt() { return &catdt; }
};
```

Icons can be connected into trees and icon "leaves" can be manipulated to grow. A sample of a resulting icon tree is shown in Figure 9-5.

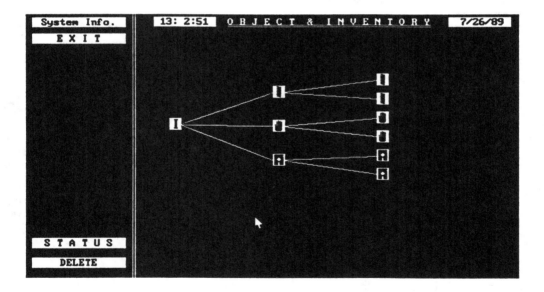

Figure 9-5. Making an Icon Tree.

These member functions are defined in Listing 9-7 or 8 to perform the required task. For example, GetInvDtFF() is defined to obtain the inventory data file, as follows:

```
int InvtIcon::GetCatDtFF()
{
    extern CATFile *CFile;

    // get the category data
    if(CFile->GetStuff(atoi(itmcode),&catdt) == FAIL)
    return FAIL;
    else
    return SUCCEED;

}
```

Class IntArea is a subclass of Bunch which puts together all the panes (icons) in the user interface area that is the right-hand side window in Figure 9-4, according to instructions from IntArea.

```
class IntArea : public Bunch {
protected:
    CataList clist;          //category list on the interface area
    Pen *foreground,*background; //background & foreground
colors
public:
    IntArea();               //constructor
    void Do(InvtIcon*);      //operation control on the clicked icon
    void Clear();            //clear the interface area
    void Draw();             //show it
    void InsertIcons();      //update all the icons on the int. area
    void AddOperat(int,InvtIcon*);  //do the "add" operation
    void DelOperat(int,InvtIcon*);  //do the "delete" operation
    void ChgOperat(int,InvtIcon*);  //do the "change" operation
    void ViwOperat(int,InvtIcon*);  //do the "viewing" operation
    void RptOperat(int,InvtIcon*);  //do the "report" operation
};
```

Using Pane's function, Draw(), IconConn draws lines (line panes) between icons to connect them together, as shown in Figure 9-5.

On the other hand, as a subclass of List, class CataList uses List's functions Append(), Insert(), Delete() to provide an appropriate list of inventory categories associated with the icons.

All these functions discussed for class group InvtIcon are provided in Listing 9-7 or 9-8.

Listing 9.8: Implementation File for Class Group InvtIcon

```
//
// invticon.cpp
//
// 7-11-89      Add iconlib
// 7-12-89      Add drawing icons from file
//
// Inventory icon program
//

#include "stream.hpp"
#include "invntory.inc"
#include "invntfil.hpp"

#include "stdlib.h"
#include "bunch.hpp"
#include "pane.hpp"
#include "manager.hpp"
#include "icon.hpp"
#include "intarea.hpp"
#include "invticon.hpp"

//
// InvtIcon constructor
//
InvtIcon::InvtIcon(int invtype,char invcd[],char *icpat,IntArea *ia,int d,int e)
: (icpat,d,e,16,16)
{
    type = invtype;
    target = ia;
    status = 0;
    xmax = 16-1; ymax = 16 - 1;
    newfgcolor = new Pen(FG_BLACK);
    newbgcolor = new Pen(FG_WHITE);
    strcpy(itmcode,invcd);
    pat = icpat;
}
```

continued...

```
//
// InvtIcon::Handle()
// if user clicked on the inventory icon, tell the InvArea class do something
//
void InvtIcon::Handle(Event &e)
{
    if (e.eventType & E_LEFTDOWN) {
    Pen *temp;
    temp = newbgcolor;
    newbgcolor = background;
    background = temp;
    temp = newfgcolor;
    newfgcolor = foreground;
    foreground = temp;
    Draw();

    extern InvtIcon *curic;
    curic = this;          // set 'curic' as the clicked icon
    target->Do(this);

    Pen *temp1;
    temp1 = newbgcolor;
    newbgcolor = background;
    background = temp1;
    temp1 = newfgcolor;
    newfgcolor = foreground;
    foreground = temp1;

    }
}


//
//InvtIcon::SetStatus
//Set the status flag
//
void InvtIcon::SetStatus(int s)
{
    status = s;
}
```

continued...

```
//
//InvtIcon::GetCatDt()
//Get the Category data
//
int InvtIcon::GetCatDtFF()
{
    extern CATFile *CFile;

    // get the Category data
    if(CFile->GetStuff(atoi(itmcode),&catdt) == FAIL)
    return FAIL;
    else
    return SUCCEED;

}

//
// InvtIcon::GetType()
// Get icon type
//
int InvtIcon::GetType()
{
    return type;
}


//
// InvtIcon::GetItmCode()
// Get icon item code
//
char *InvtIcon::GetItmCode()
{
    return itmcode;
}

//
// IconConn constructor
//
IconConn::IconConn(int a,int b,int c,int d)
```

continued...

```
{
    x0 = a;
    y0 = b;
    x1 = c;
    y1 = d;
    foreground = new Pen(FG_HIGHLIGHT);
    xmax = abs(x1-x0)+1;
    ymax = abs(y1-y0)+1;
}

//
// IconConn::Draw()
// Draw the connction lines among the inventory icons
//
void IconConn::Draw()
{
    if(y1 = y0)
    foreground->Line(this,0,0,xmax,ymax);
    else
    foreground->Line(this,0,ymax,xmax,0);
}

//
// Auxilliary function for initializing inventory data
//
void initinvdt(struct INV_DAT *ivdt)
{
    ivdt->desc[0] = '\0';
    ivdt->price = 0L;
    ivdt->unit[0] = '\0';
    ivdt->cost = 0L;
    ivdt->tax = 'Y';
    ivdt->catcod = -1;
    ivdt->vendor[0] = '\0';
    ivdt->locat[0] = '\0';
    ivdt->relevl = 0;
    ivdt->qtyonhnd = 0;
    ivdt->qtyonodr = 0;
}
```

continued...

```
//
// intarea.hpp
//
// Inventory interface area header file
//

#define ICONLEN        32
#define ICONNMLEN      15
#define INVTYPE1       1          //root icon type
#define INVTYPE2       2          //Category icon type
#define INVTYPE3       3          //inventory item type

class InvtIcon;

//
// linked list of inventory object
//
struct Ivlist {
    char itmcd[15];       //item code
    int  catcd;            //its cat. code
    int  iconid;          //its icon id
};

class InvList : public List {
public:
    InvList();
    void Append(struct Ivlist *n) { List::Append((void *)n); }
    void Insert(struct Ivlist *n) { List::Insert((void *)n); }
    void Delete(struct Ivlist *n) { List::Delete((void *)n); }
};

inline InvList::InvList()
{ head = 0;}

//
// linked list of Category
//
struct Ctlist {
    int catcod;                //category id
    int iconid;                //its icon aid
    InvList ilist;         //inventory item list
};
```

continued...

```
class CataList : public List {
public:
    CataList();
    void Append(struct Ctlist *n) { List::Append((void *)n); }
    void Insert(struct Ctlist *n) { List::Insert((void *)n); }
    void Delete(struct Ctlist *n) { List::Delete((void *)n); }
};

inline CataList::CataList()
{ head = 0;}




//
// User interface area
//
class IntArea : public Bunch {
protected:
    CataList clist;           //category list on the interface area
    Pen *foreground,*background;  //background&foreground colors
public:
    IntArea();              //constructor
    void Do(InvtIcon*);     //operation control on the clicked icon
    void Clear();           //clear the interface area
    void Draw();            //show it
    void InsertIcons();     //update all the icons on the int. area
    void AddOperat(int,InvtIcon*);  //do the "add" operation
    void DelOperat(int,InvtIcon*);  //do the "delete" operation
    void ChgOperat(int,InvtIcon*);  //do the "change" operation
    void ViwOperat(int,InvtIcon*);  //do the "viewing" operation
    void RptOperat(int,InvtIcon*);  //do the "report" operation
};

//
// intarea.cpp
//
// Inventory interface area class
//

#include "stream.hpp"
#include "invntory.inc"
#include "register.inc"
#include "invntfil.hpp"
```

continued...

```
#include "bunch.hpp"
#include "pane.hpp"
#include "manager.hpp"
#include "icon.hpp"
#include "iconlib.hpp"
#include "invticon.hpp"
#include "invtmenu.hpp"
#include "iconmenu.hpp"
#include "diagbox.hpp"
#include "invtdiag.hpp"
#include "intarea.hpp"

//
// IntAea constructor
//
IntArea::IntArea()
{
    foreground = new Pen(FG_HIGHLIGHT);
    background = new Pen(FG_LIGHT_BLUE);

    xmax = 450;
    ymax = fg_displaybox[FG_Y2]-2*8;

    struct Ctlist *tem;
    struct Ivlist *tem1;
    struct CATCODE *tem2;
    struct INV_DAT *tem3;
    extern CATFile *CFile;
    extern IdxFile *InvIdx;

    //read in Category objects
    int x = CFile->GetCatNo();
    for(int j=1;j<=x;j++)
    {
    tem = new struct Ctlist;
    tem->catcod = j;
    tem2 = new struct CATCODE;
    CFile->GetStuff(j,tem2);
    tem->iconid = tem2->iconid;
    clist.Append(tem);
    }
```

continued...

```
   //read in inventory item objects
   struct INV_IDX *t;
   t = InvIdx->GetInvIdx();
   struct INV_HDR *t1;
   t = InvIdx->GetInvIdx();
   t1 = InvIdx->GetInvHdr();
   for(int i=0;i  <t1->blklen;i++)
   {
 tem3 = new struct INV DAT;
 InvIdx->GetStuff((t+i)->stokn,tem3);
 ListIterator cwi(clist);
 struct Ctlist *cpp;
 while (cpp = (struct Ctlist *)cwi())
     {
   if(cpp->catcod == tem3->catcod)
   {
   tem1 = new struct Ivlist;
   strcpy(tem1->itmcd,(t+i)->stokn);
   tem1->iconid = tem3->iconid;
   tem1->catcd = cpp->catcod;
   (cpp->ilist).Append(tem1);
      }
 }
 delete(tem3);
  }

  InsertIcons();
}

//
// IntArea::Clear()
// Clear the IntArea window
//
void IntArea::Clear()
{
   background->FillRect(this,0,0,xmax,ymax-4);
}
```

continued...

```
//
// IntArea::Draw()
// Draw the user interface window
//
void IntArea::Draw()
{
    Clear();
    Bunch::Draw();
}


//
// IntArea::Do()
// Someone clicks on one of the objects in this area
//
void IntArea::Do(InvtIcon *ic)
{
        extern Manager m;
    extern InvtMenu *mnu;

    m.Insert(mnu,0,200);
    mnu->Draw();
    mnu->Run();
    int i = ic->GetType();     //get the icon type
    int op = mnu->GetOpFlg();
    switch(op)
    {
        case ADD:
      AddOperat(i,ic);
      break;

        case  DEL:          //click on "delete"
      DelOperat(i,ic);
      break;

        case CHG:           //change contents
      ChgOperat(i,ic);
      break;

        case VIW:           //view the object's content
      ViwOperat(i,ic);
      break;
```

continued...

```
        case RPT:              //report the object's contents
     RptOperat(i,ic);
     break;
    }

    mnu->SetStatus(0);
    mnu->SetOpFlg(-1);
    m.Remove(mnu);
}

//
//IntArea::InsertIcons()
//
void IntArea::InsertIcons()
{
    //Root icon
    ListIterator wi(paneList);
    Pane *p;

    while (p = (Pane *)wi()) {
    Remove(p);
    }

    InvtIcon *invic,*invroot,*invic1;
    IconConn *invcon;
    char     *icpatt,*icnam, ctn[15];
    struct Invlist *tem1;
    struct CATCODE *tem2;
    extern IconLib *iclib;
    extern Manager m;
    extern void ErrorProc(char*);

    ListIterator ci(clist);
    struct Ctlist *cp;
    struct Ivlist *ip;
    int x = 0;      //# of cat.
    int y = 0;       //# of invntory items
    while (cp = (struct Ctlist *)ci()) {
    x++;
    ListIterator ii(cp->ilist);
    while(ip= (struct Ivlist *)ii())
        y++;
    }
```

```
    int a2 = ymax/2;              // root icon
    invroot = new InvtIcon(INVTYPE1,"1000",Invicon,this,FG_YELLOW,FG_RED);
    Insert(invroot,10,a2);
    int a4 = invroot->yrel+invroot->ymax/2 - ((x-1)*30+x*16)/2;// bottom line
of the cat. icons.
    int a8 = invroot->yrel+invroot->ymax/2 - ((y-1)*10+y*16)/2;// bottom line
of the inventory item icons.


   //draw cat. icons
   int  j = 0;
   int  k = 0;
   //insert Category objects
   ListIterator ci2(clist);
   while (cp = (struct Ctlist *)ci2())
   {
sprintf(ctn,"%d",cp->catcod);
icpatt = new char[ICONLEN+1];
icnam = new char[ICONNMLEN+1];
if(iclib->load_icon(icpatt,icnam,cp->iconid) == FAIL)
{
    ErrorProc("Error: load_icon");
    m.Draw();
}
invic = new InvtIcon(INVTYPE2,ctn,icpatt,this,FG_YELLOW,FG_RED);
Insert(invic,invroot->xrel+invroot->xmax+120,j*(30+invic->ymax)+a4);
invcon = new IconConn(invroot->xrel+invroot->xmax,invroot->yrel+invroot-
>ymax/2,invic->xrel,invic->yrel+invic->ymax/2);
  if((invic->yrel+invic->ymax/2)= (invroot->yrel+invroot->ymax/2))
      Insert(invcon,invroot->xrel+invroot->xmax,
          invroot->yrel+invroot->ymax/2);
  else
      Insert(invcon,invroot->xrel+invroot->xmax,
          invic->yrel+invic->ymax/2);


  //Insert inventory item icons
  ListIterator ii(cp->ilist);
  while(ip= (struct Ivlist *)ii())
  {
      icpatt = new char[ICONLEN+1];
      icnam = new char[ICONNMLEN+1];
      if(iclib->load_icon(icpatt,icnam,ip->iconid) == FAIL)
      {
  ErrorProc("Error: load_icon");
```

continued...

```
    m.Draw();
      }
      invic1 = new InvtIcon(INVTYPE3,ip->itmcd,icpatt,this,FG_YELLOW,FG_RED);
      Insert(invic1,invic->xrel+invic->xmax+120,k*(10+invic1->ymax)+a8);
      invcon = new IconConn(invic->xrel+invic->xmax,invic->yrel+invic->ymax/2,
  invic1-xrel,invic1->yrel+invic1->ymax/2);
      if((invic1->yrel+invic1->ymax/2) = (invic->yrel+invic->ymax/2))
    Insert(invcon,invic->xrel+invic->xmax,
        invic->yrel+invic->ymax/2);
      else
    Insert(invcon,invic->xrel+invic->xmax,
        invic1->yrel+invic1->ymax/2);

      k++;
  }

  j++;
    }
}


//
// IntArea::AddOperat()
// Do the "add" operation
//

void IntArea::AddOperat(int i,InvtIcon *ic)
{
      extern Manager m;
  extern InvtMenu *mnu;
  extern IconLib  *iclib;
      extern CataDiagbox *ctdb;
      extern SysDiagbox *sysdb;
      extern InvtDiagbox *db;
  extern IconMenu *icnmnu;
  extern void ErrorProc(char*);
  extern CATFile *CFile;

      m.Insert(icnmnu,fg_displaybox[FG_X2]-20*8,6*8);
      icnmnu->Draw();
      icnmnu->Run();
      int  icd = icnmnu->GetIcId();
      char *ict = icnmnu->GetIcTxt();
```

continued...

```
   icnmnu->SetStatus(0);
   m.Remove(icnmnu);
   switch(i)
   {
case INVTYPE1:       //root icon
      int g = CFile->GetCatNo();
      m.Insert(ctdb,150,0);
      ctdb->Clear();
      ctdb->PutId(g+1);
      ctdb->PutDesc(ict);
      ctdb->Draw();
      ctdb->Run();
      struct CATCODE *data;
      data = ctdb->GetCataDat();
      ctdb->SetStatus(0);
      m.Remove(ctdb);

      data->iconid = icd;
      if(CFile->AddStuff(g+1,data)==FAIL)
      {
   ErrorProc("Error: Addstuff");
      }
      else
      {
   struct Ctlist *tem2 = new struct Ctlist;
   tem2->catcod = g+1;
   tem2->iconid = icd;
   clist.Append(tem2);
   InsertIcons();
      }
      break;

       case INVTYPE2:          //cat. icon
      int cj = atoi(ic->GetItmCode());
      m.Insert(db,150,0);
      db->Clear();
      db->PutTx('Y');
      db->PutCatCd(cj);
      db>-Draw();
      db->Run();
      struct Ivlist *tem3;
```

continued...

```
    struct INV_DAT *ivdt;
    ivdt = db->GetInvDat();
    char incd[15];
    strcpy(incd,db->GetItmCd());
    db->SetStatus(0);
    m.Remove(db);

    ListIterator cwi(clist);
    struct Ctlist *cpp;
    while (cpp = (struct Ctlist *)cwi())
    {
if(cpp->catcod == cj)
{
    break;
}
    }

    ivdt->iconid = icd;
    int ret;
    if((ret = InvIdx->AddStuff(incd,ivdt)) == -1 || ret == -2)
    {
ErrorProc("Error: in add invt. item");
    }
    else
    {
tem3 = new struct Ivlist;
strcpy(tem3->itmcd,incd);
tem3->iconid = icd;
tem3->catcd = cj;
(cpp->ilist).Append(tem3);
    }
    InsertIcons();
      break;

    case INVTYPE3:              //inventory item icon
    ErrorProc("Error: No deeper level stuff");
    break;
}
}
```

continued...

```
//
// IntArea::DelOperat()
// Do the "delete" operation
//
void IntArea::DelOperat(int i, InvtIcon *ic)
{
        extern void ErrorProc(char*);
        extern CATFile *CFile;

        switch(i)
        {
    case INVTYPE2: //delete the Category object
        ListIterator ci(clist);
        int flg = 0;
        int j = atoi(ic->GetItmCode());
        struct Ctlist *cp;
        while (cp = (struct Ctlist *)ci())
        {
        if(cp->catcod == j)
        {
            ListIterator cii(cp->ilist);
            if(cii())
            {
        flg = 0;
        break;
            }
            clist.Delete(cp);
            flg = 1;
            break;
        }
        }
        if(flg == 0)        //no such cat.
        {
    ErrorProc("Error: please delete all items first");
        }
        else
        {
    while(cp = (struct Ctlist *)ci()) //make up the hole
        {
            cp->catcod--;
            //change the invt. item's catcode
```

continued...

405

```
          struct INV_DAT *tem3;
          struct Ivlist *ippp;
          ListIterator ciii(cp->ilist);
          while(ippp = (struct Ivlist *)ciii())
          {
               tem3 = new struct INV_DAT;
               InvIdx-GetStuff(ippp->itmcd,tem3);
          tem3->catcod--;
          InvIdx->ChgStuff(ippp->itmcd,tem3);
          delete tem3;
          }
      }
      //delete the cat. in file
      if(CFile->DelStuff(j) == FAIL)
      {
          ErrorProc("Error: DelStuff");
      }
        }
        InsertIcons();

        break;

    case INVTYPE1:       //delete root
        ErrorProc("Error: you can't delete it");
        break;

    case INVTYPE3:       //delete inventory item
        ListIterator cii(clist);
        int fg = 0;
        char ij[15];
        strcpy(ij,ic->GetItmCode());
        struct Ctlist *cpp;
        struct Ivlist *ip;
        while (cpp = (struct Ctlist *)cii())
        {
      ListIterator ii(cpp->ilist);
      while(ip = (struct Ivlist *)ii())
      {
          if(!strcmp(ip->itmcd,ij))
          {
```

continued...

```
            (cpp->ilist).Delete(ip);
            fg = 1;
            break;
              }
                }
        if(fg == 1)
            break;
        }
        if(fg == 0)            //no such cat.
        {
        ErrorProc("Error: in delete");
        }
        else
        {
        if(InvIdx->DelStuff(ij) != 0)
        {
            ErrorProc("Error: delete stuff");
        }
        }

        InsertIcons();
        break;
        }
}


//
//IntArea::ChgOperat()
//Do the "change" operation
//
void IntArea::ChgOperat(int i, InvtIcon *ic)
{
        extern Manager m;
        extern CataDiagbox *ctdb;
        extern SysDiagbox *sysdb;
        extern InvtDiagbox *db;
        extern void ErrorProc(char*);
        extern CATFile *CFile;
```

continued...

```
    switch(i)
    {
case INVTYPE2: //change the Category object
    int j = atoi(ic->GetItmCode());
    m.Insert(ctdb,150,0);
    ctdb->Clear();
    ctdb->SetCatDt(ic->GetItmCode());
    ctdb->PutCatDat();
    ctdb->PutId(j);
    ctdb->Draw();
    ctdb->Run();
    struct CATCODE *data;
    data = ctdb->GetCataDat();
    ctdb->SetStatus(0);
    m.Remove(ctdb);

    // change the cat. in file
    if(CFile->ChgStuff(j,data) == FAIL)
    {
   ErrorProc("Error: ChgStuff");
    }
    break;

case INVTYPE1:      //change root's contents
    extern SYSFile *SFile;
    m.Insert(sysdb,150,0);
    sysdb->Clear();
    sysdb->PutSysDat();
    sysdb->Draw();
    sysdb->Run();
    sysdb->SetStatus(0);
    m.Remove(sysdb);
    SFile->ChgStuff(sysdb->GetSysDat());
    break;

case INVTYPE3:      //change inventory item's contents
    m.Insert(db,150,0);
    db->Clear();
    db->SetItmCd(ic->GetItmCode());
    db->SetInvDt();
    db->PutInvDat();
```

```
        db->Draw();
        db->Run();
        struct INV_DAT *data1;
        data1 = db->GetInvDat();
        db->SetStatus(0);
        m.Remove(db);

       // change the cat. in file
        if(InvIdx->ChgStuff((ic->GetItmCode()),data1) == FAIL)
        {
    ErrorProc("Error: ChgStuff");
        }
        break;
    }
}


//
//IntArea::ViwOperat()
//Do the "viewing" operation
//
void IntArea::ViwOperat(int i,InvtIcon *ic)
{

        extern Manager m;
        extern CataDiagbox *ctdb;
        extern SysDiagbox *sysdb;
        extern InvtDiagbox *db;
        extern void ErrorProc(char*);
        extern CATFile *CFile;

        switch(i)
        {
    case INVTYPE2: //change the Category object
        int jj = atoi(ic->GetItmCode());
        m.Insert(ctdb,150,0);
        ctdb->Clear();
        ctdb->SetCatDt(ic->GetItmCode());
        ctdb->PutCatDat();
        ctdb->PutId(jj);
        ctdb->Draw();
```

continued...

```
            ctdb->Run();
            ctdb->SetStatus(0);
            m.Remove(ctdb);
            break;

        case INVTYPE1:      //change root's contents
            extern SYSFile *SFile;
            m.Insert(sysdb,150,0);
            sysdb->Clear();
            sysdb->PutSysDat();
            sysdb->Draw();
            sysdb->Run();
            sysdb->SetStatus(0);
            m.Remove(sysdb);
            break;

        case INVTYPE3:      //change inventory item's contents
            m.Insert(db,150,0);
            db->Clear();
            db->SetItmCd(ic->GetItmCode());
            db->SetInvDt();
            db->PutInvDat();
            db->Draw();
            db>-Run();
            db->SetStatus(0);
            m.Remove(db);
            break;
        }
}


//
//IntArea::RptOperat()
//Do the "rpt" operation
//
void IntArea::RptOperat(int i,InvtIcon *ic)
{
    extern void ErrorProc(char*);
    ErrorProc("Caution: Is your printer ready?");
}
```

ICON LIBRARY

Class IconLib provides a foundation to build an icon library in conjunction with InvtIcon. IconLib provides functions to save, load icons and retrieve an icon id from the icon pattern. (see Listing 9-9). IconLib is a root class, using a system file, stream.hpp; it has two functions to perform the required tasks:

```
int   save_icon(char*,char*,int); //save an icon
int   load_icon(char*,char*,int); //load an icon
```

The two functions are straightforward and can be found in Listing 9-10.

Listing 9-9 Header File for Class IconLib

```
//
// iconLib.hpp
//
// Icon library class
//


#define ICONLEN     32      //icon size
#define ICONNMLEN   15      //icon name length
#define FAIL        -1
#define SUCCEED      0

#include "stream.hpp"

class IconLib {
    char *fnm;              //library file name
public:
    IconLib(char*);        //constructor
    int   save_icon(char*,char*,int); //save an icon
    int   load_icon(char*,char*,int); //load an icon
};
```

Listing 9-10 Implementation File for Class IconLib

```
//
// iconLib.cpp
//// Icon library class
//

#include "iconlib.hpp"

//
// IconLib::IconLib()
// constructor
//
IconLib::IconLib(char *fn)
{
    fnm = fn;
}

//
// IconLib::save_icon()
// function for saving the icon in the icon library.
//
int IconLib::save_icon(char *ic,char *icnm,int pos)
{
    FILE *fd;

    fd = fopen(fnm,"a");
    fseek(fd,0L,0);
    fseek(fd,(long)(pos*(ICONLEN+ICONNMLEN)),0);

    if(fwrite(ic,1,ICONLEN,fd) != ICONLEN)
    return FAIL;
    if(fwrite(icnm,1,ICONNMLEN,fd) != ICONNMLEN)
    return FAIL;

    fclose(fd);
    return SUCCEED;
}
```

continued...

```
//
// IconLib::load_icon()
// Auxilliary function for loading the icon from the icon library
//
int IconLib::load_icon(char *ic,char *icnm,int pos)
{
    FILE *fd;

    fd = fopen(fnm,"r");
    fseek(fd,(long)(pos*(ICONLEN+ICONNMLEN)),0);
    if(fread(ic,1,ICONLEN,fd) != ICONLEN)
   return FAIL;
    if(fread(icnm,1,ICONNMLEN,fd) != ICONNMLEN)
   return FAIL;

    fclose(fd);
    return SUCCEED;
}
```

BUILDING A FILE CLASS--CLASS GROUP OURFILE

Class group OurFile is used to prepare and manage the relevant files in the sample inventory accounting system when they are activated by the user. Because of the size of the files in the sample systems, file classes are divided into indexed and non-indexed files. All files are classified into categories for an appropriate arrangement of icons and menus on the screen, because the screen can take only a limited number of menus and/or icons each time.

Class OurFile is a root class where three file subclasses originate to organize both indexed and non-indexed files. For indexed files, class IdxFile records index file names, file id's, size of the record, number of data records, and pointers to the index block. The three subclasses and structure of class OurFile are shown in Listing 9-11.

Listing 9-11   Header File for Class InvFile

```
//
// invntory.inc
//
#define MAXIDXIN    100

struct INV_HDR {
   int indxn;        /* # of Index records in CAINVNTR.IDX*/
   int cublkn;       /* current index block # in memory*/
   int blklen;       /* size of each index block(in record)*/
};

struct INV_IDX {
   char stokn[16];
   int     iconid;
   int dtrecn;
};

typedef struct INV_IDX INVDX;

struct INV_DAT {
   char desc[15];
   double  price;
   char unit[5];
   double  cost;
   char tax;
   int catcod;
   char vendor[5];
   char locat[5];
   unsigned int      relevl;
   unsigned int      qtyonhnd;
   unsigned int      qtyonodr;
   int     iconid;            //icon index
   struct {
       unsigned int      qty;
       unsigned long int sals;
       unsigned long int cost;
   } mnthdat;
   struct {
       unsigned int      qty;
       unsigned long int sals;
```

continued...

```
        unsigned long int cost;
    } yeardat;
};

struct CATCODE {
    char  desc[15];       //description
    int         iconid;       //icon id
    unsigned long int sals;   //sales
    unsigned long int cost;   //cost
    int         delflg;
};

typedef struct CATCODE CATCD;

//
// register.inc
//

#define SYSLEN    98   /* length of the SYSTEM.ARG record*/
#define DALEN sizeof(struct DTHDR) /* length of DTHDR in bytes*/
#define DBLEN sizeof(struct DTITEM) /* length of DTITEM in bytes*/

//
// DEFINE SOME SYSTEM INFORMATION  DESCRIPTED AS BELOW
//
//
struct SYSTEMARG {
    struct IVHDR {          /* INVOICE HEADER TO BE PRINTED */
        char storid[31];      /* name of the store*/
        char storadd[26];      /* address of the store */
        char storcty[16];      /* city of the store*/
        char storsta[3];     /* state of the store*/
        char storzip[6];     /* zip code of the store*/
        char storphn[11];      /* phone # of the store */
    } ivhdr;
    double txrat;       /* Tax Rate for a local area*/
    char  finchg[5];
    double finrat;
    char ivprtr[5]; /* printer name of an invoice report*/
    char rcvprtr[5];/* printer name of a simple recieve report*/
    unsigned int ivno;   /* current invoice #, init 0*/
};
```

continued...

```
typedef struct SYSTEMARG SYSARG;

struct TERMCODE {          /* structure for terms code*/
    char desc[6][16];
};




/*
** invntfil.hpp
** Inventory File Manager
*/

#define FAIL       -1
#define SUCCEED    0
#define MAXFILENM 15              //max length of the file name

#include "stream.hpp"

//
// Parent class of the  index file and the non-index file
//
class OurFile {
    char    fname[MAXFILENM];
    FILE    *fdatp;
    friend class IdxFile;
    friend class CATFile;
    friend class SYSFile;
public:
    OurFile(char fnm[]) { strcpy(fname,fnm); }
    ~OurFile() { ; }

    virtual int GetStuff() { ; }
    virtual int AddStuff() { ; }
    virtual int DelStuff() { ; }
    virtual int ChgStuff() { ; }
    virtual int SrchStuff() { ; }
};
```

continued...

```
//
// Inventory Index file class
//
class IdxFile : public OurFile {
    char    fidxname[MAXFILENM];// index a file
    char    fdelname[MAXFILENM];// delete a file
    FILE    *fidxp;         // index a file id
    FILE    *fdelp;         // delete a file id
    int     ixblksiz;      // the size of an index record
    int     dtblksiz;      // the size of a data record
    unsigned int Inv_Dat_N;   // # of data records
    struct INV_IDX *Inv_Idx;  // points to the index block
    struct INV_HDR Inv_Hdr;   // used for search an index block
public:
    IdxFile(char[],char[],char[],int,int);// constructor
    ~IdxFile();            // destructor

    unsigned int GetInvDtN() { return Inv_Dat_N; }// get the # of data records
    struct INV_HDR *GetInvHdr();// get the index pointers
    struct INV_IDX *GetInvIdx();// get the index block pointers
    int  GetStuff(char[],struct INV_DAT*);// Get the inventory data
    int  GetStuff(char[],struct CUS_DAT*);// Get the customer data

    int  SrchStuff(char[],int*);   // search the index file for an item

    int  AddStuff(char[],struct INV_DAT*);// add an item in the index file
    int  AddStuff(char[],struct CUS_DAT*);// add a customer in the index file

    int  DelStuff(char[]);       // delete an item from the index file

    int  ChgStuff(char[],struct INV_DAT*);// change an item in the index file
    int  ChgStuff(char[],struct CUS_DAT*);// change a customer in the index file
    int  Idx_Ins(struct INV_IDX,int);  // insert an index in
//the index file
    int  Idx_Del(int);         // delete an index from the index file
    int  Inv_B_Srch(char[],int*);   // binary search
};

//
//Inventory system arguments file class
//
class SYSFile : public OurFile {
    struct SYSTEMARG    *sysarg;
public:
```

```
    SYSFile(char fn[]);
    ~SYSFile();

    struct SYSTEMARG *GetSysArg() { return sysarg; }
    int  ChgStuff(struct SYSTEMARG*); // change system args. in
// the data file
};

//
// Category file management class
//
class CATFile : public OurFile {
    int      catno;        //# of cat. in the data file
    struct   CATCODE   *cat;      //cat. data
public:
    CATFile(char fn[]);
    ~CATFile();

    int  GetCatNo() { return catno; }
    struct CATCODE *GetCat() { return cat; }
    int  GetStuff(int,struct CATCODE*);   // get the Category data
    int  AddStuff(int,struct CATCODE*);  // add a cat. in the data file
    int  DelStuff(int);        // delete an item from the index file
    int  ChgStuff(int,struct CATCODE*);// change a cat. in the data file
};
```

OurFile provides virtual functions to perform tasks that will be conducted slightly differently in each subclasses for various files, as follows:

- virtual int GetStuff(): get data.

- virtual int AddStuff(): add an item in the index file.

- virtual int DelStuff(): delete an item in the index.

- virtual int ChgStuff(): change an item in the index.

- virtual int SrchStuff(): search the index file for a given item.

Even though the principles of these functions are similar, they are defined differently to meet the need of the task in each subclass. For example, GetStaff() is defined for classes IdxFile and CATFile, respectively, as follows:

```
// Get the inventory data for IdexFile
int  IdxFile::GetStuff(char itcode[],struct INV_DAT* data)
{
   int pos,dtrecn;

   if(this->SrchStuff(itcode,&pos) != 0)
   {
     return FAIL;
   }

   dtrecn = (Inv_Idx+pos)->dtrecn;
   fseek(fdatp,(long)(2+dtblksiz*dtrecn),0);
   fread((char*)data,dtblksiz,1,fdatp);

   return SUCCEED;
}

// get the category data
int  CATFile::GetStuff(int catcode,struct CATCODE* data)
{
   int pos,recn;

   if(catcode > catno+1 || catcode< 1)  //cat. code not existed
   {
       return FAIL;
   }

   strcpy(data->desc,(cat+catcode-1)->desc);
   data->iconid = (cat+catcode-1)->iconid;
   data->sals = (cat+catcode-1)->sals;
   data->cost = (cat+catcode-1)->cost;

   return SUCCEED;
}
```

Since the structure of the three files are different, the member functions for these classes vary accordingly. For example, extensively detailed methods are provided for manipulation of indexed files, including:

```
    struct INV_HDR *GetInvHdr();// get the index pointers
    struct INV_IDX *GetInvIdx();// get the index block pointers
    int  GetStuff(char[],struct INV_DAT*);// Get the inventory data
    int  GetStuff(char[],struct CUS_DAT*);// Get the customer data

    int  SrchStuff(char[],int*); // search the index file for an
item

    int  AddStuff(char[],struct INV_DAT*);// add an item in index
file
    int  AddStuff(char[],struct CUS_DAT*);// add a customer in
index file

    int  DelStuff(char[]);        // delete an item from index file

    int  ChgStuff(char[],struct INV_DAT*);// change an item
//in the index file
    int  ChgStuff(char[],struct CUS_DAT*);// change a
// customer in the index file
    int  Idx_Ins(struct INV_IDX,int);  // insert a index in
// the index file
    int  Idx_Del(int);            // delete a index from the index file
    int  Inv_B_Srch(char[],int*);     // binary search
```

A destructor (~IdxFile()) is used to save memory space due to the size of data which can be processed. Figures 9-6 and 9-7 depict sample category input and detailed inventory data input.

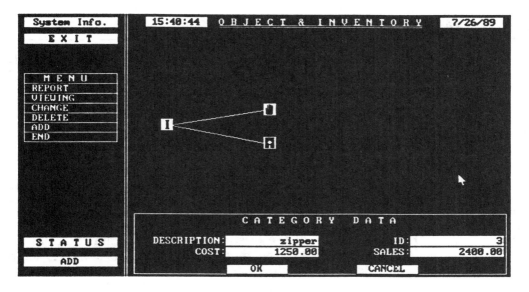

Figure 9-6. Sample Category Input.

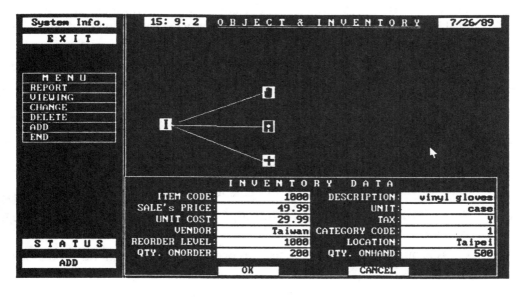

Figure 9-7. Sample Inventory Input.

SUMMARY

- This chapter presents methods and examples of adopting an object-oriented environment to a C program by using the basic classes discussed in Chapters 5 and 6.

- Depending on the complexity of the software package, programs can be significantly improved by incorporating an object-oriented environment to act as a facade where a standard graphical interface can be established for the user.

- To bring an increased degree of user-friendliness into Smalltalk- or MacApp window-like (Macintosh) graphical interface, the following three steps are recommended:

  > Build a "facade" of the existing software program to act as an interface manager using the basic classes, for example, Icon, Menu, Pen, and Bunch.

  > Develop an icon library to host meaningful specialized icons for a given domain problem, using Icon and other related classes.

  > Build a file class group to interface icons and menus with relevant existing files, using an object-oriented language, such as C++.

- An appropriate combination of the above three components will enable you to design an interface system where many desirable layers of windows can be built .

- The four class groups required to build a facade for a software package include:

  > Title: provides system information around the outskirts of the screen .

  > DiagBox: provides user dialog boxes.

  > InvtMenu: provides menu items for the user to select.

  > InvtIcon: provides icon items for the user.

- An existing Inventory Accounting System is used to demonstrate feasibility to test the concept.

- Class group Title enables the user to organize windows, menus and icons on the screen.

- The following classes need to be included in the Title class group:

> Title: to organize all the panes appearing on the screen.
>
> TitlePane: the pane for the title.
>
> DatePane: the pane for the date.
>
> TimePane: the pane for the current time.
>
> InfoWin: the pane for system information.
>
> StatusWin: the pane for operation status.
>
> ExitPane: the pane to provide an exit any time.
>
> DividLine: the pane that provides lines to divide the system control and the interface areas .

- Class group DiagBox allows inputs from the keyboard and the buttons and displays the results on the screen.

- Class Group InvtMenu enables you to program menus with icons for the user to select. Menus and icons are application-specific and can be created case by case.

- Class group InvtIcon is used to make icons for providing users with icon selection. When an icon is chosen, appropriate actions implied will be taken by the computer.

- Class IconLib provides a foundation to build an icon library in conjunction with InvtIcon. IconLib provides functions to save, to load icons and to retrieve an icon id from the icon pattern.

- Class group OurFile is used to prepare and to manage the relevant files in the sample inventory accounting system when they are activated by the user.

- Class OurFile is a root class which originates the three file subclasses to organize both indexed and non-indexed files. For indexed files, class IdxFile records index file names, file id's, size of the record, number of data records, and pointers to the index block.

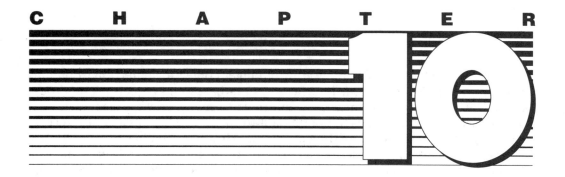

OBJECT-ORIENTED APPLICATONS TO DATA BASES

In the discussion of Chapter 9, the user learned how to adapt an object-oriented environment to an existing C program using classes of icons, menus, and mouse operations developed in Chapters 5 and 6. This chapter presents another type of object-oriented application: integrating intelligent object-oriented environments into data bases.

The two approaches used for integrating intelligent object-oriented environments into data bases are intelligent interface to data bases and object-oriented data bases. The user can build intelligent interface to many existing dispersed data bases when a program needs to obtain data from them. This intelligent interface can be a preprocessor to an existing program. However, an object-oriented data base is more than an interface; object-oriented programming is used to build a data base system that is different from the conventional hierarchical or relational data bases.

This chapter focuses more on the intelligent data bases interface by integrating classes discussed in Chapters 7, 8, and 9. Theoretical approaches, general procedures and a simplified example using the Inventory Control System for an intelligent data base interface are detailed in the presentation. However, for object-oriented data bases, a general discussion on sample object-oriented data bases is presented, because these data bases are too complicated to be discussed in a short chapter.

Chapter 10 consists of sections, adding intelligent interface to data bases using object-oriented programming, and expert system technology (OOP/ES). A general procedure for using OOP/ES is to make an intelligent interface, and to build object-oriented data base systems.

Using Expert System Technology (OOP/ES)

Data base management systems (DBMS) currently employed in processing raw input data often are cumbersome and application- dependent. Wide dispersal of data bases to various locations has created a problem of information system interface for users who are required to make rapid and crucial decisions.

The Drug Enforcement Administration, for example, has to interface many data bases located in different areas of the United States. These bases record different aspects of information on suspects. The timely use of these data from various information sources can be a substantive challenge for many operators. The preparer and data user are currently required to act as an information access expert, learning the structure of the data bases, as well as the DBMS. This requires mastering the techniques and knowledge to retrieve, update, and interface the systems with other commercial software packages.

Management of information resources is now entering a new stage. Evolution of object-oriented programming and expert systems makes it feasible to pursue an intelligent information system interface. If time and economics permit, an intelligent information system, interface mechanism can be developed. This system will reduce the time required for the preparer and user to learn information management systems, such as CAD/CAM packages, graphics, and statistics. These packages will be integrated into the information management system and automatically made available by the OOP/ES when a need is detected.

As shown in Figure 10-1, the optimum architecture of the intelligent interface mechanism consists of four components in response to the need for a particular application:

- Master Expert System, the master controller that dispatches the remaining three interface modules.

- Network Interface, in response to the need for local area network application by the user.

- Data Base Interface, in response to the need for data base management system in handling the data base.

- Software package Interface, in response to the need for standard package applications.

Master Expert System is the interface dispatch center that monitors and employs various software packages. This system formulates the queries and updates sent to the Network Interface by the preparer and user and processes replies from other components. Using the knowledge base of meta knowledge about the preparer and user, software packages, and data base, the Master Expert System provides the following: performs syntactic translations for queries and replies, applies specific software packages, and prepares data transformation for those packages.

Network Interface provides the actual interface with the user/preparer/operator. The interface communicates queries and updates between the user and Master Expert System by identifying the need of the user, determining the level of communication skill of the user, and translating the queries in an appropriate form. The Network Interface has three major functions:

- Meta-knowledge about the user: The system can apply meta- knowledge about the user, including the experience, and intentions of the user to refine the search. If the system knowledge base includes information about users and their organization, such as size, type of ownership, and location, then the system may give greater weight to a variety of potential responses. The system will evaluate projects performed by similar organizations in similar environments.

- Specialized domain knowledge: Browsing a given domain may apply specialized knowledge about that domain to facilitate searching for information to respond to the user's query. The system may contain a set of heuristic rules about searching for experiments that closely correspond to the query. Heuristic searching may act independently of other types of searching or in conjunction with a prioritization method, such as a weighted keyword search where rules are used to assign higher priority to certain types of terms.

- Keyword extraction--the system selects pertinent terms from the user's query to search the data base. Extraction can be limited to a list of predetermined keywords or it can include all significant words (for example, all except articles, prepositions, and conjunctions). The purpose of this extraction is to locate references that most closely match the query, using a combination of linguistic, statistical, and empirical methods such as query term weighting, and term frequency weighting.

Data Base Interface acts as an intelligent front-end for data base management systems in querying and updating the data base. This interface accepts queries from the Network Interface through the Master Expert System and performs the syntactic translation for queries and replies. Data Base Interface contains deductive rules for specifying general knowledge to extract information from a set of specific facts. For instance, a user can obtain data on the cost per sample object in a particular experiment, while the database contains only the total cost of the experiment and the sample size. A very simple deductive rule to obtain the data for this case includes:

```
(cost per sample object) = (total cost)/(sample size)
```

More complex rules can be included to answer the user's queries.

Finally, Software Package Interface accepts commands and transformed data from the Master Expert System. These commands are dispatched, the specific required software packages are operated, and the appropriate results are returned to the Master Expert System. For example, the Software Package Interface can determine the availability and applicability of a CAD/CAE software package and return the condition back to the Master Expert System. Software Package Interface has the following two functions:

- Statistical and mathematical queries--in a data base, users obtain data on aggregate results of their experiments. Intelligent data base interface provides these results through a knowledge based interface to a statistical package and/or a library of mathematical routines. The knowledge based interface contains information about invoking the requested functions and passing and receiving data. For example, a user could ask for average, maximum, minimum, and standard deviation of the total cost for the experiments in a particular query, such as "past experiments on air condition systems and power cells used in spacecraft."

- Interfaces to complicated computer programs, such as CAD software tools-in some cases, a user would like to apply computer programs to answer the question, "what kind of results could that experiment have produced for my flight?" Such models can be linked through a knowledge based interface that describes the capabilities of the model, input required, and output supplied. A wide variety of existing tools then can be integrated under the umbrella of the intelligent interface to the database.

Four components of intelligent interface work closely as a team to satisfy the need of the preparer and user in acquiring and updating information from the data bases.

Three Pragmatic Approaches of Intelligent Interface

Three pragmatic approaches on intelligent interface to data bases and complicated software with object-oriented programming and expert system technology include:

- **Intelligent "user"**: acts as a database for complicated software packages users. Interaction with the software package and database is not its primary objective, but merely a convenient means to access data.

- **Intelligent "representative"**: uses mathematical logic to represent general facts about data in the software package and database to increase usefulness in responding to queries.

- **Intelligent "prober"**: supports browsing through a data base and also supports query modification either to narrow or to broaden the scope of the request to make it more understandable.

Most of these approaches are implemented only in large workstations. Some examples for each type will be discussed.

OOP/ES As Intelligent Users

OOP/ES can be developed to serve as intelligent users of complex conventional software programs, such as data base management systems. Two distinctive types of OOP/ES can be developed to accomplish this objective: OOP/ES that act as "assistants" and OOP/ES that act as "controllers."

Most commercial PC packages in the joint application of OOP/ES and data bases employ knowledge-based systems that act as software packages and database assistants. These systems query optimization and data access through natural language front-ends, and deductive data bases. In most existing coupled systems, the expert makes direct calls to the standard DBMS through a hand-craft interface. This approach implements a tight coupling of OOP/ES to a designated data base. Typical examples of intelligent front-end systems which include: GURU by Micro Data Base Systems, Javelin by Javelin Software, Paradox by Ansa Software, REVEAL by McDonnell Douglass, and Superfile ACLS by Southdata.

Most of these systems are tightly coupled to a specific DBMS. Each system contains varying levels of built-in, system-specific knowledge about its data base/software packages. The coupling of standard software packages to a data base is time-consuming and package-dependent. A hand-craft interface is required for each new package added into the data base.

The more flexible approach is an intelligent interface between the applications and the data base when the OOP/ES acts as a controller. The interface integrates each standard software package on an as-necessary basis without hard-craft linking and allows each component to function independently. The intelligent interface (an OOP/ES) can reason about components, their requirements for interface, and data communications of the packages being connected. An OOP/ES uses knowledge of the packages being linked to provide communication and data sharing and uses meta knowledge regarding the capabilities of the packages to optimally select and employ software programs to meet the user's requirements. For example, a user may not be aware of the need to use a statistical package or may not know which statistical package to use. The intelligent interface will connect a software package, after determining from past experience that a particular statistical package cost-effectively shows a given aspect of the data the user has requested or acquired.

The flexibility of this interface mechanism relies on: OOP/ES's reasoning capability, the content of the data base, and the data spaces of standard software packages. The data boxes are interfaced in response to the need for data processing and data descriptions of the software packages.

Transformation of data representations and translation of data manipulation languages are required in communication between the data base, standard software packages, and the preparer and user. These are mapping: semantic mapping for transformation and syntactic mapping for translation. Since each individual software package uses a different organization for equivalent data or represents the data at different levels of detail, semantic mapping is required to transform data among software packages.

Different software packages may employ their own data manipulation languages. Mapping between these data manipulation languages is a syntactic translation. For example, the algebraic and calculus query languages used for relational data bases need to be translated syntactically for use in other software packages, such as graphics.

Two examples are cited showing the two types of OOP/ES that have served as intelligent users of software packages. SICAD (Standards Interfaces in CAD) acts as an expert-system assistant to standards processing in CAD. This package employs a custom knowledge base and a hard-craft inference mechanism to gain access to design standards. The knowledge base contains three elements:

- Classifier trees that relate engineering terminology to provisions of a standard.

- An information network that consists of decision tables written in FORTRAN representing the provisions of a standard.

- Mapping that relates data items in a standard to data items in a design data base.

SICAD was developed to assist a design program that performs compliance checking. SICAD acts as an assistant to the design program in identifying and checking applicable provisions. Compliance checking uses backward chaining to determine all data required to evaluate a provision.

KADBASE (Knowledge Aided Database Management System) acts as an expert-system controller to database management systems. The objective of KADBASE was to develop a flexible, intelligent interface that enables multiple OOP/ES and multiple data bases to communicate as autonomous, self-descriptive units with a CAD system operating in a distributed, computing environment.

KADBASE consists of three major parts:

1. The knowledge-based system interface formulates the queries and updates sent to other components and processes replies from them.

2. The knowledge-based data base interface acts as an intelligent user of a DBMs that accepts queries from other components and returns appropriate replies regarding the data base.

3. The data base access manager actually performs interface by decomposing queries, issuing the appropriate subqueries to the local data base, obtaining and processing the data, and formulating the replies.

Intelligent Representatives

OOP/ES acting as intelligent "representatives" use logic to represent facts about data in the data base or a complex software program to facilitate queries. They can be integrated to a complex database or software packages. If these intelligent "representatives" are integrated to data bases, they are called intentional data bases (IDB) which are a collection of axioms, such as rules, postulates, constraints, and general facts. These axioms can be viewed alternately as data integrity constraints, data definitions, or logical inference rules and are represented in mathematical logic.

Two examples are discussed to demonstrate the differences between the two categories, MRPPS and DADM. MRPPS (Maryland Refutation Proof Procedure System) is an integrated system based on mathematical logic. Knowledge and data are combined in a semantic network that consists of the following:

- a semantic graph (a classification structure)

- a data base (including conventional data base and the IDB).

- a dictionary (a listing of relations, constants, and functions).

- a semantic form space (consisting of definitions of constraints to be imposed on predicates and their arguments). The elements of the semantic graph are referenced by the knowledge base index to facilitate quick access.

A query to MRPPS is a conjunction of clauses. The first step in query processing checks that the query is consistent with the acceptable syntax and structure. The system uses a refutation proof procedure search for a solution to the query. The refutation proof procedure first assumes negation of the desired clauses and attempts to prove a contradiction from rules and facts in the knowledge base.

DADM (Deductively Augmented Data Management System) is an intelligent front-end system that represents a combination of a file in general knowledge with an inference engine and a file of specific knowledge with searching mechanism. General knowledge consists of a set of domain-specific assertions whose order is expressed predicate, calculus, and file of specific knowledge. This file is supported by a single relational DBMS. The system was implemented in heterogeneous hardware environments: an inference engine running on a LISP machine, a relational data base supported by a specialized data base machine, and a query and reply translator running on a DEC VAX 11/780.

The inference engine uses the specific knowledge on the problem domain to develop search strategies for locating answers from the queries. The queries then are sent to the translator for conversion to data base syntax that are passed to the data base machine for processing. Replies from the data base machine follows a reverse path.

The applications of DADM include "Manager's Assistant" to aid in corporate project monitoring, planning, and intelligent assistant for information resources managers [10].

Intelligent "Probers"

OOP/ES acting as intelligent probers provide support capability including browsing through a data base or program, probing for information and determining specific information about alternative queries best suited for the user's needs. This effort is based on rules that describe relationships between predicates. For instance, if Employ (x, John)-- that is, finds all persons who John employs--fails, the intelligent prober can try queries Teach (x, John), Employ (x, Mary), or supervise (x, John) according to rules on relationships between predicates. Motro provided an example in discussing a system for browsing in a loosely structured data base [11].

Using OOP/ES to Make an Intelligent Interface to Data Bases

The three major components required for an intelligent Interface are observed, as follows:

- Frame structure

- Rule structure

- Querying and Deriving Knowledge (Inference Engine) (Chapter 8)
  - Forward chaining
  - Backward chaining
  - Reasoning/search

- Graphical User Interface (Chapters 5, 6 and 9)
  - Windows
  - Icons
  - Menus

All or part of these components can be used to build an intelligent interface to given data bases. Significant attention has been paid to the object-oriented-programming rule, that each program should be modular. Appropriate subcomponents can be rapid-prototyped to build an intelligent interface that satisfies the need of the situation.

To use the C++ class and function name overloading effectively, the following procedure is recommended in building the intelligent interface system:

1. Structure the problem to:

    1.) Define the functions and modes to operate.

    2.) Select appropriate data types in different data bases.

    3.) Establish communications links.

2. Use an OOP/ES tool (IQ-200) to rapidly prototype an expert system.

3 Debug and refine the prototype until it is satisfactory.

4. Use C+ +/C and the library functions to convert the final prototype system.

The Inventory Control System will be used to demonstrate the procedure.

An Example-- Intelligent Interface to dBase and Lotus I-2-3

The Inventory Control System (ICS) is the complementary of the Inventory Accounting System. The ICS problem discussed in Chapters 1 and 7 is recited as follows: three Mazda automobile dealers maintain small inventories in different locations using various data bases written in dBase or Lotus 1-2-3 on the most common parts requested by their customers. A system of communication between the warehouse and the dealers is needed for maintaining optimal supplies of the most frequently ordered Mazda parts at each of the dealers. In addition, there is no means of communication between the various computer networks.

The ICS is an intelligent information system that allows a parts dealer or shop owner to: cost-effectively control their inventory, maintain an optimal level of stocks, record translations, reorder stocks, and check at any moment the condition of a given part, such as the cost, degree of customer satisfaction, and supplier's delivery schedule.

The minimum functionalities for a complete system include:

1. Communicating with other information systems containing the necessary information, for example, dBase III.

2. Organization of parts inventory information in an easy-to-understand manner.

3. Accepting rules about parts sold, purchased, priced, and other heuristic knowledge.

Organization of parts and rules have been discussed in Chapters 7 and 8. This chapter presents the communication among data bases and an overall integration of all the components of the ICS developed in various chapters.

A hybrid object-oriented language, IQ-200 (see detailed technical summary in Appendix B), is used to prototype the ICS.

Rapid-prototyping the ICS with IQ-200

Listing 10-1 shows the source code in IQ-200 for the ICS prototype. The listing includes the following files:

```
ICSINT1.BPL    ;interface commands
ICSHOST2.BPL   ;host, program, operating system definitions
ICSOBJ3.BPL    ;knowledge base objects
ICSKS4.BPL     ;remote knowledge source objects
```

Listing 10.1: A Sample Program for the Inventory Control System Prototype Using IQ-200

```
#|
****************************************************************
******

    Inventory Control Demo INTERFACE

****************************************************************
****** |#


(define-interface 'inventory-control
   :banner " Inventory Control System Demonstration "
   :hot-keys '((224 (start-help)) (238 (quit-interface)) ; f1
and f2
         (#\c-d (dos)) (#\c-r (redraw-screen)) (#\c-m (mouse-ini-
tialize)))
   :hot-keys-doc " F1: Help  F10: Quit  C-D: Dos  C-R: Redraw
C-M: Init Mouse "
   :help-file-pathname "c:\\iq200\\examples\\icshelp.txt")


;;;_____MODES

(define-mode 'inventory-control 'toplevel-mode " Inventory
Toplevel "
   '(("Dealership" (run-mode 'dealership-operations-mode))
     ("Warehouse" (run-mode 'warehouse-operations-mode))
     ("System"  (run-mode 'system-operations-mode))
     ("Help" (start-help 'toplevel-mode))
     ("Quit" (quit-interface)))))

(define-mode 'inventory-control 'Dealership-Operations-Mode "
Dealers "
   '(("Inventory" (view-dealer-inventory) :doc "Inventory of a
dealer")
     ("Purchase" (request-sale) :doc "Purchase an item")
     ("Order" (order-part) :doc "Enter order from warehouse")
```

continued...

```
    ("Show Outstanding" (view-outstanding-orders)
        :doc "Show outstanding orders")
    ("Show Processed" (view-processed-orders) :doc "Show
processed orders")
    ("Check-Dealers" (check-dealers) :doc "Check dealers for
part")))

(define-mode 'inventory-control 'warehouse-Operations-Mode "
Warehouses "
    '(("View Inventory" (view-warehouse-inventory) :doc "View en-
tire inventory")
    ("Price" (Get-Price) :doc "Get discounted price of part")
    ("Process Orders" (process-orders) :doc "Process Outstand-
ing Orders")
    ("Low Inventories" (check-low-inventories) :doc "Check Low
Inventories")
    ("Sales Percentage" (sales-percentage) :doc "Part % of
total sales")))

(define-mode 'inventory-control 'system-operations-mode " Sys-
tem "
    '(("Redraw" (redraw-screen) :doc "Redraw the screen")
    ("Go to DOS" (dos))))


;;;_____DEALER PROCEDURES

;;;DEALER INVENTORY
(defprocedure view-dealer-inventory
    (deactivate-rule-set 'basic-rule-set)
    (activate-rule-set 'userint-rules)
    (activate-rule-set 'd-inv-rules)
    (query '(show-dealer-inventory))
    (user-pause))


;;;PURCHASE
(defprocedure request-sale
    (deactivate-rule-set 'basic-rule-set)
    (activate-rule-set 'userint-rules)
    (activate-rule-set 'request-rules)
    (query '(request-part))
    (user-pause))

;;;ORDER PART
(defprocedure Order-Part
    (deactivate-rule-set 'basic-rule-set)
    (activate-rule-set 'userint-rules)
    (activate-rule-set 'order-rules)
    (query '(order-part))
    (user-pause))
```

continued...

```
;;;VIEW CUSTOMER ORDERS
(defprocedure View-Outstanding-Orders
  (deactivate-rule-set 'basic-rule-set)
  (activate-rule-set 'userint-rules)
  (activate-rule-set 'view-outstanding-rules)
  (query '(view-orders))
  (user-pause))


;;;VIEW PROCESSED ORDERS
(defprocedure View-Processed-Orders
  (deactivate-rule-set 'basic-rule-set)
  (activate-rule-set 'userint-rules)
  (activate-rule-set 'view-processed-rules)
  (query '(view-processed-orders))
  (user-pause))


;;;CHECK DEALERS
(defprocedure Check-Dealers
  (deactivate-rule-set 'basic-rule-set)
  (activate-rule-set 'userint-rules)
  (activate-rule-set 'request-rules)
  (query '(dealer-check))
  (user-pause))


;;;_____WAREHOUSE PROCEDURES

;;;WAREHOUSE INVENTORY
(defprocedure View-Warehouse-Inventory
  (deactivate-rule-set 'basic-rule-set)
  (activate-rule-set 'userint-rules)
  (activate-rule-set 'w-inv-rules)
  (query '(show-warehouse-inventory))
  (user-pause))


;;;PRICE
(defprocedure Get-Price
  (deactivate-rule-set 'basic-rule-set)
  (activate-rule-set 'userint-rules)
  (activate-rule-set 'price-rules)
  (query '(display-price))
  (user-pause))
```

continued...

```
;;;PROCESS CUSTOMER ORDERS
(defprocedure Process-Orders
  (deactivate-rule-set 'basic-rule-set)
  (activate-rule-set 'userint-rules)
  (activate-rule-set 'process-order-rules)
  (stash '(value-of part-found nil))
  (query '(process-orders))
  (user-pause))

;;;LOW INVENTORIES
(defprocedure Check-Low-Inventories
  (deactivate-rule-set 'basic-rule-set)
  (activate-rule-set 'userint-rules)
  (activate-rule-set 'low-inv-rules)
  (stash '(value-of part-found nil))
  (query '(identify-critical-inventories))
  (user-pause))

;;;SALES PERCENTAGE
(defprocedure Sales-Percentage
  (deactivate-rule-set 'basic-rule-set)
  (activate-rule-set 'userint-rules)
  (activate-rule-set 'percentage-rules)
  (stash '(value-of total-sales 0))
  (stash '(value-of part-sales 0))
  (query '(get-sales-percentage))
  (user-pause))


#|
********************************************************************
******

    Baldur Host Setup file.

 \'s for the c regexpr parser must be doubled (for lisp)
********************************************************************
****** |#

(define-host 'baldur :phone-number 7329715 :password 'changeme1
      :password2 'changeme2 :os 'dos
      :programs '((dbase3 "c:\\dbase\\") (sql "c:\\sqlbase\\"))
      :toplevel-program 'baldur-server
      :documentation "Hayward AT #1: God of light and Joy
(Helios)")
(define-host 'odin :phone-number 7329716 :password 'changeme1
      :password2 'changeme2 :os 'dos
      :programs '((dbase3 "c:\\dbase\\") (sql "c:\\sqlbase\\"))
      :toplevel-program 'baldur-server
      :documentation "Hayward AT #2: Lord of the Gods (Zeus)")
```

continued...

```
(define-host 'thor :phone-number 3276521 :password 'changeme1
        :password2 'changeme2 :os 'dos
        :programs '((dbase3 "c:\\dbase\\") (sql "c:\\sqlbase\\"))
        :toplevel-program 'baldur-server
        :documentation "Menlo Park AT #1: The War-God (Ares)")
(define-host 'ymer :phone-number 3253860 :password 'changeme1
        :password2 'changeme2 :os 'dos
        :programs '((dbase3 "c:\\dbase\\") (sql "c:\\sqlbase\\"))
        :toplevel-program 'baldur-server
        :documentation "Menlo Park AT #2")
(define-host 'tyr :phone-number 3269106 :password 'changeme1
        :password2 'changeme2 :os 'dos
        :programs '((dbase3 "c:\\dbase\\") (sql "c:\\sqlbase\\"))
        :toplevel-program 'baldur-server
        :documentation "Stanford AT #2: The father of the Gods
(Kronos)")
(define-host 'loki :phone-number 3234754 :password 'changeme1
        :password2 'changeme2 :os 'dos
        :programs '((dbase3 "c:\\dbase\\") (sql "c:\\sqlbase\\"))
        :toplevel-program 'baldur-server
        :documentation "Stanford AT #1: The mischievous God")


#                                                                    |
*******************************************************************
***


            Inventory Control System Demo OBJECTS

   This file contains all the objects for use with the ICS Demo.
*******************************************************************
******  |#


;;;_____RULE SETS

(create-rule-set 'dealer-rules)
   (create-rule-set 'request-rules :superset 'dealer-rules)
   (create-rule-set 'order-rules :superset 'dealer-rules)
   (create-rule-set 'd-inv-rules :superset 'dealer-rules)
   (create-rule-set 'view-outstanding-rules :superset 'dealer-
rules)
   (create-rule-set 'view-processed-rules :superset 'dealer-
rules)


(create-rule-set 'warehouse-rules)
   (create-rule-set 'w-inv-rules :superset 'warehouse-rules)
   (create-rule-set 'price-rules :superset 'warehouse-rules)
   (create-rule-set 'low-inv-rules :superset 'warehouse-rules)
```

continued...

```
   (create-rule-set 'process-order-rules :superset 'warehouse-
rules)
   (create-rule-set 'percentage-rules :superset 'warehouse-
rules)

(create-rule-set 'userint-rules)

;;;
****************************************************************
******
;;; Rules to determine what parts, dealers, and warehouses
exist.

;;; Parts list rules
(create-variable 'parts-list :constraint :list)

(create-rule 'get-parts-list :rule-set 'userint-rules
       :premise '(and (format "~%Compiling list of parts...")
          (set-of ?name
            (entity ?x is-a san-fran-inv
              with name = ?name)
            ?p)
          (or (not (equal ?p nil))
         (format "no parts found at San-Fran!!")))
       :action '(stash '(value-of parts-list ?p))
       :conclusion '(get-parts-list ?p))

(create-rule 'Part-List :rule-set 'userint-rules
       :premise '(and (cut)
          (or (value-of parts-list ?list)
         (get-parts-list ?list)))
       :conclusion '(get-list :part ?list))

;;; Warehouse & Dealer list rules

(create-rule 'Warehouse-List :rule-set 'userint-rules
       :premise '(set-of ?x (entity ?x is-a warehouse) ?list)
       :conclusion '(get-list :warehouse ?list))
(create-rule 'Dealer-List :rule-set 'userint-rules
       :premise '(set-of ?x (entity ?x is-a dealer) ?list)
       :conclusion '(get-list :dealer ?list))

;;;_____SPECIAL I/O RULES

;;; Supports types of :dealer :warehouse :part
;;; (achieve '(pick-value "Enter dealer to use" :dealer
?answer))
```

continued...

```
(create-rule 'pick-value :rule-set 'userint-rules
     :premise '(and (get-list ?type ?list)
         (cut)
         (menu-choose ?list ?string ?result))
     :conclusion '(pick-value ?string ?type ?result))

;;;************************************************************
*********
;;;                   DEALERSHIP OPERATION RULES
*
;;;************************************************************
*********

;;;_____DEALER INVENTORY

(create-rule 'display-dealer-inv :rule-set 'd-inv-rules
     :premise '(and (pick-value "Enter dealer to use" :dealer
?dealer)
        (entity ?dealer is-a dealer with inventory = ?inv)
          (entity ?ent is-a ?inv with name = ?part-name
             with cil = ?cil)
          (format "~%Part-Name: ~A, Number in Stock: ~A"
             ?part-name ?cil)
           (fail))
     :conclusion '(show-dealer-inventory))

;;;_____REQUEST SALE
(create-rule 'new-request :rule-set 'request-rules
     :premise '(and (pick-value "Enter dealer to use" :dealer
?dealer)
          (or (and (remote-dealer ?dealer) (cut)
          (format "~%Sorry, ~A is a foreign dealer and cannot"
              ?dealer)
             (format "~%accept purchases at this location.")
             (fail))
          (succeed))
           (pick-value "Enter part to use" :part ?part-name)
           (menu-input "Enter number desired" :integer ?num)
           (format "~%Looking in ~A's inventory for ~A"
             ?dealer ?part-name)
           (request ?dealer ?part-name ?num))
     :conclusion '(request-part))

(create-rule 'process-request :rule-set 'request-rules
        :premise '(or (and (num-available? ?curr-deal ?part-name
?num)
```

continued...

```
        (format "~%Part ~A is in stock in ~A.  Reducing inventory..."
          ?part-name ?curr-deal)
        (reduce-inv ?curr-deal ?part-name ?num))
        (format "~%Part ~A not available at ~A.~%Try checking other
 dealers or ordering part."
          ?part-name ?curr-deal))
      :conclusion '(request ?curr-deal ?part-name ?num))


(create-rule 'remote-dealer :rule-set 'request-rules
      :premise '(and (inventory ?dealer ?inv)
          (entity ?ks is-a knowledge-source
            with class-defined = ?inv))
      :conclusion '(remote-dealer ?dealer))

(create-rule 'reduce-inventory :rule-set 'request-rules
      :premise '(and (inventory ?curr-deal ?inv)
          (entity ?ent is-a ?inv with name = ?part-name
            with cil = ?old)
          (- ?old ?num ?new)
          (format "~%Inventory at ~A reduced from ~A to ~A."
            ?curr-deal ?old ?new))
      :conclusion '(reduce-inv ?curr-deal ?part-name ?num)
      :action '(stash '(cil ?ent ?new)))


(create-rule 'Available :rule-set 'request-rules
      :premise '(and (inventory ?source ?inv)
          (entity ?ent is-a ?inv with name = ?part-name
            with cil = ?cil)
          ( ?number ?cil))
      :conclusion  '(num-available? ?source ?part-name ?number))



;;;_____ORDER PART
;;; Top level backward chaining rule.
(create-rule 'order-new-part :rule-set 'order-rules
      :premise '(and (pick-value "From which dealer?" :dealer
?curr-deal)
          (pick-value "Choose part to order" :part ?part-name)
          (choose-values
            ((num :prompt "Number to order: " :constraint :integer
              :mandatory? t)
        (cust :prompt "New customer name: " :constraint :name
              :mandatory? t)
        (date :prompt "Order date: " :constraint :date
              :mandatory? t))
            "Enter Customer information"
            ?num ?cust ?date)
          (print-arrival-info ?cust ?part-name))
      :conclusion '(order-part)
```

continued...

```
        :action '(create-entity '?cust :class 'Stanford-Custs
               :name '?cust :dealer '?curr-deal
               :part '?part-name :quantity '?num
               :order-date '?date))

;;; Gets arrival information from the warehouse.
(create-rule 'calc-days-to-arrival :rule-set 'order-rules
        :premise '(and (entity ?ware is-a warehouse)
              (format "~%Looking for a warehouse that stocks ~A"
                 ?part-name)
              (inventory ?ware ?inv)
              (entity ?ent is-a ?inv with name = ?part-name
                 with order-time = ?days)
              (format "~%Warehouse ~A has the part.  Computing arrival
certainty" ?ware)
              (or (adjust-certainty ?part-name) (succeed)))
        :conclusion '(days-to-arrival ?part-name ?days)
        :certainty 0.9)

(create-rule 'print-arrival-info :rule-set 'order-rules
        :premise '(and (certainty-of (days-to-arrival ?part-name
?days) ?cf)
              (format "~%The certainty of the order for ~A arriving in
~A days is ~A." ?cust ?days ?cf))
        :conclusion '(print-arrival-info ?cust ?part-name))

;;; Adjustment for unreliable part deliveries.
(create-variable 'unreliable-parts :value '(parking_brake cool-
ing_fan)
        :constraint :list
        :documentation "Parts whose delivery is more uncertain")

(create-rule 'adjust-certainty :rule-set 'order-rules
        :premise '(and (value-of unreliable-parts ?up)
              (eval (member '?part-name '?up) ?result)
              (not (equal ?result nil))
              (format "~%Delivery of part ~A found unreliable; adjustin
arrival certainty." ?part-name))
        :conclusion '(adjust-certainty ?part-name)
        :certainty .7)

;;;_____VIEW CUSTOMER ORDERS

;;;need OR rule for no order condition
(create-rule 'view-order :rule-set 'view-outstanding-rules
    :premise '(and (pick-value "Which dealer's customers?"
:dealer ?deal)
          (entity ?deal is-a dealer with customers = ?deal-custs)
          (entity ?cust-ent is-a ?deal-custs with name = ?n
            with part = ?pd)
          (entity ?cust-ent is-a ?deal-custs with quantity = ?nd
            with order-date = ?od)
```

        continued...

```
         (format "~%Customer: ~A, Part: ~A, Quantity: ~A, Ordered:
~A" ?n ?pd ?nd ?od)
         (fail))
      :conclusion '(view-orders))
```

```
;;;_____VIEW PROCESSED ORDERS
```

```
(create-rule 'view-processed-order :rule-set 'view-processed-
rules
      :premise '(and (pick-value "Which dealer to view orders
from?" :dealer
              ?dealer)
        (or (processed-order ?dealer ?cust ?part-name ?num)
            (and (format "~%No orders processed for ~A" ?dealer)
            (cut) (fail)))
        (format "~%Order Processed for ~A:  Cust: ~A,  Part: ~A,
Number: ~A." ?dealer ?cust ?part-name ?num)
        (fail))
      :conclusion '(view-processed-orders))
```

```
;;;_____CHECK DEALERS
```

```
(create-rule 'Dealer-Check :rule-set 'request-rules
        :premise '(and (pick-value "Enter part to check" :part
?part-name)
          (menu-input "Enter number desired" :integer ?num)
          (format "~%COMMENCING FOREIGN DEALER INQUIRY...")
          (entity ?dealer is-a dealer)
          (format "~%~A..." ?dealer)
          (or (and (num-available? ?dealer ?part-name ?num)
              (format "has ~A ~As in stock" ?num ?part-name))
        (format "does not have enough ~As" ?part-name))
          (fail))
        :conclusion '(dealer-check))
```

```
;;;**********************************************************
*********
;;;                    WAREHOUSE OPERATION RULES
*
;;;**********************************************************
*********
```

```
;;;_____WAREHOUSE INVENTORY
```

```
(create-rule 'display-warehouse-inventories :rule-set 'w-inv-
rules
      :premise '(and (pick-value "Choose warehouse to display"
          :warehouse ?ware)
        (inventory ?ware ?inv)
```

continued...

```
        (entity ?ent is-a ?inv with name = ?part-name
          with cost = ?cost with discount = ?discount)
        (format "~%Part-Name: ~A, Cost: ~A, Discount: ~A."
          ?part-name ?cost ?discount)
        (fail))
   :conclusion '(show-warehouse-inventory))
```

```
;;;_____GET PRICE
```

```
(create-rule 'display-price :rule-set 'price-rules
    :premise '(and (pick-value "Enter warehouse to use"
:warehouse ?ware)
        (pick-value "Pricing for which part?" :part ?part-name)
        (format "~%Requesting pricing information from warehouse")
        (or (and (inventory ?ware ?inv)
        (entity ?ware-ent is-a ?inv with name = ?part-name
          with cost = ?cost with discount = ?discount)
        (true-cost ?cost ?discount ?true-cost)
        (format "~%Current price of ~A (including $~A discount): $
          ?part-name ?discount ?true-cost))
      (format "~%Pricing information on ~A not found."
        ?part-name)))
    :conclusion '(display-price))
```

```
(create-rule 'True-Cost :rule-set 'price-rules
    :premise '(and (format "~%Evaluating discount costs")
      (- ?cost ?discount ?tcost))
    :conclusion '(true-cost ?cost ?discount ?tcost))
```

```
;;;_____PROCESS CUSTOMER ORDERS
```

```
;;; this will transfer a part for every customer
(create-rule 'Process-Order :rule-set 'process-order-rules
    :premise '(and (pick-value "Enter warehouse to process or-
ders"
        :warehouse ?ware)
        (subclass ?customer customer)
        (entity ?cust is-a ?customer with name = ?name
          with part = ?part-name)
        (entity ?cust is-a ?customer with dealer = ?dealer
          with quantity = ?num)
        (format "~%Transfer needed for customer ~A:" ?name)
        (format "~%  ~A ~A from ~A to ~A"
          ?num ?part-name ?ware ?dealer)
        (transfer ?part-name ?num ?cust ?ware ?dealer)
        (eval (stash '(value-of part-found t)))
        (fail))
    :conclusion '(process-orders))
```

continued...

```
(create-rule 'notify-no-orders-to-process :rule-set 'process-
order-rules
     :premise '(and (value-of part-found nil)
         (format "~%There are no more current orders."))
     :conclusion '(process-orders)
     :priority 5)

(create-rule 'transfer-from-ware/delete-cust :rule-set
'process-order-rules
     :premise '(and (inventory ?ware ?ware-inv)
         (or (and (entity ?dealer is-a dealer)
             (not (remote-dealer ?dealer)))
            (and (format "~%  Dealer ~A does not exist locally"
               ?dealer)
            (fail)))
         (or (entity ?part-inv is-a ?ware-inv with name = ?part-name
            with cil = ?cil)
            (and (format "~%  Could not confirm that warehouse ~A
stocks this part"
               ?ware) (fail)))
         (or (and ( ?num ?cil)
            (- ?cil ?num ?new-cil)
            (format "~%  ~A ~A transfered to ~A for ~A."
               ?num ?part-name ?dealer ?cust))
            (and (format "~%  Transfer unsuccessful, insufficient
supply at ~A" ?ware)
            (fail))))
     :conclusion '(transfer ?part-name ?num ?cust ?ware ?dealer)
     :action
     '(do-all (delete-entity '?cust)
         (stash '(and (cil ?part-inv ?new-cil) ; only do this if
local!!
         (processed-order ?dealer ?cust ?part-name ?num)))))

;;;_____LOW INVENTORIES

(create-variable 'part-found :constraint :boolean)
(create-variable 'threshold-inventory :value .25 :constraint
:fraction)
(create-rule 'quarter-inv :rule-set 'low-inv-rules
     :premise '(and (pick-value "Enter warehouse to use"
:warehouse ?ware)
         (value-of threshold-inventory ?thres)
         (format "~%Parts for warehouse ~A." ?ware)
         (inventory ?ware ?inv)
         (entity ?ware-ent is-a ?inv with name = ?name
            with cil = ?cil with oil = ?oil)
         (/ ?cil ?oil ?ratio)
         ( ?ratio ?thres)
         (* ?ratio 200 ?%ratio)
         (eval (stash '(value-of part-found t)))
```

```
          (format "~%Critical inventory on ~A:" ?name)
          (format "~%  Current inventory is ~A% of optimal" ?%ratio)
          (fail))
     :conclusion '(identify-critical-inventories))

(create-rule 'notify-no-low-invs :rule-set 'low-inv-rules
     :premise '(and (value-of part-found nil)
          (format "~%No parts with critically low inventories."))
     :conclusion '(identify-critical-inventories)
     :priority 5)


;;;_____SALES PERCENTAGE


(create-variable 'total-sales :constraint :number)
(create-variable 'part-sales :constraint :number)


(create-rule 'calc-sales-init :rule-set 'percentage-rules
     :premise '(and (pick-value "Enter warehouse to use"
:warehouse ?ware)
          (pick-value "Enter part to use" :part ?part-name)
          (format "~%Initializing warehouse query for ~A at ~A."
            ?part-name ?ware)
          (get-part-totals ?part-name ?ware)
          (calc-sales-perc ?part-name))
     :conclusion '(get-sales-percentage))

(create-rule 'calc-stats :rule-set 'percentage-rules
     :premise '(or (and (sales-records ?ware ?sr)
          (entity ?ent is-a ?sr with total-sale = ?total-sale)
          (add-value-to-variable total-sales ?total-sale)
          ; if the part is the one we want, add its sales
               (part ?ent ?part-name)
          (add-value-to-variable part-sales ?total-sale)
          (fail))
          (succeed))
     :conclusion '(get-part-totals ?part-name ?ware))


(create-rule 'calc-sales-percentage :rule-set 'percentage-rules
     :premise '(and (value-of total-sales ?total-sales)
          (value-of part-sales ?part-sales)
          (not (= ?total-sales 0))
          (eval (* 200 (/ ?part-sales ?total-sales)) ?per)
          (format "~%Sales statistics on ~A: " ?part-name)
          (format "~%Part Sales = $~A.  Total Sales = $~A"
            ?part-sales ?total-sales)
          (format "~%Percentage of Total Sales = ~A%" ?per))
     :conclusion '(calc-sales-perc ?part-name))
```

continued...

```
(create-rule 'notify-part-not-found :rule-set 'percentage-rules
    :premise '(format "~%No sales for part requested.")
    :conclusion '(get-sales-percentage)
    :priority 5)

(create-rule 'add-value-to-variable :rule-set 'percentage-rules
    :premise '(and (value-of ?variable ?old)
        (+ ?old ?value ?new))
    :conclusion '(add-value-to-variable ?variable ?value)
    :action '(stash '(value-of ?variable ?new)))

;;;THE END


#|
******************************************************************
******

    Class and Knowledge Source definitions for ICS demo.

******************************************************************
******|#


;;; Class definitions for dealer and warehouse inventories on
car parts.
(create-class 'Location :documentation "Represents a location"
        :slots '((address :constraint :string)
            (phone :constraint :number)
            (inventory :constraint (:subclass inventory))))
(create-class 'Warehouse :documentation "Represents an actual
warehouse"
        :superclass 'location
        :slots '((sales-records :constraint (:subclass sales-
records))))
(create-class 'Dealer :documentation "Represents an actual
dealer"
        :superclass 'location
        :slots '((customers :constraint (:subclass customer))))

(create-class 'Inventory :documentation "Inventory information
on a part"
        :slots '((name :constraint :name)       ; part name
            (cil :constraint :integer)    ;current invent level
            (oil :constraint :integer)))   ;optimal invent level

(create-class 'Warehouse-Inv :superclass 'inventory
        :documentation "A Warehouse inventory on a part"
        :slots '((cost :constraint :number)
            (discount :constraint :number)
            (min-order :constraint :integer)
            (order-time :constraint :integer)))
```

continued...

```
(create-class 'Dealer-Inv :superclass 'inventory
        :documentation "A dealer inventory on a part")

(create-class 'Customer :documentation "Dealership customer"
      :slots '((dealer :constraint :name)
           (name :constraint :name)
           (part :constraint :name)
           (quantity :constraint :number :when-needed 1)
           (order-date :constraint :date)
           (time :constraint :number)))

(create-class 'Sales-Records)

;;;
*****************************************************************
******
;;; Let's create a warehouse

(read-lotus123-class 'San-Fran-Sales-Records
           :filename "c:\\iq200\\examples\\ware.wk1"
           :superclass 'Sales-Records
           :slot-names-row 0
           :deleted-rows '(1)
           :deleted-columns '(1))

(create-class 'San-Fran-Inv :superclass 'warehouse-inv
        :documentation "Inventory of parts for San Francisco
Warehouse")
(define-knowledge-source 'San-FranKS :host :local
  :program 'dbase3
  :filename "c:\\iq200\\examples\\ware.dbf"
  :class-defined 'San-Fran-Inv
  :slot-with-entity-name nil
  :name-constrained-slots '(name)
  :slot-name-translations '((min-order min_ord) (order-time
order_time)))

#|
(read-dbase3-class 'San-Fran-Inv
        :superclass 'warehouse-inv
        :filename "c:\\iq200\\examples\\ware.dbf"
        :slot-with-entity-name nil
        :name-constrained-slots '(name)
        :slot-name-translations '((min-order min_ord) (order-time
order_time)))
|#
(create-warehouse 'San-Fran :inventory 'san-fran-inv :phone
7329715
        :address "230 Geary St."
        :sales-records 'san-fran-sales-records)
```

```
;;;
******************************************************************
******
;;;; Let's create some dealers

;;;; Stanford dealer
(read-dbase3-class 'Stanford-Inv
         :filename "c:\\iq200\\examples\\dealer1.dbf"
         :superclass 'dealer-inv
         :documentation "Stanford Inventory")

;;;; local customers
(read-dbase3-class 'Stanford-Custs
         :filename "c:\\iq200\\examples\\cust1.dbf"
         :superclass 'customer
         :slot-with-entity-name 'name
         :name-constrained-slots '(name dealer part)
         :slot-name-translations '((order-date order_date)))

(create-dealer 'stanford :inventory 'stanford-inv :phone
3269106
         :customers 'stanford-custs)

;;;; Palo Alto dealer

(create-class 'Palo-Alto-Inv :superclass 'dealer-inv)
(define-knowledge-source 'Palo-AltoKS :host :local ; 'odin
  :program 'dbase3
  :filename "c:\\iq200\\examples\\dealer2.dbf"
  :name-constrained-slots '(name)
  :class-defined 'Palo-Alto-Inv)

(create-class 'Palo-Alto-Custs :superclass 'customer)
(define-knowledge-source 'Palo-Alto-CustKS :host :local  ;
'baldur
  :program 'dbase3
  :filename "c:\\iq200\\examples\\cust2.dbf"
  :slot-with-entity-name 'name
  :class-defined 'Palo-Alto-Custs
  :name-constrained-slots '(dealer name part)
  :slot-name-translations '((order-date order_date)))

(create-dealer 'palo-alto :inventory 'palo-alto-inv :phone
3276521
  :program 'dbase3
  :filename "c:\\iq200\\examples\\cust2.dbf"
  :slot-with-entity-name 'name
  :class-defined 'Palo-Alto-Custs
  :name-constrained-slots '(dealer name part)
  :slot-name-translations '((order-date order_date)))
```

continued...

```
(create-dealer 'palo-alto :inventory 'palo-alto-inv :phone
3276521
         :customers 'palo-alto-custs)

;;; Hayward Dealer
(create-class 'Hayward-Inv :superclass 'dealer-inv)
(define-knowledge-source 'HaywardKS :host :local
  :program 'dbase3
  :filename "c:\\iq200\\examples\\dealer3.dbf"
  :name-constrained-slots '(name)
  :class-defined 'Hayward-Inv)

(create-class 'Hayward-Custs :superclass 'customer)
(define-knowledge-source 'Hayward-custKS :host :local
  :program 'dbase3
  :filename "c:\\iq200\\examples\\cust3.dbf"
  :slot-with-entity-name 'name
  :name-constrained-slots '(dealer name part)
  :class-defined 'Hayward-Custs
  :slot-name-translations '((order-date order_date)))

(create-dealer 'hayward :inventory 'hayward-inv :phone 7329723
         :customers 'hayward-custs)
```

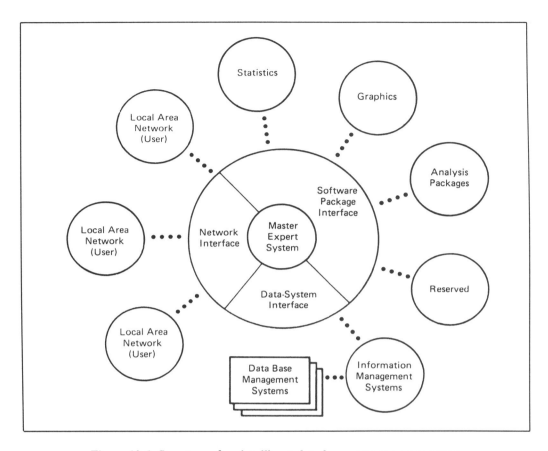

Figure 10-1 Structure of an intelligent data base management system

Defining User-interface Options

The ICS prototype is briefly explained below. To create a real application, use the library command DEFINE-INTERFACE. Information will be added concerning the functions to be implemented.

```
(define-interface :name 'inventory-control
   :banner " Inventory Control System "))
```

This command creates an interface that can be selected while in IQ-200 by pressing the F2 (go-to-interface) keyboard or selecting Applications in the Utilities menu.

First, a list of top-level function calls that will control the various modes of operation (that is, warehouse vs. dealer), will be defined. Each of these modes will have a "sensitive" item in the System Menu of the application; selecting the item will present the commands of the mode in the Mode Menu:

```
(define-mode 'inv-control 'toplevel-mode "Inventory
Toplevel"
'(("Dealership" (run-mode 'dealership-operations-mode))
("Warehouse" (run-mode 'warehouse-operations-mode))
("Quit" (quit-interface))))
```

This command provides us with the following:

```
App Name:  inv-control
Mode Name:  toplevel-mode  ;top level mode of all applications
Doc: "Inventory Toplevel"
Choice-List:  Dealership, Warehouse, Quit  ;three commands
```

The modes in which the functions will run have now been created, and should declare function names for the functions themselves, placing them in the proper modes (dealership operations will be used as an example):

```
(define-mode 'inv-control 'Dealership-Operations-Mode "Dealers"
   '(("Request-Sale" (request-sale) :doc "Sell an item")
   ("View-Inventory" (view-inventory) :doc "View inventory")))
```

This command provides the following:

```
App Name:  inv-control
Mode-Name:  Dealership-Operations-Mode
Doc:  "dealers"
Choice-list:  Request-Sale, View-Inventory  ;two commands
```

Now create the functions that will run when the commands created above are selected. Use the View-Inventory function as an example:

```
(defprocedure view-inventory
(deactivate-rule-set 'basic-rule-set)
(activate-rule-set 'inventory-rules)
(assert-rule 'view-all-parts)
(user-pause)
(activate-all-rule-sets))
```

This procedure states that when View-Inventory is called, all the library functions in the procedure will be evaluated sequentially.

Creating Hosts/Knowledge Sources

Define the remote hosts and knowledge sources that will contain the external information. First, the knowledge source for the warehouse will be defined:

DBASE file contains fields for name, cil, oil, cost, and discount for the parts at the warehouse.

```
KNOWLEDGE-SOURCE Warehouse-Parts
HOST  baldur
DBPROGRAM dbase3
DB-FILE "ware"
CLASS-DEFINED san-fran
SUPERCLASS warehouse-parts
FIELDS (name cil oil cost discount)
```

Now define the host computer, Baldur:

```
HOST      Baldur
phone-number   7329716
PASSWORD      changeme1
PASSWORD2        changeme2
OS       baldur-dos
SETUP-STRINGS ((dbase3 "c:\\rcd c:\\\\dbase\\r"))
TOPLEVEL-PROGRAM    baldur-server
```

Each knowledge (data) source, dealership, warehouse and sales record is defined in Listing 10-1. ICS prototype then is thoroughly tested and refined.

Converting the ICS to C+ +/C

The ICS can be converted straightforwardly to C++/C:

- Modify the graphical user interface classes discussed in Chapter 9 to build a friendly user-interface for the ICS.

- Use C++ to convert frames, entities, slots, and member functions, as shown in Listings 7-1 and 7-2. The organization of the ICS C++/C programs are shown in Figure 10-2.

- Use the rule structure in Listing 7-4 to convert rules into C.

- Prepare queries for the user by using Listing 8-3.

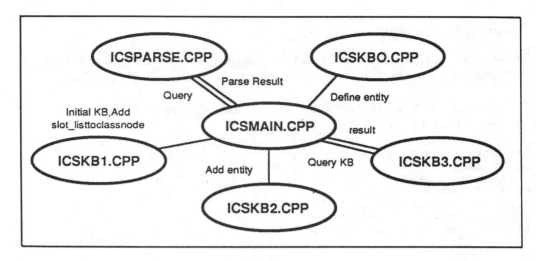

Figure 10-2 Organization of ICS components.

Because of the time limitation, the ICS conversion is incomplete. Code for the intelligent interface to dBase and Lotus1-2-3 has not been completely converted into C++; only the principle of conversion is demonstrated. Further all the codes in the listing require further refinement for improved efficiency.

Object-Oriented Data Base Systems

Object-oriented data base systems encompass a wide variety of data bases which integrate object-oriented principles. They may be classified into two groups:

- Object-Oriented Data Base Management Systems
- Object-Oriented Intelligent Data Bases
- Object-oriented data base management systems merge the capabilities of an object-oriented programming language and data base systems. However, an object-oriented intelligent data base integrates an additional capability: expert system (artificial intelligence) technology.

Object-Oriented Data Base Management Systems

An object-oriented data base management system in general combines the capabilities of an object-oriented programming language, such as Smalltalk with the storage management functions of a data base management system. The object-oriented programming language is employed to handle data base design, access, and applications. Three systems belong to this category:

- GemStone
- OZ+
- ODDESSY (Object-Oriented Data Base Design System).

GemStone is discussed in a separate section as an example to demonstrate the usage of an OOP in design of object- oriented data bases. GemStone is selected because it employs Smalltalk-like language (based on C)and relatively complete information on the system is provided in the open literature.

GemStone data base system, developed at Servio Logic Corporation uses Smalltalk-like data base management language. Consequently, the three principal concepts of the GemStone system are object, message, and class. The OOP language is extended to meet the requirements of a data base management system for a multi-user, disk-based environment. It is enhanced to cover the requirement of data integrity, large object space, data physical storage management, and access from other programming languages. GemStone was initially implemented on a VAX under VMS, see Section "A Sample Object-Oriented Data Base Management System, the GemStone Data Base System" for further discussion.

OZ+, developed at the University of Toronto [13] merges OOP concepts derived from Smalltalk and Actors [14] with those of data base systems. OZ+ is intended for use in modeling office activities and to provide efficient methods for storage and retrieval of persistent data in a multi-user office surrounding. OZ+ employs OOP concepts with a slight variation, such as objects, contents (object's data), and rules (object's operations), events,and messages. These OOP concepts are enhanced to control object persistency, to manage objects on disk, and to support true concurrency of object execution. The OZ+ system prototype was implemented on a Sun 3/50.

ODDESSY (Object-Oriented Data Base Design System) is implemented in Smalltalk for computer-aided data base design (CADD) [15]. ODDESSY uses objects, messages, and rules (treated as objects) for the design language. A sequence of messages is used to specify information about an entity, such as "employee." Two types of messages are used:

- The first type is a vertical modifier and is used in data entry to define or to refine the meaning of the design object in terms of relationships with other objects in the hierarchy, for example: hasAttributes (the object has attributes), hasIdentifiers, in "employee".

- The second type is a horizontal modifier which describes the property of each individual object, for example, is Primary (is a primary key), upTo-One (has up to one number in the attribute). The metatype (a collection of two modifiers) and metabases (a repository of objects in a metatype) are used for queries and views. Design tasks, such as creating or deducing functional dependencies, normalizing relations, and performing record analyses are made through the use of rules. Rules are formulated via the same messages which are used for specifying design.

Object-Oriented Intelligent Data Bases

An object-oriented, intelligent data base in general combines OOP, data base systems, and expert system (artificial intelligence) technology. These systems are intended to meet the emerging, complex data base applications, such as office automation, artifical intelligence (expert systems), engineering test and measurement, CAD (computer-aided design, and CAE (computer-aided software engineering) for hardware and software. Two systems, Iris and ORION, are included in this category.

Iris, developed at Hewlett-Packard Laboratories [16], is designed to meet the needs of rich modeling constructs, direct database support for inference, novel data types (for example, graphic images, voice, text, vectors, matrices), lengthy dynamic data base interactions spanning over days and many versions, and interfacing with many OOP languages. The center of Iris includes the Object Manager and the Storage Manager. The Iris Object Manager supports the query and update function of a conventional data base management system by using object-oriented languages/models; however, the Storage Manager is based on a conventional relational storage system.

The conventional SQL is extended into an Object SQL. In addition, written in Objective-C, the Graphical Editor enables the user to browse and to update interactively the Iris-defined data supertypes and interobject relation structures, such as a tree structure of the entire related data. Iris uses objects (C or Lisp), functions, and rules (nested functions) to update and to control versions for the applications that need special version control, such as CAD/CAE and office automation. The Iris system prototype was implemented in C on HP-9000/350 UNIX workstation.

The ORION Object-Oriented Database System, developed at Microelectronics and Computer Technology Corporation [17], is a single-user, multitask data base system intended for applications in artificial intelligence, multimedia documents for office information systems, and CAD. ORION is empowered with advanced features, such as version and change notification, transaction management, and multimedia management.

ORION architecture consists of four subsystems:

1. The message handler, receiving all messages which include user-defined methods, access messages, and system defined functions.

2. The object subsystem, providing high-level functions, for example, the evolution of data base schema (the class definitions and the inheritance structure of the class framework), version control, query optimization, and multimedia supervision.

3. The storage subsystem managing the allocation and deallocation of pages on disk, locating and storing objects, and indexing attributes of classes to speed up the evaluation of associative queries.

4. The transaction subsystem, managing multiple concurrent transactions and providing concurrency control and recovery mechanism.

0RION was implemented in Common Lisp on a Symbolics 3600 Lisp machine and on a Sun UNIX workstation.

The GemStone Data Base System

The design issues of the GemStone system are discussed below to demonstrate the integration of OOP in a data base management system. The GemStone is written in Smalltalk-like language (written in C).

The discussion is based only on the literature provided; no actual hands-on experience is performed. In using Smalltalk to design the GemStone system, principal features are created on the basis of two distinctive different concepts:

- OOP Concepts for Data Bases
- Extensions to OOP for Data Base Management.
- The two groups of concepts are discussed below, separately.

OOP Concepts for Data Bases

The three principal OOP concepts used in GemStone are object, message, and class, which correspond approximately to record, procedure call, and record type in a conventional data base system, as shown in Table 10-1.

Table 10-1 Approximate Equivalences between OOP and Data Base Terms

OOP (GemStone)	Data Base
object	record or set instance
instance variable	field, attributes
instance constraint	field type, domain
message	procedure call
method	procedure body
class	record type, relation scheme
class hierarchy	data base scheme
class instance	record instance, tuple
collection class	set, relation

Objects are divided into fields, and instance variables, which hold values . Values can be another object. For example, an "employee" object will have the following five instance variables, as shown in Figure 10-3:

```
EmployeeName    PersonName
SSNo
Address         HomeAddress
Department      DeptName
                Supervisor
Salary
```

The three instance variables, EmployeeName, Address, Department, all have one or more classes as their values.

Messages and methods are used to manipulate data in GemStone, for example, the message:

```
employee1 firstName
```

will return a string of the first name of the employee #1. All the named instance variables, such as EmployeeName, SSNo are accessible to methods and can be modified by them.

```
Object: Employee

EmployeeName      PersonName
                     firstName
                     lastName

SSNo              SmallInteger
Address           HomeAddress
                    stNumber
                    street
                    city
                    state
                    zipCode

Department        DeptName
                    deptName
                  Supervisor
                    firstName
                    lastName
Salary            SmallInteger
```

Figure 10-3 An employee object in OOP

Every class is represented by a class-defining object (CDO) that describes the structure and behavior pattern of class instance variables and position in the class hierarchy. Message "class" will return a CDO class. For example, if variable "dict" holds an object of class Dictionary, the message

```
dc := dict class
```

will cause dc to be assigned a CDO class of Dictionary.

GemStone provides a class hierarchy to maintain the structure and behavior of class entities. A subclass inherits structure and behavior including methods from its superclass and can implement messages of its own, such as, titledName:

```
employee1 titledName
```

in a subclass of PersonName. The above statement will return a string of the titled name of employee #1.

Because Smalltalk is implemented as a single-user, memory-based system, extensions are required to meet the need of a multiple-task, multiple-user, and disk-based data base management system.

Extensions to OOP for Data Base Management

Three major extensions to OOP for data base management are concurrency, authorization, and indexing.

Allowing multi-tasking and multi-user in the system, enhances optimistic concurrency control scheme and authorization. GemStone supports multiple concurrent users by providing each user session with a workspace containing a shadow copy of the object table derived from the most recently modified one, the shared table. This shadow copy always is updated, so the pointer references the latest copy. Access conflicts (read-write or write-write conflicts at the transaction) are checked at the commit time, since the objects that each transaction has read or written are being tracked. The scheme ensures that read-only transactions never conflict with other transactions to prevent deadlocks.

Objects can be segmented through class "Segment" by the user. Segmentation provides a means for ownership and authorization. Each user has at least one segment and can place objects into their segments. The user may grant read or write permission from one segment to another.

Indexing is used to improve the efficiency of selection and location of objects or attributes, and can enhance storage management. Indexing can be made on the collection, class, or attributes, depending on the the speed and storage requirement. For more details on the issue, see the discussion on storage management of ORION.

SUMMARY

- This chapter presents the second type of object-oriented applications: integrating object-oriented environments into data bases.

- The two approaches in integrating object-oriented environments into data bases are intelligent interface to data bases and object-oriented data bases. Users can build intelligent interfaces to many existing dispersed data bases when the program has to obtain data from them. This intelligent interface can be a preproceesor to an existing program. However, an object-oriented data base is more than an interface; the features of object-oriented programming are used to build a data base system that is different from the conventional hierarchical or relational data bases.

- If time and economics permit, an intelligent information system, interface mechanism can be developed to reduce the time required for the preparer and user to learn information management systems, DBMS packages, CAD/CAE, graphics, and statistics . These packages will be integrated into the information management data base system and automatically made available for use by the expert system when a need is detected.

- Three pragmatic approaches on intelligent interface to data bases and complicated software with the object-oriented programming and expert system technology (OOP/ES) include:

  - **Intelligent "user":** acts as a database and complicated software package. Interaction with the software package and database is not its primary objective, but merely a convenient means to access data.

  - **Intelligent "representative":** uses mathematical logic to represent general facts about data in the software package and database to increase the usefulness of the package and database to respond to queries.

  - **Intelligent "prober":** supports browsing through a database or program and also supports query modification either to narrow or to broaden the scope and understanding.

- OOP/ES can be developed to serve as intelligent users of complex conventional software programs, such as data base management systems or CAD/CAE programs.

- To use the C++ class and function name overloading effectively, the following procedure is recommended in building the intelligent interface system:

1. Structure the problem to:

   1.) Define the functions and modes to operate.

   2.) Select appropriate data types in different data bases.

   3.) Establish communication links.

2. Use an OOP/ES tool (IQ-200) to rapidly prototype an expert system.

3. Debug and refine the prototype.

4. Use C++ and the library functions to convert the final prototype system.

- The Inventory Control System is used to demonstrate the procedure to build an intelligent interface to dBase and Lotus 1-2-3.

- Object-oriented data base systems encompass a wide variety of data bases which integrate object-oriented principles. They may be classified into two groups:

  - Object-Oriented Data Base Management Systems

  - Object-Oriented Intelligent Data Bases

- An Object-Oriented data base management system in general combines the capabilities of an object-oriented programming language and a data base system. Three systems belong to this category, GemStone, OZ+ and ODDESSY (Object-Oriented Data Base Design System).

- An object-oriented intelligent data base in general combines OOP, data base systems, and expert system (artificial intelligence) technology. These systems are intended to meet the emerging, complex data base applications, such as office automation, engineering test and measurement, CAD (computer-aided design, CAE (computer-aided engineering) for hardware, and software. Two systems, Iris and ORION, are included in this category.

- The design issues of the GemStone system are discussed below to demonstrate the integration of OOP in a data base management system. The GemStone is written in Smalltalk-like language (written in C).

- In using Smalltalk to design the GemStone system, principal features are created on the basis of two distinctively different concepts:

  -OOP Concepts for Data Bases

  -Extensions to OOP for Data Base Management

- The three principal OOP concepts used in GemStone are object, message, and class, which correspond approximately to record, procedure call, and record type in a conventional data base .

CHAPTER REFERENCES

[1]Micro Data Base Systems, Guru Product Description,
Lafayette, IN 1985.

[2] Javelin Software, Javelin Product Description, Cambridge, MA, 1985.

[3] Ansa Software, Paradox Product Description, Belmont, CA, 1985.

[4] McDonnell Douglas, REVEAL Product Description, 1985.

[5] South Data, Superfile ACLS Product Description, U.K., 1985.

[6] Lopez, L. A., Elam, S. L., & Christopherson, T., "SICAD: A Prototype Implementation System for CAD," Proceedings, ASCE Third Conference on Computing in Civil Engineering, San Diego, CA, American Society of Civil Engineers (ASCE), 84-94, (April 1984).

[7] Rehak, D. & Howard, H., "Interfacing Expert Systems with Design Databases in Integrated CAD Systems," Computer-Aided Design, 17, (9), November 1985.

[8] Minker, J., "Search Strategy and Selection Function for an Inferential Relational Database," Transactions on Database Systems, ACM, 3, (1), 1-31, March 1978.

[9] Kellogg, C. "The Transition from Data Management to Knowledge Management," Proceedings, International Conference on Data Engineering, Los Angeles, CA, IEEE Computer Society Press, 467-472, April 1984.

[10] Kogan, D., "The Manager's Assistant -- An Application of Knowledge Management," Proceedings, International Conference on Data Engineering, Los Angeles, IEEE Computer Society Press, 592-595, April 1984.

[11] Motro, A. "Browsing in a Loosely Structured Database," ACM SIGMOD, 14, (2), 197-207, June 1984.

[12] Maier, D., A. Otis & A. Purdy. "Object-Oriented Data Base Development at Servio Logic." Database Engineering. 18, (4), December 1985.

[13] Weiser, S. P. & Lochovsky, F. H. "OZ+: an Object-Oriented Database System," Object-Oriented Concepts, Databases, and Appli cations. Eds. by Kim, W. & Lochovsky, F. H. Addison-Wesley, 309-337, 1989

[14] Agha, G. Actors: A Model of Concurrent Computation in Dis tributed Systems. MIT Press, Cambridge, MA, 1986.

[15] Diederich, J. & Milton, J. "Objects, Messages, and Rules in Databases Design," Object-Oriented Concepts, Databases, and Appli cations, edited by Kim, W. and Lochovsky, F. H. Addison-Wesley, 177-215, 1989

[16] Fishman, D. H., D. Beech, H. P. Cate, E. C. Chow, T. Connors, J. D. Davis, N. Derrett, C. G. Hoch, W. Kent, P. Lyngback, B. Mahbod, M. A. Neimat, T. A. Ryan & M. C. Shan, "Iris: An Object-Oriented Database Management System." ACM Transactions on Office Information Systems. 5, (1), 48-69, January 1987.

[17] Kim, W., Ballou, N., Chou, H. Garza, J., & Woelk, D. "Features of the ORION Object-Oriented Database System," Object-Oriented Concepts, Databases, and Applications, > Eds. by Kim, W. & Lochovsky, F. H. Addison-Wesley, . 251-282, 1989

Smalltalk Classes And Methods

This appendix presents the hierarchy of Smalltalk/V 286 classes, the definitions of classes, and a list of methods. The details of classes and methods are described in the user's guide entitled *Smalltalk/V 286: Tutorial and Programming Handbook*, by Digitalk, Inc., Los Angeles, 1988.

HIERARCHY OF SMALLTALK CLASSES

The hierarchies of the main Smalltalk/V classes are shown in Figure A-1. Class Object is the root class of all other classes in Smalltalk.

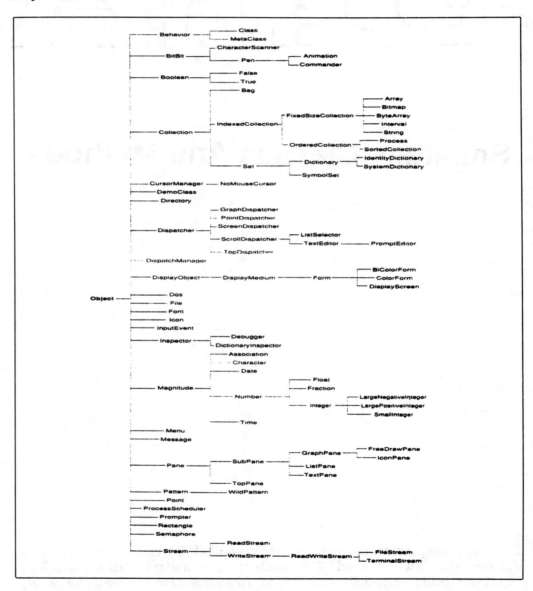

Figure A-1. Hierarchy of the Main Smalltalk/V Classes

DEFINITION OF SELECTED CLASSES

Class Name	Definition
Animation	A collection of pens representing the objects being animated.
Array	A collection of any objects accessed through a fixed range of integer indices as the internal keys.
Association	Providing the means of associating two objects known as the key/value pair, and defining the protocol to manipulate them.
Bag	A collection of unordered elements in which duplicates are allowed.
Behavior	The abstract class that defines and implements the common protocol for all the classes in Smalltalk.
BitBlt	Grouping together all the basic graphics operations.
Boolean	An abstract class which defines the common protocol for logical values.
ByteArray	A fixed size indexable sequence of integers in the range 0 through 255.
Character	The protocol for all the characters in the system (ASCII codes from 0 to 255).
CharacterScanner	Converting characters represented by ASCII values into displayable bit patterns.
Class	The superclass of all class classes (i.e., metaclasses) in Smalltalk.
ClassBrowser	Implementing a window on all the methods for a single class.
ClassHierarachyBrowser	Implementing a window on all the classes in Smalltalk/V.
ClassReader	Supporting Smalltalk source code reading and installation (compilation) from a stream, and writing to a stream.
Collection	The superclass of all the collection classes; collections are the basic data structures used to store objects in groups.
Commander	Governing an Array of pens.
CompiledMethod	Produced by the Smalltalk/V compiler and interpretively executed by the Smalltalk/v virtual machine.

Compiler Converting Smalltalk source code to compiled methods and for evaluating Smalltalk expressions.

Context Containing method temporaries and arguments and describing blocks of code (enclosed in square brackets).

CursorManage Containing the bit pattern to display a cursor shape.

Date Representing a particular day since the start of the Julian calendar.

Debugger A window application which allows debugging a Process in two different windows: a single pane walkback window and a four pane debugger window.

DemoClass Containing a few methods for demonstrating graphics.

Dictionary A collection of key/value pairs of objects that are stored as a set of associations.

DictionaryInspector Implementing a window on a dictionary which allows entries of a dictionary to be viewed and changed.

Directory Representing a DOS directory with a device letter and a path name string.

DiskBrowser Implementing a window on the complete directory hierarchy on a disk.

Dispatcher An abstract class which provides the common protocol for its subclasses.

DispatchManager Scheduling windows by providing messages for adding and removing windows, displaying all the windows.

DisplayMedium An abstract class without any instance variables.

DisplayObject An abstract class which provides the common protocol for transferring a rectangular block of characters from the receiver display object to a DisplayMedium.

DisplayScreen A special kind of form whose bit map address and size is determined by the display adapter.

False A single instance, false, representing logical falsehood.

File Providing sequential or random access to a DOS file.

FileControlBlock	An array of bytes whose structure is defined by DOS.
FileStream	Allowing streaming over the characters of DOS files for read and write access.
FixedSizCollection	An abstract class for all the indexable fixed-size collections.
Float	Defining the protocol to perform arithmetic operations on floating point numbers.
Font	Defining the bitmap patterns and characteristics of all font characters necessary for display.
Form	Containing a bit map and other instance variables to describe the bit map as a two dimensional array of bits.
Fraction	Defining the protocol to perform arithmetic operations on rational numbers.
GraphDispatcher	Handling the user input directed to a GraphPane.
GraphPane	Allowing the user to do generalized graphic drawing in the pane.
IdentityDictionary	A collection of key/value pairs of objects that are stored in two parallel array structures.
IndexedCollection	An abstract class providing the common protocol for all the indexable collection subclasses.
Inspector	Implementing a window on an object which allows the instance variables to be viewed and changed for that object.
Integer	An abstract class used for comparing, counting, and measuring instances of its subclasses representing integral numbers.
Interval	Representing mathematical progressions.
LargeNegativeInteger	Defining the data structure for instances of integral numbers less than -16384.
LargePositiveInteger	Defining the data structure for instance of integral numbers greater than +16383.
LCompiler	Converting Prolog source code to compiled methods.
ListPane	Providing functions to display and scroll a portion of the data held by the pane.
Magnitude	An abstract class used for comparing, counting, and measuring instances of its subclasses.

Menu	Defining the protocol for an application to present a menu of items to the user.
Message	Defining a data structure with an Array of message arguments and a message selector to describe a Smalltalk message.
MetaClass	The class of all metaclasses in Smalltalk (e.g., of Array).
MethodDictionary	A special kind of identity dictionary used to describe the compiled methods for each class.
NoMouseCursor	Containing the bit pattern needed to display a cursor shape.
Number	An abstract class used for comparing, counting, and measuring instances of its numerical subclasses.
Object	The superclass of all classes defining the protocol common to all objects.
OrderedCollection	A dynamic array, stack or queue.
Pane	An abstract class which provides the common protocol for all its subclasses; a subarea of a window.
Pattern	Containing a finite state pattern to be used to match against another object.
Pen	Providing a turtle graphics type of interface.
Point	Representing a position in two dimensions.
PointDispatcher	Defining or modifying a rectangle on the screen.
Process	Containing a copy of the hardware stack for the purpose of saving the state of the current process which may later be resumed.
PromptEditor	Processing input for its associated TextPane in a Prompter.
Prompter	A window with one TextPane which allows an application to pose a question and solicit an answer from the user.
ReadStream	Allowing streaming over an indexed collection of objects for read access, but not write access.
ReadWriteStream	Allowing streaming over an indexed collection of objects for read and write access.
Rectangle	Representing a rectangular area described by an origin (top left corner) and a corner (bottom right corner) point.

ScreenDispatcher	Processing the user input directed to the background window.
ScrollDispatcher	An abstract class which processes scrolling-related inputs from either the keyboard or mouse.
SelectorForm	Providing the bitmap image of the text selector which denotes the insertion point in a TextPane.
Set	Representing an unordered collection of unique objects with no external keys.
SmallInteger	Defining additional protocol for numbers in the range of -16384 to +16383.
SortedCollection	Containing elements sorted according to the two argument block of code known as the sort block (sortBlock).
Stream	Used for accessing files, devices and internal objects as a sequence of characters or other objects.
String	A fixed size indexable sequence of characters (ASCII codes from 0 to 255).
StringModel	A text holder assisting the TextEditor class by performing editing functions on the text it contains.
SubPane	An abstract class which provides the functions that are common to the ListPane and TextPane classes.
Symbol	A fixed size sequence of characters guaranteed to be unique throughout the system.
SymbolSet	A set used to record all the symbol instances.
SystemDictionary	Containing all the global variables.
TerminalStream	Defining the streaming protocol to and from the terminal.
TextEditor	Processing input for its associated TextPane.
TextPane	Providing functions to display and scrolling a portion of the text held by the pane.
TextSelection	Remembering the two points of a selection in the TextPane, and understanding all the messages for manipulating the selection.
Time	Representing a particular time of day to the nearest second.
TopDispatcher	Processing input for its associated TopPane.

TopPane	Responsible for all the operations related to its entire window.
True	A single instance, true, representing logical truth.
UndefinedObject	A single instance, nil, used to identify undefined values.
WildPattern	Containing a finite state pattern for efficient matching which includes at least one wild card character.
WriteStream	Allowing streaming over an indexed collection of objects for write access, but not read access.

LIST OF SELECTED METHOD SELECTORS

&	accessEmptyCollection
*	activate
+	activatePane
,	activateWindow
.	active
/	add
//	add:
<	add:after
<=	add:afterIndex:
=	add:before
==	add:beforeIndex:
>	add:name:color:
>=	add:withOccurences:
@	addAll
\\	addAllFirst:
	addAllLast:
abs	addClasses:at:
absobCharsOf:	addClassVarName:
accept	addDays:
accept:from:	addDependent:
acceptClass:from:	addFirst:
acceptPrompt	addLast:
acceptReplt:form:	

addSelector:withMethod:	amountToScrollLeft
addSharePool:	amountToScrollUp
addSubClass	and:
addSubclass:	andRule
addSubpane:	appendChar:
addTime:	appendText:
adjustBox	arcCos
adjustPoint:	arcSin
adjustSize	arcTan
after:	areaOnFormOf:
after:ifNone:	arguments
again	asArray
allClasses	asArrayOfSubstrings
allClassVarNames	asAsciiZ
allDependents	asBag
allInstances	asCharacter
allInstVarNames	asciiValue
allSubclasses	asDate
allSubdirs	asFloat
allSuperclasses	asInteger
amountToPageLeft	asLowerCase
amountToPageUp	asObject

asOop

asOrderedCollection

asPrinterErrorFlag

asSeconds

asSet

associationAt:

associationAt:ifAbsent:

associationsDo:

asSoredCollection

asSortedCollection:

asString

asSymbol

asUpperCase

at:

at:ifAbsent:

at:put:

atAll:put:

atAllPut:

atEnd

ATTmono

backColor

background:

backgroundColor:

backspace

backspacePoint:

backspaceSelection:

backup

backupWindow

baseDay

basePoint

basicAt:

basicAt:put:

basicHash

basicNew

basicNew:

basicSize

become:

becomeSymbolTable

before:

before:ifNone:

beginMenu

beginScroll

beginSelect

bell

between:and:

bitAnd:

bitCoordinate:

bitInvert

bitmap

bitOr:

bitShift:

bitXor:

black

black:

blank:width:

blankRestFrom:

boldLine:

border

border:

border:clippingBox:rule:mask:

border:rule:mask:

border:widthRectangle:mask:

border:

    widthRectangle:

    mask:

    rule:

bottom

bounce:

bounceBall

bouncingBox

broadcast:

broadcast:with:

broadcastChangesIn:

    upTo:

    withExcess:

browse

build:

buildDirectoryList

byteValueAt:put:

byteValueAtX:Y

calendarForMonth:year:

cancel

cancelPrompter

cantReturn

canUndersstand:

ceiling

center

center:in:

centerText:font:

change

change:

changed

changed:

changed:with:

change:with:with:

changeFileMode

changeModeOf:to:

changeNib:

changeTo:

charsInColumn

charsInRow

charSize

charWidth:

ckeckArgument:

checkCharacter:

checkDay:month:year:

checkDay:year:

ckeckIndex:

ckeckMode:

chkdsk

class

class:

classes

classPool

classVariableString

classVarNames

classVarNames:

clearScreen

clipRect

clipRect:

clipRectAll:

clockEvent:

clockOffPrimitive

clockTickPeriod:

clockTickPrimitive:

clockTicksOff

close

closeIt

closeWindow

codeFor

collapse

collapsed

collect:

combinationRule:

compile:

compile:in:

compile:in:notifying:ifFail:

compile:notifying:

compile:notifying:in:

compileAll

compileAllSubclasses

compilerError:at:in:for:

compress:

compressChanges

compressChangesOf:into:

compressSources

compressSourcesOf:into:

computeInstSize

conditionalHide:

configureAs:

containsPoint:

contents

contextFor:

continue

continueScroll

controlBreak

convertToString:

copy

copy:form:

copy:form:to:rule:

copy:to:

copyAll:from:

copyBits

copyChars

copyFile

copyFrom:to:

copyReplaceFrom:to:with:

copySelection

copyStack

copyWith:

copyWithout:

corner

corner:

cos

countBlanks

cr

create

create:

createDirectory

createFile

current

currentDateInto:

currentTimeInto:

cursorOut:

cutSelection

cycle

cyclePane

cyclePane:

darkGray

dateAndTimeNow

day

day:

dayIndex

dayName

dayOfMonth

dayOfWeek:

dayOfYear

daysInMonth

daysInMonth:forYear:

daysInYear

daysInYear:

daysLeftInMonth

daysLeftInYear

deactivate

deactivatePane

deactivateWindow

debug

decompress:

deepCopy

defaultDispatcherClass

defaultNib:

degreesToRadians

delay

delete:

deleteCharIn:

demoMenu

denominator

dependents

dependsOn:

desForm

destForm:	digitValue
destForm:sourceForm:	digitValue:
destForm:	dir
sourceForm:	direction
halftone:	direction:
combinationRule:	directories
destOrigin:	directory
sourceOrigin:	directory:
extent:	directoryListMenu
clipRect:	directorySort
destOrigin:	disappear
destRect:	diskLabel
destX	dispatcher
destX:	dispatcher:
destY	dispatchers
destY:	display
detect:	display:
detect:ifNone:	display:at:
deviceType	display:from:at:
deviceType:	displayAll
dictionaries	disPlayAt:
dictionary:	displayAt:clippingBox

displayAt:font:

displayAt:rule:

displayBox:

displayChanges

displayForm:at:rule:

displayGap

displayLabel

displayOn:

    at:

    clippingBox:

    rule:

    mask:

displayPatch:

displayScreen

displaySelection

disPlayWindow

do:

doesNotHandle

doesNotUnderstand:

doIt

Doit

doIt:

doItResult:error:

dosError:

dosMenu

dotProduct:

doubleCneter:

down

downArrow

dragon

dragon:

drawBox

drawFrom:to:

drawLoopX:Y:

drawTo:

drive

drive:

dropFrame

dropSenderChain

dropTo:

dumpOn:for:

edit

EGAcolor

EGAlowRes

EGAmono

eightLine

elapsedDaysSince:

elapsedMonthsSince:

elapsedSecondsSince:

ellipse:aspect:

ellipsePrim:aspectX:Y:

endBypt

equals:

eqv:

erase

error:

errorAbsentElement

errorAbsentKey

errorAbsentObject

errorInBounds:

errorInDay

errorInMonth

errorNotIndexable

evaluate:

evaluate:in:to:notifying:ifFail:

evaluating:

even

execute

exit

exit:

exp

expandBy:

expontent

extendOrigin:

extendSelect

extendTo:

extent

extent:

extractDateTimeFrom:

extractFileNameFrom:

extractFlagsFrom:

extractSizeFrom:

factorial

failAt:with:

fanOut

file

file:

fileExtension

fileId

fileIn

fileInFrom:

fileItIn

fileListMenu

fileName

fileName:extension:

fileOut

fileOutOn:

files

fill:

fill:clippingBox:rule:mask:

fill:rule:mask:

fillAt;

fillAtX:andY:

find:ifAbsent:

findCurrentLine

findElementIndex:

findFirst:

findKey:ifAbsent:

findLast:

first

firstDayInMonth

firstDayOfMonth

fixedWidth

floatError

floor

flush

flushFromCache:

font

for:

forBox:ofMinSize:perform:

forceEndOntoDisplay

forceMode

forceSelecdtionOntoDisplay

forClass:

foreColor

forgetImage

form:

formatted

formCoordinate:

formCoordinates:

formPrint

fourteenLine

frame	getSourceClasses
frame:	glyphs
frameAt:offset:	go:
frameAt:offset:put:	goto:
framingBlock:	gotoDos
framingRatio:	gray
free:toExecute:withPause:	gray:
freeDiskSpace	graySelection
from:to:	grid:
from:to:by:	grow
fromDays:	growSize
fromDisplay	growTo:
fromDisplay:	hair
fromDisplayAlligned:	halt
fromInteger:	hand
fromSeconds:	hasCursor
fromString:	hash
fromUser	height
fromUserSize:	height:
gcd:	hercules
getCurrentPen:	hide
getIndex:	hideCursor

hideGap

hideSelection

hideShow

hierarchy

hierarchy:

highlightLabel

home

homeContext

homeCursor

homeFrameOf:

hotSpot

hours

ifFalse:

ifFalse:ifTrue:

ifTrue:

ifTrue:ifFalse:

image

implementedBySubclass

implememtors

implementorsOf:

includes:

included:with:

includesAssociation:

includesKey:

includesSelector:

increment:

indesOf:

indexOf:ifAbsent:

indexOfMonth:

init

initBegin:end:incr:

initDependents

initFlags

initHighRes

initialize

initialize:

initialize:font:

initialize:font:dest:

initialize:hotSpot:

initializeClass

initializeDosErrors

initializeTranscript

initialSize

initialState

initLowRes	instances
initPen:	instanceVariableString
initPositions	instSize
initScanner	instVarAt:
initSystem	instVarList
initTopCorner	instVarNames
initWindowClip	instVarNames:
inject:into:	integerCos
input	integerSin
insetBy:	intern:
inspect	internalForm
inspectMenu	intersect:
inspectSelection	intersects:
installFixedSize:	invalidAdd
charSize:	invalidMassage
startChar:	isAlphaNumberic
endChar:	isBefore:
basePoint:	isBits
instance	isBytes
instance:	isControlActive
instanceClass	isControlWanted
instanceHeaderOn:	isDigit

isEmpty	key:
isFixed	key:value:
isGap	keyAtValue:
isGapSelection	keyAtValue:ifAbsent:
isKindOf:	keys
isLetter	keysDo:
isLowerCase	kindOfSubclass
isMemberOf:	label
isNil	label:
isPointers	labels:lines:
isSeparator	labels:lines:selectors:
isSwapped	last
isThereInput	lcm:
isUpperCase	leapYear:
isVariable	leapYearsTo:
isVowel	left
isWords	leftArrow
jumpDown	leftButton:
jumpLeft	leftPattBefore:
jumpRight	lightGray
jumpUp	lineAt:
key	lineDelimiter

lineDelimiter:

lineInPane:

linesIn:

lineToRect:

lineUpFrom:to:

ln

loadEntireFile

location

log:

logEvaluate:

logSource:forClass:

logSource:forSelector:inClass:

lowRes

magnify:by:

magnifyBy:

makeSelectionVisible

mandala

mandala:diameter:

mask

mask:

match:

match:index:

matchBlock:

max:

menu

menu:

merge:

message:

method

method:

   receiver:

   agruments:

   tempCount:

   frame:

methodAt:

methodAt:put:

methodDictionary

methodDictionary:

methods

millisecondClockValue

milllisecondsToRun:

min:

minBoxExtent:

minimumSize

minimumSize:

minutes

misc

model:

modified

modified:

monthIndex

monthName

monthNameFromString:

mouseClockValue

mouseOffset

mousePrimWith:

mousePrimWith:width:

mousePrimWidth:with:with:with:

mouseScroll

mouseSelectOn

move

move:by:

moveBy:

moveCursor:

moveOrSizeBox:

moveTo:

multiEllipse

multiMandala

multPentagon

multiPolygon:

multSpiral

mustBeBoolean

mustBeSymbol:

name

name:

name:

    environment:

    subclassOf:

    instanceVariableName:

    variable:

    words:

    pointers:

    classVariableName:

    PoolDictionaries:

    comment:

    changed:

nameOfDay:

nameOfMonth:

negated	nextTwoBytePut:
negative	nextWord
new	noChanges
new:	normal
newDay:month:year:	normalLine:
newDay:year:	north
newFile:	not
newLabel	notEmpty
newMethod	notifier:content:at:
newNameSymbol:	notifier:content:at:menu:
newSize:	notNil
next	now
next:	numerator
next:put:	numerator:denominator:
nextBytePut:	occurrencesOf:
nextChunk	odd
nextEntryInto:using:	offset
nextLine	offset:
nextMatchFor:	on:
nextPiece	on:from:to:
nextPut:	oopAt:
nextPutAll:	open

open:in:

openClassBrowser

openIn:

openIn:name:extension:
openOn:

openWindow

openWorkspace

or:

origin

origin:

origin:corner:

origin:extent:

orRule

orThru

other

output:head:tail:

outputToPrinter

outputToPrinterUpright

over

overClickDelay

pageSize

pane

pane:

paneScanner

pasteSelection

pathName

pathName:

pathNameVar

peek

peekFor:

perform:

perform:with:

perform:with:with:

perform:with:with:with:

perform:withArguments:

performMenu

pi

place:

pointer:word:variable:

pointFromUserDisplaying:

polygon:sides:

popUp:

popUp:at:

popUpAt:for:

position

position:

positionAtBeginning

positive

previousWeekday:

primitiveChangeModeOf:to:

primitiveClose

primitiveCreate:

primitiveFailed

primitiveFailed:

primitiveForPrinterOutput

primitiveFreeDiskSpace

primitiveNextPut:

primitiveRemove:

primitiveRename:to:

primitiveSenseDirInto:

promiteSetTo:

print

printBanner

printerMode

printerMode:

printFile

printFraction:

printIt

printLimit

printOn:

printOn:base:

printPaddedTo:

printRecursionOn:

printRounded:

printScreen

printString

processClock:

processControlKey:

processFunctionKey:

processInput

processInputKey:

processKey:

processLastInput:

prompt:default:

prompt:defaultExpression:

promptForPathName

promptWithBlanks:default:

putHeaderOf:into:

putMethod:withIndex:to:

putSpaceAfter:

putSpaceAtEnd

putSpaceAtStart

quickExit:

quo:

radiansToDegrees

radix:

raisedTo:

raisedToInteger:

read

readBuffer:atPosition:

readInto:atPage:

readInto:atPosition:

readLimit

readPrimitive

receiverAt:

reciprocal

recompile:

rectangleFromUserOfSize:

rectangleFromUserOfSize:
    initSize:

redraw

reflectDrawX:Y:

reframe

reframe:

reframeLabel

refreshAll

refreshFrom:fro:atX:Y:

rehashFrom:

reinitialize

reject:

release

rem:

remove

remove:

remove:ifAbsent:

removeAll:

removeAssociation:

removeClassVarName:

removeDirectory

removeFile

removeFirst

removeFromSystem

removeIndex:

removeKey:

removeKey:ifAbsent:

removeLast

removeSelector

removeSelector:

removeSharedPool:

removeSubclass:

rename:

rename:in:
rename:to:

renameFile

replace:withChar:

replace:withText:

replaceAll

replaceAllOld

replaceAtColumns:by:

replaceAtColumns:by:startAt:

replaceAtPattern:by:

replaceCrsIn:

replaceFrom:to:with:

replaceFrom:to:with:startingAt:

replaceFrom:to:withObject:

replaceLines:with:

replaceString:

replaceWithChar:

replaceWithLf:

replaceWithTab:

replaceWithText:

reply

reply:

reset

resetPrinter

reSort

respondsTo:

restart

restartAT:

restore

restore:

restoreDirList

restoreSelected:

resumable:

resume

return:

returnIndex:

reverse	scanBlocks:
reverse:	scanner:
reverseContents	scanTemps:
reversed	schedule:
reverseDo:	scheduleWindow
reverseLine:	scroll
reverseScreen	scrollBarFini
right	scrollBarIncludes:
rightArrow	scrollBarInit
rightButton:	scrollBarUpdate
rightPartAfter:	scrollDelay:
rounded	scrollDownAt:
roundTo:	scrollHand:to:
run	scrollLeft:
runDemo	scrollTopCorner:
save	scrollUp:
saveAs	scrollUpAt:
saveExit	search
saveImage	searchBack
scaleBy:	searchBack:for:
scaleTo:	searchForActiveDispatcher
scaleArgs:	searchForActivePane

searchForLineToShow:

searchForm:for:

searchInit

searchOld

seconds:

select

select:

selectAfter:

selectAll

selectAtCursor

selectAtEnd

selectBefore:

selectDirectory:

selectedString

selectEnd

selectFrom:to:

selectInstance:

selection

selection:

selectLines:height:

selector

selector:

selectorFor:

selectorMenu

selectors

selectors:

selectTo:

selectToCursor

selectToShifted

selfCopyToX:Y:

senders

sendersOf:

sense

setBackground

setClass:

setCollection:

setDispatchers

setFont:

setForeColor:backColor:

setInstList

setLimits

setLoc

setName:setDirectoy:

setOffsetX:Y:

setSysFont:

setTo:

setToEnd

setUpSymbolTable

setValueArray

setWidth:height:

shallowCopy

sharedPools

sharedPools:

sharedVariableString

shiftRate:

show:

showCurrentLine

showCursorLine

showGap

showPartialFile

showSelection

showSelection:to:

showWindow

sign

significand

sin

sixteenLine

size

skip:

skipName

skipPunctuation

skipTo:

solidEllipse:aspect:

sort:to:

sortBlock

sortBlock:

sortBy:

sortByDate

soryByName

sortBySize

sortMenu

source

sourceCodeAt:

sourceForm:

sourceIndex

sourceIndex:sourcePosition:

sourceOrigin:

sourcePosition

sourceRect:

sourceString

sourceString:

sourceX

sourceX:

sourceY

sourceY:

space

species

speed:

speedSpace

spiral:angle:

splitPath:

spread:

    from:

    by:

    spacing:

    direction:

spreadForm:

    to:

    width:

    startAt:

mask:

sqrt

squared

stackOverflow

startPosition:endPosition:

startScrollUp

startUp

status

storeOn:

storeString

strictlyPositive

string

string:

stringCoordinate:

stringHash

stringIn:

stringWidth:

structure

structure:

subclass:

    instanceVariableNames:

    classVariableNames:

```
      poolDictionaries:          tan

subclasses                       tell:bounce:

subclasses:                      tell:direction:

subclassOf:                      tell:go:

subdirectories                   tell:place:

subDirectory:                    tell:turn:

subtractDate:                    template

subtractDays:                    tempList

subtractTime:                    tempValue

superclass                       text

superclass:                      textMenu

superpane:                       textMenuInit

swapIn                           textModified

swapInAndRestore:                textPane:

symbol                           timesRepeat:

symbotTable                      timesTwoPower:

systemDispatcher                 to:

systemMenu                       to:by:

systemTranscript                 to:by:do:

tab                              today

tabStringAt:                     top

take:form:                       topCorner
```

topCorner:	update:
topDispatcher	update:width:
topPane	update:with:with:
totalLength	updateLastByte
totalSeconds	updateSortPane
transcriptMenu	upTo:
transientWriteFini:	userPrimMissing
transientWriteOn:	value
translateBy:	value:
tramspose	value:value:
trim:	valuePrim:value:
trimBlanks	values
truncate	variableByteSubclass:
truncated	classVariableNames:
turncateTo:	poolVariableNames:
trun:	variableSubclass:
under	instanceVariableNames:
unloadMemory:	classVariableNames:
unopened	poolDictionaries:
unusedMemory	volumeLabel
up	walkback
upArrow	walkback:

```
walkBackFor:Label:              withAllSubclasses

walkBackMenu                    withBlank:

walkBackOn:                     withCrs

walkLine                        workSpaceMenu

whileFalse:                     write:

whileTrue:                      writeBuffer:ofSizePosition:

white                           writeFrom:toPage:for:

white:                          writeFrom:toPosition:for:

width                           writeLimit

width:                          writePage

width:height:                   x

width:height:initialByte:       x:

wildcardChar                    xor:

windowClip                      y

windowClip:                     y:

windowLabeled:frame:            year

with:                           yourself

with:do:                        zapBackup

with:from:to:                   zeroDivisor

with:with:                      |

with:with:with:                 ~ =

with:with:with:with:            ~ ~
```

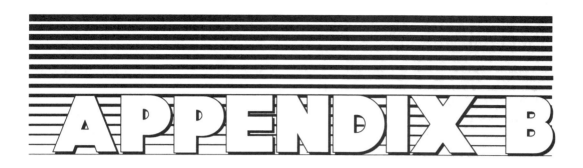

IQ-200: Technical Summary

I_{Q-200} is an applications support and development environment with powerful rule-based reasoning tools and database communication capabilities. It is designed to support applications that require interaction with many databases, both locally and over remote connections, including those which require rich reasoning and knowledge representation capabilities.

Using IQ-200, a database administrator or programmer can integrate artificial intelligence and object-oriented techniques with conventional databases and communications.

Data Integration

IQ-200 allows the integration and management of knowledge from many different sources: Data from the user, or from static, relational, remote, or spreadsheet databases is handled all within one uniform, transparent data management mechanism. IQ-200 uses *knowledge sources* to define connections to remote databases. Once defined, all machine-specific protocols, such as logging on, opening files, and making queries, are handled by the knowledge source.

Rule-Based Reasoning

Additionally, IQ-200 provides *rule-based reasoning* over distributed knowledge sources. The integration of AI techniques of rule-based reasoning brings active power to previously static databases, allowing them to conclude new information based on inferences drawn from existing data.

FUNCTIONALITY OVERVIEW

Integration of Database Sources

IQ-200's **Knowledge Source** System connects to and reasons over *distributed* databases. IQ-200 takes care of the headaches of multi-data-source management and provides the user with one uniform, powerful environment for manipulating all of the attributes. The following kinds of PC data files can be accessed directly from disk:

- Lotus 1-2-3 spreadsheet files.
- dBaseIII dbf files.
- IQ-200's own IQDB knowledge base files.

Alternatively, if no direct access to data files is available, IQ-200 will link with programs that **do** have access:

- A remote dBase III database can be accessed via a modem.
- A PC SQL database program can be accessed over a modem connection.
- A Mainframe-based SQL system, such as DB2 can be accessed over a network or modem connection.

(Note: Please contact Baldur Systems regarding compatibility with specific SQL products)

Logic Based Approach

Like most advanced Database systems, IQ-200 is fully declarative in style: When making a query, specify WHAT is wanted, but never HOW to get it; the rule-based logic will make that determination. Additionally, the logic-based approach gives it advantages over current DBMS's.

- **Deduction**. IQ-200 can DEDUCE information not explicitly represented in the database.

- **Recursion**. Queries that are difficult if not impossible to make in a typical database system can be solved easily using rules and recursive relations.

- **Explanation**. The logic used to solve a query can be explained by IQ-200. This advanced logic allows the user to check that the answer is correct and provides what the user requested.

- **Uniformity**. Any fact or query can be represented in a uniform, first order predicate logic language.

Knowledge and Data Representation

Object-Oriented FRAMES

- **Model-based reasoning**. A model of the data universe can be created by using *objects* to represent things in the real world.

- **Inheritance**. Unlike conventional database tables, IQ-200 frames simplify the creation of a structured database environment. By using Frame Inheritance, the parent-child relationships can be defined between frames, thus avoiding respecifying attributes that are common to both.

- **Active slot values**. An access to a slot of an object can invoke any procedure or computation, automatically.

Knowledge Sources

Defining a connection to an external database system is easy. By linking a frame to a database table using a Knowledge Source, database communication details and information retrieval are transparent to the user.

Predicate Fact Base

ANY kind of information expressible through logic can be stored in the predicate fact base. Each piece of information has an associated certainty factor that can be used to express the validity of the information and results.

Rule Base

Logical dependencies, heuristic information, and computational procedures can be represented as RULES in IQ-200.

Reasoning System

IQ-200's reasoning facilities were designed to provide maximum flexibility for the programmer. Using the reasoning system, queries can be solved that depend on arbitrary combinations of objects, tables, variables, facts, spreadsheets, defaults, and even external functions. Reasoning system features include:

- Complete **pattern matching** rules with variables.
- Complete combinations of **not, and** and **or** in rules.
- **Backward** (goal-driven), **forward** (event-driven), or **both** kinds of reasoning can be used at the same time.
- **Rule Sets** and **Priorities** for meta-level control of inference.
- **Certainty factors**. Every fact in IQ-200 has an associated "degree of belief."
- **Justification system**. Every solved query can be **explained** by IQ-200.
- Solutions with incomplete information: Defaults, When-Needed active values.
- Advanced reasoning constructs like Prolog: **cut, fail, and succeed.**

Communications System

IQ-200 includes a remote communications system, IQCOMM, which allows IQ-200 to communicate with other computers.

- IQ-200 can enable a PC to automatically call up another computer, or a database program, and to retrieve information from a database file.

- The IQ-200, IQCOMM package provides a server program that will run on any PC, and results in a database server. The PC then can be called up by the main IQ-200 system and queried for information.

- The user may directly use IQCOMM by setting up one PC as the server. The user then can dial into the system using any standard modem software and then can log in and run command-line programs, or transfer files.

- IQCOMM will also allow communications to other computers through networks. Please contact Baldur Systems regarding compatibility with specific network systems.

User Interface

An (optional) mouse driven menu interface provides access to most of IQ-200's functions. Through this interface data structures can be created, modified, queried, and saved. This allows interaction with database files, and querying of remote database systems. A context-sensitive help facility allows the user to obtain increasing levels of technical information on all aspects of the system.

IQ-200's Natural Language templates can shield the user or programmer from the details of a query language. The programmer can choose to use either predicate logic or simple English-like statements to create, modify, or query IQ-200 knowledge.

By means of IQ-200's interface-generation facility, the user can create screen-based, mouse-supporting end user interfaces to IQ-200 applications. An IQ-200 context-sensitive help facility can even be provided to the end user.

Interface to Other Programs

IQ-200 can bring expert system, object-oriented, database, and communications capabilities to other application programs. The IQDB extension library of functions is accessible both from the Lisp and C languages. Also, support for the Microsoft Windows-like environment is available.

EXAMPLE

This system has been designed to allow a warehouse to get order information from dealers in several cities. Imagine that each of the dealers enters their daily orders in a dbase file in a PC, and that the warehouse has a Lotus1-2-3 spreadsheet with historical records of orders over the past year. Using IQ-200, first define the ORDER classes representing each of the remote dealer order databases. Then, define Knowledge Sources to link each class to the respective remote data file. To make adjustments based on seasonal variations, define rules to access the local Lotus 1-2-3 file to determine orders from historical ordering patterns. All of this could be done using IQ-200's mouse-driven menu system.

Now, the warehouse shipping agent wants to know the quantities of each part that should be shipped to each dealer per week. The agent would query the system (possibly using natural language templates), asking IQ-200 to determine shipment quantities. IQ-200 will receive the query, determine if the answer already exists (maybe somebody just asked five minutes ago), and displays the answer. If the answer is not known, the program will automatically call up the dealer PC's, getting the information from the database files being used.

If one of the dealers hasn't yet updated orders for the week, IQ-200 could look at the historical order records from last year, and deduce a reasonable order quantity. If the historical records aren't available; then IQ-200 could ask the shipping agent directly for an order projection. If the user questions a projection, IQ-200 can be asked to explain its reasoning.

SYSTEM REQUIREMENTS

The following is required to run IQ-200 :
- IBM AT or 100% compatible PC.

- 1.5 Megabytes extended memory.

The following are recommended:
- PC-compatible Mouse.

- Color monitor.

The following is required to use the IQCOMM communications system:
- Hayes-compatible modem for each machine (workstation & servers):

- For dBase III database server: an installed dBase III program .

- For SQL database server: Please contact Baldur Systems Corp. regarding connection to specific SQL products.

- 128K bytes for each server.

The following is required to use the IQCOMM network communication system:
- Please contact Baldur Systems Corp., 3423 Investment Blvd., Suite 12, Hayward, CA 94545, (415) 732-9715, regarding specific network requirements.

The following is required to use the IQ-DB Lisp library of functions:
- Gold Hill's Golden Common Lisp version 2.2 or greater (please specify).

- Up to 700K of Lisp space (depending on the subset used).

Zortech Variables and Functions Used in the Book

This appendix lists the variables and functions in the Zortech Flash Graphics library that are used in classes presented in this book. Flash Graphics is a set of graphics routines for the IBM PC (and clones) to interface to the Zortech C compilers. Flash Graphics supports Hercules, EGA (both color and monochrome), CGA, and VGA boards, and Toshiba 3100.

For simplification, similar variables or functions are grouped together, for example:

FG_X1
FG_X2
FG_Y1
FG_Y2

In the discussion, the name of the variable(s) or function(s) are listed first, followed by a short description of objective(s) and a set of examples for programming the variable(s) or function(s).

VARIABLES

fg_displaybox

Description: the bounding box of the display
Example:
```
int x;
x = fg_displaybox[FG_X2];
```

fg_charbox

Description: the bounding box of a character
Example:
```
int y;
y = fg_charbox[FG_Y2];
```

FG_X1
FG_X2
FG_Y1
FG_Y2

Description: Variables used as indexes into boxes and lines, as in fg_displaybox,[FG_X1] refers to the x coordinate of the left side of the display
Example:
```
fg_charbox[FG_X2];
```

FG_BLACK
FG_GREEN
FG_RED
FG_PURPLE
FG_YELLOW
FG_WHITE
FG_LIGHT_BLUE
FG_HIGHLIGHT

Description: Available colors
Example:
```
fg_fillbox(FG_RED,FG_MODE_SET,~0,fg_displaybox);
```

FG_MODE_SET

Description: Mode value for setting colors onto the screen
Example:
```
fg_fillbox(background,FG_MODE_SET,~0,fg_displaybox);
```

FG_LINE_SOLID
Description: One of the line types
Example:
```
fg_drawlineclip(FG_GREEN,FG_MODE_SET,~0,FG_LINE_SOLID, line,clipbox);
```

FUNCTIONS

atof,atoi,atol

Description: Converts the string into a double(atof), integer(atoi), or
              long(atol)
Example:
```
strcpy(idata-unit,dt[2]);
idata-price = atof(dt[3]);
idata-cost = atof(dt[5]);
```

bioskey

Description: Passes the flag to the BIOS keyboard interrupt
Example:
```
if(bioskey(1))
{
}
```

fclose

Description: Closes the file
Example:
```
fp = fopen("fool.txt","r");
if(fp != NULL)
      fclose(fp);
```

fg_drawbox

Description: Draws the outline of a box on the screen
Example:
```
fg_box_t box;
box[FG_X1] = -10;
box[FG_X2] = 0;
box[FG_Y1] = 20;
box[FG_Y2] = 30;
fg_drawbox(FG_WHITE,FG_MODE_SET,~0,FG_LINE_SOLID, box,fg_displayb
```

fg_drawlineclip

Description: Clips the line to clipbox and draws the remainder
Example:
```
fg_line_t line;
line[FG_X1] = paper-xoff+x1;
line[FG_Y1] = paper-yoff+y1;
line[FG_X2] = paper-xoff+x2;
line[FG_Y2] = paper-yoff+y2;
fg_drawlineclip(color,mode,~0,linetype,line,paper->clipbox);
```

fg_drawmatrix

Description: Draws a matrix on the screen
Example:
```
fg_box_t b;
b[FG_X1] = b[FG_Y1] = 0;
b[FG_X2] = sx-1;
b[FG_Y2] = sy-1;
fg_drawmatrix(color,mode,~0,FG_ROT0,x+paper-xoff,y+paper-yoff,pat,b,paper-clipbox)
```

fg_fillbox

Description: Fills the box on the screen with the specified color
Example:
```
fg_box_t box;
box[FG_X1] = min(x1,x2)+paper-xoff;
box[FG_X2] = max(x1,x2)+paper-xoff;
box[FG_Y1] = min(y1,y2)+paper-yoff;
box[FG_Y2] = max(y1,y2)+paper-yoff;
fg_fillbox(color,mode,~0,box);
```

fg_flush

Description: Flushes any pending output to display
Example:
```
Bunch::Draw();
fg_flush;
```

fg_init

Description: Initializes the graphics mode
Example:
```
fg_init();
```

fg_init_all

Description: Determines the type of display graphics that is available and opens that display device
```
Example:
if(fg_init_all() == FG_NULL)
{
    exit(1);
}
```

fg_term

Description: Closes the display device
Example:
```
fg_term();
```

fopen

Description: Opens a file
Example:
```
FILE *fp;
fp = fopen("fool.txt","a");
```

fread

Description: Reads elements from the file
Example:
```
int numread;
numread = fread(dest,size,number,fp);
```

fseek

Description: Sets the file position
Example:
```
fp = fopen("fool.txt","a");
seek(fp,0L,SEEK_END);
```

ftell

Description: Returns the current position in the file
Example:
```
position = ftell(fp);
```

fwrite

Description: Writes elements to the file
Example:
```
wrtn = fwrite(buffer,size,n,fp);
```

int_off

Description: Turns off the 8086 interrupt via a "clear" interrupt flag instruction
Example:
```
int_off();
```

int_on

Description: Turns on the interrupt via a "set" interrupt flag instruction
Example:
```
int_on();
```

msm_init

Description: Initializes the mouse device
Example:
```
msm_init()
```

msm_term

Description: Closes the mouse device
Example:
```
msm_term();
```

msm_hidecursor

Description: Hides the mouse cursor from the screen
Example:
```
msm_hidecursor();
```

msm_showcursor

Description: Shows the mouse cursor on the screen
Example:
```
msm_showcursor();
```

msm_getstatus

Description: Gets the status of the mouse
Example:
```
msm_getstatus(&x,&y);
```

msm_setareax,msm_setareay

Description: Sets the range of x and y coordinates
Example:
```
msm_setareax(fg_displaybox[FG_X1],fg_displaybox[FG_X2]);
msm_setareay(fg_displaybox[FG_Y1],fg_displaybox[FG_Y2]);
```

sprintf

Description: A formatted print routine
Example:
```
p = (Display *)iter();
sprintf(buf,"%lf",temp->finrat);
p->Put(buf);
```

strlen

Description: Returns the length of the string
Example:
```
xmax = strlen(text)*8;
ymax = fg_charbox[FG_Y2];
```

time

Description: Returns the current time in seconds elapsed since 00:00:00, 1 January 1970

Example:
```
time_t ltime;
time(&ltime);
```

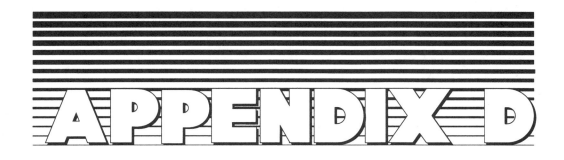

Selected Object-Oriented Companies and Their Products

Apple Computer, Inc.
20525 Mariani Ave.
Cupertino, CA 95014
TEL: 408-973-4831
Products: MacApp (a development framework)

AT&T/Bell Laboratories
Crawford's Corner Road
Holmdel, NJ 07733
TEL: 201-949-3000
CONTACT: Gregory Vesonder, Director, Tech Group
Products: C++

Baldur Systems Corporation
3423 Investment Blvd., Suite 12
Hayward, CA 94545
TEL: 800-736-4716
Products: C++ User-Interface Environment Libraries
(libraries/source codes to create environments)

Boeing Computer Services
P. O. Box 24346/MS 7A-03
Seattle, WA 98124
TEL: 206-763-5392
CONTACT: George Roberts, GM, Advanced Tech

Carnegie Group, Inc.
Commerce Court and Station Square
Pittsburgh, PA 15219
TEL: 412-642-6900
Products: KBS (Knowledge-Based Simulation system)

CNS, Inc.
7090 Shady Oak Rd
Eden Prairie, MN 55344
TEL: 612-9440170
Products: C-Talk (a language and environment)

Digital Equipment Corporation
Three Results Way
P.O. Box 1003
Marlborough, MA 01752
TEL: 508-467-4806
Products: Trellis/Owl (a language and environment)

Digitalk Inc.
9841 Airport Blvd., Suite 604
Los Angeles, Ca 90045
TEL: 213-645-1082
CONTACT: Mike Tang
Products: Smalltalk/V, 286 , MAC (languages and environments)

Ford Aerospace and Communications Corporation
Aeronutronic Division
Dept. A703-001
Ford Road
Newport Beach, CA 92660

General Motors Research Laboratories
Computer Science Department
Warren, Michigan 48090-9057
TEL: 313-575-3101

General Research Corporation
7655 Old Springhouse Road
McLean, VA 22102
TEL: 703-893-5915

GTE Laboratories
Box A3, 40 Sylvan Road
Waltham, MA 02254

Graphael, Inc.
255 Bear Hill Rd.
Waltham, MA 02154
TEL: 617-890-7055
Products: G-BASE (DBMS) and G-LOGIS (a language)

Guidelines Software, Inc.
P.O. Box 749, #CL
Orinda, CA, 94563
TEL: 415-254-9393
Products: Guidelines C++ (an interpreter)

Hewlett Packard Labs
1501 Page Mill Road
Palo Alto, CA 94304
TEL: 415-857-4233
Products: IRIS (a data base research prototype)

Honeywell Systems and Research Center
3600 Technology Drive
Minneapolis, MN 55418
TEL: 612-782-7599
Products: GAIA (an Ada environment framework)

Hughes Research Laboratories
3011 Malibu Canyon Road
Malibu, CA 90265

IBM
1501 California Avenue
Palo Alto, CA 94303- 0821
TEL: 415-855-3938

Iconix Software Development, Inc.
2800 28th St., Suite 320
Santa Monica, CA 90405
TEL: 213-458-0092
Products: AdaFlow (a software design tool)

Interactive Software Engineering, Inc.
270 Storke Rd., Suite 7
Goleta, CA 93117
TEL: 805-685-1006
Products: Eiffel (a language and environment)

International Meta Systems, Inc.
23844 Hawthorne Blvd., Suite 200
Torrance, CA 90505
TEL: 213-375-4700
Products: Max2 (OOPS board)

Level Five Research
4980 South A1A
Melbourne Beach, FL 32951
TEL: 305-729-09046

Lifeboat Associates, Inc.
55 S. Broadway
Tarrytown, NY 10591
TEL: 800-847-7078
Products: Advantage C++ (an interpreter)

Knowledge Garden
473A Malden Bridge Rd.
Nassau, NY 12123
TEL:518-766-3000
Products: KnowledgePro (a language)

Knowledge Systems Corp.
2000 Regency Pkwy.
Suite 270 Cary, NC 27511
TEL: 919-481-4000
Products: The Smalltalk Collection (a Smalltalk library)

Martin Marietta Data Systems
98 Inverness Drive East, Suite 135 (P193)
Englewood, CO 80112
TEL: 303-790-3404

Matrix Software Technology Corp.
One Massachusetts Technology Center
Harborside Dr.
Boston, MA 02128
TEL: 617-567-0037
Products: Layout (development systems)

McDonnell Douglas Knowledge Engineering
20705 Valley Green Drive, VG2-BO1
Cupertino, CA 95014
TEL: 408-446-6553

Mitre Corporation
Burlington Road
Bedford, MA 01730
TEL: 617-271-2000

National Instruments Corp.
12109 Technology Blvd.
Austin, TX 78727
TEL:512-250-9119
Products: Labview 2.0 (a language)

Oasys, Inc.
230 Second Ave.
P.O. Box 8990, Waltham, MA 02254
TEL: 617 890-7889
Products: Designer C+ + (a language and environment)

Ontologic, Inc.
47 Manning Rd. Billerica, MA 01821
TEL: 508-667-2383
Products: Vbase (a database)

Oregon Software, Inc.
6915 SW Macadam Ave., Suite 200
Portland, OR 97219
TEL: 503-245-2202
Products: Oregon C+ + (an environment)

ParcPlace Systems Inc.
2400 Geng Rd.
Palo Alto, CA 94303
TEL: 415-859-1000
Products: Smalltalk-80, Cynergy, Navigator (languages and environments)

The Rand Corporation
1700 Main St.
Santa Monica, CA 90406
TEL: 213-393-0411
Products: ROSS (Rule-Oriented System for Simulation, a language)

Schlumberger-Doll Research
P.O. Box 307/Old Quarry Road
Ridgefield, CT 06877
TEL: 203-431-5000
Products: STROBE (a language)

Servio Logic Development Corp.
15025 Southwest Koll Pkwy., 1A
Beaverton, OR 97006
TEL: 503-644-4242
Products: GemStone (DBMS)

SRI International
333 Ravenswood Avenue
Menlo Park, CA 94025
TEL: 415-326-6200

The Stepstone Corp.
75 Glen Rd.
Sandy Hook, CT 06482
TEL: 203-426-1875
Products: Objective-C 4.0 (a compiler)

Software Architecture & Engineering, Inc.
1500 Wilson Boulevard, Suite 800
Arlington, VA 22209
TEL: 7032-276-7910

Symbolics, Inc.
Four Cambridge Center
Cambridge, MA 02142 TEL: 617-876-3635
Products: FLAVORS (a language)

Tektronix, Inc.
P.O. Box 500, M/S 50-470
Beaverton, OR 97077
TEL: 503-627-1497
Products: Color Smalltalk (a language and environment)

TGS Systems, Inc.
1127 Barrington St., Suite 19
Halifax, NS, Canada B3H 2P8
TEL: 902-429-5642
Products: Prograph (a pictorial dataflow language)

Traveling Software, Inc.
18702 North Creek Pkwy.
Bothell, WA 98011
TEL: 206-483-8088
Products: Papillon (applications)

United Technologies Research Center
Silver Lane
East Hartford, CT 06108
TEL: 203-678-7553

The Whitewater Group
Technology Innovation Center
906 University Place
Evanston, IL 60201
TEL: 312-491-2370
Products: Actor (a language)

Xerox Special Information Systems
250 North Halstead St.
P.O. Box 5608
Pasadena, CA 91197
TEL: 818-351-2351
Products: Analyst Assistant Humble (Smalltalk applications), LOOPS (a language)

Zortech, Inc.
366 Massachusetts Ave., Suite 303
Arlinton, MA 02174
TEL: 617-646-6703
Products: Zortech C++ Compiler (a compiler)

PUBLISHERS

Addison-Wesley Publishing Co.
Reading, MA 01867

Cambridge University Press
32 East 57th Street
New York, NY 10022

John Wiley & Sons, Inc.
605 Third Avenue
New York, NY 10158
TEL: 1-800-526-5368

Kluwer Academic Publishers
190 Old Derby Street
Hingham, MA 02043
TEL: 617-749-5262

MIS: Press
524 North Tillamook
Portland, OR 97227

The MIT Press
28 Carleton Street
Cambridge, MA 02142

Morgan Kaufman Publishers, Inc.
Dept. A1, 95 First Street
Los Altos, CA 94022

Object-Oriented Programming Glossary

C++	An object-oriented programming language; a superset of the C language with a class structure.
Class	A collection of objects which have similar characteristics.
Class-based programming	A language that supports object classes, such as "clusters" which allow objects to be collected and "bundled" in templates.
Concurrency	Achieving sequencing and synchronization with the commit operator and read-only annotations.
Data hiding	A property that makes available only names that a user needs to know and hides the rest.

Dynamic binding	The class of object types and their method implementation are not defined at the compile time but at the run time.
Encapsulation	Preventing an object from being manipulated except by its defined external operations.
Inheritance	The data and methods (member functions) of the parent class are passed down (made accessible to) children classes.
Inheritance hierarchy	A tree of all classes in which generic, non-specialized classes like Object is at the root, and very specialized classes such as myPen at the leaves.
Instance	An object is an instance of a given class, if it belongs to children classes of that class.
Instance method	A procedure that an instance of a class can perform.
Instance variable	A variable created for an instance of a children class.
Multiple inheritance	Allows an object to inherit from multiple superclasses.
Message	A command request "sent" to an object for that object to be executed appropriately on the data.
Member function	A procedure in the class that implements a message.
Method	A method is the implementation of a message. It is called member function in C++.
Object	An encapsulated module containing data and procedures.
Object-based programming	A language that allows direct modeling of objects in the real world, such as parts, machines, cars, ships, people, or bank accounts.
Object-Oriented programming	A language that is object-based and supports classes which allow inheritance.
Objective-C	An object-oriented language.
Operator overloading	One of the basic features of object-oriented programming, in which the same operator names can be repeatedly used in the same program.

Polymorphism	Same as operator name overloading.
Private	The information defined in the private part can be used only by its implements.
Protected	Same as private except accessible to subclasses.
Protocol	A group of messages that can respond to instances of a class.
Public	The information defined in public part presents an interface to users of the type and is available to anyone.
Receiver	The object which receives the message.
Root class	The origin of all of the classes in a class organization.
Selector	A unique name for a method.
Self	A command used to refer to the instance variable receiving the message in an instance method.
Slot	The attribute of a class.
Smalltalk	An interactive object-oriented programming environment.
Static binding	Data type with method implementations are defined at the compile time.
Subclass	The newly defined class of the original parent class.
Superclass	The parent class of the class being created.

SELECTED BIBLIOGRAPHY

Afsarmanesh, H., D. Knapp, D. McLeod & A. Parker. "An Object-Oriented Approach to VLSI/CAD." *Proceedings of the International Conference on Very Large Data Bases*, August 1985.

Agha, G. *Actors: A Model of Concurrent Computation in Distributed Systems*. MIT Press, Cambridge, MA, 1986.

Ahlsen, M., A. Bjornerstedt, S. Britts, C. Hulten & L. Soderlund. "An Architecture for Object Management in OIS." *ACM Transactions on Office Information Systems*, vol. 2, no. 3, pp. 173-196, July 1984.

Alexander, James M. "Painless Panes for Smalltalk Windows." Proceedings of OOPSLA '87. Special issue of *ACM SIGPLAN Notices*, vol. 22, no. 12, pp. 287-294, December 1987.

Association of Computing Machinery. *The Object-Oriented Programming, Systems, Languages and Applications (OOPSLA) '88 Conference Proceedings*. New York, NY, 1988.

Atwood, T. "An Object-Oriented DMBS for Design Support Applications." *Proceedings of the IEEE COMPINT 85*, pp. 299-307, September 1985.

Banerjee, J., W. Kim & K.C. Kim. "Queries in Object-Oriented Databases." *Proceedings of the 4th International Conference on Data Engineering*. Los Angeles, CA, February 1988.

Barstow, D., P. Barth & R. Dinitz. SPHINX: *Exploiting the Differences Between Programming Environments and Runtime Environments*. Technical Report, Schlumberger-Doll Research, 1986.

Barth, P., S. Guthery & D. Barstow "The Stream Machine: a Data Flow Architecture for Real-Time Applications." In *Eighth International Conference on Software Engineering*, 103-110, London, England, September 1985.

Barth, P. S. "An Object-Oriented Approach to Graphical Interfaces". *ACM Transactions on Graphics Special Issue on User Interface Software*, 5, (2), April 1986.

Beech, D. *Towards an Object Model of the Representation and Use of Information.* Hewlett-Packard Technical Report, June 1985.

Beech, D. & B. Mahbod. "Generalized Version Control in an Object-Oriented Database." *IEEE 4th International Conference on Data Engineering*, February 1988.

Bobrow, D. G., K. Kahn, G. Kiczales, L. Masinter, M. Stefik & F. Zdybel. "CommonLoops Merging Common Lisp and Object-Oriented Programming." *Proceedings of the ACM Conference on Object-Oriented Programming Systems, Languages and Applications*, " Portland, OR, September 1986.

Bobrow, D. G. & M. J. Stefik. *"The LOOPS Manual."* Technical Report, Xerox PARC, December 1983.

Borning, A. "The Programming Language Aspects of ThingLab, a Constraint Oriented Simulation Laboratory." *ACM Transaction on Programming Language and Systems*, October 1981.

Brady, M. & R. C. Berwick, editors. "Computation Models of Discourse." Cambridge, MA, MIT Press, 1983.

Brown, G.P., R. T. Carling, C.F. Herot, D.A. Kramlich and P. Souza. "Program visualization: graphical support for software development." *Computer*, August 1985.

Brown, J. S., *"From Cognitive to Social Ergonomics and Beyond."* Hillsdale, NJ, Lawrence Erlbaum Associates, 1986.

Barstow, D., Howard E. Shrobe & Erik Sednewall. *Interactive Programming Environments*. New York, NY, McGraw Hill, 1984.

Brown, M.H. & R. Sedgewick. "A System for Algorithm Animation." *Computer Graphics*, 1984.

Buchanan B.G. & E.H. Shortliffe. *Rule-Based Expert Systems:* The MYCIN Experiments of the Stanford Heuristic Programming Project. Reading, MA, Addison-Wesley, 1984.

Borning, Alan, & Robert Duisberg. "Constraint-Based Tools for Building User Interfaces." *ACM Transactions on Graphics*, 5, (4), 345-374, October 1986.

Campbell, R.H. & W.J. Kubitz. "The Professional Workstation Research Project." *IEEE Computer Graphics and Applications*, 1986.

Cardelli, L., & P. Wegner. "On Understanding Type, Data Abstraction, and Polymorphism." *Computing Surveys*, December 1985.

Carey, M., D.J. DeWitt, J.E. Richardson & E.J. Shekita. "Object and File Management in the EXODUS Extensible Database System. *Proceedings of the 12th International Conference on Very Large Data Bases*. Kyoto, Japan, August 1986.

Ciccarelli, E.C., IV. *Presentation-Based User Interfaces*. PhD thesis, MIT, August 1984.

Clinger, W. D., *Foundations of Actor Semantics*. AI-TR-633, MIT Artificial Intelligence Laboratory, May 1981.

Cox, Brad J. *Object Oriented Programming: An Evolutionary Approach*. Reading, MA, Addison-Wesley, 1986.

Dahl, O. J., B. Myrhaug, & K. Nygaard. *Simula67 Common Base Language*. Norwegian Computing Center, 1984.

Deppish, U., H. B. Paul & H. J. Scheck. "A Storage System for Complex Objects." *Proceedings of the International Workshop on Object-Oriented Database Systems*, September 1986.

Derrett, N., D.H. Fishman, W. Kent, P. Lyngbaek & T.A. Ryan. "An Object-Oriented Approach to Data Management." *Proceedings of Compcon 31st IEEE Computer Society International Conference*. San Francisco, CA, March 1986.

Derret, N., W. Kent & P. Lynbaek. "Some Aspects of Operations in an Object-Oriented Database." *Database Engineering*, 8:4, December 1985.

Digitalk, Inc. *The Smalltalk/V 286: Tutorial and Programming Handbook*. Los Angeles, CA, 1988

Dodani, M.H., C.E. Hughes, J. M. Moshell. "Separation of Powers." *BYTE*, March 1989.

Duisberg R.A. "Animated Graphical Interfaces Using Temporal Constraints." In *Human Factors in Computing Systems: CHI'86*.

Fishman, D. H., D. Beech, H. P. Cate, E. C. Chow, T. Connors, J. D. Davis, N. Derrett, C. G. Hoch, W. Kent, P. Lyngback, B. Mahbod, M. A. Neimat, T. A. Ryan & M. C. Shan, "Iris: An Object-Oriented Database Management System." *ACM Transactions on Office Information Systems*. 5, (1), 48-69, January 1987.

Foley, J.D. & C.F. McMath. "Dynamic Process Visualization." *IEEE Computer Graphics and Applications*. March 1986.

Goldberg, A."*Smalltalk-80: The Interactive Programming Environment.* " Addison-Wesley, Reading, MA, 1984.

Goguen, J. A. & J. Meseguer. "Unifying Functional, Object-Oriented, and Relational Programming with Logical Semantics." In *Research Directions in Object-Oriented Programming*. Ed Shriver and Wegner. MIT Press, Cambridge, MA, 1987.

Goldberg, A. & D. Robson. *Smalltalk-80: The Language and Its Implementation*. Reading, MA, Addison-Wesley, 1983.

Guideline Software Inc. "*Guideline C+ + Installation Guide and Release Notes,*" Orinda, CA, 1988.

Gullichsen, E. *BiggerTalk: Object-Oriented Prolog*. STP-125-85, Austin, TX, MCCSTP, 1985.

Hansen, P.B. *Distributed Processes: A Concurrent Programming Concept*. CACM, 1978.

Haynie, M. N. "The Relational/Network Hybrid Data Model for Design Automation Databases." *Proceedings of the IEEE 18th Design Automation Conference*, 1981.

Hoare, C. A. R. *Communicating Sequential Processes*. CACM, August 1978.

Hoare, C.A.R. *Monitors: An Operating System Structuring Concept*. CACM, October 1974.

Ishikawa, Y., & M. Tokoro. "Orient 84K: An Object-Oriented Concurrent Programming Language for Knowledge Representation." In *Object-Oriented Concurrent Programming*. Ed. Yonezawa and Tokoro. Cambridge, MA, MIT Press, 1987.

Johnson, Ralph E., & B. Foote. "Designing Reusable Classes." *Journal of Object Oriented Programming*, 1, (2), June/July 1988.

Krasber, E. Glenn, & S. T. Pope. *A Cookbook for Using the Model View-Controller User Interface Paradigm in Smalltalk-80*. Palo Alto, CA, ParcPlace Systems, January 1988.

Kahn, K., E. Tribble, M. Miller & D. Bobrow. "Vulcan: Logical Concurrent Objects." In *Research Directions in Object-Oriented Programming*. Ed. Shriver and Wegner.

La Croix, M. & A. Pirotte. Data Structures for CAD Object Description. *Proceedings of IEEE 18th Design Automation Conference*, 1981.

Laff, M. R. & B. Hailpern. "SW 2: An Object-Based Programming Environment." *Proceedings of SIGPLAN 85 Symposium on Language Issues in Programming Environments*, ACM, 1985.

Lieberman, H. "Using Prototypical Objects to Implement Shared Behavior in Object-Oriented Languages." In *Proceedings of OOPSLA' 86*.

Lifeboat Associates Inc. "*Advantag C++ Users' Guide*," Tarrytown, NY, 1986.

Liskov, B., A. Snyder, R. Atkinson, & C. Schaffert. *Abstraction Mechanisms in CLU.* CACM, August 1977.

Liskov, B., & R. Scheifler. *Guardians and Actions: Linguistic Support for Robust Distributed Programs*. TOPLAS, July 1983.

Maier, D., A. Otis & A. Purdy. "Object-Oriented Database Development at Servio Logic." *Database Engineering*. 18, 4, December 1985.

Maier, D., & J. Stein. "Indexing in an Object-Oriented DBMS." *Proceedings of the International Workshop on Object-Oriented Database Systems*, September 1986.

Maier, D., J. Stein, A. Otis & A. Purdy. "Development of an Object-Oriented DBMS." *Proceedings of the ACM Conference on Object-Oriented Programming Systems, Languages and Applications*, September 1986.

Manola, F. & U. Dayal. "PDM: An Object-Oriented Data Model." *Proceedings of the International Workshop on Object-Oriented Database Systems*, September 1986.

Meyrowitz, N. "Intermedia: The Architecture and Construction of an Object-Oriented Hypermedia System and Application Framework." *Proceedings of the ACM Conference On Object-Oriented Programming Systems, Languages and Applications*, September 1986.

Meyrowitz, N. Ed. *"OOPSLA '88* Conference Proceedings." Special Issue of *SIGPLAN NOTICES*, 23, (11), November 1988.

Moon, D. "Object-Oriented Programming with Flavors." *Proceedings of OOPSLA '86.*

Nierstrasz, O.M. "A Survey of Object-Oriented Concepts." *Object-Oriented Concepts, Databases, and Applications*. Ed. W. Kim and F. Lochovsky. Reading, MA, Addison-Wesley, 1988.

Oasys "*Designer C++: Product Description*," Waltham, MA, 1987.

O'Brien, P., B. Bullis & C. Schaffert. "Persistent and Shared Objects in Trellis/Owl." *Proceedings of the International Workshop on Object-Oriented Database Systems*. September 1986.

Oregon Software Inc. *"Oregon C++ Software Product Description,"* Portland, OR, 1988.

Ossher, H. L. *Language Features for Object-Oriented Programming with Multiple Views.* Center for Integrated Systems, Stanford University, 1985.

Penney, D. J., J. Stein & D. Maier. *"Mixed Mode Concurrency Control in the GemStone Object-Oriented DBMS."* Manuscript in preparation.

Plouffe, W., W. Kim, R. Lorie & D. McNabb. "A Database System for Engineering Design." *Database Engineering,* 7, 2, June 1984.

Reiss, S. P. "An Object-Oriented Framework for Graphical Programming." *ACM SIGPLAN Notices,* 21,(10), 49-57, October 1986.

Schmucher, Kurr J. *Object-Oriented Programming for the Macintosh.* Hasbrouck Heights, NJ, Hayden Book Company, 1986.

Shriver, Bruce & P. Wegner, eds. *Research Directions in Object-Oriented Programming.* Cambridge, MA, MIT Press, 1987; second printing, 1988.

Smith, R. G. "Strobe: Support for Structured Object Knowledge Representation". In *Proceedings of the Eighth International Joint Conference on Artificial Intelligence,* pp. 855-858, August 1983.

Smybolics, Inc. *FLAV Objects, Message Passing, and Flavors, Symbolics.* Cambridge, MA, 1984.

Snyder, A. "Encapsulation and Inheritance in Object-Oriented Programming Languages." *ACM Conference on Object-Oriented Programming Systems, Languages and Applications,* 38-45, Portland, OR, September 1986.

Spooner, D. L., M. A. Milican & D. B. Fatz. "Modelling Mechanical CAD Data with Data Abstractions and Object-Oriented Techniques." *Proceedings 2nd International Conference on Data Engineering.* February 1986.

Stefik, M., & D. G. Bobrow. "Object-Oriented Programming: Themes and Variations." *The AI Magazine,* 40-62, January 1986.

Strom, R. S. Yemini, & P. Wegner. "*Viewing Ada from a Process Model Perspective.*" International Ada Conference, Paris, May 1985.

Strom, R., & S. Yemini. *NIL: An Integrated Language and System for Distributed Programming.* Proceedings of the SIGPLAN '83 Symposium on Language Issue in Software Systems, June 1983.

Stroustrup, B. *The C++ Programming Language,.* Reading, MA, Addison-Wesley, 1986.

Thomas, D. "What's in an Object?" *BYTE,* March 1989.

Thompson, C. "Object-Oriented Databases." *Texas Instruments Engineering Journal., vol. 3, pp. 1, January/February 1986.*

Thompson, T. "The Next Step." *BYTE,* March 1989.

U.S. Department of Defense, *Ada Reference Manual*, July 1980.

Usenix Association. "*C++ Workshop Santa Fe ,NM Proceedings, November 9-10, 1987,*" Berkeley, CA, 1987.

Wegner, P. "Dimensions of Object-Based Language Design." In *Proceedings of OOPSLA '87.*

Wegner, P. "The Object-Oriented Classification Paradigm." In *Research Directions in Object-Oriented Programming*. Ed. Shriver and Wegner. Cambridge, MA, MIT Press, 1987.

Wegner, P. "Learning the Language." *BYTE,* March 1989.

Wegner, P. & B. Shriver, (Eds.). *Proceedings of the Object-Oriented Programming Workshop*, IBM and Brown University, Yorktown Heights, *SIGPLAN Notices*, October 1986.

Wegner, P. & S. Zdonik. "Inheritance as an Incremental Modification Mechanism, or What Like Is and Isn't Like." *Proceedings of the ECOOP 1988*, LNCS no. 322. New York, Springer-Verlag, 1988

Wiener, Richard S., & L. Pinson. *An Introduction to Object-Oriented Programming and C++*. Reading, MA, Addison-Wesley, 1988.

Weiner, Richard S., & L. Pinson. *Introduction to Object-Oriented Programming in Smalltalk*. Reading, MA, Addison-Wesley, 1988.

Weisner, S. P. "An Object-Oriented Protocol for Managing Data." *Database Engineering,*. vol. 8, pp. 4, December 1985.

Wetmore, Russ. *MacApp 2.0 Viewedit User's Guide*. Apple Computer, 1988.

Wirth, N. *Programming in Modula-2*. New York, Springer-Verlag, 1982.

Woelk, D., W. Kim & W. Luther, "An Object-Oriented Approach to Multimedia Databases." *Proceedings of the ACM SIGMOD Conference on Management of Data*. Washington, D.C., May 1986.

Woelk, D. & W. Kim. "Multimedia Information Management in an Object-Oriented Database System." *Proceedings of the International Conference on Very Large Data Bases*. Brighton, England, September 1987.

Yonezawa, A., J. Briot, and E. Shibayama. The Tokyo Institute of Technology, *Proceedings of OOPSLA '86*, 1986.

Zdonik, S., & P. Wegner. "Language and Methodology for Object-Oriented Database Environments." *Proceedings Nineteenth Annual Hawaii International Conference On System Science*. January 1986.

Zortech Inc. *Zortech C++ Product Description*, Arlington, MA, 1988.

A

Actors 123
Ada 28
add 70
add subclass 43,67
addSubpane 74
advantages 248
aForm 60
algorithms 40,79
aMessage 49
animation 60
array 32,80
artificial intelligence 24,238
asCharacter 46
ASCII characters 46
asSet 54
at 53
at:ifAbsent 53
atEnd 48
attributes 50

B

backward chaining 244
bag 51,54
best-first search 312
between 44
bit-mapped windows 131,132
bitBlt 54,57,80
bitmapped graphics 80
bits 56
black 59
blank-terminated string 159
Boolean 7,13
breadth-first search 312
browse 67
browse class 40,67
browse disk 64
Bunch 166,182, 183,210
burst 134
button 56
byte arrays 67
bytes 40

C

H

halt 72
handle() 91,180
header files 82,83
height 56
hide/show 67
home 59
host/knowledge sources 455
HScroller 91

I

icon 207,209,210,215
Icon 169
IconLib 411, 412
Iconmenu 373
IconMenuItm 373
ICS class constructors 269
  deriving knowledge 318
  search and query 303
ifFalse 36,37
ifTrue 36, 37
image control 208
implementers 68
implementation file 82,195
in-line function definition 103,105
increment 60
incremental code modification 103,105,106
index 35
  indexed instance variable 67
  indexing statements 78
inference engine 24, 299
inheritance 89,92
inheritance of attributes 15,19,20,25
inherited 5,9,10, 28
initialization of classes 96
initialize slots 312
input next:anArray 49
input pane 76
input operation 159
input/output 133
inputMenu 76
insert() 185
insetBy 56
inside() 180
inspect 53,63,69,70

M

N

O

R

raise() 185
raisedTo 45
rapid-prototyping 435
ReadStream 47
reciprocal 45
rect 171
rectangle 54, 55,80
redraw () 91,134
reference parameters 82,87,88
reject 38
reject:iterator 38
rem 45
remove 64,68,70,185,193
  remove:aString 50
rename 65
replay pane 76
resume 72
right 56
root class 5,8,9,40
rounded 45
rules 241
  building rule structures 286,292
  rule action 291
  rule certainty 291
  rule conclusion 291
  rule explanation 291
  rule premise 291
run() 210
runtime message system 121

S

save 39,40,41,43,68,69
scrolling 162
search strategy 302
select 38,52
  select:iterator 38
self 117,124
sender 68
Sensor 166
set 51,54
setAttribute 141
show it 39,71
sign 45
simple polymorphism 19,25

Please send additional information on the following products:

1.   The C++ OOP Source Code Disk ($24.90 + shipping)

2.   C++ Object-Oriented Environment Libraries ($95.00 + shipping)

3.   C++ OOP Developer's Toolkit ($495.00 + shipping)

4.   C/C++ for Expert Systems ($24.9 0 + shipping)

5.   The C/C++ Expert Systems Source Code Disk ($24.90 + shipping)

6.   The C/C++ Expert System Library ($49.50 + shipping)

Name:_____

Address:_____

City:_____ State:_____ Zip:_____

Telephone:_____

FAX:_____

To order/inquire about these products, call 800/736-4716, 415/732-9715, or FAX 415/732-9716.

Or write to: Baldur Systems Corp.
                      3423 Investment Blvd. #12
                      Hayward, CA 94545
                      U.S.A.

**FOR MORE INFORMATION
about products described in this book,
use this handy tear-out card.**

FOLD AND TAPE OR STAPLE

Baldur Systems Corporation
3432 Investment Blvd. #12
Hayward, CA 94545
U.S.A.

ORDER FORM

PROGRAM LISTINGS ON DISKETTE

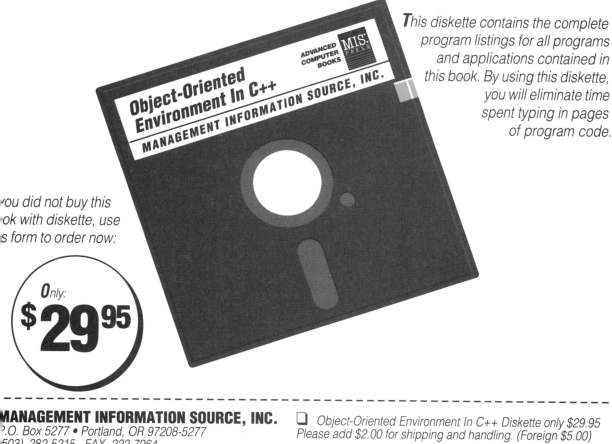

*T*his diskette contains the complete program listings for all programs and applications contained in this book. By using this diskette, you will eliminate time spent typing in pages of program code.

*ou did not buy this
ok with diskette, use
s form to order now:*

*O*nly:
$29⁹⁵

MANAGEMENT INFORMATION SOURCE, INC.
*.O. Box 5277 • Portland, OR 97208-5277
503) 282-5215   FAX 222-7064*

❑ *Object-Oriented Environment In C++ Diskette only $29.95
Please add $2.00 for shipping and handling. (Foreign $5.00)*

Check one:

❑ *VISA* ❑ *MasterCard* ❑ *American Express*

❑ *Check enclosed $_____*

AME(Please print or type)

ddress

ITY   *STATE   ZIP*

ACCT.

EXP. DATE

all free
1-800-MANUALS

SIGNATURE

M A N A G E M E N T   I N F O R M A T I O N   S O U R C E ,   I N C .